Circles and Settings

SUNY Series in Gender and Society
Cornelia Butler Flora, Editor

Circles
and
*Role Changes of
American Women*
Settings

Helena Znaniecka Lopata

State University of New York Press

Published by
State University of New York Press, Albany

For information, address the State University of New York Press,
State University Plaza, Albany, NY 12246

Production by Bernadine Dawes
Marketing by Dana Yanulavich

Library of Congress Cataloging-in-Publication Data

Lopata, Helena Znaniecka, 1925–
    Circles and settings : role changes of American women / Helena
Znaniecka Lopata.
        p. cm. — (SUNY series in gender and society)
    Includes bibliographical references and index.
    ISBN 0-7914-1767-0 (hardcover : alk. paper) — ISBN
0-7914-1768-9 (pbk. : alk. paper)
       1. Sex role—United States—History. 2. Woman—United States—
Social conditions. 3. Woman—United States—Psychology.
I. Title. II. Series.
HQ1075.5.U6L66   1994
305.42'0973—dc20   93-14927
                                            CIP

Dedicated to
Allisa Menasco
Caitlin Eileen Lopata
Colleen Elizabeth Lopata

Contents

Preface

The role involvements of Americans have changed considerably since the 1950s when I was a foreigner to America. I first became fascinated by the gap between how its women were self- and other defined and the contributions they were actually making to the society. Upon the birth of our daughter, and while I finished my Ph.D. at the University of Chicago, my husband and I moved from Hyde Park to suburban Skokie. We were convinced that this move was "best for the children," even though I was leery about leaving the academic community to dwell among American housewives in the "wilderness," which was described so negatively by many observers.

To my surprise and pleasure, I found suburbia and its women very different from the stereotypes. Armed with Znaniecki's dynamic theory of social roles as sets of social relations, and the methodology of symbolic interactionism, which I acquired from many theoretical ancestors through Herbert Blumer, I decided to study this gap between the American portrayal of women (as believed by the women themselves) and the actual behavior of the women I observed around me. Howie Becker's concept of "becoming" (from "becoming a marijuana user"), and the concepts of "life space" and "life cycle" from the Chicago School of Human Development, enabled me to develop a social role definition for the American "housewife." I interviewed many suburban and urban housewives as well as women with paying jobs. My questions focused on women's conceptions of their major roles, how these roles changed from their grandmother's time, and how they expected them to change by the time their own daughters reached adulthood. I also asked them about their perceptions of past and future changes in the roles of men. I learned what the home, neighboring; couple companionate interaction and friendship, as well as community involvement, meant to these respondents.

Over the years, my interest in the involvements, self-concepts, and life spaces of American adult women became evident through numerous studies and efforts to develop middle-range concepts and theories that would help answer some of the sociological questions. The studies focused on the congruity of constructed reality, commitments, and changes over the life course, including role modifications produced by the death of a husband, and the effect of support systems on widows. Remembering Everett Hughes, I continued to be interested in the occupations and professions, the meaning of different kinds of jobs, and how people pull roles together into role clusters. Using the symbolic interactionist framework, I continued to turn to women for the answers. I even managed, while studying Polonia, to look at the roles of women in the Polish American community. References to these studies are made throughout this book.

I finally decided to combine as much of this knowledge as possible into a single volume on role involvements, as seen from the perspective of a feminist symbolic interactionist. The venture has been an exciting one, assisted by the contributions of an overwhelming variety of scholars. There is an abundant body of knowledge concerning American women, not only as a result of the feminist revival, but also as a response to the dramatic changes in the roles and life spaces of all people. In addition, symbolic interactionism has progressed in many directions from its original founding fathers, and I have drawn freely on the work of such scholars as Goffman, Becker, Turner, Rosenberg, Stone, Daniels, Denzin, Maines, Strauss, Gusfield and others. In recent years there has also been an increasing number of women combining feminist and interactionist perspectives in their research.

It is impossible to thank individually the many persons and formal groups with whom I have interacted and who have helped me in the various ventures, but some need special recognition. Let me first list my funding sources: The Midwest Council for Social Research on Aging, Roosevelt and Loyola Universities, the Administration on Aging, and the Social Security Administration. Hank Brehm of the Social Security Administration also provided invaluable assistance in dealing with vast quantities of data needed by a qualitatively trained sociologist. The National Opinion Research Center of the University of Chicago and the Survey Research Laboratory of the University of Illinois, Chicago, conducted the interviews of the larger studies.

I can't help thinking back over my own role as a student, especially now that so much biographical data about our cohort at the University of Chicago are coming out. I was fortunate in having Blumer, Hughes and Wirth on my dissertation committee, and some great colleagues in my study groups. The University of Illinois provided me with a wonderful background, thanks to E. T. Hiller, William Albig and Donald Taft. Obviously, my debt to my father, Florian Witold Znaniecki, and my mother, Eileen Markley Znaniecki, is enormous, not only for sociological imagination, but also for having created such an exciting home atmosphere on both continents.

The major research of the last twenty-plus years has been carried forth from the Center for the Comparative Study of Social Roles at Loyola University of Chicago. Many people have taken part in these projects. The main contributors to the various studies in which women are featured include: Kathleen Fordham Norr, Cheryl Allyn Miller, Debra Barnewolt, Frank Steinhart, Sister Kim, and Monica Shoemaker. Ligaya McGovern, Rebecca Morrow-Nye, Kandace Pearson and Colleen Carpenter have been involved with the recent studies.

I have spent many hours of informal discussion with colleagues at meetings of the Society for the Study of Social Interaction, Sociologists for Women in Society, and the Society for the Study of Social Problems. I also happen to be a person who has gained much from the American Sociological Association (more in recent years than during some of the more formal, male-dominated eras of the past). I have become increasingly involved in comparative research and

international events—which I enjoy tremendously—with the help of
Jan Trost, Irene Levin, Lea Shamgar-Handleman, Stella Quah and
James Beckford. Judith Levy, Nona Glazer, Joe Pleck, Warren Peterson,
Beth Hess, Millie Seltzer, Lillian Troll, Robert Atchley, Rhoda Blumberg,
David Maines and many others have my gratitude for all the ideas
and idea testing related to *Circles and Settings*.

I am very fortunate in the colleagues I have had at Loyola
University of Chicago. Ideas have been formulated in discussions
with Judith Wittner (she has an enormous fund of knowledge as to
the roles of women), Kathy McCourt, Peter Whalley, Kirsten Gronbjerg,
and Phil Nyden of our very companionate department of sociology.
I would have been stuck many a time with the (now greatly appreci-
ated) PC had it not been for Richard Block, Ken Johnson, Anne
Figert, Fred Kniss and Chris Fry.

As before, I have looked to my nonsociological friends for
discussion and have even asked them to review manuscripts to see
if they think the ideas reflect life as they see it. This includes Teddy
Lopata Menasco, Dennis Menasco, Stefan Lopata, and Peggy Lopata,
Dick Lopata, Helen Janus Lopata Burns, Cele Shure, Pat Benoliel,
Carol Hanke, Juliet McNamara, and recently, Jule Grady Barry, Joan
Sullivan and Jeanne Goulet. Literally thousands of women have
contributed directly to my research, or to the research of scholars
whose studies I have used here. I hope that they get a chance to read
the results and that they enjoy them.

Very direct editorial help with this book has been provided by
Michael Ames, Judith Levy, Ronnie Steinberg, Catherine Surra, Rose
Coser, Judith Wittner, and an anonymous reviewer. I am especially
grateful to Wendy Nelson, an outstanding and imaginative copyeditor.
It is hard to write alone and see alternative ways of organizing and
explaining ideas. The staff of the sociology department at Loyola
University of Chicago has been extremely cooperative. This has
included, over all the years, Peggy Cusick, Maureen Abraham, Dorothy
Blumental, Tracy Wood, Karen Chase, and Mary Ellen Folk.

1

Social Roles of American Women

Enormous changes have occurred in the lives and role involvements of American women in the past century and a half. Our grandmothers led lives different from those of our mothers, who, in turn, experienced different lives from our own. How can we understand these differences and any abiding similarities?

This book examines some of the ways American women have been modifying their social roles. It is guided by the idea that the historically recent processes of modernization or social development affected men and women, urban and rural residents, upper and lower classes differently, but that in general there has been a movement toward greater societal and individual complexity and autonomy (Inkeles and Smith 1974; Inkeles 1983).[1] These processes involve three ideal-typical periods: the traditional, the transitional, and the modern. Ideal type analysis accentuates the differentiating characteristics of the phenomena (Weber 1949). The fact that we can trace these periods in the history of American women does not mean that all women currently living in this society are involved in modern

1

type roles. Modernization has affected women in different settings differently, as stated above. In fact, most American women are involved in transitional forms or types of family roles, and many even remain in traditional roles of, for example, wife and mother. The complexity of the society and the mobility of world populations insure the presence of all three types in even as modern a society as the American one. The vast majority of the world is still situated in traditional times, as far as women's roles are concerned.

Traditional, preindustrial society embedded women and men in an extended family system, organized usually along patrilineal lines, with patriarchal authority and patrilocal residence. Women's roles were formalized and established in this familistic intergenerational structure. According to Aries (1965), most European men and women were living in one of two worlds prior to the eighteenth century: that of the manor house or that of the village. Within each world each person was involved in a complexity of social roles. Life was public, which meant that each person had multiple obligations to many others and enjoyed multiple rights in relations with them. Mothers were assisted in child care and rearing by extended families, all the residents of households, and even communities. Children moved among adults and other youths with relative freedom but simultaneously were active in contributing to the economic maintenance of the social units. The role of wife was equally complicated by the multiplicity of people with whom she interacted precisely because she was the wife. These roles were embedded in an extended kinship network. The role of homemaker was equally complex—many women managed large households, whether in a village or in a manor. Aries (1965) found manor homes to contain as many as two hundred persons living inside or nearby who operated as a household, with many more coming and going for different reasons. The roles of neighbor and friend, of community and societal member, certainly varied by social classes and by age as well as gender, yet there appears to have been a relative similarity in the life spaces of men and women within each class. Upper-class daughters were educated by the same tutors as were their brothers, since they had to become knowledgeable about managing complex social units. However, formal public education (as in universities) excluded women until relatively recent centuries. Women ruled households and principalities in the absence of men, or in their own right. Each person operated within his or her *okolica*, as the authors of *The Polish Peasant in Europe and America* (Thomas and Znaniecki 1918–

20) called the territory within which a person's reputation was contained. Among the upper classes, this could include a vast territory with the help of communication and transportation networks. Among the peasants, emergencies and daily life necessitated a tight interdependence of more localized people.

The transitional period of social development, which lasted since the middle of the eighteenth century and even up to recent years in some parts of Europe and America, started to introduce dramatic changes in women's roles (Lerner 1958). Industrialization and urbanization disorganized the ascribed, i.e. assigned, familial and community roles. Mass education and mobility diminished the power of these social units. The combination organized increasing segments of work into jobs away from the ongoing life, and specialized roles emerged in other institutions. The effects of increasing societal complexity first affected middle-class urban men, freeing them from dependence upon the male family line and the local community. The public world of economic and political life, judged to be of primary importance by the blooming American society, became dominated by men. The home lost much of its centrality, and the settings and social circles of women narrowed considerably into a "woman's sphere" (Ehrenreich and English 1979; Sicherman 1975). Although women were freed from the control of the male kin network, they were transformed into personal dependents of their fathers and husbands (Eichler 1973).

This artificial division of the world into two spheres, one much smaller than, and judged inferior to, the other, became difficult to maintain in rapidly developing, complex societies. As the transitional period moved closer to modernization in the last few decades, women started revolting over the restrictions on them and increasingly ventured into male-dominated public arenas. However, the separation of women's and men's interests and developed abilities was so embedded in American society that change was very, very difficult for these pioneers. Structural and sociopsychological barriers often made it necessary for women to focus either on the private domain, centered in the home and family, or on the public, in the form of occupations, careers, and organizational involvements.

Increasing modernization allegedly has made it necessary for all members of a society to share the complexity of its life. Mass education, the demands of democracy, and ideological reconstructions of reality by various social movements, especially that of women, are increasingly individuating people's self-concepts and patterns of behavior. Women, and in some relations men, are creating or entering negotiated, rather than formalized, social roles.

The uneven rate of social development means that no matter how "modern" or developed a society is considered to be by those labeling social change, many traditional or transitional aspects of major institutions exist side by side with new technology and occupations. This means that not all women have as yet benefited from these changes (if we can call these changes "benefits")—far from it. Poverty, lack of education, discrimination, sexism, and racism keep the majority of women from exercising free choices in their role involvements and limit their rights of negotiation with circle members of many roles. In fact, most men have not benefited fully from social development. Many are stuck in the transitional stage of rigid settings, roles, and schedules. Both men and women are carrying the double burden of traditional and modern role involvements, and are feeling the strain and conflicts. We must acknowledge that even American society has not become fully "modern," if by that we mean providing equal opportunity for the development of human potential. But increasing proportions of Americans are living within, and enjoying, a complex, flexible, and negotiated social life space.

We will examine the changing roles of American women through the perspective of a symbolic interactionist form of social role theory.

Social Role as a Set of Social Relations

A *social role* is a set of patterned, mutually interdependent relations between a social person and a social circle, involving negotiated duties and personal rights (Znaniecki 1965; see also Lopata 1966, 1969b, 1971b, and 1991a).[2] The *social person* is that "package" of characteristics with which an individual enters a specific role. The *social circle* contains all those persons with whom the person interacts in the performance of *duties or obligations* and from whom she or he receives *personal rights*.[3] These definitions and the analyses that stem from them are based on a symbolic interactionist perspective.[4]

The *social person* carries the title of the social role, although it is only in relationship with circle members that the role actually exists. A social person is that package of characteristics that an individual pulls together to enter and carry forth her or his part of the role. The total individual has many characteristics, consisting of a constructed reality, sentiments, and emotions, as well as behavior, that are not called for or needed in each social role. Human beings live in a symbolic world whose meaning or reality they construct (Blumer 1969). The person of a student is quite different from that of a girlfriend, daughter, or waitress. Thus, a woman wishing to enter a specific social role prepares herself through anticipatory socialization—the process of learning necessary behavior and visualizing the self in the role. She becomes a candidate and, upon acceptance by the social circle, carries forth the duties, and receives the rights of that role. Or she can pull together a social circle and assign duties and rights, as in the role of homemaker.

The title of a role contains the typified, categorical identification, or the ideal image, of how a person is expected to fulfill the role's basic purpose (see Gerhardt's 1980 discussion of Simmel, Weber, and Schutz). A mother must give birth or adopt a child and take on the role in cooperation with others. If she is judged unfit, the child may be taken away from her. She must have the characteristics that will guarantee cooperation from all circle members besides the child, since she cannot take care of the child herself.[5] The social circle can include the father, relatives on either side, pediatricians, teachers, representatives of the state, and so forth. The title of mother is carried by her into interactional situations (Simmel 1971). It serves as a label, an anticipation of behavior by potential circle members, and as a means of evaluating her as a social person. The title, however, is not the social role itself, since that requires continued relationships between the social person and the social circle.

The whole process by which an existing social circle such as an employing organization selects a social person is indicative of the qualifications deemed necessary for the role. Often latent criteria are evident only in the characteristics of the persons who are rejected. The Catholic church is convinced that women cannot be good priests. Management consulting or law firms have frequently argued (allegedly only in the past) that they would love to hire a black or a woman consultant or lawyer, but that their clients would not accept persons with those identities.

The social person must have the sort of personality that is assumed to be necessary for meeting the purposes of the relations and for interaction with circle members, and must be able to "take the role of the other," as George Herbert Mead (1934) called the process of empathetically understanding other human beings. Physical characteristics such as sight or hearing and locomotion are often demanded of the social person, unless she or he can prove she or he has the ability to function in the negotiated manner without them.

The *social circle* of a role contains all those people toward whom the social person has duties and who have obligations toward him or her that are that social person's rights that enable him or her to carry forth the role in the agreed-upon manner. The social person's relationships with each segment of the social circle are negotiated, unless enforced by other segments or outside powers. No matter how clearly each contributor to the role has defined it prior to involvement, the actual set of relations always requires flexibility of interaction that must be negotiated. The social circle can best be literally visualized as a circle, as in figure 1. At its center is the social person, with duties and rights of self-maintenance necessary to carry forth other duties.

All social circles contain "clients" or beneficiaries, who in turn have duties toward the social person that are part of her or his rights. These rights may simply be the permission to the social person to perform her or his duties. The title of a role often contains a presupposition as to the beneficiary. University professors profess to students, judges judge defendants, architects design buildings for clients. Social roles tend to contain assisting segments of the social circle, which vary enormously in the amount of work they contribute and the duties that must be directed toward them. Each member of the assisting segments must be related to the beneficiary, with duties and rights connected to what they do for him or her. In fact, the beneficiaries do not necessarily receive the greatest amount of direct attention by the social person, as in the case of patients of physicians who have a large staff of receptionists, nurses, laboratory technicians, medical specialists, and hospital personnel who serve as intermediaries. In modern times the doctor often spends more time with these circle members than with the patient for whom all the activity is carried forth.

Many roles contain a "colleague" segment—people carrying forth the same role in the same organization—with whom cooperation is often necessary and without whom there would be no role for the social person. A saleswoman needs others selling goods in a large store. The segment containing suppliers includes anyone whose objects or services make possible the person's performance of her duties.

A social person may have rights to include or exclude members of a preexisting social circle. If she creates her own circle, she will

Fig. 1.

THE SOCIAL ROLE OF HOMEMAKER*

Beneficiaries

Suppliers and Assistants

* The size of the area represents its relative significance to the role, performed at a complex level. Modified from Helena Znaniecka Lopata, *Occupation: Housewife*. (New York: Oxford University Press, 1971), 138.

include those she thinks necessary for the carrying forth of her duties, or those whom she may not be able to avoid. A wife may have to relate with the in-laws who come into her circle with the husband. The social circles of different persons in the same type of role can vary considerably due to the influences of size, setting, the number and social class of beneficiaries. Hillary Clinton, as the manager of the household of the president of the United States, has a different social circle than she had when she lived a more private life.

The *duties* of a social role's central person are of two major sorts: those deemed necessary by all involved to meet the role's purpose, and the relational duties that make the whole process possible. These duties are not necessarily determined by what we would consider logical methods, since they tend to be lodged in history and beliefs about life held by the participants. Certainly, some duties are made inevitable by the nature of the role's purposes. As far as social science has discovered, a social mother is universally supposed to care for the physical welfare of her child, directly or through the cooperation of others. Her duties become even more complex in societies that do not believe that children are born with an already formed personality (Ehrenreich and English 1979). The relatively new theory of the developmental needs of human potential places a heavy burden on the main socializer. The more people that are involved in each child's social circles, the more people with whom the mother must interact to meet the role's purposes. Cultures and even subcultures differ in what is defined as proper care of children and the means used to achieve it. The mother must also recognize and relate to all the circle members, accepting their duties as her rights and giving them the resources they need to help her.

The *personal rights* of a social role include all those resources that must be supplied to the social person so that she can perform her duties as negotiated with circle members. Her rights also include circle members' obligations toward her. The personal rights of a social role must contain the permission to carry forth the duties. As Hughes (1971) and other sociologists of work point out, many roles cannot be carried out without the person's learning "guilty knowledge" about circle members. Priests, psychiatrists, physicians, and newspaper reporters claim and usually receive the right to gain, and not to divulge, confidential knowledge about people with whom they work, no matter how important that information is to others. The right to safety, unless waived by the social person—as in the case of military personnel in time of war—is an important right, as is the right to be recognized and to have one's performance of one's duties acknowledged. Rights in roles with similar functions vary by societal norms regarding what is necessary to the person.

Cooperation from circle members must be built into personal rights, because duties cannot be carried forth otherwise. The rights and duties of a role are often paired. The duty to exert authority must be accompanied by the right to obedience. If initiating behavior is not required, then someone else must direct the person. All roles are located in one or more social settings, such as houses, factories, or streets, with specific rights and duties of access and management of the space and objects.

Role Strain

The fact that social circles can be large and complicated may result in a great deal of role strain. One of the sources of strain is *role overload,* which occurs when there is too much to do in general, or when too many circle members make too many demands, each considering his or hers as most important (Goode 1960). The social person may be deeply committed to her role and frustrated by obstacles or barriers to adequate performance, such as the lack of cooperation from others. Role strain also arises when members of the social circle make conflicting or inconsistent demands. Fathers and children sometimes demand contradictory behavior from the mother. Strain also occurs when a circle member makes conflicting demands, creating a double-bind situation. Problems can also arise when the role demands behavior that the person considers to be objectionable or incompatible with her or his abilities and desires (Turner 1978 and 1981).

The social person can handle role strain in several ways, such as compartmentalization (dealing with each demand separately), delegation of duties, or negotiation. She or he can ignore a troublesome member of the circle. And, if things are too bad and there are alternatives, she or he can leave the role or that role relationship. Divorce is an established way out of a marriage, and jobs may be quit. All kinds of culturally approved explanations are available to people who fail to meet some role expectations, while barriers against intrusion can prevent circle members from claiming rights (Becker 1951; Scott and Lyman 1968). Some people, of course,

thrive in roles that require constant negotiation and flexibility, preferring these to roles in which all relational problems are allegedly
minimized.

Social circles, especially organized groups, can be aware of
problems built into their roles and may introduce strain-reducing
mechanisms (Goode 1960). Roles can be shifted in the structure;
third parties (such as therapists) may be brought in to mediate
conflict; norms of adequacy of role performance can be redefined;
and people of "the right persuasion" or the "right" color or other
characteristics can be hired to produce greater trust among circle
members. Kanter (1977) found corporation men unwilling to admit
women to their circle because they did not trust them.

The Role Cluster and Social Life Space

Each human being is involved in numerous social roles, at any time
and throughout the life course. The *role cluster* changes over time,
as some roles are exited, new ones are added, modifications are
introduced to current ones, and hierarchies are adjusted. In order to
explore the connections among roles in an individual's cluster, I
have developed the concept of "social life space" (Lopata 1969b and
1987e), adapted from the work of Kurt Lewin (see Deutsch 1954),
who used the term *life space* to refer to a field or total situation of
action containing the actor.[6] My housewife interviews (Lopata 1971b
and 1987e) indicated a very logical way of organizing the social life
space: We can look at roles within the same institutional dimension
as sharing a similar cultural base and so as enabling more effective
negotiation than do roles in different institutions.

People vary in the *dimensional richness* of their social roles, that
is, in the number of roles in which they are involved within a single
institution and also in the relative importance assigned each role.
Sociologists refer to an institution as a set of patterned procedures
by which a major area of societal life is carried forth. We can thus
compare different women within the same society, or cross-cultur-
ally, or women to men, in terms of the richness of their involvement
in any of the major institutions, such as educational, family, political,
economic, religious, and recreational institutions. People also vary
in the complexity or multidimensionality of their social life spaces,
in that they undertake roles in different institutions (see figure 2).

This perspective is central to my analysis of the changing roles

Fig. 2.

A MULTIDIMENSIONAL LIFE SPACE WITH VARIED
"RICHNESS" OF INSTITUTIONAL DIMENSIONS

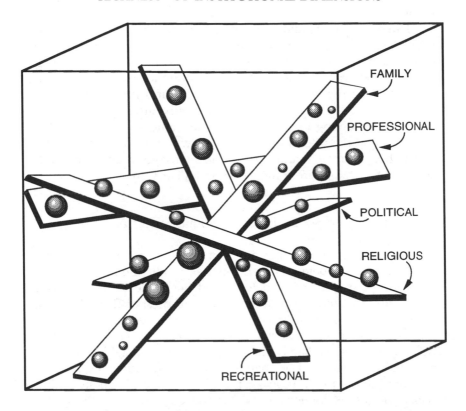

Modified from Helena Znaniecka Lopata, "Women's Family Roles in Life Course Perspective." Pp. 381–407 in *Analyzing Gender: A Handbook of Social Science Research,* edited by Beth B. Hess and Myra Marx Ferree (Newbury Park, Calif.: Sage, 1987), p. 384.

of American women. The process of modernization appears to proceed first from the destruction of a full life space within a traditional community, flattening women's life spaces into the domestic/ family sphere, and men's into the public sphere, during the transitional period. Only gradually does modern society provide opportunities for socialization and education to expand people's life spaces again to new multidimensionality, this time within a greater scale of complexity. Modern life requires the presence of many multidimensional people, able to manage roles in most institutions and even roles bridging two or more institutions. However, not all members of even modern societies have such complexity of self. Most people still exist in relatively "flat" social life spaces, focusing on one institution.

The presence of multiple roles can create *role conflict,* similar in sources to role strain. One of the ways people try to diminish role conflict is by organizing their role clusters into a hierarchical system, either temporarily, as roles surface in importance due to events, or in more or less rigid structures (Lopata 1969b and 1987e; Lopata and Barnewolt 1984; Stryker 1980). Social groups also try to decrease role conflict among their members. The Catholic church decided long ago that the role of priest conflicts with the roles of husband and father, and it continues to forbid marriage in spite of much pressure for change from the clergy in recent years.

The Location of Social Roles in Social Systems

Social roles can be placed in different types of social systems, one of which I have labeled "chart positions," modifying Davis's (1966, 68) concept of "office," which "would designate a position in a deliberately created organization, governed by specific and limited rules in a limited group, more generally achieved than ascribed." The concept of "chart position" is broader and may be used in describing roles in a family, a kinship network, a neighborhood, or a formal association. The chart shows each member the lines of communication and authority, and the province of activity within which the role is connected to other social roles.

Another system within which social roles can be positioned is that of prestige, often accompanied by power or its legitimated version of authority. In American society, men are located at a higher-status position in the gender stratification system than are women. Such a location has very important consequences for the status of other roles available to men and permeates the availability of choices of many objects, such as kitchens or airplanes, within the culture.

People entering social roles as social persons or members of social circles usually have a fairly good idea of what to expect, because models of roles are contained in cultures. Most roles have a historical base and are performed by more than one person at any given time. The models are more or less visible parts of the culture, learned at home and in other primary and secondary groups such as neighborhoods and schools. Established roles vary by specialized function, alternative ways of meeting purposes, and relationships of members. Thus, there are two ways in which social roles influence societies and their members: as actual sets of relations (e.g., waitresses at a Four Seasons restaurant) and as cultural models of relations (e.g., our image of waitresses in general).

The Life Course of Role Involvements of American Women

The presence of cultural models of roles does not guarantee the match between social persons and the social circles that makes the life of the society possible. In order for the whole thing to work, new societal members must be socialized into "humanness" and the necessary knowledge, identities, and motivations to become involved in all kinds of interactions and social roles. Social groups develop whole socialization and educational systems to guarantee that enough people want to, and are able to, carry forth needed roles.

One important form of socialization is into pervasive identities that are deemed appropriate to different roles, and one of these identities is gender. Every society identifies each newborn as male or female on the basis of its visible genitals. The implications of such classification, however, vary considerably the world over, because it contains assumptions as to personality and potentials for action throughout childhood and adulthood. Socialization insures that each individual develops the appropriate *gender personal identity,* which is carried everywhere and is more or less intrusive in all social roles.

One of the problems with discussions of gender identity has been the recent introduction into the social sciences of the theoretically and actually inappropriate concept of "sex roles." There are, simply, no sex roles in America any more than there are race or class roles (Lopata and Thorne 1978; see also Thorne 1982). There is no set of relationships of social persons with social circles whose main function is gender identity (Lopata, Miller, and Barnewolt 1984).

There are only gender or racial identities—and probably class identities at the self-conscious extremes of the class structure.

In order that sexual identification of people by others and socialization into gender identity be possible, the culture must contain images of "typical" girls (and boys), and young, middle-aged, and old women (and men). In order for the self and the others to include gender in their consideration of selection and interaction in roles, they must have indicators of such identity. Girls and boys have traditionally worn divergent hair and clothes styles, enabling easy identification. Visitors entering a home usually receive multiple clues as to the gender of a child, and adult roles often utilize uniforms as aids to classification. Changes in visual cues that occurred when the Catholic church allowed nuns to remove their identifying and isolating clothing made it easier for nuns to leave their orders. One of the major functions of the habit is to camouflage those aspects of gender identity that were traditionally associated with the roles of wife and mother, roles considered more normal for women in American society.

Language also contains clues as to gender identity. Girls must learn to talk like girls, and women allegedly share a universe of discourse apart from that of males.[7] In fact, Jessie Bernard (1981) developed a complex analysis of this in *The Female World*. Dale Spender (1980) devotes a whole volume to the analysis of "man-made language," pointing out, for example, that *master* and *mistress* have different meanings. M. Johnson (1988, 5) noted the same variation in the phrases *mothering a child* and *fathering a child* (see also Thorne, Kramarae, and Henley 1983). The world of discourse of different areas of life can keep unwanted people out of a role or group. There is much documentation of the difficulties faced by women trying to function in male-dominated occupations (Lopata, Miller, and Barnewolt 1986; Walshok 1981). Even the idea of high levels of achievement in competitive fields assumed to be masculine can lead young women into "fear of success," according to Matina Horner (1972). The initial popularity of that concept indicates that it must have some relevance even in modern America.

Children gradually develop their self-concepts, going through the stages G. H. Mead so carefully analyzed: awareness of the physical self, *playing at a role,* and *game playing* leading to the incorporation of a *generalized other* (Mead 1934). As a girl grows, she becomes increasingly conscious of how she looks in the eyes of others, not just physically, but as an actor in social roles. She learns to apply to herself the standards others seem to be applying to her, and to feel certain sentiments, such as pride or mortification, in response (Cooley [1902] 1922). She can try to change these responses, if she wishes. Unfortunately, life is not that simple. She learns that she frequently cannot fully control her environment, especially others within it.

It is obvious that people do not remain in the same social roles all their lives, and that involvement in any one social role changes over time (C. A. Miller, 1981). In order for a woman to enter a social role she must be aware of its existence and must take the necessary steps to enter its social circle—unless she pulls together a new one. For example, let us say that a woman wants to take on her first full-time job. First, she must choose one or more occupations, out of the welter available to women nowadays, that she thinks she might like and for which she feels probably qualified. There are special agencies that can help her at this stage, including career counselors at schools and employment agencies. She will probably place some other limitations on her search—territorial, geographical, or social (e.g., she may be unwilling to move out of state or to venture into a very large corporation). Next, she must learn from newspaper advertisements, or other search agents about the various organizations that can provide the circle within which her role can be carried forth. She must learn the potential employer's hiring criteria and eliminate those potential employers that she knows will never accept her, or take the time to better prepare herself to meet their standards. She then selects the one (or ones, in case she does not get her first choice) she prefers and goes through a process of application. After testing, which usually includes personal interviews by people trained to fit workers into slots, she may get the job. She must follow the same procedures, with more or less complexity, any time she enters a new social role in an established organization. Of course, not every woman goes through such calculated procedures to find a new job. Some simply hear of one through a friend or go to a place that is likely to hire persons of their capabilities.

That is not, however, the end of the entrance stage of involvement in a social role. Regardless of prior formal preparation, the person must learn the rules of the game in that particular circle. Anticipatory socialization is a process by which she learns by anticipating what she might need to know. Some schools or job training programs may provide opportunities to role-play the future occupation, with other trainees enacting the duties and rights of circle members. Reading about the job, even in fiction, may enable the applicant to go through dress rehearsals for her own performance. Talking to others in the same or a similar role can also provide clues, as does the simple process of asking people about their jobs.

Entering a social role requires forming relationships with all circle members, which is a gradual process, since the person usually does not come into contact with all at the same time. Involvement in a social role important to the woman requires, in greater or lesser degree, "becoming" the title bearer (a mother) (a wife) (see Becker 1953; Lopata 1971b). This is a process of placing oneself within the role, seeing oneself as a "natural" center of the circle and the role as part of one's role cluster and self-concept. Gradually, the person quits being a novice and enters the regular performer stage. Relationships are established and modified only by events in the lives of partners, or by the exits and entrances of circle members. Role strain has been decreased by negotiations, or the person has learned to live with it. Duties become standardized, sometimes to the level of boredom. Several paths can lead from this stage. The person can be fired for losing enthusiasm and the ability to innovate; she can be retained in a dead-end position until the phase-out stage (Kanter 1977); or she can start to again socialize herself anticipatorily into another role—one of higher status in the hierarchy or in another organization, or of a completely different type. Effective preparation can lead to promotion, until the person is no longer willing or able to socialize herself to the new role. The process of phasing oneself out of one role is influenced by one's stages of involvement in other roles.

The concept of *life course involvements* can be applied not only to roles but also to the individual's total life. A life course is usually defined in terms of stages; transitions are bounded by cultural norms of timing and the consequences of being "off time" or not at the typical time of life. Some social roles cannot be entered until certain age-related criteria are met. The biological system refuses to allow a woman to become impregnated and carry a child to birth until a certain stage of development. Most societies have motherhood norms related to schooling, official adulthood, or marriage age. At the other end of the life course, some roles must be left. Women cannot bear children after a certain age; retirement policies force or encourage the dropping of major occupational roles. Some circles put definite age parameters on candidates because of assumptions about age-related abilities. In traditional societies, it was impossible to be an "expert" in most social roles until at least adult age. One of the problems of modern society, based as it is upon traditional but rapidly changing culture, is that young people are learning the new technology required in many roles faster, earlier, and more exclusively than are their elders, which often lands them in positions of authority over their seniors.

Social Psychological Aspects of Role Involvement

A person's involvement in a particular social role can be conceptualized as including nine sociopsychological aspects. The first set consists of the *hierarchical importance of the roles* in the role cluster, the *richness of each institutional dimension* in which the roles are located, and the *multidimensionality of the social life space* (Lopata 1969b).

As mentioned above, women tend to diminish role conflict by developing, more or less consciously, a hierarchy within the cluster of roles they are performing at any one time. The role order changes with the introduction of important new roles to the cluster. For the most part, occupationally committed American women do not face competition from the two roles considered most important to their gender—wife and mother (Lopata and Barnewolt 1984). Once these roles are added, the whole cluster changes. The role of mother was generally considered most important for women with young children, even more so than the role of wife, if both are active in the role cluster (Barnewolt 1986). More-educated husbands in higher status jobs often rank higher for these women than their children do, but then the duties of these wives are often more complex than those of wives of men in less "greedy" jobs (L. Coser 1974; Lopata 1971b; see also the discussion in chapter 2 on the role of wife). Some women see life-course changes in their role hierarchies, explaining that they now have to focus on being mothers, because of the needs of small children, but that they will return to a focus on wifehood in the future (Lopata and Barnewolt 1984).

We can assume that involvement in a social role is also influenced by the richness of the dimension in which it is located. On the one hand we can predict that a woman with multiple roles in one institution will receive much support in each role from circle members in other roles in that institution. A mother can count on support with minimum conflict from her other roles in the family institution. On the other hand, members of the circles of her roles of wife, daughter, granddaughter, sibling, aunt and cousin may compete for her attention and complicate her life. Having to be a daughter-in-law may make life miserable for her in her role of mother.

The complexity or multidimensionality of the social life space is also important. Social roles in other dimensions can compete severely with roles in the family dimension, and vice versa. Although a mother may understand the priority her daughter gives to her children, the daughter's boss may not.

The next three aspects of role involvement deal with the role itself. People vary in their *assignment of importance to the different segments of the social circle,* in the extent to which they are *task-* versus *relations-oriented,* and in whether they see the duties as a set *of unrelated actions or processes* or in terms of *product* (Lopata 1969b, 290–92). Mothers may be more concerned with how their in-laws view their child rearing than with how the child is affected. Women differ in their perceptions of the duties of any role, seeing them variously as a series of disjointed incidents or events, as a set of processes, or in terms of product alone (Lopata 1969b, 291). Many homemakers are so overwhelmed by daily existence that they move from one task to another without seeing patterns or end results. Others plan the sequence of processes, with a rhythm of start, work, and finish, moving from one sequence to the next. Finally, there are many women who, for example, do not concentrate on what they do, but concentrate only on maintaining or restoring things to their proper state. Their work is done when the house is clean or the laundry finished.

The final set of aspects of role involvement are those of "style" or of being the self in the role. People can vary along the continuum of *passive-reactive-initiating approaches,* the type of *sentiments* experienced as a result of being in that role, and the *judgments of the self* in it (Lopata 1969b, 292–96). Both the passive and the reactive person in a role are noninitiating, but the first responds only to outside pressure without thinking about it or preparing herself for the onslaught of demands. The reactive person knows that she must respond and is prepared to do so, seeing that as the function of the role rather than as a natural response on her part. People can carry forth all three stances, usually in separate roles but often in relation to different segments of the same role. A mother can wait passively for the children to come home from school and make demands on her, she can prepare hygienic lunches for them because she knows what the school demands, and she can arrange a birthday party, inviting grandparents. The historical past of many societies demanded either passive or reactive stances toward the public sphere by the vast majority of their members. This is not desired, or possible, in a democratic society. The changes accompanying modernization and the feminist movement in America, at all stages, have pushed toward the self- and other-definition of women as initiators in their role selection and behavior. Education and the ability to see the wider scene within which one's role is located enable people to make such decisions and know where to push for rights. Conflict occurs when circle members do not respond to a person's changes of approach. Families may object to a wife/mother's refusal to be passive or reactive to their demands.

People differ in the sentiments they feel about various aspects of their roles. Women may hate the role of homemaker in which they feel they must be involved; they may dislike certain duties, or feel antagonistic to some segments of the circle that benefit from their work (such as in-laws). The same task may be greeted neutrally, or even with pleasure, by others. The concept of sentiments, merged by symbolic interactionists with that of emotion, is very important for the understanding of role relations.

Finally, women can vary in how they see themselves in each role or parts of it. They judge how well they are doing, aware that others are also judging them, and they feel certain ways in response to these judgments. "I am very good with the children, I read and play with them, but I can't follow a tight schedule. They get to bed when I get them to bed—this irritates their father," a woman once stated in an interview.

Thus, there are many ways in which people differ in their involvement in any role. This is not surprising, since each individual gradually builds her own social self or adjusts to the characteristics needed to enter social roles. She learns from the past, practices anticipatory socialization, interacts with circle members, and experiences the various aspects of involvement discussed here.

Commitment

The end result of the social psychological aspects of role involvement is role commitment (Lopata 1992d). People differ in which role they are most committed to, the degree of commitment they have to any role, and the kinds of "side bets" they have placed in order to insure continued participation and success (Becker 1960). Side bets include investment in education and job training, the search for and performance in an appropriate role, and the selection and arrangement of other roles so that they do not conflict or interfere with the commitment role.

The shift in women's ideology from total commitment to family roles to involvement in broader life choices accompanying modernization has moved women toward direct involvement in the public sphere. Simultaneously, it has reaffirmed the commitment of some women to motherhood and wifehood (Lopata, 1987). Some of these women have little choice, and their commitment is quite defensive; but many of them are relatively young, highly educated mothers who experienced success in occupations and then decided to stay home. They, however, unlike women in traditional or transitional times, consider such commitment to be temporary, to be followed by a return to commitment to an outside career (see also Lopata, Barnewolt, and Miller 1985).

Summary

We have now examined the basic theoretical framework guiding our analysis of the changes in social roles and life spaces of American women and some of the basic concepts to be used throughout this book.[8] The framework applies social development or modernization theory to such women. The conceptual model hinges upon the definition of social role as a set of patterned, mutually interdependent social relations between a social person and a social circle, involving task and relational duties and personal rights.

Social roles are located in the role clusters and social life spaces of individual members of the society, either within a single institutional dimension or multidimensionally in several separate institutions. Involvement in social roles influences not only the life spaces but also the identities of human beings. The models for such sets of relations are contained in a society's cultural base, while actual, situated roles are located in several social systems, organizational charts, or status structures.

Socialization into feminine gender identity and appropriate behavior begins as soon as the baby is identified as female. Girls are assigned relevant roles, or they are so heavily encouraged to antici-patorily socialize themselves in those directions that purposeful deviation is hard to accomplish. This female identity is carried through-out life, entering more or less intrusively into all other social roles. The social structure of a society constantly reminds people of their pervasive identities, which can block or open opportunities for role involvements.

Social roles have their own life courses, and each individual fits them into her total life course. Social psychological aspects of in-volvement in any particular role include the role's rank order of importance and the individual's stances vis-à-vis its various compo-nents. The complexity of the social life space influences not only the breadth of perspective with which life is constructed, but also the manner in which role conflict is resolved.

We now turn to the examination of the social roles of American women in their traditional, transitional, and modern variations.

2

The Role of Wife

All societies known to us have some institutionalized arrangement for mate selection and for the formation, continuation and dissolution of the roles of wife and husband. The complexities and changes in the role of wife over the past few generations and in comparison to other societies are too extensive to develop in detail. Therefore, I will provide only a brief analysis of the traditional role of wife that is still much in evidence in other parts of the world. I will concentrate, however, on the changing role of wife in America: from one dependent upon the traditional patriarchal family, through the "personal dependent" of the transitional type, to the emerging "modern" one. In traditional families, and especially in other parts of the world, the role of wife was basically controlled by the husband's family, in transitional times, by the husband, and in modern times it is negotiated with flexibility between the husband and wife. The role variations in transitional times, which stretch from the period of extensive industrialization and increasing societal complexity to all but recent decades, is of itself so complicated that I have broken it down by social class, with some attention to racial and ethnic variations.

Traditional Times, Traditional Places

In traditional families of the world and in America's traditional past, a girl was selected to become a wife by the two families, hers and the potential husband's. The qualities for which a future wife was chosen depended upon the culture, with strong class restrictions and in some societies caste restrictions. Three sets of criteria were considered. The most important was the match in social status of the families. Family alliances brought about by marriages of the young have been socially important. They have been used to prevent wars (or initiate them), provide for economic exchanges, and insure other privileges. In turn, the status of each family was influenced by the excellence of the match, verified by the amount of dowry or bride-price. A second set of criteria was provided by cultural norms. Among many contemporary traditional Asian families (and some American, if we are to believe the *National Enquirer*), soothsayers are also consulted to determine whether the match will be auspicious.

The social person characteristics of the future wife, which became the third layer of consideration, counted in the balance of negotiation, after the major family-matching considerations were taken care of. In societies deeply concerned over "bloodline purity" of each offspring, an important criterion was the bride's virginity. Families went to great lengths to insure this, creating Purdah-like isolation of girls from any contact with non-family males (Papanek and Minault, 1982). Other societies were more concerned with the woman's ability to bear children, even if biologically fathered by other men, although pregnancy by the future husband could be favored. Families in such cases provided opportunities for impregnation of their daughters. Other social person characteristics of the potential wife included proper appearance and such abilities as were deemed important by the social class of the families. The personal preferences of the man or woman, if known or allowed, were often overridden for benefit of the families. As Westernization spread the world over, these preferences were taken into consideration with increasing frequency; today the parents are simply asked for their consent and marriages even take place without their approval.

The husband's family formed a major segment of the social circle of, and had the greatest influence upon, the role of wife in traditional families. In many situations, the wife's duties toward, and rights from, her family of orientation into which she was born, decreased dramatically upon marriage. Her duties to the husband varied considerably from place to place, ranging from the minimal one of allowing sexual access and contributing to the family work group to being almost his and his family's servant. The demands considered appropriate within the norms of the male group could be extreme, even to the point of causing her death. The wife's right to safety has not been universal. Companionship and empathetic understanding have also not been common to marital roles.

Bohannan (1963) concluded his comparative analysis of marriage in traditional families with four sets of rights that men acquired in women upon marriage: rights to sharing a domicile, rights to sexual access, *in genetricem* rights of filiation of the children with their male line, and economic rights, including rights to goods she brought with her in marriage, goods they produced together, and sometimes even those she produced alone. In the extreme situation of a patriarchal, patrilineal, and patrilocal system, the wife had no rights over any economic goods, and her children remained behind if she decided to quit the marriage. In return, the remaining wife had the rights to a domicile, the product of sexual access (which is usually not pleasure but offspring), and maintenance till death. The woman who produced sons for the family was guaranteed their care, inheritance and other privileges of membership in the male line.

In general, the higher the evaluation of the wife's contribution to the husband's family, the higher is her status, although this does not translate automatically into freedom of action. As Goode (1963) and Ward (1963) point out, a woman's power in a family system is often influenced by her control over economic goods.

Wives in ancient Europe did not fare well, as far as their legal and personal rights were concerned. The British system, upon which much of American legal policies and culture were based, operated by "common law" by which the husband and wife formed a single legal unity, of which he was the representative. Common law disenfranchised wives, who were legally minors and had few legal rights until relatively recently (Chapman and Gates 1977). However, it also laid on the husband the duty of supplying the wife with what the lawyers called "necessities," that is, with those things that seemed essential for her existence, and such other things as accorded with the standard of life he was able to maintain (Abbott 1938, 600).

The rights to legal guardianship of the family meant that "in the nineteenth century females were not allowed to testify in court, hold title to property, establish business, or sign papers as witnesses" (Chafe 1972, 5). Other men were even appointed guardians in the absence of a husband/father, holding property until a male child reached adulthood. These policies did not mean that the wife was completely powerless in intrafamily relations, as the husband was also economically dependent upon her work in agriculture, in the informal urban marketplace, or, by the eighteenth century, in the cottage industry.

The Transitional Form of the Role of Wife

The traditional forms of economic interdependence of husbands and wives began to modify with the increasing complexity or scale of the societies within which families were located. Many technological and ideational changes contributed to this complexity in Western Europe and America, including industrialization and the increasing influence of a money economy. According to Weber ([1904] 1958), the Protestant ethic provided justification for a man to concentrate his energy upon economic activity, confirming his heavenly predestination through earthly success, rather than passively waiting for a better life in the afterlife.

Families were transformed through these changes in a two-step fashion, freeing the nuclear unit from the power of the male line. The first step freed the man, the second his wife and children. Sons could obtain formal education and job training away from the family of orientation, marketing their abilities for an income to maintain themselves in varying levels of comfort. Their success was to be won individualistically, without dependence on the family of orientation—although it could provide a foundation.

In fact, the cultures of much of Europe and subsequently America, influenced by this Protestant ethic, focusing upon the economic institution, pushed the values and reference groups of other institutions into the background. One of the major functions of the family became the support of the male earner and the reproduction of future earners. The educational institution became limited to preparing men for their participation in the economic sphere. The religious institution and the state were allowed to interfere with economic freedom only minimally.

This dramatic push toward the economic institution was accompanied by the removal of women from direct participation in its formal, public life, through very convoluted ideological and behavioral changes. When paid work first entered the economy, women and children followed (Kessler-Harris 1982; Oakley 1974b). However, as P. Laslett (1971) explains:

> The factory won its victory by outproducing the working family, taking away the market for the product of hand labour and cutting prices to the point where the craftsman had either to starve or take a job under factory discipline himself. (P. 18)

Men became increasingly interested in paid employment, and their wives and children ended up as "personal dependents" upon the men's earnings as sources for their independent income dried up (Eichler 1973). As the public domain of life grew in size and importance with all the societal changes, men developed or tightened their masculine, homosocial monopoly over it, squeezing women out (Lipman-Blumen 1976b).

The removal of women from paid employment in all but a few occupations was accompanied, in chicken-or-egg sequence, by ideological shifts. There were several components to the ideology. One was protective legislation that redefined women (who were previously considered able to do heavy work in agriculture, mines, or elsewhere) as persons of weak physique and disposition. (Actually, the reformers were more interested in the welfare of children these women could produce than of the women themselves). "Protective" legislation of the 1800s in England, and later in America, changed conditions under which women could work in industry, with an unanticipated result of making them less attractive to employers.

The Victorian upper-class image of women's delicacy and refinement also began filtering to the new middle classes and as far down the social structure as husbands could afford to keep their wives protected from work in the new competitive world. As Bernard (1981, chapter 9) concluded, a wife was stripped to a considerable extent of her access to cash-mediated markets, and left without legal rights and her own source of income. She could not be economically self-sufficient or visibly contributing a major share to the economic welfare of the family unit. Obviously, her contributions as a homemaker could be evaluated as equal to those of the man only if what each does is measured as equally important (Krauskopf 1977, 105–6). Working for money was more prestigeful than other economic activity and by law wives were kept from taking on roles that would make them economically independent.

The importance assigned to the public sphere of life led to an ideological division of the world into two spheres, accompanied by a stereotyping of personalities of each gender. According to the two-sphere sociopsychological perspectives, men are best suited to the highly competitive public sphere. They are so aggressive, controlled in their emotions, instrumentally oriented, and involved in being "the good provider" (Bernard 1983) that they do not have the interest, time, or energy to devote to other aspects of life, such as the family. Women, in this imagery, are nurturing, they care for husbands, small children, and animals, and they are passive and patient. They are expected to be weak in abilities required for the public world, such as mechanical skills, logic, mathematics, and long-range complex thinking. The ideal situation was for the husband and wife to function cooperatively out of their own spheres, meeting both instrumental and expressive functions through specialization by person rather than by activity (Parsons and Bales 1955).

The result of all these changes made the woman who became a wife in transitional times economically dependent upon the husband; she had lower status than the man and little recognition of her contribution to the unit. Rosaldo (1974), comparing many societies, developed the following structural model:

> women's status will be lowest in those societies where there is a firm differentiation between domestic and public spheres of activity and where women are isolated from one another and placed under a single man's authority, in the home. (P. 36)

Class Differences

The transitional role of wife in American society is not woven of a single fabric. It varies especially by social class. In different classes the ideal characteristics desired of a wife, and her duties and rights, can be quite different, and the social circle can vary considerably. It may contain multiple assistants and suppliers, as well as associates of the husband, or a simple set of co-workers. The social psychological aspects of role involvement vary likewise.

Working-Class Wives. Much of the literature on the role of wife in the socioeconomically lower classes in America is closely related to ethnicity—which is not surprising, since the majority of America's large-wave immigrations were composed of members of those classes. People doing well elsewhere generally stayed, unless pushed out by political or religious problems. Although the immigrants have come at different times, and from highly divergent cultures, most have shared certain characteristics (see Mindel, Habenstein, and Wright 1988). Generally speaking, their societies have been highly patriarchal, and the role of wife has been dependent upon male-defined rights and duties. For example, Kourvetaris (1988) found many vestiges of patriarchal power among first-generation Greek Americans. Cultural norms are still constantly reinforced among Puerto Rican immigrants (Sanchez-Ayendez 1988) and Mexican immigrants (Becerra 1988) by the frequent movement back and forth to the homeland, delaying the "Americanization process." However, the very process of migration increased the power of wives, compared to their traditional situations in the home countries, as found by Wrobel (1979) and myself (Lopata 1976b and 1994) in the Polish American community. They could establish their own homes, if the husband's family did not come over and thus could not back up his demands. The husband was much more dependent upon his marital partner than was true of village situations in Poland. The first generation of immigrants tried to preserve patriarchal family traditions, but rights of husbands (e.g., duties of wives) became more flexible by the second generation, much to the frustration of the elders. That does not mean that the newly emerging middle-class American ideal of wife-husband egalitarianism has permeated down through lower social classes or outward into ethnic groups socialized into different norms. As Schoolcr (1984) argues, "serfdom's legacy" continues into the ethnic world in America. The newer, or newly expanding, immigrant groups from Asia also bring with them the ideal of submissiveness of women, as found among the Chinese and Japanese by Sue and Morishima (1982).

The gender-segregated lives of working-class wives are found to continue across generations of Italian Americans (Whyte 1956 and Gans 1962), even into the third and later generations, according to Johnson (1985). Komarovsky (1962), Rainwater and his associates (1959) and Rubin (1976) describe the role of the wife in such groups as very difficult. The women marry young, hoping for a better life and often in order to escape unpleasant situations in their parents'

homes (Rubin 1976). Their romanticized expectations of married life
are obtained from the mass media, rather than from their families'
problematic relations (Rainwater, Coleman, and Handel 1959). The
stage of becoming a wife is full of frustration, and later years bring
passive acceptance rather than positive change. The husband is
unable to provide the emotional support both wish for, and both are
disappointed in themselves and in each other. The man dominates,
sometimes becoming violent under the influence of alcohol or in
response to his own problems and insecurities (Rubin 1976, 1983).
Sexual difficulties combine with those of finances and child rearing
to create an oppressive environment (see Komarovsky 1962).

The wife's problems can be so disabling that they push her into
"hysterical" behavior, which the husband handles by trying to maintain a "logical" (i.e. distant) stance (Warren 1987). For marriages like
this in the 1950s, when the whole culture was inundated with what
Friedan (1963) called the "feminine mystique" demanding passive
stances by women, personal emotional problems were often defined in psychiatric terms (Warren 1987). A woman depressed by the
restrictions of "true womanhood" could become classified as a
"madwife" and subjected to hospitalization and even to shock or
electroconvulsive therapy (Warren 1987). Her social circle in the
role of wife did not come to her defense, since she deviated from
what its members considered necessary behavior. She was declared
cured of her madness when she acquiesced in her roles.

According to Rainwater, Coleman, and Handel (1959, 58–66),
the workingman's wife lacks the ability to change her roles because
of several characteristics of her construction of reality. She accepts
things as given, has little interest, energy, or skill to explore things
for herself, lacks faith in her personal efficacy, experiences limitations on self-command due to strong and volatile emotions, and is
oriented toward the present and her immediate surroundings rather
than the future and planning.

Much of what is known about the working-class wife comes
from research of decades ago, although more recent studies support
these basic theses (Langman 1987). The transitional aspect of such
a woman's role of wife is the role's location in a traditional, male-
dominated, often violent circle, combined with dreams of intimacy,
mutual self-disclosure, companionship, and sharing that are contained in new images of husband-wife relationships (Rubin 1976,
120). Her relationship with the husband is strained by the fact that
he does not share the dream, wishing her to simply be like his

mother, without these "crazy ideas" that require from him acts that he is incapable of undertaking. He openly resents giving up any of his traditional masculine rights—such as his right to sexual access when he wants it and not in negotiation with the wife. Such a man has no models for behavior that expresses feelings and meets some of the woman's needs. He thus often has extreme reactions to any demands that he change, whether by considering the wife's sexual desires or "helping" her with the roles of mother or homemaker. He does not discuss his world, including his job, with her, considering it too technical for women, and he thinks that talking about frustrations is too much like "griping," which men should not do. He wants work and home to be kept separate, not wishing to hear the wife's side of life (Komarovsky 1962, 152–55). Cross-gender communication requires a different socialization and educational background than has been true of blue-collar couples.

The life cycle of the role of wife appears to have changed less from traditional to transitional times among working-class families than among middle-class ones. The birth of children creates a common bond between husband and wife, unless their presence is fraught with problems, as in cases of unwanted or difficult offspring. Few other subjects form a bridge between the worlds of men and women. Money, friendships, and in-laws are all possible sources of strain. Desertion and divorce are fairly frequent, with the wife gaining little power or benefit from such action. Working-class women are generally distrustful of governmental or other formal agencies and do not have the resources to demand their rights. Social security or welfare can help, especially if it brings steady income compared to a husband's irregular employment or contribution to the family maintenance (Lopata 1979).

The general picture of the social psychology of role involvement presents the women as focused on the role of mother, hoping that all will go well—or at least not too badly—in marriage. They tend to be passive or reactive, meeting demands as they are made, and do not consider themselves as especially good wives or persons. They fear sexual temptation from outside of marriage and tend to be impulsive in most of their actions (Rainwater, Coleman, and Handel 1959). Such women settle into their marriages as the years go by, still within the gender-segregated home and relations with others.

Middle-Class Wives. Transitional middle-class families in America have also varied considerably, mainly by the degree of crystallization of their life-styles and closeness to either their lower- or their upper-class counterparts (Langman 1987, 226–29). Mate selection has increasingly become a matter of personal choice, preceded by dating rituals but not frequently by the cohabitation more typical of modern times. Dating and the honeymoon allegedly provide opportunities for self-disclosure and learning about the other. The social circle of the wife is relatively free of control by the families, and though in-laws are generally recognized and interacted with. The circle is now more likely to contain couple-companionate relations and the husband's work associates. Middle-class couples in transitional marriages tend to communicate more with each other than do transitional couples of lower status. Berger and Kellner (1970) found such couples, especially the wives, active in reconstructing reality upon marriage. The change of name and of relationships with others by the woman is accompanied by frequent modifications of the past in memory and of her anticipated future through shared communication with the husband.

Actually, marriage often does not change life dramatically unless each partner has to cease, or restrict, prior outside activities. Both the man and the woman tend to continue their main occupational or educational activities. The greatest amount of change in the role of wife usually accompanies the birth of the first child, specially if the mother quits her job to take care of the offspring, as she tends to do in transitional families. This shift is a major component of what researchers have labeled the "crisis" in the role of wife due to early parenthood. The wife is often too tired to pay attention to the husband, appears more interested in the baby than in him, and is prohibited from, or uninterested in, sexual interaction. The couple's finances are stretched by the loss of her earnings and the cost of the pregnancy, birth, and the child, and leisure is either interrupted or requires advance preparation and added expenditure. The wife often feels like, and appears to the husband to be, a different woman from the one he married. The multidimensional world they shared in the past has become for her a single-dimensional one, focused on the home and motherhood.

On the other hand, the lives of many middle-class transitional wives are shaped to a considerable degree by their husband's occupations and their couple-companionate activities.

The Two-Person Single Career. A wife in a transitional middle-class marriage can, and is expected to, do much to help her professional, entrepreneurial, or corporate-management husband in his career. Many men are in jobs or organizations defined by L. Coser (1974) as "greedy institutions." These require total commitment and heroic effort, not only on the part of the man, but also by his wife. In transitional families she is not expected to have a career of her own or any serious involvements that might interfere with her contribution to the husband's career. Papanek (1973) described this situation as a two-person single career in which the man holds the occupational or office title and receives the rewards directly, while the wife is the backup person and benefits vicariously. The role of a wife is influenced in two major ways by her husband's position or occupation, as summarized by Finch (1983) from a large literature on this subject. First, the husband's job structures the wife's life through income, time, space, and social relationships. Characteristics of his job also impinge on what she can do in other roles. Second, his job can require contributions from her in the form of supportive work as well as family-status-production work that "affects the family's relation with others in the community or reference group" (Papanek 1979, 775).

When a husband's earnings constitute the total family income, the effect upon the role of wife is easily discernible. The amount he earns, whether his income is dependable, the method of payment, the additional perquisites, and his uncompensated work-related expenditures—all influence the life she can create for the family. Although the earnings provide resources, a woman's lack of control over their characteristics and the way they reach her is a major problem. Even when the wife contributes to the family income, she usually contributes a smaller proportion than he does, and her earnings are not formally recognized by the husband. Bird (1979) classified the attitudes of transitional families toward the wife's earnings into four categories. The portion of her earnings identified as "pin money" is kept out of sight, for her to spend as she wishes:

> The object is not to give her independence to flout his wishes—but to save him from the pain of seeing it. . . . Earmarker Couples are neo-traditionalists. They deal with the threat of her money by building a Chinese wall around it to show that the family is "really" living on his pay alone. . . . Pooler Couples deal with the threat of her money by insisting that it doesn't matter where it comes from. . . it becomes "our money." . . . Bargainer Couples are radicals. They look the threat of her money full in the face and accept it at full value. (Pp. 130–35)

In all such marriages, the wife is expected to carry out her job, if she is able to hold one despite complications, without neglecting the role of homemaker and all her husband-supportive work.

The time schedule of the husband's job obviously impinges on the social life space of the wife, especially if she is also a home manager and mother. She must synchronize the activities of all family members around those of her husband and prevent interference with the timing of his work. Irregularity or unusual scheduling of the husband's job may preclude the wife's seeking a job of her own. Some jobs, such as those of consultant or traveling salesman, require absence from home for extended periods of time, consigning total family management to the wife and complicating her relations with other circle members and in her other social roles.

A major complaint of wives of entrepreneurs, professionals, or corporation workers is the "spillover" of concerns and even work into home time. Many middle-class workers are unable to leave the work behind, carrying it home at least in their heads and often physically. The family must compete with it, often feeling neglected and insignificant in comparison to the job.

The wife's life is also affected by the spatial elements of the husband's job. This is obvious in the case of the geographically mobile husband. The migration of men in search of a livelihood helped populate America and other lands, but it can cause family strain. Wives left behind must wait for their husbands to send back money for their journey to join them, or wait for them to return and fetch them. Corporations with branches all over the world often shift members of management as needed, regardless of family needs. The loneliness of the transferred wife can be a major problem, especially for women lacking the social skills to make new friends and enter new roles. The man's organization provides his incorporation and transfers his personal credentials, while the wife must do this on her own. Again, one of the obvious problems with the geographical mobility of a husband is the wife's lack of control over the location and timing of any particular move. Frequent moves make it unlikely that the wife will be able to find a job. A wife's refusal to give up her own life inevitably hurts the husband's career.

The spatial impingement of the husband's work on the life of the wife points to the artificiality of the division of the world into private and public spheres. This is especially evident when the husband works out of the home. Lawyers and other professionals may have their only offices in their homes. Husbands may also carry forth work activities from the home without an isolated work space, thus penetrating all areas. Others do some of the work at home, even when based elsewhere, using it as a branch office. Although having the freedom to use the home is an advantage to the employee or self-employed man, it plays havoc with "normal" households. Family routines must be organized around the worker, and activities of importance to other members are often curtailed. Apprentices or other assistants might actually live in the home, and they have to be supplied with services by the homemaker simply because her role of wife includes obligations to the husband's work circle. Spatial proximity of the husband's work can also introduce clients, customers, or representatives of a variety of organizations to the home.

A special case of interweave between the husband's job space and the wife's space in all her roles exists if the couple lives in territory provided by the employer. The clergy, officers of corporations, universities, or prisons, domestic workers, farm laborers, and many others sometimes have the right to homes owned and controlled by the organization to which the husband is attached. Although the employee receives benefits from such arrangements, in terms of closeness to work, free or adjusted rent, and services, the main beneficiary is the employer because of his or her control over the situation. The wife benefits from these rights of the husband, but faces many restrictions on her life. The uncertainty of housing also hangs over her, as she can lose her home if they divorce or the husband leaves the job or dies.

An even stronger spatial impingement on the wife occurs in institutional settings. The military can place families on bases in which they can "shop, drink, dance, attend movies, parties and planned trips at all times and at lower costs" than do others (Dobrofsky and Patterson 1977). The same is true of faculty at military schools or workers in company-owned communities. In such a total institution, much of the wife's life is controlled by the organization. Such a woman is incorporated into the hierarchy, in a peripheral and vicarious manner. She carries her husband's rank with her, in terms of her appearance, deference, and demeanor, at all times in which she is known as, for instance, "the captain's wife."

In addition to the "spillover" effect, a job can force or prevent relationships with others. Police wives, whether the husband is hired by the community or by private employers, complain that there are restrictions on whom they can develop friendships with (Young 1984). Army officers' wives are not allowed to fraternize with women whose husbands are mere enlisted men, while wives following husbands to foreign stations must formalize all relations with natives. The literature and films on the colonial wife in India or Africa document the constraints placed on her behavior (see Callan and Ardener 1984). On the other hand, relationships with superiors, work colleagues, or clients of the husband are often forced upon the wife. The wives of public figures are embedded in the community, which can be as large as a nation, with "contamination" of the private person by the occupation (Finch 1983, 36).

The contributions of the wife in a two-person career of the husband fall into four major areas: maintaining the husband's physical and psychological environment, "stroking," direct involvement in the social circle of the husband's job, and "status production" (Bernard 1973; Papanek 1979). The first area overlaps the role of homemaker. Although it is possible for a wife not to be a homemaker, most women combine the two roles. The duties of maintaining the husband physically so that he can successfully perform his job include caring for his clothes, maintaining a functioning household, preparing food, and locating needed objects. It also means protecting his "recreation" time, during which he recuperates from the strain of the job and prepares for the next stint. Domestic labor can be seen as economically productive when it contributes to the productivity of the male worker. His time, money, and energy are preserved by the work of the wife, who "oils the wheels of production" (Finch 1983, 79). Her activities can enable him to entertain at home and provide the required family appearance both inside the home and away from it. These backup services may be required consistently, as in the case of the First Lady or the wife of the president of an organization, or in emergency times only. Even if she does not do the work itself, she is responsible for seeing that it is done, when and where needed.

The provision of "moral support" is also an extremely important part of the role of wife, even to workers who do not need much direct contribution to their careers. Bernard (1973) calls this the "stroking" function. It consists of "showing solidarity, giving help, rewarding, agreeing, understanding and passively accepting" (Ostrander 1984, 39). It usually does not mean giving advice.

Participation in a two-person single career can entail even more direct, although still peripheral, duties on the part of the wife— answering the telephone or being active in wives' organizations such as the Women's Auxiliary of the American Medical Association

(Fowlkes 1980). The trips that the U.S. president's wife makes with him, especially abroad, require a great deal of preparation, including knowledge of the cultures and societies involved. Such preparation can be an awesome obligation, with possibilities for many a faux pas. In fact, it can take up most of a wife's time, even with briefing from the husband's other assistants.

Another set of activities that involve the wife directly in the job of the husband Finch (1983, 94) calls "back-up services." These are typical for wives of male academics or other male researchers and writers, as attested to by their acknowledgments: "could not have done this without the help of my wife, who found references, edited and typed the manuscript . . ." The advantage for the worker of having his wife provide such help is that she is "always on the spot" (Finch 1983, 96).

The wife can serve as an assistant in the husband's social circle to such an extent that she is an additional worker whom the organization gets for free. Sometimes referred to as part of a team, such a worker is nevertheless seen by others as peripheral to the main actors.

The combination of all these activities can involve what Papanek (1979) defines as "family status production" work, which has two main levels. For wives of upwardly mobile husbands it involves the production of status, and for already established families it consists of status-maintenance activity. It encompasses not only the role of wife, but the woman's whole role complex. While supportive effort is expected of the wife in a two-person career throughout the husband's career life, the higher his actual or potential status is, the more important is her status-productive work. Papanek (1979) places its peak mainly at midlife, when income and aspiration are still rising and there is enough discretionary income to allow the wife a wide range of activities.

The constraints and contributions connected with the role of wife in a two-person single career can be overwhelming. Role conflict can be avoided only by placing the role of wife in the top position in the role cluster, stripping away or pushing into the background social roles that are not compatible. Few such wives can devote considerable time to the role of daughter to ailing elderly parents, or even sometimes to the role of mother. Friendships are hung on the activities of the husband, as many a woman has found when dropped by erstwhile friends after her husband's death or demotion.

Wives of public figures are particularly vulnerable to the strain of trying to balance privacy with the obligation to be visible to people who feel they have the right to treat them personally. The strategies available to wives in such situations of vicarious contamination of sentiments directed to the husband are limited, and must be learned, often painfully, as a number of biographies and autobiographies of such women attest (see the various write-ups of Kitty Dukakis during and since her husband's bid for the American presidency).

All in all, however, a wife can be a major contributor to her husband's career, even if she is seldom acknowledged as such or given only honorary rewards. Outside observers may feel that she receives sufficient benefits, basking in her husband's fame and sharing more tangible privileges. The suspicion that such rewards might draw a woman into a marriage is often mentioned by the mass media when an attractive young woman attaches herself to a very successful but physically unappealing older man. Each of the two obtains what she or he considers desirable, reflecting the gender-specific values of our culture. A major problem with a wife's rights and privileges is their vicarious nature, which women in the role of wife in "modern" marriages find objectionable.

The historical facts of the focus, in the Protestant ethic, on men's occupational success, and of the feminine mystique ideology directed toward women, have been recognized by many observers. Even before World War II, a series of books by Nancy Shae, such as *The Army Wife* (1941) trained into proper behavior women married to officers of the U.S. armed services. William H. Whyte, Jr.'s *Organization Man* (1956) and subsequent articles discussed the "wife problem" of business executives. What to do with these women, since the corporation was internally organized with no place for external appendices? In addition, some wives were uncooperative and even hurt their husbands' careers and the success of the organization. Fowlkes (1980) studied the wives of men in medicine and academia in *Behind Every Successful Man,* finding the older ones fully accepting the adjunct role, while Vandervelde wrote in *The Changing Life of the Corporate Wife* (1979) about wives who refused to fit into the mold. Kanter's classic *Men and Women of the Corporation* (1977) devoted a whole chapter to wives, their duties and rights. Actually, the wives had few rights, since they were seen as external to the system and partially replaced by the "office wife," or secretary, who meets many of the needs of the managers. Margolis

(1979) reported many contributions of wives in *The Managers*. Helen Hughes (1977) described her personal experiences as a Ph.D. sociologist married to a member of the University of Chicago faculty during years when nepotism rules were used by organizations to prevent the employment of more than one member of a family. Chapters in the Callan and Ardener (1984) volume *The Incorporated Wife* cover similar situations of wives within academia, the police, the armed services, overseas branches of corporations, settler families in Northern Rhodesia, and several colonial locations.

Situations in which the wife has a powerful public position while the husband must perform the backup duties, as in the case of the former prime minister of Britain, make people most uncomfortable. Interestingly enough, males accompanying public women are often referred to as "escorts," even when they perform much more important functions directly contributing to the job. When two independent persons "escort" each other in a modern marriage, but the husband's only function is to insure that his wife can perform her important duties as effortlessly as possible, that is another matter. Having the wife as the major partner in a two-person career goes against two cultural norms: that the wife should be the supporting partner who adjusts to the husband's needs, and that the husband should not be in the subordinate position of the backup person.

It is probably not surprising that many women in public roles either do not have husbands or are married to men with independent careers.

Of course, many of the impingements of the husband's job upon the wife's social life space and the contributions she makes to his career are also experienced by working-class wives, and, especially, upper-class wives.

Middle-Class Black Wives. The situation of middle-class black families appears to be similar to that of their white counterparts, but there are important variations. The black community has long encouraged and rewarded educational and economic involvement by its married women, as a natural outgrowth of the fact that whites discriminated much less against them than against black men. Families often had to depend on the earnings of the wife, who was more likely than her husband to have a steady white-collar job.

The interviews in *Occupation: Housewife* (Lopata 1971b, 122–35) from the 1950s and 1960s showed the middle-class black wives to be very supportive of their husbands. One of the full-time homemakers, aged twenty-three, explained the complexity of her role as wife as including

> dividing each thing into its proper place and trying to be able to give your man the type of warmth or consolation he needs when he feels that he is not being treated fairly outside of the home. (P. 133)

The need to be emotionally supportive of the middle-class man who is facing discrimination from the white world is expressed over and over in these and later interviews. Most of the middle-class black respondents who are employed fall easily into the role of the wife in the "modern marriage" category. The same conclusion was reached by Willie and Greenblatt (1978) from a review of four "classic" studies of power relationships. In fact, they, as well as Staples (1988, 312), point to the fact that middle-class black women have been virtually absent from the women's movement in America, mainly because their concerns are economic and less oriented against sexism than against racism. Awareness of the depth of prejudice and discrimination facing the black man in the middle-class world, the shortage of men in the black community, and the problems of "finding and keeping a mate" (Staples 1988, 313) decrease the probability of anti-male stances on the part of these women. Middle-class married couples of other racial and ethnic minorities in America also resemble their dominant-group counterparts.

Upper-Class Wives. Ostrander (1984) defines upper-class families as being in that position because of unique characteristics in addition to income, occupation, and education, which are used to classify other families.

> In conceptual terms then, "upper class" is defined here as that portion of the population that owns the major share of corporate and personal wealth, exercises dominant power in economic and political affairs, and comprises exclusive social networks and organizations open only to persons born into or selected by this class. (P. 5)

The mate selection process of the upper classes in American society has been of special interest to sociologists as well as to the mass media (see Rosen and Bell 1966). Social Register families insure appropriate partners for their offspring by structuring the environment, sending the young to the proper schools, joining clubs, and arranging opportunities for contact at a geographical and social distance from members of lower classes.

Women who enter the role of wife in this social class are well aware of the enormity of their responsibility. Their husbands run the economic and political life of the society, and definitely of the community within which they reside. The wives realize that this will not be an egalitarian marriage. Even those who inherit wealth in their own right tend to turn it over to the husband to manage (Ostrander 1984). This is one of the extreme cases of patriarchal control and personal dependency, even though it is not the husband's oldest male relative, but the husband himself, who has all the power. Both in-law families influence their lives, opening doors to major social clubs and supporting the wife's status-maintenance activities. Most of these women do not have status-production duties, since the families are already established. Theirs are the status-maintaining obligations, and their rights include having funds available for such activities. They conduct their lives to maintain the general standard of family position, rather than to influence the husband's job.

These are the women who always place the role of wife first in line of importance, even over that of mother; in this they are quite different from working-class wives, who almost invariably focus on the children, or middle-class transitional wives, who tend to have life-course commitments (Lopata and Barnewolt 1984). Upper-class wives have to be always available to fulfill duties in the role of wife, even if it means shifting obligations to others. They know they cannot take a full-time job, although the husbands worry that they may wish to do so. Even voluntary-organization activities, necessary for status maintenance, must never appear to be more important than actions directly in response to the husband. The marital relationships described by Ostrander (1984) do not appear close, warm, or empathetic.

Actually, we know less about the role of wife in this class than in others, as there are so few women in it and they have complex means of protecting their privacy. They are conscious of the importance of reputation, transmitting only such information about themselves as they wish to publicize. They have both the space and the social distance to keep away strangers. Servants intercept even social scientists, and participant observation is difficult when entrance into interaction centers is restricted.

The Modern Form of the Role of Wife

It is actually hard to determine the characteristics of the role of wife in modern marriages, since we have not, for the most part, moved far from the transitional female-male relationships of this type. If we follow Inkeles (1981; see also Inkeles and Smith 1974), "modern" people are highly individuated and competent to function in a complex, industrialized society. Even in transitional phases of social development—maybe particularly then—marriage certainly did not involve two independent persons in a relationship in which they were cooperative and interdependent but equal in power and status. There is evidence of change, however, even if we are not quite sure where it will lead.

Indices of Change

One of the dramatic indices of change in the relations between women and men has been sexual. Allegedly, the double standard of sexual "freedom," which has a long history and allows the man other relationships while the woman is supposed to stay a virgin and then a "chaste" wife, is in the process of vanishing (Reiss and Lee 1988). The whole subject of what is still called "premarital" sexual permissiveness is complex, and it is uncertain how it influences the role of wife. An important aspect of the changes, however, is cohabitation of unmarried couples. Trost (1979) defines cohabitation as "sharing a bedroom during at least four nights per week during at least three consecutive months with someone of the opposite sex" (p. 13).

Initial conclusions of research on cohabitation in the United States showed differences in the attitudes of women and men. The women saw cohabitation as a trial marriage or a step toward wifehood. Men allegedly spoke of many conveniences without strong marital commitment (Ehrenreich 1983). Defining it simply as an "expanding dimension of the courtship process" (Henze and Hudson 1974, 725) implies increasing commitment during dating but includes the possibility of impermanence. But then, even marriage now no longer means lifelong involvement.

The current interest of women in developing their own careers and feelings of personhood prior to marriage, combined with increasing sexual permissiveness, makes cohabitation unsurprising. Such heterosexual couples face many of the same problems experienced by married couples, except that it is harder for them to build trust in each other concerning money, work, or sexual matters (Blumstein and Schwartz 1983). Power still accrues to the one with the higher paycheck and the person who has least to lose if the relationship dissolves.

Whether seen by participants as a trial marriage, a nonpermanent relationship, or just a convenience, cohabitation provides a certain amount of preparation, socialization, and task learning that can be useful for entrance into the role of wife. This includes decisions as to location, furnishings, financial obligations, friendships, and so forth. However, our definition of social roles disqualifies this relation from being that of wife-husband, for various legal and social-circle reasons and because the participants appear to be "playing at the roles" rather than actually involved in them. Trost (1979) asks, Why do cohabiting couples, or any couples for that matter, marry? The reasons include the wish to have "legalized" children, security and safety, freedom from outside criticism, and the belief that marriage is morally better.

The modern wedding is apt to be planned fully by the couple (rather than by the woman's parents as in the past) to the extent that they define its rituals and even pay many of the costs. This frees them from dependence upon their families of orientation and allegedly provides each partner with equal power for the future.

The modern woman is inevitably involved in a multidimensional life prior to, and at the early stages of, marriage, being more educated and middle-class in her life-style and aspirations than were her grandmother or mother. Even the 1956 suburbanites of the *Occupation: Housewife* study claimed that "modern woman" has many more rights than her grandmother had, although many added that she has many more responsibilities (Lopata 1971b). The modern woman is able to pull together her own social circle within the role of wife, being freed from many family- imposed and societal restrictions. She can even ignore her in-laws, if that is what she and her husband have negotiated.

The 1989 respondents saw modern women as having much more choice, and they expressed fewer worries and concerns than bothered the feminine mystique wives. The answers had a much freer feeling than those in the 1950s.

The woman of modern times has been influenced by revised feminism, whether she is conscious of it or not. She tends to have planned her life course in addition to and beyond marriage, if she considers marriage at all. Whether young or rethinking her involvements, she intends to work in a relatively demanding job and to have a "career." Although this latter aspect of life is vaguely conceptualized, the woman is likely to prepare for a specific occupation much more often than did her mother, and she intends to "have it all" in terms of success in the roles of wife, mother, and career woman. She does not count on marriage as a solution to all problems, and she expects to have to support herself if it breaks up. Thus the role of wife is not seen as the major commitment of the future.

It is interesting to note here that students in my sociology classes, and in those of other professors with whom I have talked, are quite split in their view of marriage: The women expect to continue in their interesting jobs with the help of a "sharing" husband, while the men want wives who will support them in the two-person single career style. They had better not marry each other!

In *The Marriage Contract* (1981) Weitzman studied a phenomenon that appears to have gained popularity in modern times. A marriage contract establishes the rights and duties of the husband and wife regarding each other and often regarding other members of their social circles and even their commitments to other social roles. Whether they formalize them to this extent or not, many more couples than in the past discuss their future expectations and negotiate major subjects over which they anticipate problems.

Another subject recently drawing both public and social science attention is that of intermarriage. One of the historical, though not common, trends in the African American community has been marriage of successful black men to white women, thereby decreasing even more the pool of eligible black males for black women (Staples 1988, 315). Interestingly enough, three of the five couples featured in a recent *Chicago Tribune Magazine* section devoted to intermarriage included a black spouse, but in two cases the African American was the woman, not the man (Emmerman 1990). Intermarriage appears to be increasing in recent years, as ethnic and racial enclaves and subcultures have loosened their hold on people, and educational or occupational interests have brought previously separated individuals together (see Stephan and Stephan 1989 for this trend in Hawaii and the American Southwest, and Kitano and associates 1984 for both Los Angeles and Hawaii).

The Negotiated Marriage: Rights and Duties

One of the major characteristics of the role of wife in modern marriages is its flexibility in consequence of negotiation with not only
the husband but the whole social circle. The negotiations and the
resources available to each partner to work out the relationship they
want focus around three major areas of life. Gone are the chattel,
senior-junior partner, and other marital combinations described by
Scanzoni and Scanzoni (1981), and the sub rosa games involved in
prior relationships.

One subject of negotiation that is a dramatic break from the past
is the right of equality in sexual behavior and satisfaction. There still
appears to be a difference between women and men in styles of
lovemaking since women are reportedly still trying to get men to
broaden the interaction beyond sexual intercourse to include ten-
derness and affection (Cancian 1987). Alternatives to a particular
sexual partner are much more easily available to modern wives,
now that they are able to continue or resume a multidimensional life
at any stage of the life course. Homosexual relationships have either
expanded in frequency or simply become more visible. Sexual
interaction is one of the three major subjects of constant negotiation
among all couples, whether heterosexual cohabiting, married, lesbian or gay (Blumstein and Schwartz 1983). The fact that it remains
a subject that has to be negotiated shows that it remains a problem.
Various experiments, such as an "open marriage" that allows each
partner full freedom in extramarital relationships, "swinging," or
various forms of group marriage, have not worked out for people
who, after all, were not socialized into such rights (Reiss and Lee
1988, 259). Although there appears to be a trend in recent years back
to strictly monogamous sexual interaction, this time adhered to by
both husbands and wives, Reiss and Lee (1988) hypothesize: "What
many in America are seeking today is a combination of a deep love
relationship in marriage and some lesser level of intimacy outside of
marriage" (p. 279). Of course, fear of AIDS is encroaching with
apparent speed upon sexual promiscuity, and even more limited
sexual exploration, in very recent years.

A second major subject for negotiation in modern marriages is
money. It is not that marital financial problems had been absent in
previous centuries, but that the base has shifted with the growing
economic independence of the wife. Women entered traditional

marriages with a dowry or a hope chest that was their economic contribution. With the spread of a money economy, many wives also worked in paying jobs. However, their contributions were discounted, especially when they had no legal power over family property.

The restructuring of the American economic system and changing ideologies are creating an environment that supports women's outside employment. Many couples realize that they cannot maintain a desired standard of living unless the wife brings in earnings. Although the modern wife still does not contribute 50 percent to the family income, she has a stronger base for negotiation than when her earnings were not considered important because the man was the main breadwinner. In addition, financial negotiations can focus not only on how the money is spent, but also on how the couple should invest in each other's careers. No longer is the total investment in the husband.

This brings us to the third subject of negotiation among marital partners of modern, and future, times: commitment to work, not only within the family, but also in jobs. The modern wife is negotiating for rights unusual in past marriages, such as the right to decide when and where to have a job, and to have it influence family time and space, including where they live and couple relationships. Equally on the table is her need for supportive behavior from her husband, similar to, if not as extreme, as what wives have provided to husbands in two-person careers. Bird wrote already in 1979 in *The Two-Paycheck Marriage* that a daunting problem faced by "revolutionary" couples of modern times is the "two-career collision course." Both ordinary daily routines and crisis situations are affected by a person's "greedy" occupation, but when both spouses have such occupations, this creates possibilities for serious conflict. Whose career must be put on hold while the partner meets a new challenge? Who meets emergencies in shared roles without bothering the other? In other words, whose career is most important and should be placed first when its demands appear on the scene? Who gives up a job to follow the spouse in situations of transfer? Thus far, most research points to a failure of wives and husbands to reach a "modern" arrangement with equal treatment of the demands of jobs in two greedy organizations. Underneath it all is the usual lurking suspicion that the family could not exist on the earnings of the wife and that the possibility of parenthood would throw it into dependency on the husband's paycheck. Bird (1979) points to a few examples of "the cool supercouples," but the mass media are full of stories of the women Harvard M.B.A.s who drop out of the corporate structure when they reach the "baby panic" years of life, or after trying to be "supermoms." It is interesting that they are not referred to as "superwives," possibly because the fight on that front has already been won. This would mean that the wives have negotiated a refusal to function in two-person careers of a husband. The reverse will probably never develop, but limited involvement of each partner in the other's job appears to be emerging.

The topic of shared home management and parenting has not as yet progressed beyond discussion level. As Hochschild (1989) and many other social scientists have documented, the declared necessity for a second paycheck has not resulted in shared "second shifts" of work and responsibility at home and with children in more than a very few families. Part of this delay of responsiveness to perceived economic need for the wife's employment is due to the ever-threatening career-scheduling system that punishes women and, it is feared, will punish men if adjustments are made to the two-career family.

There are other aspects of the role of wife that have been, or are being, modified in modern families. The decrease of significance of the husband's associates in the wife's social circle may increase his involvement in her job's circle. The couple can negotiate kinship involvement; the wife is no longer forced to associate with his male line. Dramatic changes are occurring in all American institutions that will reflect back and forth on changes in the role of wife. Observers of the occupational structure point to increasing flexibility of employers in response to the needs of families. Modifications are occurring in the ideological, political, educational, and religious realms of our lives. All these shifts reflect back on the resources and wishes brought by women into marital negotiations. Sources of strain remaining in marriages are partly vestiges of problems embedded in traditional or transitional ones. As Settles concludes in "A Perspective on Tomorrow's Families" in the massive *Handbook on Marriage and the Family* (Sussman and Steinmetz 1987), adjustments to all these shifts will be made primarily by the woman, indirectly affecting the role of husband. And Goode (1982) reminds us that men resist the changes demanded of them because they signal, and actually involve, a loss of power.

In view of all the uncertainties as to what the role of wife will be in a "modern" marriage, we are safe in simply hypothesizing great

variations and life-course flexibility, and not just along societal subgroup lines, such as social class.

The Life Course of the Role of Wife

A woman takes on the role of wife through a series of stages. Contact
must be established between herself and those representatives of
the social circle who are involved in the selection process. In modern times and places, a woman focuses first on the potential husband (and vice versa), and then gains or selects most of the other
circle members. Of course, it is usually difficult to ignore people to
whom the selected husband is already attached, and in-laws can
become an unavoidable addition to the role of wife. A second stage
in becoming a wife involves mutual testing of partners, whether by
families or in dating situations. The characteristics for which the
testing takes place depend upon the perception by the tester as to
future duties and rights of the role, which is sometimes, although not
often, seen in life-course perspective. The sequence of announcements of the decision to enter the role of wife is the third stage. Each
segment of the future circle is informed in acceptable sequence.
People who will not be involved, such as former boyfriends or
associates with whom relations must be cut off because of the
woman's becoming a wife and the man's becoming a husband, must
also be told. In past times in this society, employers were to be
informed, and employment terminated upon marriage.

The procedures of entrance into the role of wife are often very
elaborate, depending not just on the wishes of the marital unit, but
also on those of the circle influenced by its social importance.
Weddings are traditional events carried forth into modern times,
although with innumerable variations. The final stage of becoming
a wife involves the incorporation of that identity into the woman's
self-concept and the reconstruction of reality to fit the marriage and
her marital status. The depth of the changes in her self-concepts and
construction of reality is allegedly greater for traditional and transitional women than for men, and it definitely varies among women
depending on the other sociopsychological aspects of role involvement. Bernard (1973, 42) refers to the "shock theory of marriage" for
women; that marriage involves "dwindling into a wife." The woman
leaves behind her birth name and becomes Mrs. John Doe. Most

observers claim that major legislative reforms are needed before full partnership becomes possible in marriage.

Over the life course a wife's social relationships vary considerably in the content of the circle and of interaction. Any changes in the life of the woman and the lives of the other family members can modify this role. Parents who must be cared for, the movement of the husband up the patriarchal family line in seniority, promotion of the husband or the wife in modern times, addition of the role of mother, health problems, and aging, for example, can have consequences upon relations with the husband and others in the circle. Changes in the husband's job, especially when they involve geographical mobility, can add or remove people from the wife's social circle. Of course, divorce, desertion, and the death of the husband modify the role of wife.

The husband-wife relationship can change from its own dynamics. Sexual interaction may recede in importance as years go by. Conflict over children may diminish as the children grow up. Some couples drift onto different paths, becoming less frequently joined. In fact, Pineo (1966) claims that the later years of marriage bring "disenchantment." Wives and husbands who have taken each other for granted while pursuing their own interests may come to find competing roles less engrossing and wish for more satisfaction from the marriage. However, by that point they have little in common. Levinson (1978) and associates found middle-aged men in a "midlife crisis," worrying about death and feeling they missed many good years by concentrating so hard on financial success. They wish to "modify their life structures," leave their wives for younger women, and start new families. The wives, even those who have not divorced but who find no vitality in the marriage, ask themselves, according to Rubin (1979), "What do I do with the rest of my life?" On the other hand, some studies find that, as the spouses decrease involvement in other roles, each may turn to the other for companionship and more leisure-time activity, revitalizing the marriage (Deutscher 1964).

The Social Psychology of Role Involvement

Not all wives grant the role of wife first importance in the hierarchical arrangement of their role clusters. The rank also varies in relation

to the other roles in the family dimension and the multidimensionality of the life space. The richer the dimension, in terms of the
number of family roles within it and the importance assigned each,
and the more complex the life space, the less significant or all-
encompassing is the identity of wife. In addition, women can vary
the importance they assign to the duties and rights connected with
the husband, in comparison to those involving other members of the
social circle. For example, a wife in a highly patriarchal family may
feel, or may have to express, greater allegiance to the parents of the
husband than to the husband. Many a wife is more task- than
relation-oriented in her interactions with her husband, feeling that
physical duties of providing for his comfort are more important than
empathetic ones. She can also see herself as simply responding to
his demands, rather than anticipating his needs and or considering
their mutual needs. Thus, her stance of responsiveness can be
passive or reactive, without necessarily including deep sentiments
of love or a view of herself as a loving wife. In fact, such an
involvement in the role of wife is true of many lower-class women,
according to research regarding many countries and times. Middle-
class women with more education and more comfortable living
styles tend to be more empathetically involved in this role.

   Those who study marital happiness and its effect on life satisfaction face the problems of both defining these sentiments and forming methodologies for their research. Americans generally declare
their marriages to be happy, although there has been a decrease in
such statements by wives in recent years. Increases in divorce do not
prove rejection of marriage itself, as evidenced by the frequency
with which women reenter this relationship.

> In the middle and late 1970s, when many journalists and lay persons
> believed that the soaring divorce rate meant that the institution of
> marriage was declining if not disintegrating, many family social scien-
> tists, including us, took the position that marriage was just as impor-
> tant to Americans as ever, and that the increase in divorce partly
> reflected the fact that marriage was so important to people that they
> were becoming less willing to tolerate unsatisfactory marriage rela-
> tionships. (Glenn and Weaver 1988, 317)

So, with decreased economic dependence of wives on husbands
and the increased ease and acceptability of divorce, observers assume
that women who remain married are satisfied with this relationship.

One problem with that argument is the frequency with which abused wives remain in their marriages. As Wittner (1990) reports in her study of the domestic violence court, the whole structure of the society and its system of protecting people from violence is so complicated and ineffectual as to make a wife's efforts to leave an abusive marriage extremely difficult. And reports of violence and psychological abuse have abounded in recent years, though so have the number and variety of self-help and other groups attempting to deal with such marital problems.

The role of wife is affected by the retirement of the husband; he is no longer absent during the working day, making constant contact inevitable or providing time for leisure-time activity. The wife may demand greater cooperation in her role of homemaker. Reduced finances can be a consequence, but so can reduced costs. Of course, the wife's adjustment to changes in the husband's social circle depends also upon her involvements outside of the home. Employed wives are less satisfied with their marriages than are full-time homemakers, though the latter are more frequently depressed (Shehan and Rexroat 1986).

The Ex-Wife or Widow

In highly patriarchal families, a woman often did not have the right to divorce, nor could she continue to live with the husband's family if he divorced her, which left her with few choices. In some situations she could return to her family of orientation, but she could not take the children with her, because they belonged to the husband's line. Divorce has been forbidden by the Catholic church and is against the norms of many societies. Until very recent times, divorcées were ostracized, a reflection of the status of women. Situations in which whole families are involved in arranging the marriage, especially when economic goods are exchanged, usually discourage divorce, since it complicates the lives of so many. The modern increase in divorce can be partly accounted for by the independence of the marital unit from external pressures, such as powerful families or communities from which the partners could not escape.

The subject of divorce has attracted a great deal of attention in America in recent times simply because of its frequency, in face of the traditional assumption, written into most religious ceremonies, that marriage is "till death does us part." Wives traditionally were not expected to leave this role except in dire circumstances defined by law, religion, or custom (Halem 1982). As mentioned above, the importance of the patriarchal system and the concern over patrilineal inheritance insured that men could more easily substitute wives than women could substitute husbands. Of recent times, divorce has been of special concern to the husband's family, since the woman has the right to remove the children from contact with it. Thus, two sets of social groups have been threatened by women's ability to obtain divorce: those who consider marriage a permanent relationship and those concerned with patrilineal continuity. Of course, in many societies the woman who has wished to leave a marriage has had no place to go, since there have been so few alternative ways in which she could maintain herself and no groups that would accept her.

The loss of the role of wife through divorce or widowhood can be a major life-disrupting event even in modern times, since it affects not only the marriage, but also other of the woman's roles. Although these two means of exiting the major aspects of the role of wife are very different, there are some similarities. Many factors influence the degree of disorganization of self, social roles, and life-style produced by divorce or the death of the husband. Of signal importance is the degree of psychological, social, and economic dependence of the wife upon the husband and upon being married. Some women never develop strong emotional ties with the husband and live quite independently from him and other members of the social circle. Others build their identities upon the husband and live vicariously through him. He can serve as their connecting link to the world outside of the household. The amount of distress felt by the wife at these events is influenced by the circumstances surrounding them: when in the life course it occurs, its degree of suddenness, the presence or absence of alternative supports and relations, and the status loss or amount of stigma in the role of ex-wife. The process of getting a divorce can be traumatic even for women at lower levels of marital integration, especially in times when such action was disapproved by the community and significant others, and when the legal procedures were demeaning. Although widows, unlike divorcees, had no choice in losing the role of wife, both can feel some blame. Women in America are expected to provide the emotional glue to the marriage. Asian Indian families of the deceased have been known to directly blame the wife for not properly taking care of the husband or not fulfilling other duties that could have prevented the death (Lopata 1972, 1987a, and 1987c).

There can be other unpleasant consequences of divorce or widowhood. Economic repercussions can be traumatic. Weitzman (1985) found that, in states with no-fault divorce, women and children were being pushed into poverty while men gained in discretionary income. A widow lacking other sources of economic support can also be impoverished, especially if she is ineligible for social security. A decrease in income can result in a need to sell the house and move into a less desirable neighborhood, breaking ties with the former community of residence. Problems arise in child rearing. Friendships can be weakened if the woman's funds are inadequate to retain her former round of activity, or because the absence of a partner makes couple-companionate "fun" awkward. In-law relations can also wither—a positive consequence if she wants independence, but negative if it means a loss of support. Social group memberships often drop, and existing roles must be modified to a varying extent. If reconstruction of reality, including of the self, occurred in the process of becoming a wife, it must again take place when the woman is no longer in that role.

There are major differences, however, between the effects of widowhood and the effects of divorce upon the former wife: The vestiges of the roles are not comparable, nor are many of the forms of resultant loneliness (Kitson et al. 1980). In the case of divorce, there is the problem of the continued existence of the ex-husband, and vestiges of the role of being his wife remain, often painfully (Ebaugh 1988). Conflict with the ex-husband over children or financial arrangements can create a life of tension and anger. So can jealousy over the ex-mate's social, sexual, and emotional life. Some wives wish to return to the marriage, others are lonely for many aspects of the prior life but don't want their husbands back. In any case, there are many emotional "hang-ups" associated with divorce, even in modern times when divorce is allegedly so easy.

There are some problems unique to widowhood. Caring for an ill husband for years can be debilitating, while sudden death can leave a lot of "unfinished business." In either case, the woman feels powerless. A widow often feels obligated to continue the social existence of her late husband, sometimes even to the point of sanctifying his memory, a process which interferes with her social relations (Lopata 1981b). She is also expected to insure that the children remember their father positively. Often she is older and does not have the personal resources to reengage in a new support network or modify the existing ones after the period of grief is over. A voluntaristic society demands knowledge of its resources and initiative in social integration, characteristics that are often absent among women brought up to depend on the family and the domestic sphere of life. The loss of traditional support systems leaves many an urban American widow in a relatively restricted social life space (Lopata 1973c and 1979; see also chapters in Lopata 1987c and 1987e).

A major problem in widowhood, experienced in somewhat different ways following divorce, is loneliness. A widow can experience any or all of these forms of loneliness: loneliness for that particular man, for having a love object, for being a love object, for a sexual and physically intimate partner, for a companion, for an escort to public places, for a partner in couple-companionate interaction, for someone around whom to organize time and work, for another presence in the home. She can be lonely for the social life she used to enjoy when married. Friendships with married friends need to be dropped and auxiliary memberships in groups made inoperative; activities connected with the husband's occupation and person no longer are demanded or possible. Widows even miss some of the duties their role of wife required, and the rewards that came from their performance. Thus, the whole life-style can be affected by the death of the husband, to the extent that his presence or other forms of contribution are needed for its continuance (Lopata 1969a). The Widow-to-Widow programs, existing in many communities on the model developed by Silverman (1987) at Harvard Medical School, aim to help widows solve some of these problems by serving as emotional supports and as providers of resource information. The emotional supports include an opportunity to talk about the deceased and the circumstances of death as well as current problems. Other associates often do not want to hear the story again. Widows report that other widows "really understand," having gone through the same experience themselves.

On the other hand, divorce or the husband's death can remove many restrictions in life and self-concept. Divorcées and some widows report that, after the period of grief for the husband or the marriage is mainly over, they blossom. Many others report feelings of independence, a fuller self-concept, and an interesting life. Among widows, however, the vestiges of the prior role usually contain the obligation to remember the deceased and to insure that his children and others with whom he had important relationships keep him socially alive—that is, alive in their memories. Segments of the social circle of the role of wife may still remain in interaction with her.

Reentry into the Role of Wife

Remarriage, or reentry into the role of wife, has its own dynamism. After all, there are still the vestiges of the prior marriage, often in the form of children, and a socioeconomic life-style produced by the marital team working together. The former or late husband is still around, in consciousness if not physically. Some women are simply unwilling to remarry, because they enjoy their independence and do not wish to invest in that role again. Divorcées may not wish to go through another failure; widows may feel that no one can replace the deceased or that they do not want to care for an ill man again (Lopata 1979 and 1988b). Others report that children fear loss of inheritance if they remarry, or resent anyone taking their father's place. On the other hand, remarriage can solve the problems of loneliness and emotional and financial insecurity.

Of course, the older the woman, the less the probability of finding a new mate, in view of the statistical shortage of eligible men. Divorcées are more apt to remarry than widows but not as likely as divorced men (Cherlin 1981, 29). Younger women are more apt to enter that relationship than are older ones. Remarriage is, of course, dependent upon the ability to go through all the stages of meeting an appropriate candidate for husband, developing a relationship, and "becoming" a wife. There appears to be a higher-than-by-coincidence probability that a widow will marry someone she knows from the past, often a widower from a prior network. Groups such as Parents Without Partners or Spares provide opportunities for cross-gender contact, and the mass media are full of advertisements for mates and for "singles" events. Contact can also be established through special-interest groups that draw both men and women of the appropriate age, racial, or other qualifying characteristics.

The woman who reenters the role of wife has added not only a husband but a whole new social circle, in addition to the one that remains from her prior marriage. A factor affecting her success with the new role is her ability to keep it separated, psychologically and socially, from the vestiges of the old one. Her new husband's marital history must also be dealt with in the reconstruction of reality this time around. The quality of relationships in remarriage varies by the same factors as in the initial marriage, with some modifications due mainly to past experiences (Furstenberg and Spanier 1984). Complications result in an even higher chance of divorce than in first marriages, but McKain (1969) found that people entering older, retirement marriages were quite realistic in their requirements and expectations.

Summary

Both modifications in American society and new constructions of reality by women have introduced many changes into the relations of the wife with all circle members of that role, within relatively recent times. Social class differences complicate the movement from traditional to modern role of wife; the least change is experienced by the extremes of the lower and upper classes. The role of wife in traditional times was heavily controlled by the husband's family and by strict norms of behavior. Transitional marriages combined vestiges of the patriarchal dependency system, in which the man is head of the household and major decision maker, but with relative independence of the nuclear family from the male line. The wife becomes the personal dependent of the husband, since his job and earnings provide the basis of their life-style. Her social circle, duties, and rights are tied into the husband's involvement in an occupational role. It is in the expanding middle class that two-person single-career demands have most affected the transitional wife. As a man's job became defined as requiring total commitment, it acquired the right to impinge upon the life of the wife and to demand extreme support. Assisted by the feminine mystique, which assigned women total responsibility for the home and the family, this system functioned within the two-sphere world.

The role of wife in modern marriage is still in the process of emerging, but it will undoubtedly have two main characteristics: variation along many self-defined and negotiated lines, and great flexibility. As both men and women decrystallize the traditional life course, dependent upon life chances of family background through repeated entrances and exits in education, occupation, and other role involvements, their marital roles will of necessity become more flexible. Entrances into and exits from the role of wife will become more attuned to events in the whole role cluster. Already many women are foregoing marriage or marrying at a later date. Divorce at a later stage of life does not preclude reentry into this role. Negotiated sexual, emotional, occupational, and general supports are subject to renegotiation as self- and other-defined needs change. As of now, this flexibility and variability are most evident in the role of wife, but it is quite possible that these characteristics will become more visible in the role of husband. In the meantime, greater pressure from all kinds of people upon the established institutions may make marriage less repercussively dependent upon changes in the rest of the world.

3

The Role of Mother

The role of mother is universal. The norms surrounding it depend to a great extent on assumptions within the culture as to the needs of social mothers and of the offspring throughout their life courses. The role also depends upon other members of the social circle and how deeply they are involved in monitoring, contributing to, and benefiting from it. No woman has been able to carry out the role of mother without the cooperation of many other people. In past times in America, and currently in most places in the world, responsibility for the child was shared not only by the social father, but also by the extended kin.

A woman enters the social role of mother when she accepts that role in relation to a particular child, or children, and is accepted as such by the social circle she pulls together, more or less voluntarily. Throughout history, the biological mother did not necessarily enter the role of social mother, since the newborn could die, with or without the help of those involved, or she could give it to someone else, usually a woman. In the same vein, the social mother did not necessarily give birth to the child, being able to acquire it in other ways. In modern societies her announcement that she will mother the child has to be legally approved by representatives of the state, such as school personnel, treating her as the mother. Birth certificates assume that the birth mother will undertake social motherhood, while adoption papers recognize the separation of the two forms of motherhood. Women, and even men, can be called "mother" and may even perform many of the duties and receive many rights of that role without being granted its full identity, if they are considered substitutes.

> There are several widespread institutions that involve shifting children between domestic groups. The first is wet-nursing, which is essentially a service institution and may consist of bringing in a servant rather than sending out an infant. The second is fostering, which is often reciprocal between kin though it too may have a service component, for it is a practice that is related to the in-house nursing (nannying) of older children, to servanthood, and to apprenticeship. The third is adoption, a practice associated with the problem of heirship. (Goody 1983, 68)

This role, like that of wife, has gone through three major changes in the last century or so. In traditional families the main burden of mothering fell on the mother's shoulders. The emerging modern era is moving toward a wider circle of shared, negotiated parenting, involving the father and various nonrelated persons or groups of the community. Before analyzing these variations in the role of mother in American society, we must look at the social person characteristics of women who can or cannot enter this role.

Preventing or Insuring the Role of Mother

Decisions as to who enters, and who does not enter, the role of mother go beyond biology and have been very important in the history of humankind. There has been an interesting movement back and forth as to the rights of decision making in cases in which entrance into the role was not ascribed by biology alone.

Societies have had ambivalent feelings about children, giving varying freedom of choice to potential mothers. These feelings have been converted into ideologies, cultural norms, official policies, and even laws. Some societies at some times have not wanted some of its women, or some segments of the population, to reproduce. This was and is particularly true of societies concerned about children as a "national asset" and the "physical deterioration of the population" (Oakley 1981, 212). Sterilization of people judged mentally or physically inferior, or of those who already have children, has been state policy for centuries in India and other countries and was the policy of Nazi Germany. America's history contains references to this form of control of population "quality":

> Paul Popenoe, a leading eugenics spokesman, estimated that 10 million Americans should be sterilized on the basis of IQ testimony. By 1932 compulsory sterilization laws for the feeble-minded, insane, criminal and physically defective had been enacted by twenty-seven states. (Hartmann 1987, 96–97)

Official policies influencing motherhood have included economic rewards or punishment, sex education, funding and dispersal of birth control technologies, health care for the mother and children, and other supports or barriers. Laws define incest and intermarriage. Underlying these are the cultural milieu, the way the society is organized around gender identity, the value given to the role of mother in competition with other roles, and the socialization of children for the future. Judith Blake (1974) found America of the 1970s to be characterized by strong pronatalism, encouragement of marriage for women, high gender-role differentiation, a negative attitude toward careers for women, emphasis in higher education on fields of specialization appropriate to future family roles, an assumption of the naturalness of the desire to have children, and personality socialization into polarized social roles. Blake, as well as Betty Friedan (1963), documented the contributions of psychoanalysis and sociology to the coercive pronatalism imposed on women. On the other hand, Huber (1980) concluded that American society is antinatalistic in that it does not help families after children are born. The Reagan and Bush administrations opposed sex education in schools, the dispensing of contraceptives, and abortion, while cutting back on prenatal and child health care. These administrations claimed to be shocked by reported child abuse, yet did not wish to spend money to prevent it. No serious efforts were made to encourage employers to provide parental leave at birth or adoption, or to insure child support payments by fathers.

In times and places in which birth control has not been frequently practiced and multiple pregnancies have been desired even
by women drained by their frequency, the period of childbearing
has extended from puberty till menopause or death. The high death
rate of the young, and the contributions of children to the economic,
emotional, and old-age support of parents, as well as ancestor
worship insuring an afterlife, made frequent birthing a necessity.

In spite of the current assumption that women have a biologically determined "mothering" propensity, some mothers have killed
their children or allowed their children to be killed, sometimes even
after several years of mothering. Only occasionally have mothers
protested against their children's being sent to probable death in
wars. Infanticide has been practiced for a variety of reasons, including sacrifice to gods, deformity, illness, sex, birth order, and illegiti-
macy (Bennett, 1983, Sommerville 1982). Even European families of
the Middle Ages did not have the sentimental views about children
that developed later, but accepted as necessary the probably pre-
ventable deaths of many newborns and young babies. It must be
remembered that the strongly patriarchal systems of most of Europe
did not give mothers many rights over their children, so that they did
not have the power to prevent child abuse, even in situations in
which their attachment went against the cultural norm of indifference to, or even neglect of, sickly infants.

Modern technological advances have increased at two extremes
women's choices about whether to enter the role of mother: voluntary rejection of the role, and help for those having difficulties in
bearing children. In traditional societies of the past and present, and
in much of America, abortion was often the only way a woman
could prevent unwanted children. Russian women have allegedly
resorted to it frequently during their childbearing years. There are
thus many ways in which a woman can reject entering the role of
mother, ranging from celibacy, contraception, infanticide, to giving
the child to someone else to mother.

Voluntary childlessness was defined as a form of deviant behavior in America's allegedly pronatalistic past (Veevers 1980). Although
the reported rate of expected childlessness has varied little over
studied time in America, there appears to be a change from unwanted, as compared to chosen, childlessness. Also, it is only recently that we have a record of reasons women give for rejecting the
role of mother. Many estimate the costs to outweigh the benefits
(Houseknecht 1987). The economic costs of raising children have

become increasingly high, especially since children contribute little, if anything, to family income, and when a loss of earnings by a stay-at-home mother is included in the calculations. Sociopsychological costs can include loss of freedom, heavy responsibility accompanied by worry and anxiety, negative consequences on marriage, and interference with careers and other roles and relationships (Miller 1987, 584).[1] Some also report a general dislike of children, concern over population growth, troubled early life experiences, or the wish not to lose control over their bodies and future. Care of children can be seen as arduous and complex. Comfortable routines, self-fulfillment, and marital harmony can be seen as destroyed by the addition of motherhood to the existing role cluster. The decision can involve another person, usually the potential father, and difficulties arise if the two are not in complete agreement. It also appears that early decisions not to enter into the role of mother are sometimes questioned as the couple nears the age when pregnancy is no longer advisable or possible. The reported benefits of motherhood include primary ties and affection, stimulation and fun, expansion of self, adult status and identity, achievement and creativity, and becoming a wanted and "better" person. The Chicago women I studied also added under benefits the pleasure of "watching them grow" and "the sense of family" (Lopata 1971b). To these we can add avoiding the stigma of not being a "normal woman" (Oakley 1981, 226). These values hold for America; in other times and places, economic and religious benefits, plus care in old age, have been primary.

The technological means available to women who want to avoid becoming mothers have multiplied considerably, although American society has mixed feelings about their use. Rothman has raised a new concern in *The Tentative Pregnancy: Prenatal Diagnosis and the Future of Motherhood* (1986). Medical technology in the form of amniocentesis or ultrasound now makes it possible for women to determine early on, even before others know they are pregnant, whether they wish to accept a problem fetus, or even one of the "wrong" gender. The long-range consequences of these technologies have not been fully thought out in America, or elsewhere for that matter.

Entering the role of mother can be quite unplanned, a consequence of sexual intercourse without thought of such consequences. Accidental, or "mistimed," pregnancies can be met by the future mother with several emotional responses, depending on many factors. The circumstances of the pregnancy, such as the absence of a husband to give the child patriarchal legitimacy or a social father to share its care, or its occurrence when other roles make heavy demands, can create negative feelings. The experiences of pregnancy, including bodily changes and emotional responses of others, are important factors.

One of the situations that most Americans find "unnatural" is that of ex-mothers or "absentee mothers" (Paskowicz 1982) who accepted the role, related with the child, usually for several years, and then left or gave up custody, and thus the major duties and rights, to someone else, usually the father. Like people who give up other important roles, such women appear to go through several stages: experiencing doubts, seeking alternatives, facing a turning point, and finally creating what Ebaugh (1988) calls an "ex-role." Being an ex-mother is one of the hardest of ex-roles. Women who choose to relinquish custody usually feel incapable of performing the role adequately and consider other people and their life situations better for the child. Others lose custody in courts or through the decision of the children. The state still takes children away from mothers judged to be abusive or neglectful (Wittner 1977).

Women who cannot get pregnant although they wish to do so face a different set of problems, especially when adoption of babies judged by them and intermediaries to be appropriate is difficult. Some couples are determined to parent their own biological children. Infertility can lead to a sense of failure, marital problems or prolonged and expensive medical experimentation. New reproductive technologies are often painful and leave the woman feeling a complete loss of control over her body. In fact, Lauritzen (1990) calls the new developments a "tyranny of technology." He says such technology as artificial insemination or surrogate parenting constitutes a "dismemberment of motherhood"—in that three women, the genetic, gestational, and social mothers can be involved in the process—and calls the process a "commodification of reproduction." Social scientists have been trying hard to imagine consequences of recent reproductive technology, as evidenced by some recent titles (Rapping 1990): *The Mother Machine: Reproductive Technologies from Artificial Insemination to Artificial Wombs, Once upon a Future: The Women's Guide to Tomorrow's Technology, Made to Order: The Myth of Reproductive Progress, Test-Tube Women: What Future for Motherhood?*

Despite the critiques, reports by women who entered the role of mother with the help of the new procedures, such as surrogate motherhood, are very positive (Overbold 1988). The major problems here can be the failure of the biological mother to give up the child, and the complications of all the procedures, which involve legal and medical intermediaries. It will take time before the situation is sufficiently institutionalized to resolve its technical and ethical problems. The combined technology, including genetic experimentation, and societal redefinitions of what is "natural" may decrease the frequency of infertility and the fear of transmitting genetic problems (Rothman 1986, 67). Some women are using the technologies to become mothers, biologically and socially, without there being an acknowledged father of the child.

Traditional Times, Traditional Places

Patriarchal families controlled who could father the child to which the woman gave birth, and insisted on having sons, which was seen as the responsibility of the woman, even when people knew that the male sperm determined the gender of the child. Since the mothers were usually also responsible for managing the household, and they continued having children, they had little time for the actual care of the offspring. The kinship group, older children, or servants, among those who could force or hire others to provide such assistance, did most of the physical care and the socialization of new family members. British common law, copied by early American society, gave the "absolute right to the custody of their minor children to the father" (Lindgren and Taub 1988, 332–33). The main responsibility for the children lay with the father's family, especially in the case of male children. Girls stayed with the mother and other female members of the family, their lives controlled by the family's concerns over the possibility of their becoming impregnated at an inauspicious time.

Transitional and Modern Forms of the Role of Mother

The main characteristic of transitional families in America has been the placement of the total responsibility for the care and socialization of children upon the social mother. Aries (1965) dates from the eighteenth century the idealization of childhood as a distinctive stage of human life and of the mother as the caregiver of children.

Of course, the romanticization of children did not prevent their continued economic exploitation in early industrialization (see Sommerville's *The Rise and Fall of Childhood,* 1982). Families also fought child labor laws, considering their offspring to be necessary to their economic support. Care of the young by mothers, assisted by the role's circle, often included what would now be considered child abuse. The Puritans believed in physical punishment—that "sparing the rod" resulted in problem youth.

The reversal of the position of the child from being expendable to being a "precious" member of the family had become so strong by the mid-1900s that several authors labeled the recent past "the century of the child" (see Ehrenreich and English 1979). The increased emphasis on child protection and the importance of motherhood for the socialization of the young had a backlash effect on women in the midtwentieth century. Women had to live with "the fantasy of the perfect mother" (Chodorow and Contratto 1982). The emphasis on this role, which was less apparent in Europe, was due to American society's refusal to take responsibility for its children, the growing difficulty of mothering in the absence of traditional formulas for rearing and controlling the young, the prevailing theories of human development, and the relative isolation of mothers from the extended family (Lopata 1971b, 182–88). The main contribution of the father was to provide the economic support for the family. His prior responsibility for what the children did was thus diminished, shifted to the mother. A look at the titles of books with widespread popularity in the 1950s indicates that some Americans were concerned about the total interdependence of mother and child in relative isolation from other socializers. Mothers became accused of living vicariously through their children, and of rearing them too "permissively." Wylie's *Generation of Vipers* (1955) is a good example of the extremely negative portrayal of American women during the "feminine mystique" years. The anti-Semitic stereotype of the overprotective Jewish mother is an example of extreme "mother bashing" (R. Coser, 1992). Bettelheim (1962) went so far as to advocate child care organized by the kibbutzim movement in Israel, which took the children away from the mother for most of the time, to be reared in peer groups by caregivers on eight-hour shifts. He defined American mothers as too protective of their children, whose moral development needed contact with peers in what Mead called the "game stage."

It is very difficult to differentiate the transitional from the modern role of mother in the United States, mainly because American society has not really moved beyond the idea that the mother is the only one responsible for the child. There is a great deal of public commentary and outcry over the failure of other people to feel responsible for our youths, but little has been done to change either the ideology of perfect motherhood or the behavior of all involved. The problem of child care arose in transitional times as a result of the decreased availability of extended kin, older children, servants, and the community at large to care for the young and the organization of much work into jobs in organizations away from home, jobs entered into by individuals without arrangements for care of family members. The most recent trend of increased labor-force participation of mothers compounded the problem, because the fathers were already gone for most of the day.

Modern women who have moved into the multidimensional life space required by the complexity of social development find life complicated by the addition of the role of mother, with all its transitional characteristics (see Rossi 1968 and the discussion of role conflict in chapter 8). Employed mothers now seldom send children back to villages from which they migrated or to relatives in other locations, as they did in the past (Hareven 1978a, 1978b; Hareven and Langenbach 1978). Older children are in school and related activities, the extended family has dispersed, and its older female members, such as grandmothers, also hold jobs. Exceptions still exist in ethnic communities, in which kin care is institutionalized and/or the women live nearby and cannot get jobs.

Nonfamilial child care is expensive, servants either are no longer available or are prohibitive in cost, and out-of-home caregivers can be unreliable. American mass media are constantly reporting cases of physical, sexual, and psychological abuse by people hired to take care of the young. This does not mean that mothers themselves never abuse their children, but that caretakers paid for the service are forbidden from breaking established rules of care. These reports create great concern and guilt in employed mothers, who nevertheless need the money from their jobs (Kamerman 1980).

One solution is to allow older children to take care of themselves at home after school. Labeled "latchkey children" by the press, which has not presented this solution in a positive light, such children reportedly do not suffer any long-term social or cognitive developmental problems (Rodman 1990; Rodman and Pratto 1987). Cain and Hofferth (1989, 76) report that such self-care is usually for only short periods of time and carried out by older children of white, middle-class families who live in suburban or rural areas. Mothers are available by telephone, and some communities have developed volunteer hot-lines for troubled situations. There is little mention of fathers.

As of now, women are still held responsible for solving any problems arising out of the difficulty of being a mother in modern times and the dysfunctionality of transitional role relations. A perfect example of the double-bind situation of women is the constant public outcry over child care. It encompasses a complete refusal of the society to take on responsibility for its young, on the national or community level (see Grubb and Lazerson 1982).

Strong conflict between the role of mother of young children and the role of employee/worker/career woman is an American phenomenon. Other societies are still in traditional life patterns with extended-family and village involvement in their children or have found new ways in which the children are seen as part of the community, which shares their care (see Kamerman and Kahn 1989; Kahn and Kamerman 1975; Kamerman 1980, presents alternative responses from European countries). There are many ways in which employers, schools, community centers, organized sports, and other interest groups can contribute to the welfare of children so that the mother need not be present twenty-four hours a day. There is some evidence that American governmental and private employers are beginning to consider their responsibilities to their employees and that fathers are insisting on greater flexibility in their work schedules to enable active fathering. If these trends continue, the mother's social circle will take on much greater functions than just passive assistance to her.

The Life Course of the Role of Mother

Becoming a Mother

The process by which a woman enters the role of mother, even in adoption, takes time, during which she anticipatorily socializes herself and future circle members and is socialized by others (Rossi 1985). A mother's duties precede the child's birth, for they include self-care in order to insure the health of the newborn. Throughout human history the pregnancy and birth processes have been connected with fear, which is not surprising in view of how frequently mothers and children used to die during these processes (Miller 1987, 583). What are considered influences upon the physical and psychological welfare of the mother and the fetus vary considerably from society to society, and even among subgroups. "Experts" on childbirth abound, ranging from women already in that role, to midwives and people who will form the mother's social circle after the birth. Magical and religious rituals are performed even now to insure the protection of the fetus from all kinds of harm (Znaniecki 1965, 117). Whole books are devoted to prescriptions and proscriptions pregnant women should follow. In recent times, a large and successful profession has grown up around pregnancy, childbirth, and early childhood pediatrics (Halpern 1989). In fact, social scientists have labeled this the "medicalization," or professional regulation, of birth, taking decision making and even birth itself out of the "minds and hands" of the mother. The adopting mother can only hope that the biological mother took adequate precautions to insure that the baby she turns over is healthy.

Another duty of the future mother is to prepare in advance an adequate physical environment for the child, including clothing and related paraphernalia. Such preparations are aimed at insuring safety, health, and comfort. "Baby showers" provide many items judged necessary for the care and development of the newborn, or at least considered representative of his or her status. Complex social and religious ceremonies surround the birth and recognition of the newborn (Williams 1990).

Traumatic Events in Becoming a Mother

Of course, becoming pregnant does not guarantee entrance into or continuance in the role of mother. Demographers estimate that only about half of all infants ever born reach maturity (Miller 1987, 582). American mothers who are above the line of poverty, thus spared many of poverty's health complications, are much more likely to see their children grow into maturity than are mothers who live below that line.

An added complication to the role of mother has been the recent dramatic improvement in medical technology that enables intensive and extended care for newborns (see Guillemin and Holmstrom

1986, Frohock 1986). The technology available in the "closed world of the neonatal intensive care unit" (Guillemin and Holmstrom 1986, 141) raises important social and ethical issues. The medical staff tends to exclude the parents from the decision-making process, and the effect of this on the families is not always positive.

In spite of the modern technologies that save babies and older children, many mothers still experience the loss of a child. Research indicates that stillbirths, miscarriages, and even wanted abortions due to fetal abnormalities are highly traumatic to the woman who has already socialized herself into motherhood (Borg and Lasker 1988). Grief can be experienced even if the mother never had a chance to "bond" with the baby she carried. One would assume that it would be even harder if the child had already acquired human capacities and responsiveness. Knapp (1986) entitled her study *Beyond Endurance: When a Child Dies,* and teams of professional or volunteer assistants have recently emerged to help parents cope with caring for a dying child (Carlson 1984).

Being a Mother

Motherhood is a role for which many transitional American women feel unprepared, untrained, and inadequate. This was particularly true of the women influenced by the feminine mystique of the 1950s and 1960s (Lopata 1971a, 189). They, like mothers currently in the transitional stages of women's roles, were caught in a historical gap when traditional family child care became unavailable or rejected and before "modern" medical and social "experts" took over the responsibility of educating them into new knowledge. The proverbial postpartum depression is often analyzed as hormonal, but it is undoubtedly influenced by the enormity of responsibility suddenly thrust on the mother, especially in a society that gives so little of that responsibility to other members of the child's social circle, such as the father or kinfolk. The "parenthood as crisis" literature also points to the changes in life-style introduced into the homes of many a mother who had been in a multidimensional life space before. Such women experience a more dramatic shift in their lives with motherhood than with marriage, especially if they do not return to work or other full-time involvement after the birth.

Only in recent years have there been societal resources in the form of self-help groups or expert counselors for mothers, and even fathers, assisting with new parenthood. However, modern new mothers find themselves in a double-bind situation: resenting professional control yet anxious over their inability to meet all the demands of the role without it.

The consequences of becoming a mother are extensive in transitional and modern times. These include changes in the self, sometimes to the extent of identity crisis, or a feeling of being pushed into the background as an individual by the constant physical work and by social contacts being limited to mainly infants in a restricted life space. On the other hand, motherhood can be experienced as bringing an increase in maturity, capacities, and abilities (Lopata 1971b, 193). A third consequence is inevitably described as "being tied down." Previous freedom to come and go at will is gone. Elaborate arrangements, often expensive or involving unwanted dependencies, have to be made for child care. Mothers may face special problems in connection with the children, such as their handicaps or care for several children of different ages and with different needs. Changes in the relationship with the husband/new father are necessitated as the new role adds overlap dimensions to the one entered into before (Lerner and Spanier 1978). Lower-class women often report that becoming parents added a new tie to the marriage, while middle-class women tend to feel that it complicates and interferes with husband-wife interaction. Some families change residences after the addition of children, considering past locations less desirable for the children or for the parents (Lopata 1971b, 203; see also Rossi 1985). All in all, becoming a mother increases work and responsibility and decreases personal leisure to a level not anticipated before (Wearing 1990). These changes do not necessarily result in unhappiness, as they can be offset by the pleasure of having a child. This is particularly true of mothers who had planned not only for having a child, but also for its timing (see Michaels and Goldberg 1988).

Research of the past two decades, often undertaken on the assumption of changes in the roles of women and men due to the women's movement and other cultural modifications, invariably comes to the conclusion that responsibility for the child has remained with the mother since it became lodged there with social development or modernization (Backett 1982; Oakley 1974b). She continues to be responsible for the child's physical well-being, as were her grandmothers, but the growth of psychology and other social sciences has added the burden of also being responsible for the child's psychological development. In most of known history, personality inheritance or at least imprinting at conception or birth was taken for granted, so that the mother was not accountable for the results. Of course, the duties of a mother in insuring the psychological health of the child have varied considerably, depending on assumptions about human nature.

In addition, the mother must teach the child to be "a conscious partner in their relation" and a contributing member of present and future social circles (Znaniecki 1965, 121–22). The child must learn how to relate to other people, not just in general terms but within social roles. All societies contribute to the mother's duties and rights by adding experts in different areas of knowledge for the socialization and education of the child, be they mothers-in-law or physicians-cum-psychologists (Ehrenreich and English 1979). Some of these additions actually deprive the mother of her rights of socialization, implicitly or even quite openly informing her that she is not an adequate parent. This was the assumption behind the Head Start program in America, which is intended to insure that children not be disadvantaged in the educational system by the limitations of the "culture of poverty" (Berrueta-Clement 1984; Joffe 1977).[2] Part of the various programs of preschool or nursery care of children of immigrant or other lower-class families has been education of the parents, especially the mothers. "Friendly intruders" (Joffe 1977) have been teachers and others claiming professional license and mandate to intervene between mother and child, especially when the parent does not have the power to refuse such interference. In fact, our society's mistrust of the mother's ability to raise her children in the way the society wishes them raised has a long history.[3]

The mother can expect cooperation from the members of the social circle in her fulfillment of her duties in that role. The child has the duty of recognizing her as the mother and her demands as her rights. This usually means that the mother has the right to obedience from the child, within limits imposed by the society. Other people in the social circle of the mother can impose restrictions on her behavior, and on that of her child, to guarantee expected results. The mother's rights include the opportunity to be connected with other people, even outside of the family, especially as the child grows and becomes involved in the outside world. The decrease of embodiment in an extended family and neighborhood by women in the allegedly depersonalized and mobile urban environment increases the need for connecting links for the child, so that the mother must somehow serve as such a link to the outside world.

The growing child is expected to give the mother opportunities for vicarious experience, something that is desired especially, according to much social scientific literature, by the middle-class mother who gave up her personal ambition in taking on the role complex of wife/mother/homemaker. The mass media acknowledge this right by favoring pictures of proud mothers standing next to their famous sons (sometimes, daughters). Thus, the rights, like the duties, change over the life course of the role.

One must constantly keep in mind that the child is not just a passive lump of clay or *tabula rasa* upon which the mother simply "writes" the behavior she wants the child to exhibit, but a constantly interacting person (Mead 1934). The way the mother interacts with the child is thus deeply influenced by how the child relates to her, and by the surroundings within which all this takes place.

The social circle often, but not necessarily, includes the father of the child, especially if he is legally so recognized and is actively involved in the role. This father has specific duties and rights that can support, but sometimes interfere with, the rights of the mother. Each parent has a different involvement with the children, depending on their gender, birth order, and ages (Harris and Morgan 1990), which can create problems. For example, one parent might believe that the other is favoring or neglecting a child unfairly. Parents may disagree strongly over the best methods of socialization of the young. Arguments can be over a child's behavior—and reasons for discipline, the method of carrying it out, and the child's response to this. The mother thus must negotiate her mothering with the father. On the other hand, she is usually the only one present with the child for most of the time, especially if she is a full-time homemaker, so the father may have little input. The father's contribution to the role of mother varies considerably by social class in situations involving stepparenting or nonparental boyfriends of the mother (Jarrett 1990a, 1990b).

The circle may also include siblings of the child, i.e., other children of the mother, other relatives, on the mother's or father's side, who are interested in how the mother performs her role and in its consequences on the child (Kidwell 1981). Neighbors, school personnel, members of organized social groups to which the child belongs, the child's friends, teachers, even the community police may develop relationships with her because she is the mother of that child. These relationships can assist her in how she wants to function as a mother, but they often create role strain because of differences in values or means, or overload in demands. The paternal grandparents' ideas about how their grandchild should be reared to perpetuate the family status may differ greatly from those of the mother if she comes from a different background. The mother has duties to all these circle members, recognizing their contributions to—or interferences with—her role, making possible their access and actions in relation to the child. Variations in the composition of the social circle theme of transitional motherhood are now developing. For example, a Washington state judge has recently recognized two lesbians as a "two-mom family," the legal parents of a child. "Their daughter will now have a rare two-mother, no-father birth certificate" (Monagle 1989, 69). This legal decision made it possible for the adoptive mother to retain custody in case of the death of the biological mother, and to receive her life insurance and estate. "And if Lynn and Lisa should split, their daughter will be entitled to child support and visitation rights." Pepper Schwartz, sociologist and coauthor of *American Couples* (Blumstein and Schwartz 1983), testified in that case that "there is no discernible difference between children brought up in lesbian or heterosexual households" (Monagle 1989, 69).

The role of mother is also deeply influenced by how many children are involved. Even more than with other roles, the addition of each new child modifies the mother's relations with prior children and with other members of the circle.

The Older Mother

Both the satisfactions and the problems of the role of mother change during its life course, mainly in response to changes in the children and, in later years, in the mother. Changes are demanded of the mother by the growing child and the society, which wants the child to increasingly take on the responsibilities of full membership. These demands can be met in a variety of ways, often depending on the birth order of the child. The mother may be more protective of the firstborn child, who must fight for new rights, and the succeeding children benefit from their establishment. One of the benefits of motherhood may be learning new knowledge from the children, who keep the mothers up to date about the rapidly changing world.

The social circle of the mother changes as components of assisting segments come and go. Children develop their own social roles, more or less independent of the mother, with their own social person characteristics, duties, and rights within each social circle. Early studies of the "empty nest" stage of the life course of the role of mother concluded that it can be a source of depression. Bart (1971) studied Jewish women in California hospitalized with depression as a result of the last child's leaving home. Basing their feelings of self-worth mainly on being a mother, in traditional Jewish manner, they felt worthless once their mothering activities were severely diminished by the independence of geographically distant children. Recent analyses indicate, however, that women finally freed from most of the duties of in-house motherhood felt themselves expanding in social life space and personality (Baruch, Barnett, and Rivers 1983). This freedom may not last long. A new phenomenon is the return of children to the home after the parents have adjusted to the freedom provided by the empty nest (Schnaiberg and Goldenberg 1989). Unable to afford similar housing on their own, facing economic problems of unemployment or underemployment, married or divorced or in relationships that cannot sustain themselves, children come home, often bringing their husbands and children with them. Parents try to prevent their children's downward mobility by helping any way they can (Newman 1988). The role of mother does not necessarily decrease when the children leave home for allegedly independent lives.

Various factors contribute to intergenerational relations involving the older, often widowed mother, and her children, including the level of interdependence and personal resources of both. Mothers vary considerably in the extent to which they are dependent upon the children for economic, service, social, and emotional supports; many have other resources such as kinfolk, friends, neighbors, co-members of voluntary associations, and so forth (Lopata 1979). Middle-class American widows prefer not to live with married children, if at all possible. Not only independence of living style and rhythms, but also avoidance of conflict or irritation and housework or child-care work, encourages widowed mothers to live alone (Treas and Bengtson 1987). However, independent living is not possible for widows whose subcultures require or facilitate sharing of housing, or who cannot function in modern American cities. Some widows, such as many in lower-class black communities, take for granted continued intergenerational residence and mutual support systems (Bengtson and deTerre 1980). Independent residence can, but does not necessarily, mean social isolation or deprivation of supports. Shanas (1979a, 1979b) has repeatedly exploded the myth of the isolated older mother.

Motherhood in Retrospect

The fact that not every woman has enjoyed being in the role of mother may be partially indicated by a 1976 story by Ann Landers in *Good Housekeeping*. The article was featured on the front cover, under the headline "Why So Many Mothers Are Sorry They Had Children—a Shocking Report." Landers asked the magazine's readers, "If you had it to do over again—would you have children?" Seventy percent of ten thousand responses (80 percent from women) responded with no. Interestingly, most of those who so responded did not sign their names, while the positive responses included identification. The negative answers fell into three categories: parents of troubled teenagers, parents who stated that the children had ruined their marriage, and older people who felt unrepaid for their sacrifices. Of course, the respondents were not representative of American women, since the only selection criterion was that they were readers of that magazine, and since not all readers responded. The most likely to respond were people who were willing to openly express strong feelings on this subject. On the other hand, a 1990 Gallup poll, on a different kind of question, found that only about 4 percent of Americans are strongly antichildren: They don't have any, don't want any, or are glad they didn't have any (Gallup and Newport 1990, 3).

However women evaluate their lives as mothers, most experience a great deal of stress when their offspring encounter problems. After all, children do not just grow up and live happily ever after. Fifty-five percent of the mothers and 34 percent of the fathers studied by Greenberg and Becker (1988, 788), reported at least moderate levels of stress because of what was happening to their children or what the children themselves were doing. In order of frequency, these included problems with health, work, children (of adult child), emotions, and finances. Of special concern were problems with alcohol or marriages. In the order of the amount of stress experienced by the mother, marital, financial, emotional, and alcohol problems were the worst, while health problems created the least stress (E. Johnson 1981). The fathers felt the stress indirectly, in that the problems affected the wives first. The study concludes that the parents repeatedly act as resources to their children in spite of experiencing stress themselves. In fact, an increasing amount of research finds a downward flow of supports from the parents to their adult children for longer periods of time and in greater frequency than is true in the reverse direction. This means that parents are more often contributorsthan burdens to their children.

Social-Class Variations in the Role of Mother

Just like the role of wife, the role of mother varies by social class, which is not surprising since whole life-styles and provisions of life chances differ by social class.

Mothers of the Underclass

The American underclass, which is considered to be below the actual class system and isolated from its institutions, has become of concern to both social scientists and the mass media. Some of its characteristics are of recent origin, including the presence of many female-headed households containing children born to very young mothers and extreme poverty of a vicious-cycle nature. It consists mainly of descendants of slaves who have been deprived of their own heritage and consistently discriminated against, and who have ended up in those locales of the society from which most supportive institutions escaped. It also contains households headed by women of Puerto Rican and North American Indian background (John 1988; Sanchez-Ayendez 1988). The underclass is found in urban areas with extremely high unemployment, and its whole life-style is lodged in poverty. Corcoran, Duncan, and Hill (1988, 109) report from the Panel Study of Income Dynamics that 65 percent of persistently poor families are headed by women, and 70 percent of these are black. Seventy percent of black children are likely to have spent at least some of a ten-year period of their lives in poverty, and 30 percent were so disadvantaged for six out of the ten years. Of white children, only 30 percent were ever poor during the ten-year period, and only 2 percent spent over half of that time in poverty. One conclusion that comes from this study, supported by other research, is the temporary nature of poverty among white women, and the greater frequency of both poverty and long-lasting economic problems among African American women.

As stated above, a problem that is major and increasing for the underclass, although not limited to it, is entrance into the role of mother by teenagers, who are assumed to lack the maturity and support necessary to carry forth the role in the style deemed best by society. Wallis (1985, 82) estimated that, of the 163 pregnancies per 1,000 black teenage girls, 51 percent end in nonmarital births, 8 percent in marital births, and 41 percent in abortions. The comparable figures for whites are 83 pregnancies per 1,000 teenage girls, with 19 percent ending in nonmarital births, 35 percent in marital births, and 47 percent in abortions. Wallis's article appeared in a lead article of *Time* magazine entitled "Children Having Children: Teen Pregnancy in America." Its prominence indicates a serious American concern.

There are many reasons why girls become pregnant early in life. Most teens have limited knowledge of sexual matters, are suspicious of contraceptives, or use motherhood as a marker of adulthood. They see babies as sources of love and enjoy the idea of taking care of them. Their social circles of their own mothers and other kin and friends help them care for these babies, although not always in the best style (Furstenberg 1990).

> The centrality of the maternal role has been well documented in past literature on low-income black women. Motherhood is critical for female adult status, even when it occurs outside of marriage and particularly when other channels of mobility are locked. Within the community context, children are a symbol of womanhood. (Jarrett 1990b, 5)

These low-income black mothers have very traditional views; they wish they could marry a man with a good job but have little hope of doing so. As one explains, it would be "foolish" to have children just to get on welfare. Furstenberg, Gordis, and Markowitz (1969) found teenage girls to have very limited knowledge and much misinformation about contraception and to be very upset when they found out that they were pregnant. However, once they accepted the pregnancy and the baby, they appeared less worried about having another.

The consequences of early motherhood include reduced education, rapid subsequent childbearing and higher levels of fertility, economic deprivation and reduced asset accumulation relative to those who delay childbearing, and subsequent marital dissolution if married (Teachman, Polonko, and Scanzoni 1987, 17). As stated before, the Reagan and Bush administrations held inconsistent attitudes toward this problem. They discouraged sex education, the dispensing of contraceptives to young unmarrieds, and abortion, yet they did not adequately assist pregnant women and young mothers, or prevent the "feminization of poverty," and they promoted the punishment of mothers who, unable to control their frustrations, abused or neglected their children. The main solutions to these problems, provided through the Aid to Families with Dependent Children program, stigmatize the recipients. Critics of the program state that women take advantage of it by purposely becoming mothers. These critics do not realize the inadequacy of the support and the difficulties of caring for children and low-pay employment (Piven 1989).

Wilson's (1987) analysis of the underclass in the social structure of American society concluded that its situation is class- rather than race-based, but there is strong disagreement with that hypothesis among other social scientists, because it underestimates the consequences of racism. According to Wilson (1987), young men of the underclass cannot function as husbands and fathers, that is, cannot contribute actively to the raising of children they have fathered for mainly economic reasons. They cannot obtain adequate general and vocational education, and thus cannot find jobs in a market decreasingly needful of unskilled labor. Such unskilled jobs that remain have moved out of the American urban centers in which such men are ghettoized (Bluestone and Harrison 1982). The combination of frustrations facing such men alienate them from their families. Unable to support their children, they are unwilling to marry the mothers (see also Liebow 1967). Jarrett's (1990a, 1990b, and 1992) ethnographic study of these women finds many also choosing not to marry. Such mothers openly admit their powerlessness vis-à-vis the men and have developed a female support network of mothers and daughters (see also Omolade 1986). This does not mean that children grow up without male care or support. The separation of biological from social fatherhood, present in much of human history, makes it possible for many other men—brothers, grandfathers, boyfriends of the mother, and so forth—to be involved in parenting or other kin interactions. In many cases, the women understand the economic insecurity of the men and have fewer expectations of support than is true in middle-class families (Jarrett 1990a, 1990b).

Puerto Rican families on the mainland face similar problems. Only 46 percent of the married mothers have a husband present in the home, compared to 56 percent of Mexican Americans and 58 percent of Cuban Americans (Sanchez-Ayandez 1988). In fact, 46 percent of Puerto Rican women have children out of wedlock; feelings of responsibility on the part of these fathers reportedly are much weaker than those of legalized fathers. And, as the husband-absent figures indicate, even legal fathers may not undertake the role of social father.

On the other hand, recent research has pointed to the strength of the support systems surrounding solo black mothers and the temporary nature for many of dependence upon welfare (Jarrett 1990a, 1990b). De Anda and Becerra (1984) report the same among Hispanics, especially a close relationship between the adolescent mother and her own mother, although the father-daughter relations are weak. The mothers of the underclass have become relatively independent of long-lasting relationships with supportive adult men and solve their economic problems and child-rearing problems in a variety of other ways. One of these involves temporary relationships with limited support expectations. In fact, many do not want to be controlled by men who cannot provide the benefits of economic support due to their own economic marginality (Jarrett 1990a).

The most detailed description of such a life-style is presented by Carol Stack (1975) in *All Our Kin*. Mothers living at or below the poverty level, whose welfare benefits do not come close to meeting their needs, are quite flexible in sharing resources. Children are reared and socialized by an extended group of many real and fictive relations, mothers passing them back and forth to eat and sleep as resources become available to people. She also pointed to the separation of social from biological fatherhood. The sharing of funds, food, and all belongings has the advantage of meeting emergencies, but the interdependence and mutual obligations make it very difficult to move out of the cycle of poverty even if temporary "good fortune" comes along. The disadvantage to this support system is that all of its members are caught in the vicious cycle of poverty (Kriesberg 1970; Wilson 1987). The welfare program itself does not provide sufficient income to pull them out of poverty, but it does make the women subject to external interference with their life-style by "friendly intruders" who judge their fitness as mothers (Joffe 1977).

Thus, American society has not been able, or willing, to solve the problem of poverty. Concern with the future of the children has not extended to help in breaking poverty's vicious cycle in the underclass. Americans are embarrassed by the presence of poverty in their country, but predominant attitudes hark back to the Elizabethan poor laws of Britain, which "blame the victim" (Kriesberg 1970; Piven and Cloward 1977). Other industrial societies that provide more adequate assistance to families have decreased poverty, without detrimental effects upon the "character" of those being helped (Kahn and Kamerman 1975).

In spite of negative attitudes toward the poor, minorities, and especially women on welfare, a few efforts have been made by Americans to provide better support to pregnant adolescents. Some schools are allowing these girls to continue attendance and provide prenatal care and schedule modification. The most advanced have set up nurseries on school property to make it easier for these mothers to complete their education. Economic assistance by the state, with the help of a supportive network, allows the young mother to prepare for adult roles while she cares for the newborn.

Native American mothers have the additional problem of facing a different kind of prejudice and discrimination, which has included sterilization, child-placement programs that result in adoption by non-Indians, and missionary activity in schools that tries to remove traces of their culture (John 1988). Native American women are worried about cross-racial adoption, the loss of potential for masculine behavior of their men, and the refusal of their own communities and of the larger society to pay attention to their problems.

Working-Class Mothers

The families at the bottom of the social class ladder have usually been either members of racial minorities or voluntary immigrants of the European peasantry who brought with them a sustaining culture (Schooler 1984). The latter settled near each other and developed ethnic communities. People like the Poles built churches and schools and created multi-institutional frameworks within which mothers could rear their children (Lopata 1976b; Thomas and Znaniecki 1918–20). The Polonias (Lopata 1994), Little Italys (Gans 1962), Greektowns (Kourvetaris 1988), or Mexican American communities (Williams 1990) insured kin support in child rearing, and divorce was rare, community pressures favoring stability. Mothers generally did not hold jobs but obtained pay from boarders and lodgers, doing other people's laundry or exchanging services. Children assisted with that work or were even sent out to earn money on their own.

Whole families were sometimes employed by a single organization. Although usually able to live on a relatively stable income in good economic times, these families faced many uncertainties. The mothers reorganized their lives and budgets when hit by economic crisis, as during the Great Depression (Milkman 1979). Support networks and the ideology of upward mobility in a more or less democratic society helped create a full, if frequently uncomfortable, life. The children of the immigrants, facing cultural conflicts and the multiplicity of their parents' problems, disproportionally displayed delinquent behavior, which was frightening to the mothers, but most grew out of it and formed their own norm-following families. Although European immigrants faced some prejudice and discrimination in early culturally divergent years, they lacked the generationally transmitted physical differences that insured continued minority status, and thus they were able to melt into general society (Mindel, Habenstein, and Wright 1988).

The upwardly mobile European and, increasingly, Asian families have had the advantage of more frequent two-parent families, employed husbands and fathers and a lesser amount of long-lasting discrimination than has been true of the persistently poor (Jarrett 1990a).

Most working-class families stuck to strongly patriarchal and authoritarian norms of parent-child relationships (see Mindel, Habenstein, and Wright 1988, *Ethnic Families in America,* for details). Children were expected to be obedient and were punished physically for trespassing against the norms (Langman 1987). Rainwater, Coleman, and Handel portrayed the "workingman's wife" in 1959 as constantly worried about her children, hoping they would just sit still, not fight, not get dirty, and not get into trouble outside of the home. Although they contributed to a great deal of the mother's frustration, children also provided their mother with her major gratifications, life meaning, and evidence of personal worth. The mother spent many hours a day on their physical care but often felt that she could not understand them or influence their behavior. She wanted to teach them right from wrong, to become moral adults, but she did not even trust herself to do the same. Unlike the middle-class mother of that time, she could not, and did not, try to provide a varied back–ground of experience. Passivity and short-term satisfaction were her ideals for her children and for herself. Living in an environment that was limited both physically and in her construction of reality, she could not offer them anything else. She spent money on the children to provide them immediate pleasure rather than to achieve long-range goals.

> It is apparent that working-class mothers want to be needed and loved by their children in a way which middle-class women do not. (Rainwater, Coleman, and Handel 1950, 97)

The same orientation toward being a mother, socialization, and the future of children is found in many more recent studies, such as Rubin's *Worlds of Pain: Life in the Working-Class Family* (1976). Gender segregation of life, experienced by the mother, is translated into differences in relations with daughters and sons. There is no attempt by the mother to extend her children's adolescence by encouraging education, although most mothers wish for the continuance of early childhood years. A similar worldview has been found among the Polish Americans in Detroit (Wrobel 1979) and the Catholic Irish in America (Horgan 1988). It was also typical of the working-class Italian Americans of West End Boston:

> The West End family is an adult-centered one. Since children are not planned, but come naturally and regularly, they are not at the center of family life. Rather, they are raised in a household that is run to satisfy adult wishes first. As soon as they are weaned and toilet-trained, they are expected to behave themselves in ways pleasing with adults. . . . When girls reach the age of seven or eight, they start assisting the mother, and become miniature mothers. Boys are given more freedom to roam, and, in that sense, are treated just like their fathers. (Gans 1962, 56)

Several more-recent studies of Italian American families also point to the distance between fathers and small children, with the children's socialization and care being left to the mother (Johnson 1985; Squier and Quadagno 1988).

Some middle-class patterns of socialization of the young appear in ethnic communities as families become more affluent, but especially with increased education in the American system. Some working-class immigrants, such as Eastern European Jews, sacrificed for their children's education and have experienced strong intergenerational upward mobility (Farber, Mindel, and Lazerwitz 1988; Sklare 1971). The same pattern appears among Asian American families, such as the Chinese (Wong 1988), Japanese (Kitano 1988), and Korean (Min 1988). These groups have also displayed a high outmarriage rate, so that more of these children have a dual background and, presumably, either a more middle-class or a more conflict-ridden interaction with the mother, depending on whether she is of Asian or another culture.

Middle-Class Mothers

Mothers located in the various layers of the American middle-class are found to be much more involved in the long-range socialization of their children for success, anticipating satisfaction from their achievements as a right more than is true of mothers in lower social classes (Skolnick 1983). Motherhood involves duties of psychological development, of providing the child with tools toward self-expansion. These women have the background and current resources to link the child with the wider world.

Paid-for services are important to those middle-class families who are relatively isolated from the tight kinship support network available in some stable communities. Residence is influenced by jobs, and relatives tend to become socially diversified and distant. Upward mobility also makes many a mother unwilling to depend on her parents for child care, not wishing to reproduce their cultural patterns (Rapp 1982). Sue and Morishma's study *The Mental Health of Asian Americans* (1982) points to the refusal of younger mothers to conform in their child rearing to the strict, clearly defined roles of prior generations. These women are even drawn to intermarriage with men who allow more freedom in their mothering activities.

The American mass media have recently publicized an almost obsessive effort by more educated middle-class mothers to push their children toward very early achievement, with allegedly negative consequences of tension and anxiety. Such mothers are willing to expose their children to limited dangers, rather than constantly protect them from all threatening experiences.

Middle-class mothers in general control their children through threats of withdrawal of love, rather than through the physical punishment used by lower-class parents (Langman 1987). They try to involve the father in the socialization process and to discuss policies and actions with all circle members, including the children (Kohn 1977). Attempts at androgynous socialization are also reported, the mothers not wishing to restrict daughters or sons along traditional lines. This is particularly true of mothers of only, or a limited number of, children (Polit and Falbo 1987). However, such women are also more likely to be involved in jobs in "greedy institutions," presenting role conflict and a complexity of relations with the children, with the help of a variety of assistants (Epstein 1983; Lorber 1984). Such employment deprives many of the time and energy necessary for serving as connecting links to the community, making these mothers either more similar to working-class mothers or more dependent upon a complex social circle to accomplish this (O'Donnell and Stueve 1983). Their economic resources enable these mothers to use time- and energy-saving methods, such as using restaurants and cleaning services, and buying store-bought clothes for the children, if the mothers earn enough or have earning partners.

Mothers of the Upper Class

Upper-class mothers tend to relate to their children within a much broader world than that of their socioeconomically lower counterparts. Membership in the upper class is already established, and the task of the mothers is to have children and to ensure that they fit into the whole life-style of their position. Extended families, schools, and the other families of this social class assure that the children develop along the class lines. The children are socialized to follow the norms and control their behavior, since deviation brings notoriety harmful to the family status. They are surrounded with appropriate objects and persons, provided with boarding school and top-flight higher education, and isolated from interpersonal relations with "undesirable elements," that is, members of lower strata, unless on a status-maintaining level. Being in constant, equal power relationships with others of the same position is especially important when it comes to mate selection, mothers being very careful to provide close contact with children of eligible families. Upper-class women consider their role of mother to be of extreme importance, although subsidiary to the role of wife (Ostrander 1984). The threat of disinheritance, which would remove the child from a very nice life-style, appears sufficient to grant the mother rights of obedience. Money is also available to save the child from painful consequences of antisocial or even criminal behavior. Some amount of rebelliousness is allowed, possibly even expected, but long-range conformity is usually accomplished. Mothers, however, walk a tight line and create as many barriers to downward mobility as possible. Children whose parents fail to live up to the position within which the young were socialized often treat parents in a less-than-positive manner (Newman 1988).

Upper-class mothers participate in activities and organizations that insure continued family membership in their stratum, extending to the adulthood of their children (Daniels 1988, 7). The mothers' activities also insure the health, education, and welfare of the community in which they reside.

Other Variations in the Role of Mother

Raising Sons

There is an additional area of difficulty faced by mothers in this society: the raising of boys. The mother is expected to, and does, relate differently with sons than with daughters, with societal and subunit variations. British and American experts in psychology, medicine, social work, and mass media have been deeply influenced, especially in the past, by Freudian and neo-Freudian theories of child development (Oakley 1974b). These define boys as experiencing the oedipal complex of wanting to kill their fathers in order to sexually possess their mothers, and girls as experiencing penis envy for which there is no cure. Much of the psychological literature of recent years dealing with childhood socialization focuses on the boy's need to separate himself from a prior intense relationship with the mother, repressing tendencies toward emotional dependence and the need for close relationships (Chodorow 1978). This situation is very different from that in traditional India, where the son's tie with the mother was considered the most important (Lopata 1987e, 1991b). Less attention is paid in this literature to the actions of the mother to encourage such separation, and to the consequences upon her of this gradual, or sometimes sudden, alienation. In a society in which women have lower status than men, she obviously must encourage the son's growing awareness of her inferiority. The lower the status of the women, the more the mother must accept the fact, reinforced by others, that the son will end up seeing her as inferior to him. She must accept the change from being the child's focal point, as she is likely to be in early years, to being lumped together with other women as being of lesser status.

It is the duty of a mother to try to insure that the personalities of her daughters and sons develop gender-appropriate emotional, self-concept, world-construction, and behavioral packages. Traditional patriarchal societies insured this gender specific socialization by taking young boys away from the influence of mothers and kinswomen to interact only with other boys and men. Transitional societies changed the base of human life, rearing children together in a relatively isolated household dominated by the mother, and then in the equally isolated classroom with female teachers. For this reason, members of society who are concerned with such things worry about the socialization of boys, providing toys, male role models, and many rights to insure that these women's influence will not prevent them from developing masculine identities.

The mother is thus encouraged to accept, even reward, behavior that runs counter to her view of the world. This is apparent when mothers who actively protest against wars allow, even buy, toy guns as gifts for their sons.

> Many tired, frustrated, or otherwise overwhelmed mothers of sons . . . encourage their sons to join the military because they believe there is no place else to turn. (Forcey 1987, 15)

The gender specialization of relations with the children continues into the mother's old age. American sons are not expected, even by their mothers, to be major support providers for their mothers. American society provides many ideological justifications to the adult son for not focusing on his mother's needs, primarily because he must function as the "good provider" for his own family of procreation (Bernard 1981). This society decided in the first third of the twentieth century that offspring should no longer be held responsible for the economic supports of old or disabled family members, mainly because it could not enforce rules of such responsibility. Thus, older mothers are provided for economically through social security, Medicare, and other support systems, rather than by their sons, with few residual expressions of blame or guilt (Lopata 1991b). The son's male identity excuses him from being the primary provider of emotional supports of the mother, while his employment excuses his absence from most service supports. However, he is not totally absent from the mother's support network, specializing in such gender-segregated activity as household repairs and help with decision making (Lopata 1979; O'Bryant 1987). Interestingly enough, some mothers most enjoy being with their sons, even if a daughter provides most of the supports.

The Role of Mother in Divorce and Widowhood

Many factors contribute to the degree of disorganization suffered in her role of mother when she and the father of the children divorce. Divorce can be especially stressful for children in contested cases, in which both parents fight in court for the custody, each one trying to prove the other unfit for such care (Solnit 1984). The process can bring in outsiders, in the form of representatives of the law who must decide what is "good for the children," thereby officially declaring what is not good for them. This can be devastating for the children caught in the middle, who hear the strong accusations on all sides. The fact that contested divorces often result in problems led some states to pass no-fault divorce laws. Weitzman (1985, 339) studied the new system in California and found the situation little improved for mothers and children because fathers failed to pay support even when ordered to do so by the courts. The nonsupport of children is in fact one of the two major law-breaking actions by American citizens, the other being evasion of taxes. Weitzman's study found that the majority of mothers and children of no-fault divorce have lost, on the average, 73 percent of their previous income, while the husbands/fathers gained 42 percent. Widowed mothers often experience less economic loss than do divorcees, thanks to the Social Security Act's amendment of 1939, which brought them benefits as mothers of dependent children of the deceased (Lopata and Brehm 1986).

The problems of rearing children without the help of a previously present father in a society organized around two-parent families are legion. To begin with, the father's leaving, through death or divorce, can be very traumatic for both the wife and the children. The Chicago-area widows who participated in two of my studies (Lopata 1973c and 1979) often expressed an inability to help their children with their grief because they were so immersed in their own feelings. Some even refused to acknowledge that the children were suffering from the death of the father, claiming they were too young or too old to be affected. Others worried particularly about the sons in the absence of a supportive male. The situation is more complicated for the mother in the case of divorce, because the father remains on the scene with rights to the children. The divorce itself is likely to create strong emotions with which the mother must deal when interacting with her children.

An additional problem of mothers without another adult in the home is the care for the children while they are away at a paying job. On the other hand, divorce can relieve the mother and children of a very tense, even hurtful, home situation, as when alcoholism or physical and sexual abuse were involved. All records indicate that the mother is less likely to be the perpetrator of sexual abuse, and in most cases children are considered better off with their mothers than with their fathers.

The absence of a father may have other benefits for the mother. In the *City Women* study (Lopata, Barnewolt, and Miller 1985), our interviews with full-time homemakers aged twenty-five to fifty-four were organized according to the complexity of the households they managed. We first placed single mothers at the high end; after all, they had to solve all problems themselves and lacked the help of a male parent. We found out quite early in the analysis that their roles were in fact simpler than those in father-present households. The man proved to create work and complexity more than to decrease these. Child rearing was easier with one person making the major decisions, preventing role strain from disagreements. In fact, a majority of respondents to a national survey of divorcées reported their relationships with their children actually improved after divorce (Genevie and Margolies 1987, 375). They had more time for them with less competition for attention from fathers, and experienced greater closeness and respect, while at the same time being more independent to make their own decisions.

Both the death of, and divorce from, the father affects the social circle of the mother. In-laws may drop out, except in cases in which inheritance is of great importance. Grandparents, aunts, and uncles may remove their contributions and even create problems for the mother. The courts may have rights over the way she raises the children. A drop in income may require a move to a less desirable location, resulting in her children's having less desirable associates. On the other hand, the mother's own family and friends may increase their supports.

Mothers-in-Law

Traditional patrilocal societies gave the mother considerable power over her son's wife. There are many recorded situations, as in pre-Communist China or even current rural India, in which the mother-in-law treated the young woman as a servant and made her life so unpleasant as to push her into suicide (Barnes 1987). Transitional

America has removed much of the rights of control by a mother-in-law, who is, anyway likely to be living at a distance from the younger marital unit. The stereotype of the mother-in-law and the frequency of mother-in-law jokes indicate that there are more sources of tension with this relationship than with other in-law interactions. The role is strongly influenced by the mother-son or -daughter relation to begin with, as well as by the other members of her social circle, such as the parents of the person her child married. Mother and daughter-in-law or son-in-law do not interact in a vacuum. Complications arise out of the fact that the woman can be simultaneously the mother, the mother-in-law, and the grandmother. A husband may feel that his wife's mother has too much influence over his wife, or the young woman that her husband is too much influenced by his mother. Or both may resent any suggestions, even offers of help, from the older generation. The classic study of in-law relationships by Evelyn Duvall (1954) discussed both the comparative freedom of choice and the complications of relationships in a society that did not force the daughter-in-law to live with, and provide supports to, the relatives of her husband. Her title, *In-Laws: Pro and Con,* is indicative of the transitional situation in which the mother-in-law is likely to have traditional attitudes toward the younger generation.

In general, the wife tends to mediate relations not only between her husband and her parents but also, and even more so once children are born, between her husband and his own mother. One source of intergenerational tension can be the mother's feeling that her son has obligations toward her care that only the daughter-in-law can meet. Mothers-in-law are more "likely to have strained relationships with daughters-in-law than with sons-in-law" (Fisher 1983, 190). However, they must establish some positive relations with the son's wife if they want to be involved with the grandchildren (Fisher 1986, 130). An interesting finding is that, although the birth of children makes a woman's relationship with her own mother closer, it increases "the ambiguity in the quasi-kin, quasi-maternal relationship between mothers-in-law and daughters-in-law" (Fisher 1983, 190; see also Fisher 1986). The awkwardness of the relationship is indicated by the fact that a mother-in-law tends to give the daughter-in-law things, while the mother is more likely to perform services for her (Fisher 1983, 191). The younger woman is apt to express ambivalence over help from the in-laws and ask her mother rather than her mother-in-law for advice. The fact that in-laws are a secondary relationship, added almost as an afterthought, to the primary one between a husband and a wife, through no choice by anyone, may account for part of the problem in their interactions. Another factor is the probability, especially in a society as heterogeneous as the American, that the spouses come from different backgrounds, accentuated in their parents' generation, which may clash over ritualistic or day-by-day routines. Of course, popular culture emphasizes the alleged feeling of all mothers that the person their son or daughter marries is never good enough.

We can assume that the role of mother-in-law in modern times will involve greater freedom of communication and negotiation with circle members.

Stepmothers and Foster Mothers

Many women carry out the role of mother who are not biologically or socially "real" mothers of the children they have taken under their care. There is a vast difference between stepmothers, who acquire that role with marriage to the children's father, and foster mothers, who are temporary substitutes when children are taken away from their biological parents. The frequency of divorce and of remarriage creates complex stepparenting relationships. Many factors affect the interaction between stepmother and stepchild, such as the reason for the absence of the previous mother (death, divorce, or desertion), where the children are living, who has custody over them, the ages of all involved, whether the woman has children of her own, especially if they live in the home, and the life circumstances in which all who are involved find themselves (Visher and Visher 1979). The presence of "reconstituted" or "melded" families is increasingly being recognized by social scientists and the mass media. *Newsweek* magazine's special issue "*The 21st-Century Family* "devoted a major segment to stepfamilies (Kantrowitz and Wingert 1989, 24), pointing to the fact that "half of all people entering first marriages in the 1970s and 1980s will eventually divorce" and that, since most will remarry, there will be more and more joint families in the future. Giles-Sims and Crosbie-Burnett (1989) pulled together much of the recent literature on the stepfamily for a special issue of the journal *Family Relations*. Glick (1989, 26) estimates that 40 percent of married couple families in 1987 would be stepfamilies before the youngest child became eighteen years old. Most stepfamilies require adjustment to a new father rather than a new mother, since most women retain custody over their children.

Five residential stepfather families exist for every residential step-mother family, and 3% of remarried couple households include a stepfather and a stepmother. (Giles-Sims and Crosbie-Burnett. 1989, 20)

Even if the children of the new husband are not living full-time with the stepmother, they are apt to spend considerable time with her. The combination of mother and stepmother roles may be diffi-cult, with resentments over her attitudes and actions coming from both sets of children. Also, of course, she has to relate to the father of the stepchildren, as well as to their mother. The ages at the time the family blends together and the attitudes of the children toward their other parents may make the role of stepmother difficult, or a pleasure. Traditional women usually entered stepmothering as a result of the death of the mother. Transitional women are most strained by this role, because they tend not to have satisfactory models for dealing with the role complexities. Modern families try to work off the strains in the relationships openly and through negotiation.

The problems of foster mothers, who are paid to take children from problem families into the home to care for as substitutes for the biological and social mother, are also complex. The foster mother does not have all the rights and duties of a recognized mother and does not know how long the child will be in her care. Adjustments have to be made by the child, whose previous experiences with being mothered are likely to be negative, or whose mother is in a very difficult situation with which the child identifies. Adjustment must also be made by the foster mother, who did not contribute to the current personality and values of that child, and by all the circle members.

Other "variations on the theme," as *Newsweek* (Selingmann 1990) called gay and lesbian couples, and other domestic situations in-volving mothers proliferate in modern America.

Sociopsychological Aspects of Role Involvement

The role of mother has additional characteristics that, in combina-tion, make it unique among social roles. In the first place, it lasts a lifetime, unless the child dies, regardless of how involved the mother remains. It also changes throughout its course, especially during the first quarter or so of the child's life, when physical growth is accompanied by psychological maturation and constantly modifies the mother's duties and rights toward the child.

This role brings together multiple aspects of social psychological involvement. The birth of the first child is considered a major event of life. The role of mother is expected to be ranked as very important in the woman's role cluster. In fact, it competes with the role of wife; most women in the various Chicago-area studies gave it top priority (Lopata 1971b; Lopata and Barnewolt 1984). It frequently expands or activates other roles in the family dimension, including those of daughter, mother-in-law, and grandmother. In addition, it usually includes a great deal of emotional and sentimental, often contradictory, involvement. Although women allegedly depersonalize the role if there are "too many" children and they are too exhausted by childbearing and child rearing to differentiate among them, there is no substantial proof of such a tendency.

In American society, a mother is expected to demonstratively love her children and experience many other emotions and relational sentiments as she carries out the role, yet to control the level of these feelings. This combination can create person-role strain. Reared to control her emotions as "an adult," the mother faces the emotionally uncontrolled infant with trepidation and uncertainty. Reports of child abuse frequently point to the inability of the mother to stop the crying or anger of her child no matter what she does.

Problems of emotional involvement certainly do not end with the passing of infanthood, but they vary considerably from mother to mother and with each child. Some mothers feel possessive about their children, considering them extensions of themselves rather than persons in their own right. According to some critics (see Wylie 1955), such a woman lives vicariously through her offspring, hoping they will achieve and experience things she has visualized romantically for herself.

Most mothers experience a great deal of anxiety about child rearing and feelings of powerlessness over not being able to control the environment or the children. Often, knowing what they should do for the children does not solve the problem, in the absence of rights or resources. Some aspects of the role, such as the need to have patience, vicarious pain over children's troubles, or lack of privacy and time for herself, can be irksome to mothers. A child's problems of health or incapacity, such as in mental retardation, can be a perpetual drain upon the mother.

The duties of a mother are influenced by the attitudes and actions of other circle members, toward whom she may feel ambivalent. She has the duty to allow others to help in the socialization process of her children, and the right to be relieved of some of this work, although not of the responsibility for the result. The whole subject of child care is now receiving so much attention as to create strong guilt feelings and frustration among mothers who feel they must remain in or reenter the labor force and be away from home for many hours a day. The deeply ingrained American belief that only a mother can be an adequate caregiver for her child, and that all substitutes are of inferior quality, makes the psychological burden heavy. Forgotten are the centuries and the societies in which the socialization of children was turned over to others, often of a lower social class. The institutionalization of child care by the community, as in the kibbutz, does not apply here, where it is the private responsibility of each parent (that is, the mother) to make appropriate arrangements. It is not hard to predict, however, that public discussion of this subject will produce more community effort to help families, as is true in other societies within which the transition between traditional and modern support systems is occurring.

The weight of the ideology of motherhood contained in the concept of the "good" mother, and especially of the "ideal" mother, appears to transcend cultures, although variations exist by social class and other subunits. The characteristics of the ideal mother appear in descriptions given by women in transitional societies, especially in Westernized locales such as Sydney, Australia (Wearing 1990), as well as Chicago (Lopata 1971b) and elsewhere in America (Rainwater, Coleman, and Handel 1959). Such a mother "gives of herself," sacrificing her own needs in order to always be available and responsive to meet the needs of the children (Wearing 1990). Her role priorities place duties to the child above not only her duties in the role of wife and nonfamilial obligations, but also her duties to herself. Personal feelings, as well as such emotions as anger, must always be under control. Most women find the ideal impossible to achieve and always feel guilty for failing to meet it, for wanting time and space for themselves or for acting in "wrong" ways (Wearing 1990, 49). The image also offers many a woman the model by which she evaluates herself as less than good, with detrimental effects on her whole self-image since this is generally considered such an important role for women. This is particularly evident in cases in which the mother finally gives up the role, feeling that others can contribute to the welfare of her children more than she can.

The Chicago women's descriptions of the ideal mother reflected "passive-reacting-initiating" stances of sociopsychological involvement in interesting ways (Lopata 1971b, 219–23), reflecting their educational backgrounds. Traditional women with little formal education explain the ideal in self-sacrificing terms that reflect passivity. The mother caters to the needs of children without complaining. The reactive woman keeps up with the physical maintenance of the children, their clothes and food needs. The initiating one tries to teach them right from wrong. The less educated mothers focus on physical aspects of child care, the more educated see the ideal in psychological terms, responding to the emotional needs of the children or encouraging the children to venture and expand their horizons.

Warren (1987) found that the picture of the perfect mother that appears in the mass media, and often in stories told about other women, contributed to depression on the part of those labeled and treated as "madwifes." Chodorow and Contratto (1982) are highly critical not only of the mass media, but also of some feminist literature, for creating the "fantasy of the perfect mother" who is an all-powerful influence upon her offspring. How the children "turn out" becomes a major anxiety of mothers; the fact some turn out "OK" in adulthood is a major source of satisfaction for her, since she is given all the credit. The fact that for increasing periods of time the child is away from the home and the mother's sphere of influence leads to the mother's having feelings of powerlessness, especially in neighborhoods where drug and crime rates are high.

The image of the ideal mother as self-sacrificing can have repercussions in later life if the woman expects all those whom she has serviced to pay back past debts.

On the other hand, many mothers of the baby-boom cohort I studied simply dealt with the ideal as an unrealistic romanticization they did not need to deal with in reality. Others accepted aspects of it by which they defined themselves as good, disregarding aspects in which their performance was less than ideal. Most expressed great pleasure at "watching the children grow," seeing them healthy and happy, in spite of all the problems and frustrations. The satisfactions they reported are numerous, usually focused around love, the pleasure of providing a "good home," responsiveness by the children to their efforts, or even just enjoying the whole process of mothering, accepting the problems as part of life. The expressions of satisfaction covered wider spheres of life than did statements of problems or frustrations, which were quite specific (Lopata 1971b, 219).

Summary

These, then, are the major aspects of the role of mother, as developed in American society and contained in its cultural base. The role is lodged in the family institution, although it provides links to other institutions, such as education, religion, recreation, and the economic and even the political spheres, as when mothers function as family consumers or organize to fight for children's rights. The role, built upon a middle-class transitional-times model, assumes the presence of a rather complicated social circle, actively involving the father of the child, grandparents, and other kin in a bilateral fashion as assistants, physicians, service suppliers, and associates of the child. It assumes that these members will function cooperatively, helping the mother to care for the physical, psychological, and social welfare of the child, allowing her to be the center of her own role. The model takes it for granted that she can stay home full time and is willing and able to do everything to benefit the child, within a patriarchal structure of the family.

The model ignores two very important facts. One is that mothers seldom, if ever, have had all the resources to function at even the allegedly "average" level of role involvement. A major difficulty for most women is economic, forcing them often into a double-bind situation. The high incidence of divorce, desertion, and other reasons for the absence of a wage-earning father makes that source of income increasingly unavailable. If a mother cares for the children alone, she cannot earn money. If she takes a job, she is absent from the children and must find someone else to care for them during her work and transportation hours. The wage discrimination prevalent in this society results in her inability to earn enough to pay for child care and all the other household expenses (Steinberg 1982 and 1990; see also several chapters in Larwood, Stromberg, and Gutek 1985). The feminization of poverty is not just a mass-media creation.

But there is a much more basic problem with the role of mother at the present time: the rapid and dramatic structural and cultural changes in America have made many of the characteristics of the transitional family dysfunctional to the welfare of its members and the society as a whole. These changes are beyond the control of the family, yet family roles and their relations to other roles of its members have not been redefined. Such a reconstruction of reality and relationships would enable the parents (both the social mother and the social father) to serve as centers of organized family and community resources for the care and rearing of children. It would expand the social circle of the mother, with the help of numerous assistants all sharing not just the action but also the responsibility and emotional involvement. The transitional form of the role of mother is simply too artificial and harmful to all concerned. Those women who have expanded this role to include all sorts of circle members have actually duplicated some of the patterns of upper-class women of the past and present. They have been able to do so only because they can afford to pay for these resources in the absence of adequate assistance.

It is impossible to describe fully the role of mother in transitional and, especially, modern times without commenting on the decreasing contribution of men, in the role of father and as members of the social circle of the mother. Ehrenreich (1983) developed the argument in *The Hearts of Men: American Dreams and Flight from Commitment* that American men have been removing themselves from family responsibilities since the 1950s. Certainly the number of female-headed single-parent families, and the frequency with which male parents fail to cover child support, provide some backup to this argument (Weitzman 1985). Although the society at large, in its press and social scientific journals, expresses anger over the inadequacy of the responsibility taken for children by social and biological fathers, little is done about this situation, and the problems of female-headed households are somehow defined in terms of women alone. Maybe the recent male-consciousness movements will decrease the frequently expressed hostility of men concerning being "tied down" in marriage and fatherhood. On the other hand, contrasting macho movements appear to be moving in the opposite direction, valorizing the hero who faces the world alone.

In order for the role of mother to be brought into the modern world, there needs to be a complete change in America's attitudes toward its young. This society has either ignored family troubles brought about by its changes or, even when it turns these into recognized social problems, blamed the victims. Family members, especially mothers, are still seen as the source of problems they are helpless to control. According to many observers, and especially Kahn and Kamerman (1975; see also Kamerman and Kahn 1978; Kamerman 1977 and 1980), America does much less than other industrialized modern societies to assist families in daily life and crises. In fact, Huber (1980) calls this an "antinatalistic" society, and Grubb and Lazerson (1982) have focused the title of their book on public responsibility for children: *Broken Promises: How Americans Fail Their Children*. Other societies, and America of the future, we assume, can see the care of children as the responsibility not simply of the parents but of the community at large.

4

Social Roles in Kinship Networks

Most societies have been organized around kinship networks, which trace lines of descent and define roles for people united by marriage, birth, or adoption.[1] Roles in nonfamilial institutions have been dependent upon kinship roles. "These same kin groups may also be the property-owning units, the political units, the religious units, and so on" (Schneider 1989, vii). Transitional societies have weakened these bonds as other groups have taken on major aspects of such functions. Adams (1968) argues that the kindred form a network, not a social group, since there is frequently no organized structure within it. The networks consist of the one or both nuclear families of orientation and procreation plus other relatives in varying degrees of connection. A kin network can be differentiated from the biological grouping by the degree of actual involvement in interaction and social roles. Some societies refuse to consider the relatives of a wife coming into the husband's family as part of her children's kin. Persons who are part of the recognized family tree may be cut off from the network, or may fail to incorporate themselves into it simply by not undertaking kin roles.[2] Conflict can break communication with, or even recognition of, a whole branch of the biological family. Active involvement can be dissolved, as often happens in America between in-laws once the connecting links die or are divorced. The high degree of choice in social relationships in modern society carries over to the kin network.

World Revolution in Kinship Salience?

Traditional patrilineal and patriarchal family systems, the most common types of family systems among human beings, contain strong norms of obligation to members, however the kinship boundaries are demarcated. Patrilocal residence, with new family units of the sons settling within or nearby the ancestral dwelling, helped insure contact and control.

Goode (1963) concluded from a survey of many societies that the world revolution of modernization changed the basic family structure from that of the extended family to that of the nuclear, relatively isolated unit. He did find, however, that the elite segments of both traditional and modern societies, even those in urban settings, maintained extended familism, while the masses usually did not. His main conclusion about the unidirectional move from extended to relatively isolated nuclear families, supporting that of Parsons 1943 and Parsons and Bales 1955, produced a strong reaction from social scientists. Family sociology in the following years was full of claims of continued involvement of the nuclear unit in the wider extended network (reviewed by Sussman 1962; Adams 1968; Lee 1980; and Litwak 1965). Winch and Blumberg (1968) tested this and related hypotheses and found a curvilineal relationship between societal complexity and family organization, claiming that there are independent familial systems, that is, small nuclear units, among both the simpler, nomadic groups and in modern societies, while sedentary, agricultural societies favor extended familism. The factors that lead to the separation of the smaller family unit from the extended one include migration or mobility, independence from stationary property such as land, and freedom from the family as a unit of labor. Thus, they predicted that highly developed societies will have "relatively low extended familism" (Winch and Blumberg 1968, 86). In addition, the decline of economic functionality of extended familism in complex societies decreases men's interest in that unit. This shifts the function of maintaining kin ties to the women, who are usually less geographically mobile due to the bearing and nursing of children.

The Transitional Form of Kin Networks

The kin network is traced in America bilaterally, that is, from both the woman's and the man's lines of ascent and down through both sons and daughters (Schneider 1980). This gives the woman much more importance as the connecting link between the families than is true of kinship groups that are traced unilaterally through the male line. The American system includes grandparents, aunts and uncles, plus cousins and all their spouses and children. Marriage adds the spouse's relatives, modified by the concept of "in-law." Grandchildren and even great-grandchildren may be active members of the network.

Americans differentiate the level of relation by what Schneider (1980, 22–23) calls "modifiers," some of which are restrictive, dividing blood relatives from those who are not, and some of which are unrestrictive, providing an unlimited range of relatives. Modifiers are also applied to degree of distance, as in "first cousin" versus "second cousin." The situation is complicated in this society by the fact that so many people come from cultures that contain other symbolic distinctions. For example, a niece in a Polish American community must differentiate in her language and behavior between her father's brother and uncles from other sources. In recent years the American kinship network has been made even more convoluted by the presence of ex-relatives with whom some duties/rights packages of interaction are maintained and new relatives that come along with new marriages (C. Johnson 1988).

Of course, all the effects of "the world revolution" upon the family emerge over time and have not reached many segments of even allegedly modern societies such as America. Kinship networks performed important economic functions among immigrant groups, as well as in subgroups of recent times (Bieder 1973). American ethnic communities still contain strong interdependencies among kinfolk (see Min 1988 for Korean; Glenn 1986 and Kitano 1988 for Japanese; Wong 1988 for Chinese; and C. Johnson 1985 for Italian American families). Patterns of chain migration and arrangements for housing and jobs are clearly documented in industrial Amoskeag (Hareven and Langenbach 1978, see also Hareven 1978). The Polish peasants from Europe crossed the ocean at the initiative of relatives, and then brought more of the family over (Thomas and Znaniecki 1918–20). Kinship groups shared housing, often taking shifts in beds, and all sorts of supports (Lopata 1976b and 1994). Immigrant women were even more dependent upon the kin network than the men, since they were culturally discouraged from seeking jobs alone (Lopata 1988a). The influence of kin and ethnic job-search support is evident in the clustering of immigrants in occupations and locales.

Patterns of kin support extend even into second and third generations of immigrants, and upward mobility of some members does not necessarily break ties (Winch, Greer, and Blumberg 1967). For example, uncles were known to help nephews in less fortunate family units attain a better education or economic position (Adams 1968). Winch, Greer and Blumberg (1967) summarized studies that found a higher level of extended familism among Polish Jews than among Polish Catholics in the United States. Their explanation for this interesting difference is that the Catholics came from peasant families with extended family systems of sedentary agricultural activity, which was disorganized in urban America. The Polish Jews, who had been traders in the home country, were able to reestablish entrepreneurial activity with extended family help after migration. The occupations in which they became concentrated under the influence of anti-Semitism, unlike bureaucratic occupations in large organizations, do not require much mobility and provide opportunity for supports of younger family members.

Another situation in which kindred relationships form an important part of life is among the underclass blacks in America. Stack's 1975 classic *All our Kin* documents the interaction among many layers of relatives in an urban community living at the poverty level. Kin members

> trade food stamps, rent money, a TV, hats, dice, a car, a nickel here, a cigarette there, food, milk, grits and even children. Thus networks of domestic co-operation come into being. The social and economic lives of men, women and children become so interwoven that failure to repay a debt might mean someone else's child will not eat. (Stack 1975, 195)

However, the extensive interaction reported by Stack, in which actual and fictive relatives provide multiple supports in crisis situations, such as illness or loss of a job, which occur almost daily, has some negative consequences. It drains the resources of the persons who are doing a little better, preventing movement out of the poverty cycle. The outlay of supports may prevent individualistic upward mobility. However, the members of the two lower-class extended black families followed by Martin and Martin (1978) through several stages of formation who reached middle-class status kept in touch without apparently hurting their social movement.

Ethnic communities are not similarly involved in kinship exchanges. For example, Polish Americans are much more involved in community-status competition and organizational life than are Italian Americans, who are much more family-oriented (Lopata 1988a; Squier and Quadagno 1988). Most research on kin relationships in England and the United States, building upon Bott's *Family and Social Network* (1957), stresses social class differences. African American mothers raising younger children alone appear to be receiving more kin help with child care, finances, and emotional support than they give, especially if they are poor (McAdoo 1980, 143). Lifecourse changes being what they generally are, the recipients will undoubtedly be the heavier givers as they grow older. Women of working-class families appear to be much more oriented toward all types of relatives than are their white-collar counterparts. This is also true of upper-class families that have benefited from the status attainment of prior generations (Ostrander 1985); however, these often neglect members who have not reached the appropriate position or who have experienced downward mobility (see Newman 1988). On the other hand, the extended family may replace friendships lost through a drop in social class. "Blood ties are often 'thick' enough to endure, even in the face of the downwardly mobile family's embarrassment" (Newman 1988, 125). Middle-class families appear to be less kinship-bound than the other classes.

Kin Member and Kin Keeper

One is born into, or adopted into, a family that is usually affiliated with a more or less organized kin network. However, the role of kin member exists only if the person develops sets of social relations with others identified as relatives. Many families also develop the role of kin keeper, who serves as the core keeping the spokes of the kin network together. The extensive discussion of kinship networks above accentuates the fact that families in transitional times placed most of the burdens, and benefits, of kin involvement upon women.

The roles of daughter and sister, wife and mother, are the most central to the kinship network, and the outer layers may be pooled together into a generalized set of relationships in the role of kin member by the kin keeper responsible for maintaining contact. Even the close relatives can be so generalized, or lumped together, by a woman who sees herself as a member of the network without being its center as a kin keeper. She can carry forth limited sets of duties, forming lines of contact within the larger unit, and can be treated by others as one of the connecting links. Such action can be a bridge to her role of daughter or sister, which pulls her side of the family into the larger network. An example of the networking behavior of people who do not take on the job of kin keeper for the whole network appears in Adams's 1968 study of cousin relationships in Greensboro, North Carolina. Cousins there were unlikely to be close to each other unless the two sets of parents interacted frequently or they lived nearby or shared a common interest. What is significant for our focus on women is the importance of sister closeness for cousin interaction.

> Relationship through the mother strongly predominates among the females from a blue-collar family, while a similar but less pronounced relationship holds for young white-collar background adults. (Adams 1968, 139)

These findings that the role of kin member is more salient to women than to men are reinforced by numerous other studies. In fact, although kinship roles appear to have somewhat atrophied in current-day America, the norms or expectations underlying them, including that they should be carried forth by women, continue.

Divorce or widowhood can deprive a woman of support exchanges with her husband's relatives, as numerous studies have indicated (Anspach 1976; Lopata 1973c and 1979). This break is easier to visualize in the case of divorce than in the case of death of the person who is the connecting link, since the man's family would be expected to place loyalties to him ahead of those of an in-law in conflict situations. The fact that such connection by marriage may never have been comfortable is indicated by the absence of the male kin in the support systems of widows in several studies. The Chicago-area widows whom I studied very seldom report any supports to themselves or even to their children from the late husband's kin (Lopata 1973c and 1979).

The role of kin keeper, rather than just kin member, or the relational outgrowth of "kin-keeping work," remains a familiar concept in America (Rosenthal 1985). Di Leonardo (1987), who studied Italian Americans, defines its duties as follows:

> By kin work I refer to the conception, maintenance, and ritual celebration of cross-household kin ties, including visits, letters, telephone calls, presents, and cards to kin; the organization of holiday gatherings; the creation and maintenance of quasi-kin relations; decisions to neglect or to intensify particular ties; the mental work of reflection about all these activities; and the creation and communication of altering images of family and kin vis-à-vis the images of others, both folk and mass media. (442)

Similar complexities of kin keeping are reported for other ethnic groups. Historians and social scientists find that it is usually a middle-aged or older woman of the kin network who has kept up with the desired kin members, knowing their locations and being the organizer of family gatherings and celebrations (Rosenthal 1985).

The person maintaining kin solidarity can also be the family historian, although these functions are not inevitably tied together. One of the interesting aspects of kin keeping is the transmission of the position through generations. It is "inherited" by another woman, although not necessarily by the daughter of the former facilitator. It has to be initiated by the social person, with cooperation from others. She must of necessity come from a family with numerous potential members of the network. The probability is high that she has economic resources to undertake this role. She must also have the personality to act as a bridge even between conflicting segments of the network, and she can easily experience role strain because of such conflict. Unfortunately, from the point of view of symbolic interactionists, too few studies of kin keepers have been conducted to determine how important this role is in the person's role cluster. We do know that the family dimension must be rich, but we do not know the form of multidimensionality of the life space. The woman must be an initiator of interaction, but she can undertake it out of either pleasure or a sense of duty. Being the center of the network requires not only time and interest but also power to enforce cooperation. The social circle of the kin keeper is created by the woman herself out of available members, but its maintenance requires a great deal of cooperative effort by others, not only in terms of work but also in terms of willingness to spend the time and often the cost of continued contact. As more and more women enter the labor force full time, one of the areas of life experiencing cutbacks is personal leisure activity. This definitely could include kin work.

Ethnic groups are not the only ones still concerned with kin keeping. More affluent and educated families are also interested in such interaction because of pride in the family's past or present accomplishments and the obvious advantages of continued contact (Bahr 1976). I found, for example, that widows kept their children in more frequent, and possibly closer, contact with their in-laws in cases of high-status families than if there were fewer advantages to such interaction (Lopata 1973c).

Of course, extensive involvement as kin keeper by a member of the nuclear family may create role conflict with a husband or children, who may resent the outlay of time, energy, and financial help, much as reported in cases of daughters' supports of parents. In fact, the modern emphasis on obligations to nuclear units may make assistance to the extended family less justifiable than before. This is particularly true in America, since kinship here does not form the major organizing principle of all social life, as it does in some other societies. Few bureaucratic organizations are now willing to hire a person simply on the recommendation of a family member, unless the latter has power in the system. Nephews of powerful men undoubtedly have an edge over anonymous candidates. There are few known cases of powerful women in public positions insuring their relatives an adequate position, but such women definitely exist and can be expected to increase in number.

The Modern Form of Kinship Networks

It is hard to predict what will happen to kinship roles when the family system becomes modernized. The trends toward individualization of social relations bode them little good. The revolution against ascribed roles, or those into which one is born or assigned without choice, had accentuated the perceived burdens of kinship roles and diminished the perceived benefits. It may be that this trend will continue with even greater speed in the future, so that selected collateral relatives are converted into "friends," and close contact is maintained with only those relatives who contribute actively to one's life. On the other hand, the broadening of the social circles of major roles, with the diffusion of obligations for primary relations to both genders and the community at large, may revitalize kinship roles. Women no longer burdened with almost exclusive responsibility for parenting, "daughtering," and maintaining social relationships in marriage and other partnerships, at work, and in the community may willingly enter negotiated kinship relations. So may men, who can negotiate to close the gap between themselves and all kinds of relatives.

Daughter

Children are born into a family of orientation, so called because it provides them with socialization necessary to orient the self into the world, which is already organized symbolically and in actuality by past generations and contemporary associates. The family of orientation includes parents, by birth or adoption, and siblings. The relationships of the daughter to various people in her social circle are modified dramatically over time as she matures and enters new roles or as circle members experience changes in their lives. A significant example of this is in the daughter-mother relationship, as discussed from the point of view of the mother in the previous chapter.

The Traditional Form of the Role of Daughter

The traditional patrilineal family incorporated the nuclear family as subservient to its needs. Often combined with patrilocal residence, it tied each marital and parental unit together. Children belonged to that unit and not to the mother. Males felt the strongest identification with their sons rather than their daughters. Sons were deemed necessary for family survival, continuity of identity, contributions to the male work group, care of elderly parents, inheritance rights, and, where applicable, ritualistic actions guaranteeing the afterlife of ancestors. The value assigned to daughters depended upon their contributions to the patriarchal family's welfare. The more costly their upkeep till they left in marriage, and the more their leaving cost through dowries, the less they were valued. Their work life was limited if marriage occurred early and if they were not allowed to perform necessary family and religious rituals.

In fact, as noted before, infanticide of girls has been historically more common than of boys (deMause 1974). Sons were often killed by enemies in battles, or as a means of genocide, but daughters were put to death or allowed to die by their own families. The devaluation of female newborns and babies has not vanished entirely in recent times, as evidenced by the neglect and infanticide of girls in areas of India and in China (B. Miller 1981; Mosher 1983). The current debate over the use of abortion to select the gender of offspring indicates the continued preference for male children.

It is not surprising that strong patriarchal systems, still present in societies such as Turkey (Heisel 1987), Korea (Koo 1987) and Iran (Touba 1987), encourage the mother to develop the closest possible relationship with the sons, particularly the son who is apt to inherit the property and therefore the responsibility for her care in old age and widowhood.

> Mother-son relations were most often stressed as being of love and affection more than any other, including husband and wife which were seldom mentioned and, when they were, were spoken of as entailing dislike and hatred as well as affection. (Ross 1961, 97)

Arranged marriages are not conducive to empathetic understanding between the son and his wife, so the mother-son tie can remain the son's closest throughout life. The mother gains power as she ages, either as the wife of the patriarch or as the mother of the inheriting son. The daughter-in-law then becomes the main service supplier to the household. Her lot in traditional China, for example, was reputedly so bad that it produced frequent suicides (Barnes 1987).

In such a system, in fact, the daughter had few rights, not being an important member of her family of orientation and relatively early in life becoming only a daughter-in-law.

Before modern times in America most families were dependent upon children for work and, when possible, for household finances. Children were expected to contribute to the family's subsistence along gender-specified lines, determined by the family's activities. A major set of duties of the role of daughter was to help care for younger children and assist the mother in age-appropriate tasks. Farm families often assigned the care of small animals to girls, while the boys helped the fathers in the fields. In preindustrial times and places, home-based work was complicated and hard, involving the making of basic family-maintenance goods. Some families or villages even produced goods for barter and, at a later stage of development, objects or services for sale. Girls were trained at a very young age to contribute to such activity (Boserup 1970, 140–41). The work was both a duty and a right, as it prepared them for increasingly complex participation in a family-based work team. The skill and knowledge made them valuable additions to their family of orientation and then to that of the husband. This direct contribution of children to family support continued even into the early years of industrialization, daughters often working in cottage industries (Oakley 1974b; Tilly and Scott 1978b). Children, even daughters, were also sent out of the home to earn money. Families at the turn of the century depended upon child workers:

> Children were employed in coal mines and steel mills; even five- and six-year-olds worked in seacoast fishing industries. In the city children shined shoes, sold newspapers, wrapped cigars in sweat shops and worked in stores. (Osborn and Osborn 1978, 28)

Many immigrant families built up their resources with the help of all members, including children. For example Polish Americans had definite ideas about what work for pay was appropriate for their daughters (Lopata 1976b and 1988a). Helping mothers maintain lodging and boarding homes or with take-in laundry was favored, because it taught domestic skills. Employment in the homes of others was a preferred alternative. Lower-class girls in general were kept from school on the assumption that they could learn all they needed in life in the home, while boys were more likely to be kept in school longer because of the assumption that they needed to learn how to survive in the outside world. Factory employment that would bring the girls into contact with men of other ethnic groups was heavily frowned upon. Immigrant women in this country developed their own monopolies over certain jobs, varied by location (Mindel, Habenstein, and Wright 1988).

The history of the role of daughter has had other complicating features as traditional support systems in American society have decreased. The transformation of work into jobs, and of economic support into dependence upon money to be earned by such jobs, made mothers and children into personal dependents of a husband/ father, as discussed in the last two chapters. In the process, the children, especially the daughters, lost many rights of support. The mother frequently could not support them. The absence of an in- come-earning man has either pushed children into poverty or re- sulted in society's taking over their support. The latter process has included either their economic support (usually at quite inadequate levels) within the home with the mother, or their removal from the home. American history abounds with cases in which children—daughters for moral reasons, sons for fear of delinquency—were taken away from their mothers and placed in alternative settings such as asylums, workhouses, and orphanages (Sutton 1983; Vandepol 1982). Abbott (1938) reprinted the conditions under which the state of Illinois allowed "female infants" to be placed in "industrial schools for girls":

> Every female infant who begs or receives alms while actually selling, or pretending to sell any article in public, or who frequents any street, alley or other place, for the purpose of begging or receiving alms; or, who having no permanent place of abode, proper parental care, or guardianship, or sufficient means of subsistence, or who for other cause is a wanderer through streets and alleys, and in other public places or, who lives with, or frequents the company of, or consorts with reputed thieves, or other vicious persons, or who is found in a house of ill-fame, or in a poor house. (P. 80)

One of the symbolic developments in American society centered around life insurance for children. While the value of children was measured in economic terms, as contributors to family maintenance, such insurance, whose popularity peaked in 1882, was seen as a protection against loss of their work through death. However, people were often accused of facilitating children's deaths in order to collect the monies, and such insurance became actively opposed by the national child-saving movement of that time. Rapid industrialization, combined with child labor laws, compulsory education, and the rejection of "baby farming," decreased children's economic value. Increased emphasis on the psychological value of children led then to the view that the insurance provided ready cash for mourning rituals. Finally, as children became considered expensive consumer items, its use has been publicized by insurance companies as an investment against that cost to parents, especially as a means of providing a proper education. That is the current use of child insurance (Zelizer 1981 and 1985).

The social circle of the daughter often contained, at least in the past, religious groups and personnel whose duties were to help the parents teach ideology and normative behavior. The duties of the child were to obey and learn. The same was true of the school system, to the extent that it contributed to the role of daughter.

The Transitional Form of the Role of Daughter

Gradual modernization is creating an extremely complicated world for a daughter. It increases her freedom of choice as to how she will live in it, but perpetuates her dependence on the resources and limitations of her family of orientation early in life, and of gender stratification throughout life.[3]

In the case of a baby born to an American urban family, the city is already there, with all its institutional resources, ready to be entered for various reasons at different stages of the life course. The family into which the girl is born lives in part of that city and participates in its life in limited ways depending on its own social life space. This family has constructed a view of the world that contains its beliefs of what is true and right, its emotions and sentiments concerning all component objects, and more or less integrated patterns of action. This worldview includes definitions of that baby as an object toward which patterned as well as idiosyncratic behavior is or will be directed. Once that baby is accepted into that family, mainly through the declaration by a woman that she is her mother— by birth or adoption—this unit will take responsibility for her till an age of societally defined adulthood when self-maintenance independent of the family is judged possible (Lopata 1984). In American society, the officially accepted baby is identified by sex, individual name, family, and any other relevant categories.

It is one of the functions of the significant others in the daughter's social circle to insure that these identifying categories become her pervasive identities.

The Life Course of the Role of Daughter

The birth of each child affects the social unit she joins. The influence the daughter's sex has upon her relations depends on how important it is for her future and that of her social circle. The circle consists of others besides the mother, and its size and complexity depends upon many factors. She may have an active father, one who accepts membership in that circle. The absence of the father from that circle, in a society that emphasizes his importance, may be very difficult for the daughter. This can be especially so if his absence is due to divorce (in years before the current tolerance of such action), desertion, or imprisonment. The death of either parent also affects children deeply. A complicating problem has been the effect of the father's absence upon the mother and other members of the circle. Siblings, as well as members of the extended family, are influenced in their duties by whether or not the daughter has an involved father. Research on families of divorce indicates that divorce may deprive daughters of their rights to an extended family on the father's side (Anspach 1976; Spicer and Hampe 1975). The social circle of the children may be quite asymmetrical if their mother fails to maintain contact with the grandparents and aunts and uncles on that side of the family (Farber 1966). On the other hand, the mother's remarriage may introduce a whole new segment to the daughter's circle, including a stepfather and stepsiblings.

The Dependent Daughter. A girl's position in the family structure is determined by the timing of her birth in its life cycle, its composition, and the surrounding circumstances, such as whether her mother is married, the ages and gender of the other children, the presence and availability of other family supports, and the family's socioeconomic position in the community and society. Her anticipated future as an adult is reflected in the complexity of the circle that helps her become one. Her circle provides the life chances upon which she builds the career of her various roles. There may be a nanny, other household servants or residents without assisting functions, baby-sitters, and pediatricians. If she is a daughter to the British royal family, she may have hundreds of people in her circle, of whom she becomes more or less individually aware as she grows biologically and socially. If she is born to a poor, relatively isolated farm family, the circle may be very small.

The perceived characteristics of the daughter influence how she is treated by the circle members. As discussed in chapter 1, her identification by sex leads to gender socialization by all, influenced by cultural definitions of girls, varied by social class and other subgroup membership. Her behavior—even as early as in the womb—and her appearance can lead people to make assumptions about her personality and future roles. Her family's social class is often a good predictor of which items of future personality are selected for encouragement in anticipation of her adulthood position. Circle members are constantly commenting on the baby, comparing her to others and predicting social person characteristics from "clues."

At this early stage the duties of the daughter are simply to survive the attention and care given by others and to respond positively to what is happening around her. Negative responses can result in negative reactions. Child abuse studies indicate that the victim can actually trigger abusive behavior on the part of emotionally disturbed mothers by crying or by looking or smelling "wrong" (Lamb 1987, 153–56). It does not take long before the baby's duty becomes to recognize major caregivers, with positive signs of pleasure at their contact. Sooner or later these signs are supposed to express love—especially to parents, in America, even if they are not the major caregivers. From then on, her duties to her circle keep expanding and becoming more complicated, often full of strain and, later, fraught with role conflict. In many if not most societies they include the duty to obedience, self-control along lines related to age and gender, pleasant appearance that makes family members "proud," and in general following the appropriate norms of behavior.

The rights of daughters actually precede the conscious duties and vary considerably from society to society and from subgroup to subgroup. Rights to physical and psychological care usually include the right not to be abandoned, although some groups allow the mother to "lend" or even "give" a daughter to others more in need of such a person or because the mother feels she cannot satisfactorily provide what the child has rights to. The right to receive care may mean that she can receive life- or pleasure-giving objects and actions on demand, or else training to fit the schedule of care determined by others. Considerable literature indicates that mothers give more attention to daughters than to sons, spend more time with them, and are involved in more extensive support exchanges with daughters throughout life (Losh-Hesselbart 1987; Peterson and Rollins 1987). The definition of care, and thus of neglect, varies, of course, by the definition of children's needs. Gilligan (1982) concludes that the standard definitions of human relationships are based on a male model of need. However, the definition of need in the case of girls appears to be shifting in America toward a more careful examination of the right to protection from harm, probably due to the public exposure by the feminist movement of the seriousness and frequency of the abuse they have suffered.

The subject of protection and the definition of abuse of children has had a convoluted history in American society, as conflicting demands have surfaced at different times (Pfohl 1978). These have included the right of the family to privacy and the right of both the society and the child to socialization for nondisruptive behavior. The right of a child to be socialized into becoming an acceptable member of society, and the duty of the parent to provide this socialization, may lead to harsh methods and punishments that endanger the child's physical safety, even fatally. Thus, the daughter's right to safety and empathetic care may clash with the right to be properly socialized by the parent into the family and the society. (E. Pleck, 1983). An example would be the treatment of children in Puritan America.

The right to safety can also include freedom from certain sexual or psychological actions by others, although the definition of, and emphasis upon, this area of life has also undergone change. Recent literature indicates that many, even very young, daughters have been sexually abused by their fathers, their stepfathers, and other family members. Runaways and prostitutes have been disproportionately victims of sexual abuse. The long-term effects of such experiences include traumatic sexualization, seeing sexuality as a commodity to be used for money, or its rejection, and feelings of betrayal, powerlessness, and stigmatization (Russell 1986, 167–70). Mothers are often aware of such impingement on the child's rights, but many mothers do not protect their children, especially if they feel powerless themselves and are afraid of the perpetrator. Sexual abuse by women family members, such as mothers or sisters, is very rare, supporting the conclusion that abuse is primarily a male phenomenon, accentuated by the patriarchal culture and sex stratification in which the woman is seen as inferior to the man.

The major duty of a daughter in a transitional family, as in the feminine mystique days, where the family no longer depends on her productive or income-earning activity, is to grow up without causing her parents problems, without shaming them in front of others, proving that they are good parents. More modern families are apt to give adolescent daughters greater rights to define their own needs, make their own decisions, and lead independent lives. The age at which restrictions are lessened, however, varies, and the negotiations involved are likely to bring problems. Kingsley Davis (1940) explained years ago the inevitability of conflict between parents and children because of their different rate of absorption of the culture, especially in rapidly changing societies. Parents socialized twenty-five to forty-five years ago have a construction of reality that is very different from that of their offspring. American parents, many of whom were immigrants or grew up in ethnic families and neighborhoods of a society very different from the one their children experience are unlikely to see the world from the vantage point of the younger generation. Traditional parents are also armed with the "knowledge" that modern youths are not responsible, do not under-stand the realities of life, and so forth. Youths, on their part, have great difficulty taking the role of the parent, whose value system appears completely inadequate for life as it now is. This is true in different ways for girls and for boys, although both feel the need to establish themselves as independent people within their own worlds (Chodorow 1978).

Daughter-parent conflict is often connected to the traditional patriarchal concern over the daughter's sexual behavior. American society defines delinquent girls in those terms, while people are less concerned about heterosexual acts of boys, whose delinquency is defined in terms of impingement upon property or personal rights of mainly adults. At least this was true in the pre-AIDS days. Con-cerns about the virginity of their daughters, or at least over public violation of sexual or motherhood norms, is still part of the culture of many parents and conflicts with the modern girl's peer culture. Regardless of the importance of friends, high school daughters are highly dependent upon family approval for their self-estimation (Eskilson and Wiley 1987). Chicano and Puerto Rican families still worry about the daughter's reputation but are more tolerant of deviation than are low-income white parents (Jarrett 1990a). Role-straining mixed messages from the mother concerning indepen-dence, in what Fisher (1986) calls the "holding on and letting go" double-bind syndrome, can permeate the whole relationship. On the other hand, the daughter can be the confidante and empathize with the mother, forming a coalition against the father. Mothers can also serve as buffers, protecting the girls from the father. They can provide encouragement and all forms of emotional and social sup-port, even without conflict with other members of the family or outsiders. Jarrett (1990b) found lower-income black daughters feel-ing strong solidarity with their mothers. Atypical relationships can develop between the mother and the daughter, in which the expect-ed rights and duties are not honored, as in the case of either a remote or an overinvolved parent (Fisher 1986, 26–32). Variations in the role of daughter in a father-absent versus a two-parent household have not been fully explored, although there is some indication that the daughter undertakes many more duties toward the mother and the household in general if there is no other adult present (Lopata 1979). Daughters have been known to take on many of the respon-sibilities of the absent wife/mother/homemaker when the father is left alone, which is one of the conditions in which father-daughter incest occurs (Russell 1984).

Children of the upper classes are often, in fact preferably, sent to "finishing" or other boarding schools (Ostrander 1985). Employed Issei (first-generation Japanese American) mothers sometimes sent their children back to Japan to be raised by their own mothers and other relatives, as a last resort (Glenn 1986, 210). Becoming a student or a worker away from home usually decreases the duties of the role of daughter, with an increase of commitment to outside relations. Employed daughters sometimes contribute to family income if they live at home, but they are no longer expected to send money and provisions back to the family if they live elsewhere. There does not appear to be a uniform financial agreement between a college student daughter and her parents concerning repayment of the cost of her education.

American and European daughters tend to increase identification with the mother when they themselves reach adulthood and become involved in similar roles (Entwisle and Doering 1981, 128). In fact, the image of her own mother improves significantly after the daughter starts raising her first child. Part of this is due to the amount of help she receives from the parent, especially in the lower class, where the kinfolk are less dispersed. Middle-class women more often hire help, at least for a short period of time after the birth of a child, and mothers come in after that.

The shift of roles by the daughter also provides her with a new perspective and better empathetic understanding of the complications of motherhood. In addition, "the hierarchical nature of the relationship becomes less problematic" (Fisher 1986, 126), so that duties of obedience, which become increasingly obnoxious as a woman matures, are relaxed. Not all mother-child relations become more symmetrical, as both persons can be locked into the duties or rights of their own cohorts. A lack of reciprocity can be resented, or actually enjoyed, by either (Fisher 1986, 53). Daughters with families of their own often receive many new rights from their parents, financial assistance, empathetic understanding of daily problems, baby-sitting or even more involved care of the children, and services such as help with shopping and household work (Goetting 1989). This was definitely the pattern established by "mum" and her daughters in boroughs of London studied by Bott (1957) and Wilmott and Young (1964). The mother insured that married daughters lived nearby by scouting apartments, and the women exchanged services, visited back and forth, shared work, and even ate meals together when the husbands were absent. Social scientists studying kinship relations have documented extensive interaction and exchanges of support systems between adult children, especially daughters, and their parents, especially mothers. In early years of the daughter's life within her own family of procreation, the flow of supports is mainly downward from the mother (Adams 1968; Shanas 1979b; Sussman 1965). Recent research confirms the continuation of this flow (Barnett 1988). Ethnic traditions reinforce the tendency of parents to help their adult children, and the closeness of the tie between mother and daughter results in a "fundamental asymmetry or 'tilt' in American kinship in favor of the wife's family" (Cohler 1988, 54). Modern daughters expect many such forms of support, which sometimes are not met by the busy mother.

Allegedly, there is much more tolerance by mothers of sexual activity of unmarried daughters, even of unmarried childbearing and rearing, in underclass black communities than among other groups (Jarrett 1990a; Staples and Mirande 1980). However, recent statistics of births identified only by the mother indicate that young white women are also bearing and keeping children (Cherlin 1981). A short news item in the *Chicago Sun Times Parade* ("Unmarried Mothers," 30 September 1990, 9) stated that "approximately 25% of all babies born in the United States in 1988 were born to unwed mothers." There is little research on the unmarried daughter's rights to continued help from the mother in these circumstances in white communities, probably because the trend toward keeping the baby is so new.

The Adult Daughter of Aging Parents. The role of daughter changes as parents become decreasingly capable of providing their own care, let alone providing support systems to others. Actually, this stage in the family life cycle may arrive gradually, unless a serious health problem develops. The decrease of the power of the male line, accompanying social development, has changed the relation of adults, both daughter and son, to their parents (Lopata 1991b). Transitional American society gradually removed the pressure on the son to take full responsibility for the welfare of his parents. In fact, even main economic supports are no longer expected of him. In the meantime, the daughter has been freed from arranged marriage and the need to leave her family of orientation for that of her husband. As the son's obligation to his childhood family decreases, so does that of his wife. She is now able to retain her relationships with her own family. The mother now does not need to depend wholly upon the son and is thus able to develop closer relationships with her daughter, no longer fearful of losing her early in life. A daughter also gains more positive attention from the mother as a child than was typical in the patrilocal family system, encouraging continued feelings of closeness.

It is during the mother's older years that the increased responsibility of daughters rather than of sons appears in modern families (see Lopata 1987c, especially chapters on Iran, Turkey, Korea, and India; also Lopata 1991b). Thus, the closer relationship between the parents and the daughter, rather than the son, throughout life leads to an increase in her flow of supports toward the older generation. Social scientists, whether or not influenced by Freudian ideas, have long concluded that her contributions are more natural than those of the son and daughter-in-law (Chodorow 1978). Some social scientists claim that this supportive relationship between an adult daughter and her aging parents is undertaken voluntarily, rather than as a consequence of familial obligations as in the past (Hess and Waring 1978a and 1978b). This supports my thesis concerning the shift from the patriarchally ascribed responsibility of the son and daughter-in-law to that of the daughter, who has more comfortable, and in adulthood, more egalitarian relationships with her parents, especially with her mother.

On the other hand, it may be that the daughter who is still in the transitional stage of family development when women took on most nurturant, supportive activity has simply been socialized to a sense of obligation to the parents, especially the mother (Hess and Waring 1978a and 1978b). In one study the daughters living within fifty miles of the aged parents who were not actively supportive of them felt very uncomfortable over the fact that a sister carried the main burden. The sons were obviously not socialized into giving much care, and thus felt no guilt over their failure to do so:

> The overall feeling conveyed by the data is the discomfort of the local sisters, but not the brothers, about being in the role of secondary caregiver, even though in reality they provided more help than the brothers. (Brody et al. 1989, 537)

"Being employed significantly decreased the hours of assistance provided by sons but did not have a significant impact on the hours

of assistance provided by daughters" (Stoller 1983, 851). The importance of daughters rather than sons is evidenced by the likelihood
that at least one daughter is living within easy support distance of a
widowed mother, and the frequency with which they appear in her
support systems (Lopata 1979). The Chicago-area mothers generally
did not share housing with their children, although if the older
woman lived with a child it was much more likely to be with the
daughter's family than with an adult son, even if he were single.

Increasing frailty of parents, accompanied often by bouts of
hospitalization and definite incapacitation, is not only physically,
but also psychologically, difficult for daughters if they must "reverse
roles," treating the mother or father as a dependent who lacks even
decision-making skills. The older generation's social life space can
wither, making the daughter the main supplier of a variety of supports (Fisher 1986).

The amount of time, energy, and sometimes money involved in
caring for a parent may cause conflict with a daughter's other roles,
in the family of procreation or even in an occupation. This is especially true if the woman is an only child. Daughters have been
known to delay marriage or quit a job in order to provide supports
for a mother or father, or both. Single adult children often bear the
brunt of the care. A total of forty-two of the fifty never-married
women studied by Simon (1987) were the primary caregivers for an
ailing parent.

The families of procreation of a married daughter may express
resentment over her new priorities, while she may resent their
unwillingness to understand these (Kleban et al. 1989). Other researchers find daughter caregivers stressed by the addition of this set of
obligations to the normal work load of other roles. Brody (1989) has
drawn our attention to "daughters in the middle," caught in a complex set of high-priority obligations toward the parents, the husband, and the children.

The parents may also suffer in such situations, feeling the resentment from the caregiving daughter and being forced to acquiesce to
demands from harried caregivers. The loss of power of decision making over their own lives can be an extremely frustrating experience.
Mere contact and aid may not result in interpersonal intimacy between
generations, especially if it is felt on both sides as being only obligatory.
In fact, it may result in elder abuse by the stressed caregiver.

"Factors tending to attenuate intergenerational bonds" from the
point of view of the daughter include diminishing opportunities, the

demands of middle age, psychological barriers, and transitions. "Factors tending to preserve and prolong the intergenerational bond" include socialization and the sharing of values, role modeling, and special sentiments, as well as the presence of a healing-caring network (Hess and Waring 1978, 261).

A final duty of a daughter to her parents is to keep their memories alive, providing the grandchildren knowledge of their contributions to family lineage and heritage.

The Modern Form of the Role of Daughter

The evidence is overwhelming that the transitional stage in modernization has placed a major burden on women in the role of daughter, as it has in their other roles. Brody (1989), England and Farkas (1986), Horowitz, (1985), Lopata (1991b,) and all the other researchers studying the support systems of elderly parents report greater contribution and stressful concern on the part of the daughter than on the part of the son. Finley (1989) expects this system to continue until there is a societal reevaluation of the importance of the male source of support. At present, all agree that the institutionalization of women's housework, and the extension of this into care for others, is so strong as to resist any attempt to create a more egalitarian system of emotional and service support. Wilkinson (1988, 191) suggests the creation or expansion of extensive forms of support for dependent family members from voluntary social groups as a means of alleviating the burden placed on the female kin member, especially the daughter. If the predicted changes by which the responsibility for human welfare is better distributed among a variety of people and groups actually take place, as I believe they must for modern life to reach its potential, then the role of daughter, much like that of mother, will contain a more complex social circle. Its members can negotiate both the duties and the rights of what can now be a burden for the social person of daughter at the more dependent stage of the life course of the mother.

The Role of Daughter-in-Law

The relationship between daughter-in-law and mother-in-law appears more often in anthropological or sociological studies of more highly patriarchal family systems than of the modern American one. In the former, the younger woman is often seen as the victim (see Barnes

1987 on China; Ross 1962 on India). In a sort of hazing like in fraternities of the not-so-distant past, she often receives the same kind of treatment as did her mother-in-law when she was young. In addition, joint households often assign much of the homemaking work to the younger woman, the mother-in-law thus becoming the honored matriarch of the family.

The relation between the woman that grows out of the kinship system is expected to be difficult, since the two women are of different generations, have usually not been in contact prior to the younger woman's marriage to the son of the older woman, have had the relationship thrust on them by that event, and are in competition for the attention of the man who is the connecting link. The daughter-in-law may resent what she sees as interference in child rearing, which the older woman may perceive as simply providing help to the novice. However, the modern daughter-in-law has more power than in the past to negotiate with the husband for independence from his mother. In fact, contact can be relatively voluntary and limited. The daughter-in-law can treat the relation (with cooperation from the mother-in-law, of course) as one of friendship, minimal involvement, or "substitute mother" (Fisher 1986, 119). Although one of the duties of the daughter-in-law's role in traditional times was to respect and express positive feelings toward the husband's parents, many women are unable to feel those sentiments and are less likely in present times to control their expressions. The daughter-in-law's role may also be complicated by her husband's conflicts between his duties and rights in the role of husband and those in his role of son.

Most daughters-in-law are able to successfully separate relations with their own mothers from those with the husband's mother. Marotz and Cowan (1987) studied women who lived together on farms or ranches and who reported that they got along pretty well, using conflict-avoidance techniques. The sources of conflict were differences in values and goals, which often were not communicated adequately.

Sister

The role of sister is thrust upon a girl simply by birth or adoption and acknowledged family membership of herself and a sibling. Birth order is an important circumstance affecting the place of the newborn in the family, the social circle components, and treatment by others. The size, spacing, and gender distribution of the sibling group influence all members (Elder and Boverman 1963). It makes a great deal of difference whether the child is in the first, middle, or youngest position in the family, and whether the siblings are girls or boys. Duties and rights are assigned differently by parents and others according to such characteristics of the sibling structure. A brother will relate with a sister differently than will a same-sex sibling, and the number of years between children can generally decrease competitiveness and increase protectiveness.

An extremely important influence on the role of sister, as on all other sets of relationships, is the society within which it is carried out, with its culture and social structure. The location of the relation within that society, especially in its socioeconomic system, is also very important, as lower-class or lower-caste families usually relate differently than do upper-class ones. The role of sister can also vary among other societal subdivisions, such as religious, as in the case of the Quakers versus Catholics, or ethnic, as with Italian Americans versus Navaho Indians. It certainly makes a difference whether the sister can retain her role (i.e., relations with her circle) or loses it with marriage.

Cross-cultural analyses point to a greater interdependence among siblings in many parts of the traditional world than in middle-class America. Sibling groups share many functions, including work and responsibility, serving as substitutes for each other, being obedient to seniors, teaching and learning, playing and disciplining, and making sure that the family system operates smoothly (Weisner 1982, 308). In many such societies community and family are accentuated over individualism, and caregiving is a normal, ongoing aspect of life. The importance of the sibling group continues throughout life unless there is a geographic dispersal of members. In societies such as Egypt, for example, a sister is highly dependent on her brothers for mate selection, the provision of dowries, property inheritance, and so on. Such close interdependence fosters strong sentiments, not all of them positive.

The literature on siblings in transitional America is in interesting contrast to this cross-cultural description, in that it is scarce and often does not specify gender. Two revealing article titles are "Sibling Interaction: A Neglected Aspect in Family Life Research" (Irish 1964) and "The Sibling Relationships: A Forgotten Dimension" (Pfouts 1976). In fact, most recent studies of siblings have focused not on the role, but on the effects of such variables as birth order, gender, spacing, and "density" upon such characteristics as personality.

A few studies provide some insights. The small number and short age distance between siblings of recent decades allegedly promotes more competitiveness and cooperation in childhood and youth than was true in the past. In addition, mothers of transitional times devoted greater attention to children, again increasing the possibility of competition. Sisters reportedly feel moderately close to their siblings, more so than brothers, and more so toward their sisters than toward their brothers (Boverman and Dobash 1974). Adolescents feel closer to their older than to their younger siblings, implying an asymmetry of the relationships. Kammeyer (1967) found that the presence of younger brothers helped sisters learn feminine deference and demeanor, while the presence of older brothers made the younger sister more masculine or "modern."

Intense sibling loyalties can develop in cases of parental loss or child abuse (Bank and Kohn 1982). Such loyalty manifests itself by constant devotion, identification with the other, the ability to resolve interpersonal conflicts rapidly and openly, sacrifices for the other, the wish to be together to the point of strong negative reaction to separation, and defense of the other against outside threats. However, we need to know more about the factors that bind sisters and brothers to each other. As of now, only dire circumstances in the lives of the siblings appear to result in strong loyalty.

What happens as brothers and sisters become adults and old people? An extensive debate has been waged over the last forty years about the involvement of adult and aging siblings in each other's support systems. The discussion harks back to Parsons's (1943) statement that the modern American family is isolated from its kinship group, which includes siblings. Lee (1980) stated in his summary of the 1970s decade of research and theory on kinship that while the 1960s work was dominated by refutation of this thesis, the 1970s focused on studies of actual exchanges of supports. Most sociologists would agree that the middle-class American situation contrasts with that of working-class urban Britain, where the mother ("mum") guarantees contact among her daughters by her own activities. Even there, however, the sisters tend to disperse when the mother dies or if the sister's family of procreation moves elsewhere (Wilmott and Young 1960).

As in the ideal of friendship, which we will be examining later, other relationships and roles prevent many adult women from maintaining a strong focus on the role of sister. This is particularly true of women in the roles of wife and mother, especially if they move from the area occupied by their family of orientation, as so many Americans have done.

Most of the studies of the role of sister focus on older rather than middle-aged women and reach one of two mutually exclusive conclusions. On the one side are studies that argue that the role of sister is active among older Americans and pulls together not only the women but also male siblings. This reinforces the thesis that women take responsibility for keeping in contact with kin. Older women are more apt to communicate with their siblings than are older men. Closer sister relationships occur among older women who never married or had children than among those who had families of procreation (Shanas 1977). Thirty-one of the fifty never-married women studied by Simon (1987, 70) were sharing an apartment or house with a sister or brother in old age. Economic support, help in sickness, companionship, and emotional support were reasons for such arrangements. Several reported especially close relations with a sister. Sisters were very helpful as support providers and confidantes among black women facing serious personal problems (Chatters, Taylor, and Neighbors 1989, 764). In fact, researchers find that sisters, and sometimes brothers, are used as child and spouse substitutes (see also Shanas 1977). In addition, even for rural elderly not "enmeshed in an emotionally supportive network of kin relations," having a sister living in relatively close proximity may contribute to the life satisfaction of women (McGhee 1985, 90). It is possible that even "rivalrous feelings between sisters" may challenge them toward a livelier involvement in interaction or a fuller social life space.

In general, closeness and contact tend to remain constant over the years at whatever level is achieved in adulthood (Cicirelli 1982). Memories, however, may help increase feelings of acceptance and approval later in life. As Gold (1987) notes:

> The reduction in perceptions of resentment and envy indicate that older sisters and brothers may be able to "forgive and forget" in old age. . . . The findings here indicate that generational solidarity becomes more evident early in old age and grows throughout late life for many sibling dyads. (P. 30)

Gold adds that it is mainly the sister who contributes to such feelings of closeness, in both sisters-only and in sister-brother dyads. She focuses on the salience of the memories, rather than on more active support systems.

On the other hand, several researchers have questioned this "overheralded structure in past conceptualizations of family functioning" (Gibson 1972). A careful examination of the data used by sociologists such as Litwak (1965) and especially Sussman (1962) indicates that most of the supports flow up and down the parent-child line, rather than horizontally to siblings (Lopata 1978). "Siblings simply are not available for interaction in the metropolitan area for a large proportion of the sample. The sibling bond is not sustained at the same level throughout the life cycle, and becomes less prevalent among older people" (Rosenberg and Anspach 1973, 108). Not only is the role of sister relatively rarely activated among old women, but when it is, it can become a burden, creating strained relations with siblings. This is particularly true in cases in which one sister becomes the major caregiver while other sisters and brothers are locally available but much less active in the supports of older parents (Brody et al. 1989). In fact, there are numerous records of sibling abuse, including even homicide (Steinmetz 1987). As with other family abuse, it tends to go from brother to sister, although age is an important factor.

Siblings seldom appeared in support networks of widows in the Chicago metropolitan area, even when the respondents were given 195 chances to list a sister or brother (Lopata 1978 and 1979). We asked about four sets of supports, defined as the giving or receiving of objects or actions that the giver and the receiver perceive as supportive of a life-style (Lopata 1987b, 3). Support networks consist of people or organizations that provide supports. Support systems are sets of actions or objects and include the inflow and outflow of economic and service supports and social as well as emotional interaction. All but 19 percent of the widows have at least one living sibling, but "the average frequency of contact with such a collateral relative is just over 'several times a year'" (Lopata 1978, 357). Most of the widows do not report economic exchanges with anyone, let alone siblings. In addition, at most 10 percent of the women report a sibling within the service support system, and that is as a giver or receiver of help with decisions. Siblings appear as helpers with transportation, household repairs, shopping, yard work, child care, and so forth even less often than that. The same is true of social supports. Only 11 percent of the respondents report visiting or traveling out of town with siblings, and only 10 percent report sharing holidays with them. Fewer go to public places, share lunch, go to church, or engage in leisure games or sports with a brother or sister. Finally, and this is the most devastating finding to those who claim that close sibling relationships in adulthood and old age are common, very few siblings appear in the emotional support system. Fewer than 10 percent of the widows list a sibling as the person they most enjoy being with, to whom they tell problems, who comforts them when depressed, makes them feel important or useful, or who most often makes them angry. Only 10 percent feel closest to a sibling or would turn to one in times of crisis. All in all, siblings do not appear in 99 percent of the economic-inflow, 98 percent in the economic-outflow, 87 percent in the service-inflow, and 92 percent of the service-outflow systems. They are more frequently involved in the sentiment system, but even here, 74 percent of the women do not think of a sibling when answering those questions. On the other hand, if a woman lists a sibling, it is usually a sister and she is usually listed several, sometimes many, times (Lopata 1979 and 1987c).

Several articles in a special issue of the *American Behavioral Scientist* (Bedford and Gold 1989) devoted to the complexity of sibling relationships among older Americans, report a prevalence of conflict in many relations among sisters, the infrequency of sustained help, and the distress produced when such help is actually given. Support occurs mainly in brief crisis periods (Bedford 1989a and 1989b).

A number of factors can serve as mediators influencing the provision of supports by siblings, such as geographic proximity, social network structure, health and functional status, gender composition, and ethnicity (Avioli 1989, 57). Physical distance affects especially members of the lower social classes, who are not accustomed to using correspondence or even telephones for maintaining closeness, being mainly dependent upon face-to-face interaction, which can be hard to achieve with limited resources. Social distance, in terms of social class difference, is also important, although there is no consensus on its influence as a depressor of relationships. Bott (1957) found professional and generally more middle- and upper-class couples more involved in friendships with like-minded peers than with parents or siblings.

There are several explanations for the relative absence of siblings from the support systems of widows and of other adult or older sisters.

> The decline in the need for interdependence and shared functioning, and in the maintenance of a single family estate, is the primary underlying feature allowing for the remarkable mobility in the American sibling group. Bilateral inheritance has a great deal to do with the relatively equal investment in boys and girls in our society. The replacement of parents' material wealth with other forms of parental investment early in life, and lessened importance of having parents' skills transferred to sons, are both of enormous importance for the freedom and egalitarian treatment within the Western sibling group. (Weisner 1982, 325)

Siblings interact intensely in America, according to Weisner (1982), only when inheritance issues arise, because our "unusually egoistic family pressures" (325) increase chronic rivalry and personal possessiveness, especially among middle-class American siblings (see also Lamb and Sutton-Smith 1982).

All in all, the assumption that sibling relationships grow closer with aging has not been borne out in most research on transitional families. The growing literature on stepfamilies in modern times includes discussion of stepsisters, usually in early stages of entrance into that role. We do not know enough as yet to tell whether stepsisters retain active involvement in that role in later life.

Grandmother

One of the main advantages of old age, portrayed in highly romanticized terms, is that of being a grandparent. Images of a grandmother baking pies with her granddaughter or telling stories to the grandchildren abound in American folktales and literature. The wicked old stepmother is replaced by the kind old grandmother. The relationships are positively presented; negative aspects are not mentioned. The grandmother, deservedly in that role because she had children and raised them to value having families of their own in contact and cooperation with her, reaps all the benefits. She has companionship without constant care. The grandchildren and she are in contact for a limited number of hours, when both are on their good behavior, and then separate, leaving nothing but pleasant memories. She can read to them without worrying about their performance in schools. She can perform the traditional homemaking tasks such as cooking favorite foods without having to worry about diets or forcing the children to eat at the right time and in the right way. She can buy clothes or playthings, but need not worry about their maintenance. She can spend money on their entertainment rather than on their support. She can use money as gifts without undertaking major expenditures for teeth straightening or housing.

Although being active in the role of grandmother is voluntary, a woman has actually no choice as to when and under what circumstances it becomes available to her. Children produce their own children on their own timetables, not as a convenience to their own parents. "Normative time," so labeled by Neugarten (1973), occurs when the grandparent is ready and the community considers her to be at the appropriate stage of her life. If the event occurs too early or too late, or "off time," complications can occur, as indicated before in the case of unmarried black grandmothers (Burton and Bengtson 1985).

Traditional Times, Traditional Places

Grandmothers have traditionally had the right to help in, or even to dominate, the socialization process of the grandchildren. This was both a duty and a right in slowly changing societies in which they had accumulated knowledge and time freed from heavy subsistence work (Wong 1988). The middle generation was usually all too glad to turn over this function to the older one, being themselves too busy with social reproduction. A Puerto Rican grandmother living on the mainland reputedly has strong rights of control over her grandchildren, including that of removing them from the parents if she considers their behavior unsatisfactory (Ludwig 1977).

The right and duty to socialize the grandchildren is often accompanied by the total care of these beneficiaries in the grandmother's social circle. This is true of Thailand (Cowgill 1972), traditional China (Wong 1988; Barnes 1987), South Korea (Koo 1987), and many European countries (Mindel, Habenstein, and Wright 1988).

> Cooking, washing, cleaning, bathing are necessary repetitive chores at which grandmothers may substitute for younger mothers who may be involved in occupational roles away from home. At the same time, these grandmothers are serving as teachers and disciplinarians. In fact, it appears that it is often the grandmother who is the actual, if unrecognized, head of the household, the person who controls much of the daily routine of the members and supervises most of the activities of the children. (Cowgill 1972, 98–99)

The role can thus combine elements of the roles of homemaker and mother with those of grandmother. Role strain and role conflict often enter into this type of situation when two social persons in two different roles claim the same duties or rights. A mother and a grandmother may each feel that it is her main right to socialize a child her way, with the assistant conforming to her definitions of that situation. This occurs quite frequently between first- and second-generation immigrant families in America. On the other hand, there are situations in which the role of mother may be delegated by the biological mother willingly, or by community action, to the biological grandmother.

Conflict between the mother and the grandmother over the children is especially likely when more than one set of relationships operates concurrently in the same locale. This happens in three-generation households, when there is not a clear-cut division of authority and labor. As Ross (1962) found in urban India, and F. Adams (1972) in Mazaltepec, the grandmother can define her role more satisfactorily for herself when adult married children and their offspring reside in her home than when she lives in households dominated by the younger woman (see also Koo 1987). The higher the status of the elderly woman, the greater usually are her rights to determine her role of grandmother. In traditional and even modern China, a grandchild may be left behind by families moving away from the ancestral home or sent to the home of the grandmother to be raised by her or to care for the elderly (Barnes 1987, 213). Some American Indian communities allow children to leave their parental homes in cases of family conflict and to live with grandparents or aunts and uncles (Nelson 1988; Schlegel 1988).[4]

Transitional and Modern Forms of the Role of Grandmother

Many changes in the culture, composition, and social structure of societies have dramatically changed the real, rather than the ideological, role of grandmother. One basic conclusion by observers of these changes is that the role has decreased in importance for both the older woman and the grandchildren in transitional, urban America from times and places in which the kinship network was locally contained and mutually interdependent. Thus, the first reason given for this decrease is the weakening of the network that granted the grandmother rights and assisted her in her duties. The extended family has dispersed, and remaining members are limited in number, usually the parents of the children and possibly their aunts and uncles.

The weakening of the patriarchal structure of families means that the other grandparents, of which there can be several sets, must now be considered. Geographical separation of the grandmother and the major beneficiaries also makes their circle involvements more difficult.

Many demographic changes in the society can influence the attractiveness of grandparenting (Sprey and Matthews 1982). Modern grandmothers often are too busy to participate in that role on an extensive basis. Most have not modified their role cluster sufficiently to incorporate grandparenting, or at least to move it into prominence. Rather than making grandparenting a "career" of involvement, such women, too involved in other roles while the grandchildren are small, may find the youngest generation involved in its own life when they are ready to grandparent (Cherlin and Furstenberg 1986).

There are several recent trends that affect the age at which a woman acquires grandchildren. Among lower-class African American, Chicano, and Puerto Rican families, women can become grandmothers biologically while still in their twenties and thirties and feel very irritated over being pushed into a role that implies aging (Burton and Bengtson 1985; Jarett 1990b). They often have children and grandchildren of the same ages (Jarrett 1990a). Of course, if the present trend toward later marriage and motherhood continues, the role of grandmother may increase in importance in the future, as the new cohorts of women reach the age of retirement from public roles while grandchildren are still available.

Another reason why the role of grandmother may be decreasing in importance can be the gradual removal of major rewards. Being an active grandmother may be worth a great deal of effort not only in the absence of interesting competitive roles, but also when it is considered very important to society in general. This is likely to occur when there is power, or at least authority, connected with it, when the older woman is given the rights to determine the boundaries of the role, and when there is a complex social circle assisting and supporting her actions. Historical and anthropological research indicates that such circumstances were present in the past and in other societies, where the practical contributions of the role were valued. In such societies people envied families with grandmothers, assigned them sufficient rank that their demands on behalf of the children were honored and resources were provided for their performance of their duties. Of course, some of the descriptions of grandparents' power in other times and places may be exaggerated. Even great dowager grandmothers of future kings and queens may not have had the ultimate say in how the youngest generation was to be cared for and socialized. The social circle of grandmothers has often contained people who have equal, if not greater, say on these matters. The more important the youngster, the more complex his (and sometimes her) circle, of which the grandmother is only a small part, is likely to be. Thus, her role is influenced by the grandchild's current or future roles.

One of the characteristics of modern societies is the rapidity of social change, which makes much of the knowledge collected over years by the grandmother considered outmoded by the middle generation and its assisting personnel (Gutmann 1985; Lopata 1972, and 1976a). The children of immigrants, born and socialized in America, often resist the influence of their own parents over the children, wishing more "modern" contents and methods of socialization, as provided by Dr. Spock (1957) or other "scientific" sources (Lopata 1971b and 1976a). widows interviewed for the study *Women as Widows: Support Systems* (Lopata 1979) complained that their role of grandmother had withered into one of "baby-sitting," or simply watching that the child not be hurt or do anything destructive, rather than actively being involved in child rearing. In fact, many felt that their own children interfered with the building up of a relationship with the grandchildren.

In fact, one of the major reasons that American widows prefer to live alone, even to face loneliness, rather than share the households of their married children and their offspring, is the anticipation of intergenerational conflict. They imagine not only irritation with the grandchildren, but also, and often even more importantly, anger at their own offspring over their methods of rearing the youngsters (Lopata 1973c and 1979).

An earlier study of role modifications of older widows showed that, at the time of the interview, blacks in the Chicago metropolitan area had no advantage over their white counterparts when it came to sharing households, although many had experienced living with relatives in the past (Lopata 1971a and 1973c). The assumed centrality of matrifocal families among non-middle-class blacks led me to the assumption that many more black families would be headed by a maternal grandmother or have her living in a home headed by a daughter (Burton and Bengtson 1985). However, only a tiny number of Chicago-area widows ever had grandchildren living in the same residence. Interestingly enough the grandmother shared a home with granddaughters more often than with grandsons.

In spite of the infrequency among all the social races of three-generational households, I had expected grandchildren to be actively involved in the support systems of the widows. This hypothesis also proved incorrect. Grandchildren appeared in the economic support systems of widows, if they did at all, only as recipients of gifts of money. Only one-fifth of the references to people whom widows entertained at home, and one-fourth to those with whom holidays are spent, are to grandchildren. I also assumed a much greater contribution of such children in the emotional support systems—but was disappointed. Only 10 percent of the widows reported having a grandchild as one of the three persons with whom they most enjoy being, and about 6 percent as the person who most often makes them feel important or useful. Grandchildren are definitely not major contributors to the support systems of the vast majority of Chicago-area widows in two carefully selected samples. A few of the widows' comments about the third generation indicated irritation with the manner of deportment or lack of deference. On the other hand, some commented that they enjoyed the relationship and that it was part of their emotional support system. Cherlin and Furstenberg (1986) probed in greater depth and found that the generalized reference to "grandchildren" masked the fact that the older generation had favorites, who were emotionally very important. Even ethnically identified grandparents were not, for the most part, involved with grandchildren on a day-to-day basis. However, there was strong emotional investment in those children who were seen regularly.

The subject of grandparenting has recently drawn expanded attention from both popular and social science literature, undoubtedly accompanying increases in the numbers of the elderly and the growth of the field of social gerontology (see Bengtson and Robertson 1985).

The Social Psychology of Grandmothering

The deinstitutionalization of the role and its basic relationships has made available many alternate ways of grandparenting. The (1964) Neugarten and Weinstein study, a classic in the field, determined five different "styles" of such role involvement, all based more on companionate than on authoritarian relationships: formal, fun-seeking, surrogate parenting, as a reservoir of wisdom, and as a distant figure. This typology has been used in many studies, with additional embellishments of the basic five. The distant grandmothers can be detached or remote, passive or selectively investing themselves. A very important function of the more passive grandparents can be that of being the "family watchdog" who stands ready to help mainly in emergency situations but refrains from what might be taken as interference (Troll 1983). Many characteristics of the older woman, including her health, income, other family obligations, or personal stances to social roles, can also influence the social psychological aspects of role involvement. This role "can be either a gift or a curse, a reward or punishment for what one has done or been earlier" (Troll 1985, 135). Research on life-course changes in personality indicates a continuity of stances, a stability of styles in many roles that preceded that of grandmother.

Styles of grandparenting do not function in isolation from the social circumstances and background of interaction. We must remember that this role can be enacted with many different grandchildren. Unless all are within the same geographical area, social distance may be affected by resources available to undertake an alternative style. Add to this the changes and ambiguities of the role itself, even within each class, and other complications arise. Geographical proximity influences such relationships, as it does others. The match between expectations on the part of each generation is important: The closer these expectations are to each other and to an "ideological" view of the role, the easier it is to actually relate. The relative willingness and power of each generation to bargain and negotiate the relationship also contribute to interaction (Robertson 1977). The ages of all participants and the stages in their family cycle must be considered, according to Wood and Robertson (1973). There may be a generation gap in expectations, grandparents often expecting aspects of the role to be quite different from what the youngsters expect.

A combination of social class variables constructs the situation within which relationships flourish or remain formal or distant. Lower-class families of all social races allegedly give the role of grandmother much more centrality and vitality than do the middle classes (see Adams 1968; Staples 1988; Winch and Blumberg 1968). One change that could lead to an increase in the use of grandmothers as child rearers by middle-class mothers is the latter's movement into the labor force. However, such mothers tend to use day-care facilities, in spite of their inadequacies, rather than the grandmother, due to generational differences in ideas about human development. Other middle-class tendencies that seem to decrease the value of kin caretaking of children include an emphasis on leisure-time pursuits. Males' increasing longevity past retirement has turned the older generation toward fun rather than work. The grandparents brought up one family and resist being tied down by children. Being economically comfortable now with social security, they can pay for their own services, rather than depending on their children, which decreases their need for payback supports (Clavan 1978, 355; Lopata 1979).

Gutmann (1985) claims that Americans have repudiated gerontocracy, or the power of the elderly over the rest of the society. The middle-aged and older are refusing to face aging, wishing independence and autonomy from familism, hedonistically withdrawing from demands of closeness, narcissistically choosing only roles that provide pleasure rather than duties.

As the obligatory aspects of the role of grandparent decrease for the older generation, and as the middle generation finds alternative ways of caring for its children and focuses on nonfamilial activities, the factors facilitating voluntary relationships become more pronounced (Hess and Waring 1978a). The importance of the middle generation in either facilitating or interfering with grandparent-grandchild interaction cannot be neglected. Their feelings and viewpoints can push the others toward or away from each other. In fact, Robertson (1977) presents different dimensions of parental mediation influencing grandparent-grandchild relations. These include the parental perception of the significance of grandparenthood, of the appropriateness of the behavior of the grandparents, and of the rituals of contact. In addition, the means parents use to mediate between generations, the frequency of mediation, and the parents' attitudes about the equity of interaction are all important factors affecting the results.

A situation that recently received sociological and popular attention is the demand by grandparents for access to grandchildren in the case of divorce (Burton and Bengtson 1985, 65). The probability of continued contact is relatively high if they are the parents of the divorcée, less likely if it is the son who formed the connecting link. In modern society, the divorced wife has the right to remove the grandchildren from contact with the ex-husband's family if she wishes. This right is contrary to the traditional patriarchal system, in which the grandparents on the male line had stronger rights over the children than did the mothers. The creation of barriers to contact with grandchildren can be a serious shock to grandparents who have already developed loving relationships. The mother can even remarry and change the children's family name so that they are hard to trace. Such a cutoff is not likely to happen if the grandparents have property that can be inherited and subsequent legal battles are to be avoided. The sociopsychological aspects of involvement in grandmothering mean that some women suffer emotional withdrawal if grandchildren they had become attached to are no longer available for contact and mutual support.

Summary

Women's kinship roles, including kin keeper on either side, daughter, sister, or grandmother, have become sufficiently deinstitutionalized in the United States to allow voluntary engagement in adulthood. The forced interdependence that often created uncomfortable demands for work and subservience has decreased with independent sources of social integration. On the other hand, the prescribed, traditional support resources have simultaneously become optional, and people can, without recourse, be deprived of emotional or social comfort.

An interesting recent suggestion is to have the government allow large kinship networks to incorporate themselves as businesses, providing tax advantages in the form of write-offs for assistance with new business ventures, tuition funds, and wealth transfers (Wallis 1992, 44). Such a modern innovation could revitalize kinship in America.

Once having entered the role of daughter, even if without choice, a girl allegedly has the backing of society to insure that she receives adequate care, although many cases of neglect appear to slip by its notice. The role has a distinct life course, changing from high levels of dependence upon the mother in childhood, to comparatively egalitarian interaction in adulthood, and possibly a reversal in the parents' old age. There are also definite social class variations in how this role is carried forth and in the size and complexity of its social circle. In the extremes of social class position, greater importance is assigned to the role of daughter than in the middle classes.

An important aspect of this role in modern America is that it can be active even after marriage. In contrast to prior times and places, a woman does not have to neglect her family of orientation when becoming a daughter-in-law.

Sister relations were probably never significant in patriarchal families, since sisters dispersed upon marriage, joining the families of their husbands. Continued contact with the mother in modern times can insure sibling interaction in adulthood, but her death can weaken the link. Mobility, whether social or geographical, can decrease its salience, if positive feelings ever existed. Contact at funerals and weddings is not equivalent to continued interaction and supports. The role can be reactivated in old age, as other roles lose their significance and if circumstances permit.

There are many idealized images of the role of grandmother in all ethnic and racial subcultures in America's past. The role is now so highly deinstitutionalized that each grandmother develops, more or less voluntarily and in cooperation with circle members, her own relationships with her grandchildren. The more resources she has, the more she can demand or negotiate her terms for the role. The intermediary generation can function as her assistants, setting up the proper atmosphere and making interaction easy, or it can hinder it.

Grandmothers are known to vary considerably in their personal styles of involvement. However, it takes more than a style to carry forth a role, and many factors facilitate or impede this one. Many more women have now survived to grandmotherhood than in the past, and the deinstitutionalization of the role and the increasing individualization of American women mean that here too, as in other social roles, diversity abounds.

5

Occupation: Homemaker

One of the interesting characteristics of the role of homemaker in modern America is the high level of emotional and evaluative disagreement it draws. The woman in this role can be seen as a creative contributor not just to direct beneficiaries but to the society at large. On the other hand, the role can be seen as exploitive and demeaning to the titleholder, even if it is judged to be important to the beneficiaries.

The role of homemaker is undertaken by a woman who decides, more or less voluntarily, to manage a household and draws together a social circle involving everyone who benefits from her work and who contributes to her efforts—assistants, and suppliers of goods and services. The role can be performed by a man, who is interestingly still called a "househusband," while the older term *housewife* has been replaced by *homemaker* to include women other than wives. Very, very few men undertake the role of full-time househusband, carrying the main responsibility of managing the household and allocating tasks to circle members (J. Pleck 1983).

Housekeepers are usually defined as employees of homemakers or other managers of households.

The duties of this role, as of any other, depend upon the size and construction of the social circle and what must be done in interaction with each member. Its rights are also influenced by the relative status, or prestige location, of the homemaker and by her location in the organizational chart of the household's environment. The household is the basic unit of the role.

The social circle of the homemaker can be quite simple, consisting of a limited number of beneficiaries, residents, guests, other recipients of products and services she has created, and assistants. She could be the only beneficiary, if she were the only resident and never invited anyone into her home or offered services and products from the home without pay. Such a situation can be visualized in the case of a homemaker in a relatively isolated and self-sufficient American pioneer farm. Some circle members may be forced upon her by other decisions, as when in-laws or stepchildren move in with a husband, or residents invite guests. Most traditional homemakers have been embedded in a network of extended families and village neighbors with complicated work and product exchange systems. Modern homemakers have numerous assistants in the form of product and service suppliers. A social circle can be as complex as that of the White House, managed by the U.S. First Lady with the assistance of enormous staffs and with uncounted numbers of beneficiaries from all over the world.

Traditional Times, Traditional Places

Households have varied tremendously all over the world and throughout history. The young bride of the traditional rural Hindu family of India moved into limited quarters within the joint family household managed by her mother-in-law and had few rights until she herself became the eldest matriarch (Gujral 1987). Limited rights also went with homemaking in all ancestral homes in familistic cultures, in which each generation had the obligation to retain things for the future with little individualized change.

Aries (1965) describes the manor homes of Europe as very complicated centers of societal life, especially in countries without specialized political and economic meeting places. Within them lived a variety of people, while others visited for many reasons, often for extended periods of time. My own great-grandmother recorded in detail the work and the social activities connected with my grandfather's wedding in Poland in the 1870s (Znaniecka 1872). Literally hundreds of people, whom she had to organize, were involved as assistants, suppliers, and beneficiaries. Artificial orange trees to decorate the home were made by local women who were obviously given models, since such trees could not grow in the Polish climate. Visitors stayed for weeks, having traveled great distances in premodern conveyances.

Homemakers in charge of manor homes usually managed the whole estate when the husband was away for business or wars, even if his signature were required for legal transactions (Pinchbeck [1930] 1969). Servants and apprentices often lived within the employer's household. Many families either obtained young servants from villages or sent their own children as servants in the homes of others (B. Laslett 1973; P. Laslett 1971; Oakley 1974b). The homemaker trained and supervised these workers and provided the resources they needed to carry out their tasks. In all but recent times, this involved extensive production of goods, such as breads and clothing, from raw material (Andre 1982; Strasser 1978). Care of animals was often part of the role.

American history also provides many examples of complex social circles of homemakers. Demos (1973) details seventeenth-century family life in the Plymouth colony. Kessler-Harris (1981), Cowan (1983), Ehrenreich and English (1979), Hayden (1981), Rothman (1978), and numerous other social scientists have relatively recently reexamined American history in an effort to make more visible the work of women as homemakers and in informally paid activities and jobs. Studies of the contributions and problems of black and immigrant women trying to maintain households under extremely trying conditions emphasized the importance of the homemaker as the connecting link between the public and the private spheres of life. The creation of a home private sphere was especially difficult for women of color, due to the constant interference of public policies (Hurtado, 1989).

Many houses in American traditional times may have been relatively simple in terms of room specialization, as they were in Europe before privatization, but the large amount of work in and around them required the cooperation of numerous persons. Expansion in size changed human relationships, providing greater institutionalization of interaction and emotion. The household could contain the elderly, many children, unmarried relatives, servants indentured or in apprenticeships, boarders and lodgers, and the poor under guardianship (Hareven 1978b; Ryan 1979). All these people had to be provided space, fed, clothed, and cared for in illness; at the same time, they contributed their services in a complex of household work. Animals also had to be cared for. The establishment of homemaking was further complicated in America's early history by the absence of legal rights. European and American wives were legal minors, unable to own and control a dwelling until relatively recently. They remained in the home owned by the father until they married and entered the home owned by the husband, which then passed on to the son. Babcock and her associates (1975) document the consequences of such laws in *Sex Discrimination and the Law*:

> When a woman marries, she loses her domicile and acquires that of her husband, no matter where she resides or what she believes or intends. . . . As of 1974, only four states allowed married women to have separate domiciles from their husbands for all purposes; another 15 allowed women to have separate domiciles for voting, six for election to public office, five for jury service, seven for taxation and five for probate. (Pp. 575–76)

The extension of this norm, in the ritual of a new husband's carrying his bride across the threshold of "his" dwelling, has now been made obsolete by the simple fact that the couple usually shares a household even before marriage and that it is just as likely to have been hers to begin with as his.

Urbanization and industrialization, plus modern technology, contributed to changes in the roles of homemakers, the composition of their social circles, and the intertwinement of relationships of duties and rights. The expansion of the middle class and the increasing heterogeneity of the population added new dimensions to home management. The home changed its significance several times. By the turn into the twentieth century, "more than 70 percent of the population had lived in boarding houses at some time in their lives" (Lynes 1963, 51). Immigrants and young couples either could not afford, or did not want to maintain their own households. Apartment hotels proliferated. Charlotte Perkins Gilman ([1898] 1966) pushed for an American domestic revolution that would do away with private kitchens and introduce professional child care, but this never became popular. O'Neill (1969a) observes about Gilman:

What she could not have guessed in 1889 was the extraordinary affection Americans would demonstrate for the detached, self-contained, single family dwelling. (P. 45)

The Transitional Form of the Role of the Homemaker

The home that most American women have been managing throughout the transitional periods of social development is very different from that described by social historians of the traditional family era. It has been changing in terms of its place vis-à-vis the rest of the world, its composition, its relationships, and the values it represents. The role of homemaker in America has also been developing several unique characteristics, in contrast to other roles, and other times and places. Some of these are inherited from the past, others have evolved in recent times.

A transitional aspect of the role of homemaker is its indeterminate character, for there are great variations available to, and influencing, its titlebearer and the contributions made by others (Lopata 1966 and 1971b). Such a woman must, of course, command the necessary resources for even minimal involvement (such as money and other material goods, location, and the cooperation of others) and must operate within their limitations. A woman marrying a widower or divorced man who has custody of his children has less independence than one starting out with a new household. Even the former is likely to immediately introduce change or push for the establishment of a new home over which she has rights of selection and arrangement. Role making, as Turner (1978 and 1981) has termed the process of personal innovation in preexisting roles, is also more predetermined when the household has been established in the past than when a woman creates her own circle. In the latter case, the homemaker tends to be free of control by in-laws in location, although the husband's occupation usually imposes restrictions.

On the other hand, some of the influence by family members on the homemaker was replaced by that of "experts" by the end of the nineteenth century (Ehrenreich and English 1979; Rothman 1978). The "germ theory" of disease placed the responsibility for prevention upon the homemaker, requiring a completely different view of cleanliness than in the past. Doctors took over from household managers and midwives as the experts about what is good and healthy in daily life. The home became the haven for those who had to leave it to earn income or learn in school how to live within the modernizing world. The same trends that made the wife a personal dependent of the husband in transitional times also made the home-maker basically limited to meeting the needs of a husband and children. She is responsible in such times for making the home a virtuous, clean, healthy, safe, secure, and hospitable place for all beneficiaries.

An important characteristic of the homemaker role in transi-tional times has been the ideologically acclaimed, but usually unful-filled, potential flexibility of the social circle. Beneficiaries can become assistants, under certain circumstances, by demand or negotiation. For example, all members of the household can join together, shar-ing in preparations for the entertainment of visitors. Or the home-maker may try to negotiate with circle members to have them give up some previously established rights of beneficiaries in order to help her manage the household on a permanent basis. The expan-sion of women's role clusters, and thus attempts to change the role of homemaker, is one of the major sources of conflict within families and other residential units. Homemakers experiencing role conflict are increasingly demanding that beneficiaries become at least partial assistants, although they do not go as far as Oakley (1974a) in her recommendation that the role be entirely obliterated through a division of responsibility, with the work added to other roles of residents. The dramatic popularity of Hochschild's *The Second Shift* (1989), which illustrates the failure of this attempt to turn husbands from beneficiaries into assistants or role sharers, indicates the reality of this problem. The same can be said about the conflict homemak-ers are having with children when they attempt to change these beneficiaries into assistants (Wittner 1980).

The modern household with shared homemaking is not here in great numbers (see also J. Pleck 1983)! Observers such as Bird (1979), Matthews (1987), and Hochschild (1989) stress the impor-tance of early and explicit negotiation with future adult circle mem-bers, and socialization of children into their expected contributions. One of the problems is that arrangements for duties or rights made at any one stage of the role course may not be satisfactory later on and may have to be renegotiated again and again.

One unusual feature of the role of homemaker in this transi-tional society has been the ambivalence felt toward it by so many social persons, so that even women who claim to hate many aspects of it and who feel anger at the lack of cooperation from circle members often do not want to part with all the responsibility or identification with the role (Ferree 1987; Hertz 1986; Yogev 1981). The same can be said for circle members.

Stereotypes

One of the first things that impressed observers of the American scene for years is the stereotypical and negatively valued image of the housewife/homemaker (see, for example, de Tocqueville as quoted in Dulles 1965).[1] The devaluation of housewifery or home-making activity was actually the reason for my original study of American women that forms one of the bases for this volume. Several factors may have contributed to this situation. Within the last couple of centuries, social development dramatically expanded the public sphere of life located outside the home. The major part of productive work shifted from home-based territory to that public sphere, allegedly leaving only second-stage production to the home (Dulles 1965). The husband was removed as its co-manager, committing most of his time and energy to outside activity. The development of complex structures to meet the expanding needs for formal education into cultures beyond that shared by the family, as well as the development of organized religion, mass communication, and recreation, led many observers to also devalue the home's contribution to these institutions. The home was deprived of its location as a center of important societal events, serving instead as a place to which adults escaped from, or prepared for, the harsh, competitive outside world.

The household also shrank in complexity as unmarried older relatives, servants, and apprentices moved out (Coser 1973; Laslett 1978; Vanek 1978). For some reason, the size of the unit is associated with the importance assigned to it by many observers, who ignore the extensions of the role beyond its borders. Ignored also are the new values and technologies, such as environmentalism and consumerism, which have introduced new dimensions into the homemaker role but have not been given sufficient value to offset the loss of older tasks and relations. Observers repeatedly express surprise over the amount of time required to maintain a home, assuming that much of the activity is nothing but meaningless busywork.

The American view of the home as a simple and societally

unproductive unit has also contributed to the view of the home-maker either as a simple person engaged in repetitive and noncreative work or as completely alienated. The "domestication" of women, that is, their identification with, and limitation to, a circumscribed and privatized home, now being experienced in developing countries, has been influenced by Western ideologies (Glazer 1978; Matthews 1987; Rogers 1980).

The downgrading of the home and of the homemaker can be accounted for even more explicitly by changes in the American value system that accompanied the Protestant ethic (Weber [1904] 1958) and were reinforced by neo-Marxists' focus on the market value of work. The argument over whether domestic labor is productive or unproductive, only for private use or for exchange value, occupied major thinkers of the midtwentieth century to the extent that other systems of evaluating human activity were neglected. From the capitalist point of view, unpaid work is not of societal importance; from the point of view of the working class, unpaid work also provides no subsistence and is devalued. The early debates over use and exchange value have now been superseded by the growing recognition of the importance of unpaid work to societal welfare. The feeling that unpaid workers are inevitably being exploited remains and will undoubtedly continue until values other than market price gain importance.

The feminist movement of the 1960s and 1970s, influenced by Marxism, initially reinforced this negative stereotype of the role of homemaker, to the extent that Oakley 1974a) advocated its total elimination, as mentioned above. Ferree (1980, 110) calls the blame placed on feminism for contributing to the denigration of house-wives "blaming the messenger for the message." It certainly constricted the value placed on all nonmarketable cultural products and social activity. Even Friedan (1963) bought into that value system when she recommended that women work only for money—for instance, painting not for pleasure but only to sell the product.[2] The attempt to find the "monetary value of housework" falls into that economic sphere (see Walker and Gauger 1973 and the extensive discussions in Glazer 1984). Fromm (1947) described Americans as obsessed by the "marketing mentality," which judges a person's worth by how much he or she is worth in the market. The application of criteria of the economic institution, such as task efficiency, to other institutional areas of life inevitably downgrades the relational aspects of social roles (see also Brown 1982). A perfect example of this is contained in the otherwise excellent analysis of household work by Carmi Schooler and his associates (Schooler et al., "Housework as Work," 1984 and Schooler et al., "Work for the Household," 1984). Both discussions of substantive complexity in the role of homemaker focus on things, ignoring the complexity of dealing with people. This they do systematically for low-status jobs, although they focus on complexity in dealing with people, rather than things, when describing higher status jobs.

Matthews (1987) explains the devaluation of the homemaker role by another set of factors associated with the home economics movement. America in the first half of the twentieth century underwent a broad social movement labeled "scientific management," fathered by industrial engineer Frederick Taylor (1911). Work patterns were examined in industry to determine more efficient uses of time and worker energy, and efficiency became the motto. Attention was then directed toward the home, with home economics as a new scientific field running parallel to, but gender-segregated from, the newly professionalizing occupations. According to Matthews (1987) and Strasser (1982), the home economics movement devalued the competence of women already performing the role of homemaker on the basis of their life experiences. It thus reinforced the placement of women in the home and the separation of men from it, then defined homemakers as inefficient in that role. In addition, it gradually redefined homemaking into a role whose main function is consumer activity (Matthews 1987, 171). Strasser (1982) judges the home economics movement even more strongly:

> With their advertising, the manufacturers joined the home economist—who welcomed them from the start—in their roles as household experts, perverting the role in the interest of selling goods. (P. 8)

Americans' negative image of the role of homemaker emerges not just from its gender identification, but also from a set of criteria that assigns high importance to activity involving those stages in the production of goods and services that are counted as part of the gross national product. Glazer (1980, 253) identifies state governments as contributing to the trivialization of housework, while Glazer and associates (1979, 162) argue that "businesses, schools, stores and others who provide services related to running a home and caring for children" assume that each home has a housewife with all the necessary time to adjust to their schedules.

The Life Course of the Role of Homemaker

Becoming a Homemaker

The social person of the homemaker needs only to manage a dwelling, to declare herself in the role, and to establish relations with at least two other persons. Unless she inherits the home, she sets one up by renting or buying space that meets the qualifications of such housing, which means in most of America that it has a roof, walls, doors, and windows, is heated and electrified, and has water and waste-disposal facilities. Such a dwelling in all but extreme poverty locations is usually divided into rooms, the basic ones being kitchen, bathroom, and bedroom. Multiple and special-function rooms of great variety can be included, each then furnished with objects judged necessary by the standards and resources of the homemaker to meet the assigned functions. Again, unless the woman inherits such objects, they must be purchased and adjusted for the use of the beneficiaries. Self-defined needs tend to change over the life cycle of the role, in response to changing needs of the beneficiaries or changing resources and wishes of the homemaker. One of the complications of the patriarchal heritage of modern America in all but the very recent past has been women's lack of sufficient economic independence to purchase or rent dwellings and fill them with the objects for modern living.

One of the trends frequently referred to by observers of population changes is the frequency with which both men and women now leave the homes of their parents (or parent) to set up independent housekeeping (Masnick and Bane 1980, 20; Sweet and Bumpass 1987, 82). In fact, demographers consider this as one of the dramatic shifts between 1960 and 1980. Cohabitation with others helps solve some of the problem of cost, as does improvement in jobs and wages. Pooling of resources occurs after the "yours or mine" dwelling decision is made. There are no strict norms as to duties and rights, beyond the minimum maintenance requirements for safety and local standards of cleanliness and appearance. The beneficiaries and assistants may refuse to allow the homemaker the rights of access and action or to accept the results of her work; they may remove themselves from the home; but there are few, if any, situations in which suppliers refuse to sell to or service a homemaker. Some unmarrieds share responsibilities and the work of management with cohabitors. However, studies of even countercultural communes and the kibbutzim movement indicate the difficulty of breaking down gender roles in household and even community life, regardless of the strength of egalitarian ideology (Gerson 1978; Zicklin 1983).

Entertaining guests and learning to shop for goods to be converted for home use and for services in and out of the housing unit are the frequent early steps of "becoming a homemaker." American women managing households without a husband or other permanent adult who can share the economic maintenance, responsibility, and work are increasing in number. There are several reasons a woman may have sole responsibility for a multiperson household: Other adult members can be incapacitated, as with elderly parents or a disabled husband or child; there may have never been a co-manager; a cohabitor may have left through desertion or entrance into a total institution (e.g. prison, armed forces, or hospital); or divorce may have split a marital pair that lived together in the past. The process of becoming a homemaker is thus also an indefinite one at present, with no precise turning point and frequent humorous commentary. Modern young women are not apt to think of themselves as homemakers unless and until marriage or motherhood. The role at first appears as a simple addition to other roles such as wife or friend, without major adjustments in the cluster. Social research indicates the inevitability of assignment of the role to women by husbands and everyone involved in helping to maintain the home or benefiting from its activities. In other words, people living in or entering the home tend to assume that the "main" adult woman is the homemaker.

There has been a very interesting change in the past thirty years in assumptions about the need for training for this role. After subject-specialized mass education became organized in America, the home economics movement insisted on teaching scientific management methods for homemaking. Courses on sewing, cooking, financial accounting, and so forth were added to schools at various levels. These were initially aimed at girls only. Students of both genders in our Wisconsin town now take courses in what is still called "home economics" and in what used to be called "shop." Home economics colleges still exist in many land-grant universities, though they are often renamed and inclusive of family study and even social work. The idea behind the nineteenth-century home economics movement, favored by Catharine Beecher and her sister, Harriet Beecher Stowe (1870), was to introduce scientific principles into home management. This aim is also evident in the numerous gender-specific mass-media publications.

The tie-in between this role and that of wife is suggested in the title of a chapter by Gates in Chapman and Gates (1977), "Homemakers into Widows and Divorcées: Can Law Provide Economic Protection?" In fact, the role used to be called "housewife," as indicated by the title of my 1971 book, *Occupation: Housewife,* and by that of Matthews's *Just a Housewife* (1987).

The 1950s and 1960s Chicago-area respondents were definitely split over whether modern homemakers were properly trained for that role, and over who was responsible for such training, the school or the home (Lopata 1971b). Over half did not consider housewives trained, and they blamed both the schools and girls' lack of interest. The higher the woman's education, the higher the family income, and the younger the children, the more the woman thought that training was necessary, and the more she used a variety of sources to obtain increased "on-the-job" learning (Lopata 1971b, 146). Employed urban women were the least likely to consider the role as something for which you need training and were the most apt to perform the role at minimal levels. Transitional dependence on official experts was apparent in their lists of useful past and current sources of knowledge. Primary relations, including with the mother and the home, were listed by mainly younger urban women as either past or current sources. The suburbanites, all of whom had children, used the older generation less frequently, turning more often to the mass media and peers for advice. These were the post–World War II mothers of the baby-boom generation who used the dramatic explosion of advice to homemakers in the media to revolutionize home life. They broke away from parental and urban patterns to create new variations on old roles in a new suburban environment (Gans 1967; Lopata 1971b).

Women who were asked similar questions in 1990 were much less concerned with the adequacy of their prior preparation or on-the-job training, which is not surprising in view of the cultural shift away from such total commitment (Lopata 1993c). They did not perceive as large a gap between pre- and post-homemaking involvement in that role as did the respondents of the feminine-mystique period.

The Expanding Circle

The next stage of the role of homemaker is that of the "expanding circle," when others, usually a husband and definitely children, are added. It usually takes full-time involvement with a small child before the woman sees herself, voluntarily or in consequence of the push by others and circumstances, as the "natural" center of the role and really incorporates it into the role cluster. Of course, some women, usually the younger ones of modern times, never really shift their identities in that direction, while others, usually the older, less educated ones, focus upon it. Some new homemakers find themselves overcome by the unaccustomed features and scope of the work at this stage, responding to constant demands in never-ending sequences (Lopata 1969b; Strasser 1982). The work is very different from any they experienced in the past. Traditional and even modern resources for easing the burden of tasks do not necessarily help to decrease worry and tension about doing things well. Social isolation can be bothersome when children are small, the climate harsh, and other adults absent most of the day (Andersen 1983).

Another problem of this stage of role involvement is the change demanded of everyone, of the social person and circle members, during the early stages of the creation and expansion of the circle. Skills and knowledge learned prior to entrance or early on the job can become useless, or even dysfunctional, as the circle of beneficiaries expands. Having learned to prepare an elaborate meal requiring hours of time does not help a homemaker with tiny babies to feed. Thus, competence gained at one stage does not automatically transfer to another stage.

The Peak Stage

The work and relationships of the peak stage are influenced by a combination of factors:

1. The number and ages of the beneficiaries: children, adult cohabitors, and anyone else (such as guests).
2. Their special needs.
3. The kinds of duties undertaken by the homemaker in relation to these beneficiaries because of societal, circle, or self-imposed demands.

4. The size and complexity of the home that must be maintained.

5. The number of items that must be maintained and the activities required to keep them in good condition.

6. The number of assistants and the type of help they provide, plus the duties directed toward them.

7. The number and variety of "labor-saving" devices or conveniences (e.g., prepared foods) designed to decrease the effort or time required to perform any of the tasks, in terms of not just time but also energy (Hartmann 1981; Schooler et al., "Housework as Work," 1984; Schooler et al., "Work for the Household," 1984).

8. The number and variety of new homemaking activities requiring organizational and activity time, especially in conjunction with the roles of wife and mother.

9. The location of the household and each task in relation to the assisting segment and to useful objects, plus the versatility of these services as sources of shifting duties and activities.

10. Competition from other roles in the homemaker's cluster and the social psychological aspects of her involvement (Lopata 1966, modified).

This stage is still very demanding and often harried, especially because it contains beneficiaries with highly divergent needs, and thus a multiplicity of assistants and suppliers. Women who lack financial resources, are unwilling to pull together such circle members, or have uncooperative beneficiaries (who are unwilling to also to be assistants) can find this stage especially stressful.

The Full-House Plateau

The full-house plateau occurs when the household is not apt to have new beneficiaries added to it. The social circle can expand, however, with the addition of new suppliers of goods and services to the home, or outside of it, and new associates of the main beneficiaries who enter the home. At the same time, the young members of the household gain in the ability to take care of many of their needs, decreasing the direct work, but not supervision, by the homemaker. At this stage the full-time homemaker is likely to find the job complex, but satisfying to the extent that she has mastered the tasks, negotiated satisfactory relationships, and added flexibility to the role (Schooler et al., "Housework as Work," 1984; Schooler et al., "Work for the Household," 1984). This is similar to being in the stage of a job when one's expertise is high.

The Shrinking Circle

The "shrinking circle" stage usually begins when the children start leaving and ends when the woman is left alone. Relationships are modified by the exit of circle members; assistants and suppliers are dropped or withdraw. For example, the decrease of a husband's involvement in his job may decrease the need for entertainment or special clothes preparation, while increasing work created by his constant presence (Szinovacz 1989). Children who were both beneficiaries and assistants withdraw from both segments of the social circle. On the other hand, changes in the role involvements of the homemaker may ease her role conflicts, as when she retires. The shrinking of the circle may result in the woman's neglecting her own self-care. For instance, cooking is something women feel they do for others, not for themselves, so many a widow creates health problems for herself by not getting good nutrition (Lopata 1973c, 1979). Her incentive to keep the house, and even herself, clean and with a pleasant appearance may disappear with the shrinking of the circle of beneficiaries.

Of course, any of these stages can be interrupted, or reversed, especially in our modern, mobile society and long-lasting life courses. Divorce can decrease the circle, remarriage can increase it. Widowhood can occur before the children leave home. Children who moved out in gestures of independence can return, often bringing with them spouses and children, turning the role back into that of the peak stage. Aging or widowed parents no longer can demand of adult offspring that they return to the ancestral home as in patriarchal times, but occasionally they have to move in with daughters, or sons, and their families. Realtors in several Chicago communities report that house owners are adding not only "granny" but also "children's families" units. The expense and shortage of adequate housing brings Americans back to household sharing, whether they prefer such arrangements or not, reactivating the role of homemaker.

The life course of the role of homemaker is affected by social class, the uses made of the house by all the beneficiaries, including the homemaker, and the life courses of the roles of circle members. One of the interesting consequences of the indeterminate nature of this particular role is that it expands in conjunction with some roles, such as that of mother, but contracts with others, such as that of employee. The stages of occupational involvement by the husband, of school involvement by the children, of dying by a circle member, and so forth, all impinge on the duties and rights of the homemaker. Her rights over the home and how it is used also vary by a number of other factors, such as her relationship to the official head of the household and inheritance rights following his or her death.

The Part-Time Homemaker

Much discussion in recent decades has focused on whether women have simply added a "second shift" (Hochschild 1989) to their lives, retaining a full-time involvement in homemaking while adding on a full-time job, or whether they have cut homemaking down to a part-time occupation with the help of cohabitors or with the decrease in household complexity. Numerous studies record a definite failure by women to cut down the role of homemaker to a part-time, shared commitment (see Aldous 1982; Berk 1985; Ferree 1980; Hochschild 1989; Model 1982). The person expected to share household responsibility and work is generally the husband, and husbands do not appear to change their ways even when the wife goes into full-time employment. Working-class men allegedly "help" more, while middle-class men give more lip service to sharing the work of home maintenance. Model (1982) and J. Pleck (1983), among others who have concentrated on the amount and type of household work undertaken by the husband, usually find a continued gender-segregation of tasks and a lack of feeling of responsibility for the solution of mutual problems by the husband. This means that the major responsibility for the household remains with the woman, who must assign, or negotiate for "help" with, the work much as in the past, although there appears to be more of that help in the present.

Homemaking and Household Composition

Another way of looking at the role of homemaker is in terms of household composition (see also Hartmann 1981, 383). The full-time homemakers of the study of middle-aged women (ages twenty-five to fifty-four) of the late 1970s were organized in the analysis into four major groups, with two subgroups, by complexity of the household (Lopata, Barnewolt, and Harrison 1985; Lopata, Barnewolt, and Miller 1987). The managers of households containing only adults (husband, adult children, or both) had the most ambivalent feelings about that role. They did not see homemaking as a complex job and perceived more advantages to full-time employment and less to full-time homemaking than did any other homemakers (Lopata, Barnewolt, and Harrison 1987, 227). Two-thirds would prefer full-time jobs, but various circumstances prevent them from having one, and they have not actively sought employment of recent years. Those who are the most committed to the role of homemaker, rather than having just drifted into it, are the women in this category who had children at an early age or those in the early stage of becoming a homemaker who plan on adding children to the household in the near future.

Closest to the adults-only households are the single-parent households, whose managers would really like to get a job, especially if they are on public aid, but who do not have the resources to do so. Some of these women are widows, but the majority either never were, or are no longer, married. They lack the education, skills, day care, health care, and sufficient money to create a positive presentation of self to prospective employers, or even to enter a job search (Hartmann 1981). We had originally thought that these women have the most complex job as homemakers, since they lack the assistance of a husband/father. However, analyses of various aspects of their role indicate that a husband added to, rather than ameliorated, the burden of household management (see also Stack 1975). Homemakers in single-parent households were able to set their own work schedules and duties, not needing to build these around a man's presence (Lopata, Barnewolt, and Harrison 1987, 231). Their overall self-esteem is low, with little in their past to provide positive feedback. Most come from disadvantaged families. They are not especially happy over full-time homemaking and in general lack strong commitments to any role except that of mother.

Managers of households with small nuclear families (husband, wife, and one or two pre-adult children) tend to be white, to be the most educated, and to have had in the past the highest occupation of all the homemakers in our sample. Their family income is relatively low, mainly because the breadwinner is still young (Lopata, Barnewolt, and Harrison 1987, 235). Unlike the blue-collar women studied by Rosen (1987), they chose to give up the earnings of a job, feeling they could manage financially and that it was more important to stay home with the small children. They see the role of home-maker as above average in complexity and see few advantages to full-time employment. They often explain that involvement in full-time homemaking is temporary, since they plan to return to the labor force in the future. Thus, their relatively high commitment to the role of homemaker is based on their commitment to the role of mother. They rate themselves higher on the items combined into the self-esteem scale than do the other homemakers.

Managers of large nuclear households with a husband and more than two children are not in numbers as overwhelmingly white as those with fewer children. They do not see the role as complex, although they rank it high in opportunity for creativity, the chance to see the product of the work, and time for self-development. Thus, they have reached the full-house plateau level and mastered the tasks of homemaking. The younger the woman, the more commit-ted she is to this role. There is a negative association between this commitment and self-esteem along the leadership dimension.

Sociopsychological Aspects of Role Involvement

The women at even the height of involvement in the role of home-maker do not necessarily assign it equal importance in the role cluster; many situations contribute to its placement. For one, the role has shifted in salience in American society over the centuries, with the movement into, and then away from, the ideology of "true womanhood" (Cott 1977). The importance women assigned this role, even during the 1950s at the height of the feminine mystique era, reflected strong variations. Only a third of the Chicago-area women who were both homemakers and employees in my initial studies even mentioned it when asked in open-ended questions which roles were important to them (Lopata 1971b, 48). On the other hand, almost two-thirds of suburbanites referred to it—but then they were at the peak stage of the life cycle of that role and of the suburban revolution of the American dream of home ownership. However, when forced to make a choice among twelve social roles most often involving women, the Chicago-area respondents were able to separate wife and mother from homemaker and differed by social class in the rank assigned the last-named role (Lopata 1971b, 57). Some were home-focused, and product- rather than person-oriented. They wanted the home to look perfect by their standards, and were irritated by constant disruptions by other residents and their guests (Lopata 1971b, 60).

By the late 1970s, the home-oriented woman had pretty much vanished. The study of metropolitan Chicago women aged twenty-five to fifty-four included again a list of twelve roles, of which only the four most important were elicited (Lopata and Barnewolt 1984). Employees who were not married or had no children ignored the role of homemaker almost entirely (1 percent of 1,833 respondents listed it). In addition, only a tenth of the wives and mothers who did not hold a job outside of the home placed homemaker in one of the top ranks, while 9 percent of husbandless mothers did so (see also Luxton's 1980 study of three generations of homemakers).

In general, women who ranked homemaker as third or fourth in importance tended to have rich family-dimension involvements, which is not surprising. Those with many salient roles outside of the home were less oriented toward its management.

There are, of course, important social class variations in a woman's sociopsychological involvements in the role of homemaker. Lower-class women are often overcome by the never-ending round of work involved in maintaining a home and a family, without adequate resources, and with additional complications such as the unemployment or absence of a husband (Luxton 1980; Milkman 1979; Rubin 1976). Both socialization and structural limitations of the environment tend to produce a passive stance (Kohn 1977; Schooler et al. "Housework as Work," 1984), or lead such women to seek out solutions that make them appear passive to associates (Wittner 1990; Milkman 1979).

The *Occupation: Housewife* (Lopata 1971b) working-class respondents tended to perform the role repetitiously and reactively. When asked to explain the rhythm of their work, the least educated and poorest Chicago-area respondents described a continuous round, reflecting the old adage that a woman's work is never done (Strasser 1982). Middle-class women asked for qualifiers of time of year, week, family schedule, and the like. The upper-class homemakers studied by Ostrander (1985) and Daniels (1988) used the home as the showplace for their class position, in terms of its appearance and the complexity of activities carried forth in it or from it. A perfect example of the class influence on homemaking is contained in etiquette books for wives of military or colonial officers and protocol rules for wives of political heads. The hostess obligations of the American ambassador's wife, including especially those for official dinners, can be extremely complex. She must not only arrange for the dinner and what is to be served, but also train the servants so as to avoid all awkward situations, select the seating arrangement according to norms of protocol, and insure that conversations flow to involve everyone (Hochschild 1969).

> Since the ambassador's wife is much of the time either a hostess or a guest, and since much of her important work is performed in those roles, she finds that often she is stationary, either on her "turf" or on someone else's. There is not much time for walking around in public. Rather, in private places she is in public. (Hochschild 1969, 84)

There are two other aspects of involvement in the role of homemaker that have drawn increasing attention from social scientists: the sentiments felt about various features of the role, and the self-images of women involved in it at different levels.

Sentiments and Self-Images

As Shehan, Burg, and Rexroat point out (1986; see also Shehan 1984), "studies comparing the mental health and well-being of employed wives and housewives proliferated during the 1970s" in response to the increased participation of American women in the labor force. Most of these studies concluded that "employed wives have better psychological health than housewives." The frequency of depression among housewives is associated with the stage of the family life cycle and the number and ages of children. The larger the number of beneficiaries, and the more needful they are of her care, the more depressed the homemaker is apt to be when she does not have the necessary resources (Pearlin 1975). This is not surprising, from the vantage point of role strain theory. The woman in the rapidly expanding and full-house stages of homemaking can feel overwhelmed, especially since the roles of wife and mother require more than just the work of those roles. The early stages of homemaking include being tied down in the home, thus creating social isolation, which easily leads to depression (Shehan, Burg, and Rexroat 1986, 406).

An important aspect of a woman's satisfaction with this role, as with any other, is the fit between her expectations and reality (Ferree 1976 and 1980). Those women who purposely enter this role, voluntarily expand the beneficiary segment of the social circle, and feel that the assisting segment is meeting its obligations, tend to be satisfied with it; those who are disillusioned with major features of it are likely to feel depressed or angry (Lopata, Barnewolt, and Miller 1985; Warren 1987). The assumption that modern American homemakers are not satisfied is often connected by the media with the assumption that those who are involved in it full-time envy employed women and see their lives as being more glamorous and less confining than their own. Thus, satisfaction can be expected of homemakers when the society reinforces their decision to enter and remain in this role full-time, and dissatisfaction when it publicly rewards employed women.

One frequently sees mass-media stories about the defensive stance of women who are not in the labor force, unlike the 1950s and 1960s, when full-time homemaking was the preferred form of involvement. I had found the *Occupation: Housewife* (Lopata 1971b) respondents generally satisfied with this role, their level of satisfaction increasing with an increase in personal resources, such as education, and with instrumental resources, such as money. Friedan argued, however, in *The Feminine Mystique* (1963) this satisfaction may have been only a polite veneer, underneath which lay serious concern over "the problem that has no name"—that is, the feeling of confinement and lack of personal identity and development. The late 1970s homemakers in the *City Women* study felt much less confined by that role, unless they lacked the self-confidence to function outside of it. At the two extremes for full-time homemakers, thus, are the younger, modern women who choose that full-time involvement and those who feel trapped in it, wishing for alternatives but unable to go through the barriers they feel are surrounding them. In between are the homemakers who do not feel strongly enough to make in-or-out decisions, or who do not define the situation in such terms, moving more or less freely between various levels of involvement.

Ann Oakley's (1947b, 192) study of London housewives in the peak stage of that role also found many women dissatisfied with the work involved. They complained of monotony, a long working week, and loneliness, though they were pleased with their autonomy. Women with a history of high-status jobs were the most dissatisfied, as the various tasks connected with the role did not produce the same level of satisfaction as their former jobs had. Cooking and shopping were among the most liked activities, a sentiment found also among American homemakers (Lopata, Barnewolt and Miller

1985). Schooler and associates (Schooler et al., "Housework as Work," 1984; Schooler et al., "Work for the Household," 1984) found one of the distressing aspects about the role of homemaker to be "responsibility over things outside one's control." The fact that the role itself is not necessarily depressing—definable as only repetitious, monotonous, and demeaning—is evidenced by their conclusion that women who are ideationally flexible may choose to do substantively complex household tasks.

The literature on depression among homemakers led to the inclusion of a series of fifty-one items of areas of competence and generalized characteristics in the *City Women* interviews (Lopata, Barnewolt, and Miller 1985). In brief, we found that full-time homemakers expressed less strong, less positive identification with areas of competence connected with leadership qualities than did the employed women. The exception was among the younger and more educated women who saw themselves as only temporarily in the role of full-time homemaker and identified themselves as competent and successful. One can but speculate as to the reason other full-time homemakers do not give themselves higher competence scores. Women with high scores may be more apt to stay in or return to the labor force, or the full-time homemakers may feel that their lack of leadership qualities precludes satisfactory employment. On the other hand, we can easily conclude that the role of homemaker does not provide feedback, in looking-glass form, or self-evaluations that can lead to high self-esteem (Schooler et al., "Housework as Work," 1984a; Schooler et al., "Work for the Household," 1984; see also Rosenberg 1979).

The Homemaker and Her Home

Of great interest to symbolic interactionists are the constructions of reality within which people live, and these include the home and things within it (see also Duncan 1982, Csikszentmihalyi and Rochberg-Halton 1981). One change in the relation between the home and the homemaker since traditional times is that most young women can start out on their own, instead of living for extended periods of time in households managed by other women, such as mothers, mothers-in-law, or boarding-house managers. A household—that is, the unit living in a home—has become simplified, while the house's physical structures are more complex, with diversification of room functions among families that can afford it. For example, each child is expected to have her or his own room. However, the design of these homes has remained mainly the job of male architects, while women have been mainly able only to modify its interior or add features. Hayden (1981) predicts in *The Grand Domestic Revolution: A History of Feminist Designs for American Homes, Neighborhoods, and Cities* that this will change in the future (see also Ardener 1981).

The symbolism of "the American Dream" has traditionally contained a picture of home ownership, made possible for many after World War II by federal low-interest mortgages. The suburban respondents of the *Occupation: Housewife* study (Lopata 1971b, 178–81) felt that life was better than they had visualized as teenagers, mainly because they had not anticipated living in such nice surroundings. The home was a source of pleasure, security, and status. The working-class Levittowners were very much involved in their homes and yards, which they individuated with decorative features from the mass-production base. It was not suburbia per se that had a strong impact upon former urbanites, but home ownership:

> The single most important source of impact is undoubtedly the house, even though most of the changes it encouraged in the lives of Levittowners were intended [by the developers]. The house is both a physical structure and an owned property. . . . Modernity encouraged improved housekeeping methods and allowed a bit more space time for wives. (Gans 1967, 277)

P. Rossi (1955) speaks of the "mystery" of home ownership that pushes people in that direction, and the Polish Americans whom I studied (Lopata 1976b) worked very hard to obtain this symbol of permanence and status.

Part of reality construction is the perceived fit between the person and her surroundings. A woman is apt to dislike her home if she considers it below her as a symbol of status. She may then just bide her time until she can move to a home that is better by her standards, or try to change the one she has if such upgrading improves its fit in the neighborhood. We asked women in the 1990 exploratory study if the house they were in was their "dream home." Only about a tenth of the respondents replied yes; the others complained about size, location, and appearance, but explained that their present homes were all they could afford at the time. Those who were pleased had lived in other places before, and had house-hunted for a long time, or had had the house built to their specifications. Linking the home to one stage of life does not mean that leaving it is psychologically impossible:

> Yes! In some way it is [my dream house], but I have dreams of a bigger home. This is my first house, it is like my baby. I have furnished it and have made it our home. Everything inside the house is us, we both have put a lot of work into the house. (Twenty-five-year-old homemaker anticipating needs for more space in next stage of the role)

Another woman, however, not satisfied with her house and unable to leave for another due to financial constraints, kept adjusting it to meet her self-defined needs.

> It is not what I perceived to be the home I would live in this long. It was to be my starter home, but with each project it became more of our own. We have totally redecorated the interior and exterior of the home. We added additional rooms and made a larger expanse of living areas. We upgraded baths and kitchen. . . . I would like to add a first floor family room but this is not financially feasible. (Forty-seven year-old with a husband and six children living in the household)

Almost all of the home owners had changed something about their houses, starting with redecorating and including often considerable remodeling. Renters seldom do more than paint, feeling it to be a waste of time and money to individuate the place, even after years of residence.

The Homemaker as a Link between Home and Society

Looking at the homemaker from the woman's point of view, as Smith (1987), Glazer (1978), Bernard (1974 and 1981), and other feminists recommend, we find that she is not limited to a relatively isolated household, which other members are free to leave in order to enter roles in other institutions, while she waits for them to return to her hot soup and stroking support. Those homemakers who are committed to this role, at least temporarily, by choice rather than because of a lack of alternatives, tend to see themselves as centers of a complex social circle that reaches far beyond the confines of the home (Lopata, Barnewolt, and Harrison, 1987). Even in the midst of the feminine mystique period, women extended into the wider community in several ways. They interacted with suppliers of objects and services, they provided such to others, and they saw characteristics of life outside of the home that had their imprint. For example, they liked to dress up their children for outside events. The recent demands that their contributions be recognized by others in the public sphere have definitely been helped by the feminist movement, but the activities were there before. The importance of this work has been mainly invisible to the male world and even undervalued by the women themselves (Daniels 1988; Finch and Groves 1983; Glazer 1984 and 1988). For example, the Chicago-area women of the 1950s and 1960s studies utilized twenty-six services brought to the home and thirty-three services outside of the home (Lopata 1971b, 168–71). Over half had daily newspaper delivery, and many received local papers. Very few had a live-in maid, that service having long been gone from most American homes, although about a fourth employed a cleaning woman who came in periodically. The use of external services was complicated by the fact that women who did not have cars were limited to weekend ventures. The more affluent and more educated used a variety of services; the less privileged were more geographically limited, but they tended to go out to get supplies more often. In addition, the full-time homemakers in suburbs exchanged services and goods with neighbors. Many of the ways they served as connecting links between the home and society actually fell into the supportive functions of the roles of wife and mother. The economic and political spheres of life did little to make it easier for homemakers to function—the allegedly work-saving technology and the transportation-consumer-professional-service complex were not actually designed with them in mind (Cowan 1983; Lopata 1971b and 1980a). Although some effort is now being made by the public sphere to ease the homemaker's life, the 1950s required entrance into a tremendous variety of specialty stores, children in tow.

Homemakers frequently mention their contributions of work and products to organizations in the religious, educational, occupational, political, and combined institutions of the community. Such contributions are made by women of all social strata. Black homemakers often spend days preparing food for Sunday church affairs. Rummage sales, picnics of a variety of groups, gala events of women's auxiliaries of men's clubs, fund-raising socials for women's or school groups—all these activities are expected of homemakers in most communities. The work can take considerable time, but it also provides opportunities for interactions that continue to link the home with the outside world.

The homemakers also speak with pride of seeing the products of their work in public: their children nicely dressed for school, neighbors commenting on the festive holiday look of the home, church members congratulating them for a potluck dish (Ferree 1976 and 1980). Recent studies have documented just how dependent public life is upon the unpaid work of women who bridge not only the spheres but also the specialized and often segregated areas of each institution. Glazer (1984 and 1988) has devoted a number of years to the study of women's benefits to the economic institution and, recently, to health services (see also Weintraum and Bridges 1979). Galbraith emphasizes:

> The conversion of women into a crypto-servant class was an economic accomplishment of first importance. . . . If it were not for this service all forms of household consumption would be limited by the time required to manage such consumption—to select, transport, prepare, repair, maintain, clean, service, store, protect, and otherwise perform the tasks that are associated with the consumption of goods. (Galbraith 1973, 79; Lopata 1984, 162).

Socialist feminists of the 1970s repeatedly listed the contributions to capitalist economy made by the consumer, who is very often the woman (see Gerstel and Gross 1987b; Hensen and Philipson 1990). Pictures and news stories have documented the fact that the former Communist/socialist countries depended on (mainly) women to stand for hours in line waiting for household goods, such as meats, breads, and even toilet paper. Even buying services can take time (Weintraum and Bridges 1979). Involvement in consumption, health care, education, and religion requires efforts by the homemaker, in addition to persons who directly work in these institutions. Certainly many organizations have recently cut back on personal services to members of the society. The buyer economy supplied milk, vegetables, bread, and knife sharpening directly to the consumer. The rising costs of labor shrank the personal delivery system.

It is interesting to note that some of these changes have followed a circular path. First, the consumer, student, or patient was in the power of experts whose esoteric knowledge was accompanied by a license and a mandate to determine their fate (Haug and Sussman 1968; Hughes 1971; Lopata 1976a). Next, rather than depending upon the vendor, such as a store owner or delivery employee, to provide the "best products for the lowest price," the consumer in the homemaking role, with sufficient education and coached by experts in the media, became an expert and a comparative purchaser herself. Much of what has been written about the woman as consumer in the "consumption society" and the role of homemaker ignores the complexity of this activity, which requires a great deal of time and knowledge to define the needs of families and other beneficiaries, to study alternative means of satisfying them, to locate products and services, to obtain these, to bring them home, to convert them for personal use, and to store them (Berk and Berk 1979; Glazer 1984).

In the field of health, women are expected to ensure the prevention of illness in family members and others whom they are helping to care for, as well as nurse them during illness and the dying process. This includes medicines and other items, actual physical care, presence at times of need, transportation to health facilities, and the following of experts' prescriptions (Glazer 1988). Attempts to cut back on expenses by medical personnel have resulted in recent increases in demands upon women. They must perform extended duties as caregivers, reversing the trend of the past century or so during which the medical profession and allied fields increased control over, and care of, the health of the nation. Of course, the private sector never really stopped caring for the sick, but it had decreasing control over decisions. The control has remained with the medical profession, having been taken out of the hands of pregnant women, mothers, wives, daughters, friends, and neighbors, but an increasing amount of the work has returned into the laps of homemakers.

Time shortages for women who handle demanding jobs and manage households are evident in some of the new services that have sprung up in urban centers. Homemakers expand their social circles to include providers of fully cooked meals and clothing, carpeting, furniture, and other objects delivered to their homes (Bergman 1986). They can shop for goods using the television. We can expect this trend to expand in the future as more and more women earn sufficient money to consider it worthwhile to pay others sometimes sizable amounts of money to undertake tasks.[3]

The Modern Form of the Role of Homemaker

Two recent changes may be contributing to an increase in the status of homemakers in modern times: One is the new recognition of the contributions they make to the functioning of society; the other is the realization of how complex and necessary their work is, even when it is compressed into "the second shift" (Hochschild 1989). Feminist social scientists have begun to reexamine the dependence of capitalist (and socialist) societies upon the activities and relationships of the homemaker (Daniels 1988; Glazer 1984; Glazer et al. 1979; Seccombe 1974). They join Galbraith (1973) in pointing to the importance of the work the homemakers do as "crypto-servants" or "servants" to capitalism— work that was previously or alternatively carried forth by paid workers (Eisenstein 1979; Glazer 1980). Various economists and related scholars have attempted to estimate the monetary value of the work involved in the role. Although such estimates diminish nonmonetary activity, they establish its importance in American eyes (Glazer 1978; Pyun 1972). The largely unsuccessful attempts, by the homemaker who also carries a paid job, to change the role and to increase the contributions of others to the maintenance of the home have also drawn attention to the role's complexity.

The difficulties experienced by social scientists trying to place the homemaker role in the occupational status structure have also drawn attention to the great heterogeneity of the ways it is carried forth (Bose 1980; Nilson 1978). The transitional evaluation of the status of the homemaker as dependent upon the status of the husband ignores her role involvements. Yet there has been a connection, at least in the transitional two-person-single-career past, between the complexity of the role of homemaker and the husband's occupation.

The modern homemaker has attempted to carry out this role with great flexibility, and her negotiations for cooperation from circle members have varied with her needs. These needs are adjusted to her other roles as well as those of circle members. Thus, she may become a full-time homemaker when involved full-time in the role of mother, shifting into part-time involvement as she returns to greater participation in outside roles, converting beneficiaries into joint managers and increasing contributions of suppliers.

Of course, the expanding cost of housing in modern America makes it more difficult for women to identify the role of homemaker with the ownership of a home that is her own and that she can modify to fit her needs. This may combine with other changes, such as an increased focus on external roles, to further decrease the importance of this role.

Summary

We have now examined the complexities inherent in the role of homemaker in transitional and modern American society. The role is entered into by the woman when she becomes a manager of a household and pulls together a social circle of beneficiaries, assistants, and suppliers. It is a very indeterminate role; it has no defined boundaries or standards of performance, although extremes are commented upon by participants and observers. Women do not generally prepare for this role. They pick up some knowledge from observation and by helping in the home of their families of orientation, and they count on their ability to learn on the job. Numerous experts are available, mainly in the mass media, to guide them in becoming homemakers and through the various stages. The household of modern times contains relatively few live-in beneficiaries. New products, services, and technologies may introduce greater variation in performance than was previously true of homemakers of different social classes.

Women also vary considerably as to the social psychological aspects of their involvement in the role of homemaker. Those with a rich family dimension in their social life space tend to regard it as more important than do those with a fuller involvement in other or multiple dimensions. Many aspects of the role are not sources of satisfaction, although seeing the product of the labor can be. The negotiation that is a constant part of this, as of any role, can be a source of pleasure or a constant irritant. A major problem on the current scene is the attempt by many women to change relationships with beneficiaries, getting them to move closer to the assistants' segment of the social circle. These beneficiaries tend to resist, expecting the wife/mother/homemaker to carry forth the duties of the role as performed during the feminine mystique days by their mothers and grandmothers.

The work of the homemaker extends beyond the home and the family, as people benefit from her services and the products she has created. It extends to life in other institutions. Although the role has faced many periods of being downgraded in importance, it seems to have survived and may be increasing in public opinion as the difficulties of managing a home and the invisible work of homemakers become more apparent.

The increasing refusal of women to carry all the burden of the duties of the homemaker role, with few rights, while also contributing to the breadwinning activity that makes possible the operation of the home, family, and community, will certainly introduce more modern variations of the role. The fact is that most women are not in highly demanding stages of the role course and that the number and needs of beneficiaries have decreased. For many women, this role can be a part-time involvement. The conflicts and concern expressed in the mass media really focus upon the woman who is combining full-time homemaking with the peak stages of the roles of wife, mother, and jobholder. This covers a relatively short period of time for most modern women. Those with limited resources are still having a hard time managing complex households. Those above the level of poverty or restricted assistance are finding greater expansion of the role into societal life, forming a link between the home and the beneficiaries, on the one side, and resources, on the other side.

6

The Job: Settings and Circles

Much work in modern societies has been organized into jobs, with specified qualifications, as well as duties and rights, for the social person and the members of the social circle. The universal characteristics of jobs include these: The worker is hired by an employing organization (or is self-employed) because she or he meets the desired criteria to perform specific tasks and relational duties in a usually predesignated social circle, and the worker is paid for job-related work and can be fired if she or he does not satisfy the requirements (or the worker can leave voluntarily). All jobs have specified locations or settings, whether within a limited space (e.g., behind a counter) or scattered (e.g., among offices of clients and any combination of locales in between). Whatever formal duties and rights tie the social person and circle members together in the role, no work organization can function without a complex informal system of interaction involving the cooperation of all.

We must also remember that not all work is organized into jobs, so that it is necessary to examine carefully not only what a person is doing at any time, but also her social relations, to determine if the interaction is part of a job or part of another type of social role. For example, much of the work done by wives or mothers, volunteers or homemakers, could be restructured into paying jobs, but the social relationships would be different. For instance, some of the actions of a wife are similar to those of a call girl. The logic of this separation is lost on people who speak of a mother's "going to work," when they mean that she has taken a job, as if the role of mother did not involve work.

Jobs contain not only tasks, which are evaluated by the U.S. Department of Labor by degree of complexity, but also sets of relations, since they are true social roles (see Kohn and Schooler 1983 and related papers).[1] The tendency to see only visible tasks, or technical job descriptions, especially in less prestigeful occupations, contributes to much of the simplistic evaluation of so many jobs. A perfect example of this is the role of cocktail waitress (Spradley and Mann 1975) in a male-dominated bar, who must negotiate and play games with customers and bartenders in order to accomplish the simple tasks of transmitting orders for drinks and delivering the drinks (see Harragan 1977, *Games Mother Never Taught You: Corporate Gamesmanship for Women,* for games at another occupational level). The Department of Labor's (1977) classification scheme determines whether the major focus of a job is work with data, people, or things and then evaluates the complexity with which these are manipulated. It has been the consistent thesis of this book that all jobs, like all social roles, involve at least some complexity of dealing with people, some negotiated interaction with circle members, which is often not recognized by the Department of Labor.

Since we cannot meaningfully examine many occupations in a book devoted to a variety of women's roles, we will concentrate on two main sets of characteristics of jobs that have a major influence upon women's relations. The first of these focuses on the role aspects (social person, circle, duties, and rights) of all employees. The second is the influence of the setting upon such relations (see also Pavalko 1988). Of course, locales also vary by many other factors, but what appears especially significant is the "ownership" of that locale, be it a bench, truck, office, or whole factory within which the role must be negotiated. Control over the space within which the job is carried forth provides at least some control over the rights and duties of the workers. Other characteristics of the setting, such as its "jointness" and boundaries, accessibility, and distribution of circle members, are important. All these factors influence the amount of control an employer, associate, or beneficiary has over the worker's independence and autonomy, the ease of working with others and of obtaining resources, access from outsiders, and rights. Let us first examine the role of employee in general, then focus on jobs in different settings.

The Entrepreneurial or Self-Employed Woman

One of the ideals of the American business community has been independent ownership. Whether offering a product or a service, the self-employed businesswoman organizes her own job with more or less freedom, pulling together a social circle, defining rights and duties. Constraints, of course, abound even for the self-employed, coming from the technical or relational aspects of the job (see the chapters in Lopata 1990). Governments at all levels promulgate laws and demand payment in the form of taxes. Beneficiaries, assistants, and suppliers must constantly be negotiated with, and the amount of control each segment has over the job varies considerably. The most autonomous is the individual professional, such as a psychiatrist, who operates from her own home or office.[2] Beneficiaries come to her because they need the service, acknowledge her superior control of esoteric knowledge, and grant her many rights, including a right to high payment. Other beneficiaries can have greater control, as do restaurants contracting for certain homemade meals, or women seeking the service of a beautician. Colleagues and co-workers make their own demands, such as conformity to a code of ethics, while employees must be supplied resources and paid.

Enterprising women (Bird 1976) have always managed to create their own businesses. Wives of whalers or traders who were gone for extended periods developed businesses of their own throughout American history. Widows often organized services or served as middle persons between producers and consumers (Christensen 1987b). There has been a recent regeneration of such activity, as more educated women, caught between their interest in economic independence and the rigidity of the occupational system, have organized their own businesses, with greater choice of activity, social circle, time, and space. A report that a high proportion of women with Harvard MBAs had dropped out of the corporate world within a few years led to studies of where they had gone—and the answer was not to full-time homemaking, but to companies they formed themselves (Kleiman 1986, 10). The Small Business Administration estimates that "the number of self-employed women in the United States grew 74 percent between 1974 and 1984" (Kleiman 1986, 10).

Many entrepreneurs start out working from the home or a small rented or privately owned shop or office. Beauticians and solo professionals like physicians, psychologists, lawyers, architects, artists, social workers, and music or other specialized teachers provide services. Others create objects to be sold within the home or to external businesses. Typical of modern times are catering, baking, or gourmet cooking establishments providing foodstuffs to private households or restaurants (see also Foerstner 1987). Shops specializing in antiques or other objects are often located in homes or communities of similar businesses. The beneficiaries might either come to the home for the service or goods or deal with an intermediary and never even interact with the producer. Suppliers also come to the businesswoman, or she goes out to fetch them herself (Christensen 1987c). Assistants can be hired from the outside, or household members can be used, with varying degrees of formality in the relationship.

As in the case of home-based employees, entrepreneurs working out of the home face problems if this is also the major setting for other roles. Boundaries between the job and those roles are not easily maintained (Christensen 1988a and 1988d). Frustration and anger are common among people who try working on nonhousehold (or even household) tasks in a home containing other people with whom other roles are shared, as any writer, artist, or academic will testify. Role conflict experienced by women in such circumstances is even greater than that of men, since the former are expected to take care of all home-related matters first, with no one to protect them from impingement by family roles (Beach 1989; Christensen 1988d). Women are expected to organize space, time, and their own behavior around a home-based husband, but the same rights do not seem to be guaranteed to the home-based woman worker who is also a wife, mother, daughter, neighbor, friend, community activist, and so forth.

Some businesses that start out on a home base grow sufficiently large or complex to require separate space, an office or a factory. A special variety are family-owned businesses headed by women. There are two ways in which a woman can own her business besides starting and building one herself: She can inherit it, usually after the death of her husband or father, or she can buy one started by others. Although Ward (1987) finds that 90 percent of American businesses are family owned, started after World War II, and with a still-living founder, almost inevitably a male, he makes no reference to women owners. A major problem of such businesses is family succession, because founders often do not train replacements and have trouble letting go of the firm, especially to a relative (Danco 1982). There are cases of widows running the business founded by their late husbands, although Danco (1982) does not consider this a good practice; he claims that few women are able to understand the complexities of a firm in its final form, even if they were originally involved in it, and even if it originated in the home. In this claim he reflects many of the attitudes of traditional businessmen. Daughters are only recently written up by the mass media as inheriting management of family businesses. Such a situation is still unusual, and there are reports of strain, even conflict, with circle members accustomed to working for the male founder. Traditional businesses do not approve of women in power (see Lopata, Miller and Barnewolt 1986 for some studies of such attitudes).

The most frequently given example of a very successful company founded and run by a woman who hired family members, including two sons, is Mary Kay Cosmetics. Acceptance by the business community is easier to get if the firm is stereotyped as appropriate for women. Some of the successful women business owners have formed a nationwide association.

Working for Someone Else: The Role of Employee

A person looking for a job and an established social circle wishing to fill a vacancy must find ways of coming together. Modern societies have developed complex methods for accomplishing this, including state and private employment agencies, interviewers who come to schools, and "headhunters" or executive search firms. These use allegedly rational methods to test and fit people to jobs and organizations. A frequent method, less costly to the employer, is that of placing advertisements in mass media with a readership likely to include potential candidates. Vacancies can also be filled by word of mouth—people already working in companies letting others know of openings. There are two problems with that method. In the first place, it limits the job seeker to people she knows, who are apt to be in traditional occupations. Since most women are still secretaries, lower-grade teachers, nurses or nurses aides, and so forth, friends and acquaintances are apt to provide information about positions of the same gender-segregated type. On the other hand, good jobs can also be learned about in this manner, as when a woman executive in a corporation brings in her friends, similar to the way the "old boy" network has always worked. Thus, the use of friends is an advantage for the job seeker at a high occupational level, while it can be a limiting factor for the job seeker at a more limited level. The other problem with using personal channels is the illegality of the word-of-mouth vacancy information system in modern times. All positions must now be advertised openly to prevent discrimination against minorities and women. Of course, the methods of matching jobs and persons are seldom as rational as alleged, and they vary considerably by occupation and employer.

Job-search procedures are influenced, of course, by a woman's knowledge of the labor market and by what kind of job she thinks she would be able to get, as well as by her wishes for certain characteristics of jobs, such as location. Socialization and education usually provide knowledge as to the kind of job she would like and the kind of organization she would like to be involved with and that is likely to accept her. Women who seek out jobs in male-dominated occupations usually have a prior connection, through relatives, friends, or co-workers (see Hareven and Langenbach 1978 and Cavendish 1982 on factory jobs; Lembright and Riemer 1982 on long-distance trucking; Walshok 1981 on women in crafts; and Epstein 1983 on lawyers). Schools often encourage preparation for traditional female jobs, perpetuating gender segregation in spite of mass publicity about recent changes.

Of course, many a woman job seeker never considers, or is considered for, most jobs. The doubly disadvantaged are women of color in the U.S. labor force (Smith and Tienda 1988). That category usually includes black, American Indian, Hispanic, and Asian women. Although women of employment age, regardless of race, are least apt to be in the labor force when they have small children, single mothers are often pushed into jobs for economic reasons, and more of these are of minority than dominant groups. Women of color, however, still have a long way to go to reach equality in the American labor force with white women, and certainly with white men, as far as occupation and earnings are concerned (Smith and Tienda

1988, 78). The failure of many women of color to break out of minority-female occupations, enabling first horizontal and then upward mobility, is also documented for California Chicano and Mexican immigrant women by Segura (1989) and regarding the professions, for black women by Sokoloff (1988). On the other hand, an "enormous decline in their overrepresentation in female-dominated professions" was experienced by white women in the years between 1960 and 1980 (Sokoloff 1988, 47).

The hiring procedures and the hierarchy of qualifications by which the person and the job are matched vary considerably by the main location of the work. A woman hired as a receptionist in an office of high-status architects may need mainly "good looks" (often including "acceptable" skin color) and good clothing, a "friendly," poised manner, a certain quality of voice, and the gatekeeping ability to distinguish acceptable from unacceptable visitors (Stone 1962 and 1981). On the other hand, a woman hired for a telecommuting job operating from her home needs only relevant skills and physical ability to perform the tasks well and on time; her appearance is irrelevant. Allegedly a physician's appearance within norms of propriety (usually defined in upper-middle-class manner, according to Bucher and Stelling 1977), is less important than her proven ability to take care of patients and coopcrate with colleagues and service suppliers. As Hughes (1971) noted a long time ago, the fact that physicians have traditionally been men may interfere with a woman's attempt to pull together a social circle (see also Lorber 1984 and Walsh 1977). The gender, racial, age, and other characteristics that an employer finds acceptable in a candidate are affected by the distribution of such among circle members: administrators, colleagues, and clients (Epstein 1988).[3] The history of hiring for different jobs is replete with selection processes that focus on who can be "trusted—i.e., persons of the same gender, race, age, and so forth as those doing the hiring—and only lawsuits or governmental action have forced change in cases of gross discrimination (Kanter 1977). America has been halfhearted in administrating antidiscrimination laws.

Sex segregation of jobs in America, and elsewhere for that matter, is definitely a phenomenon that is resisting change (Hartmann 1990). For example, Cavendish (1982) observed when working in a factory in Britain that all the women were in stationary positions on the assembly line, while men had superior positions and rights of mobility. In fact, a week before the Equal Pay Act became law, everyone was shunted around so all the assembly line workers would be women, and all the supervisors and higher grades would be men, and they wouldn't have to pay higher rates to women. (P. 78)

Epstein (1988) and Reskin and Hartmann (1986) summarize explanations of barriers to the entrance of women into some occupations that leave them mainly in jobs and positions with inferior levels of pay, career line, autonomy, and other rights. These include theories that "blame the victim," explanations that women are biologically, or through socialization, unwilling and unable to take high-commitment and skill/knowledge jobs. Freudians, who influenced American culture to a large extent, claim that "biology is destiny" and that women are created mainly for reproduction, so that they should not be involved in competing roles (Epstein 1983, 198; see a strong statement of this position in Deutsch 1944). Others see women as unwilling to invest in their "human capital" or in extensive occupational preparation. Most researchers and theoreticians, however, look to structural and historical factors in order to understand sex discrimination and segregation in the world of paid work. Barriers they see include those to training and entrance opportunities, employer "taste" for workers who will fit into the ongoing system and who fight "reverse discrimination," the history of a dual economy that has relegated women to the peripheral labor market and sex-labeled jobs that make it difficult for all involved to imagine women in other occupations, and many other formal and informal institutional processes.

There are many cultural beliefs about gender and work that make choice of nontraditional jobs, or even employment in general, difficult for American women (Reskin and Hartmann 1986). These are based on the strongly held assumption that there are innate psychological differences between the genders, including that women are "too good" for politics and the "dirty, competitive" world of business and production, and that male-female relationships are inevitably reduced to sexual encounters. Even legal barriers to full employment still exist, founded on the protective laws of 1974, which are often used to justify discrimination. Some of these have just recently been rejected by the U.S. Supreme Court. People advantaged by the existing system simply do not want to lose benefits. Male workers in male-dominated and male-intensive occupations, whose egos are founded on a chauvinistic view of their work, do not want "inferiors," be they women or members of racial and cultural minorities, entering, for fear of losing prestige and many other benefits. Clients of organizations of "experts," such as management consultants, lawyers, or doctors, do not want social inferiors to tell them what to do; at least managers of such groups claim this to be the situation when they refuse to hire a woman or black (Kanter 1977; Lopata, Miller, and Barnewolt, 1986).

Regardless of how well a person prepares for a prospective job through education, formal job training, and anticipatory socialization, on-the-job training is always necessary. This may be provided through secondary sources, but most jobs involve direct contact with circle members who precede the person at the location. It is here that many of the discriminatory practices are employed by superiors or co-workers. Social circle members, such as supervisors or co-workers, may refuse to provide the information necessary for adequate performance of duties and receipt of rights, as numerous studies have documented (e.g., Walshok 1981 and Schroedel 1985 for manual workers; Jurik 1985 for female correction officers; Epstein 1970 and 1983 for professionals; and Kanter 1977 or Harragan 1977 for management).

The size, complexity, and composition of social circles of jobholders vary considerably, the layers of closeness often being influenced not only by location and the size of the total organization, but also by the importance of the job to the organization and by the presence of intermediaries, such as the assisting staff surrounding the social person. Beneficiaries may be so removed from the person that no direct interaction takes place, or they can be so scattered that the person is the only representative of the company to have face-to-face contact with each. The latter is the case with traveling salespersons. Beneficiaries may enter a territory within which a whole assisting staff is present and forms an interacting network, as does a patient of a doctor in a hospital.

A good indicator of how a woman can define her relationship with circle members on the job is whom she considers to be the main beneficiaries of her service (Lopata, Barnewolt, and Miller 1985). An equal proportion of *City Women* respondents selected their employing company, or the bosses' customers, and their own "customers, clients, patients, or students." Identification with people who benefit from one's work is certainly different when the benefit is seen as direct ("my client . . .") rather than indirect (as the responsibility of the employer).

Although the beneficiary of a product or service can be quite depersonalized, the reference group, consisting of people whose judgment of performance is important, is usually much more specific. This was true of the *City Women* responses, the supervisor's judgment of performance being the most frequently listed by workers directly under the control of such a member of the organization (Lopata, Barnewolt, and Miller 1985). The judgment of co-workers and customers was important in this regard to only about a tenth of the respondents. Over a quarter of the women listed their own judgment of work performance as the judgment they respected the most. These differences are really significant, and one can imagine a woman's concern over the judgment of her work by these different people. Variations by occupations are interesting. For example, teachers consider their students as their main beneficiaries, but colleagues (other teachers) as their reference group. The claim that the beneficiary does not have the right to judge the performance has been a major point in the development of professionalization. Professionals reserve that right for themselves and their peers. This illustration also reemphasizes the importance of seeing the social role as involving a social circle with interacting segments rather than with isolated parts of a role set, à la Merton (1957a and 1957b).

Regardless of who is the beneficiary of an occupational role, the salaried or wage-earning worker has a definite package of duties and rights, often controlled by a complex administration, in relations with the employer. These include being in the assigned place during the designated or agreed-upon time period. The number and timing of hours of work have been the subject of strong dispute between employer and employee, assisted by unions and, finally, by governmental decrees (Steinberg 1982). The employee must fulfill her contract concerning her work, within the confines of the resources, including other people's performing their jobs and providing the social person her rights.

The employer must not only pay for the work, but must provide necessary resources, another subject of conflict between labor and management. If a worker who sews at the factory does not bring her own equipment and material, then these must be provided. The resources allegedly include environmental features and adequately trained, cooperative assistants and other circle members of adequate number. Either safety, comfortable working conditions, and so forth must be supplied, or the worker must agree to work under the conditions that exist. Unfortunately, as the history of work for women, and in many cases for working-class men, shows, businesses and even governmental agencies have failed to supply their workers with environments that are sufficiently safe and comfortable, resulting in serious accidents, illness, and even death. Many unions have been male-dominated and ignored problems raised by their women members, and many women work in settings with no union supervision (Kessler-Harris 1982; O'Farrell 1988; Schroedel 1985; see also Armstrong 1982).

Since employers have not voluntarily given up control over conditions and benefits, as Edwards documents in *Contested Terrain: The Transformation of the Workplace in the Twentieth Century* (1979), and unions have often been too weak or unwilling to confront the system, frequently the only resource for women fighting injustice is the government. However, a vast literature documents the failure of many states to prevent exploitation of workers. Some do not wish to interfere with the business sector or pass laws they do not have the strength or desire to enforce. The competitiveness of capitalism, or the benefits derived by the power elite in any other economic system, combine to create a history of exploitation of employees. Thus, the only alternative for a worker may be to quit a dangerous job and thus be deprived of its benefits, meager as they may be. Labor turnover is often simply a form of protest by workers fed up with inadequate resources and rewards.

The social circle of an employee may, and in fact often does, contain people who are not part of the employer's organization. They can be the beneficiaries, as is true of diners served by waitresses, clients by social workers, or patients by physicians. In other cases they can be colleagues, as among university scholars and scientists who consider others in similar jobs all over the world as people with whom to share ideas. Even assistants do not need to be in the same organization, and suppliers of goods and services usually come in from the outside. A worker who is attached to a particular setting must have some means of transportation of goods to and from her, while a mobile worker must have permission to enter the territory of others. Of course, the fact that segments of the social circle can be outside the authority of the employer or the jobholder makes more complex the negotiations, unless the common denominator of money balances duties and rights.

Sociopsychological Aspects of Role Involvement

One of the problems facing employers is employee "loyalty" or commitment to the job and all its components, and/or to the organization. The extensive literature on job training, motivation, satisfaction, and so forth comes from two directions: externally from economics and the social sciences, and internally from divisions of the organization whose function it is to hire the "right person," to provide prior or on-the-job training, and to keep workers. Our *City Women* study of the changing commitments of women to work and family roles utilized a career commitment scale, which proved discriminating among the employees along predictable dimensions (Lopata 1993c). Defining commitment in terms of the "side bets" a woman makes to insure continued involvement and a minimum of role conflict, à la Becker (1960), we find that the women most committed to their jobs undertook a long socialization and preparation period early in life or after involvement in an unsatisfactory job, rank the job as important in the role cluster, consider the job as complex and are pleased by this, see themselves as leaders and successful women, and tend to associate with others like themselves. In addition, often they are not married—ever or any more—and are without small children. They earn more than most of the Chicago sample, although we do not know if their commitment is a consequence of or a cause for that level of reward. They are in higher-status jobs, as sales agents, managers, and professionals.

In general, the greater the perceived complexity of the occupation, and the higher its objective status in the occupational structure, the higher the women's commitment (Lopata 1993c; see also all the relevant work of Kohn and Schooler 1983). Salesclerks, who often prepared for better jobs and held such in the past, are not highly committed. On the other hand, nurse aides who come from lower socioeconomic backgrounds and have little status or pay feel that they have been trained for the job and socialized into the ideology of the medical profession sufficiently, so that they consider themselves as performing very important work of high benefit to the patients. Their inability to retain a job for long periods of time is almost entirely due to external circumstances over which they feel they have no control. Clerical jobs vary in complexity and prestige within a company, from file clerks to executive secretaries, and the commitment scores reflect this. Another interesting finding is that professionals in "object-focused" jobs, such as statisticians, drafts-women, designers, and so forth, do not possess high commitment scores, while those who deal with people, such as personnel and labor relations workers, clergy, reporters, counselors, and so forth, are highly committed. Of course, commitment to an occupation or a career line may not be translated into commitment to an employer.

All employees find some aspects of their jobs more enjoyable than others, because of either the tasks or the relations with a segment of the circle. Irritating interaction with someone important to the job can ruin one's enjoyment of the job, as reported by most of the women in the trades interviewed by Schroedel (1985). Joanne Miller and associates (1980) explain some of the sociopsychological effects of occupational conditions, confirming the fact that women, as much as men, wish autonomy in their jobs, although they appear somewhat less concerned with mobility. McIlwee (1982. 315) found women in the first year of work in nontraditional jobs satisfied with mastering traditionally male-labeled skills, with intellectual and physical challenge, with help and support from some of their male co-workers, with the pay, with anticipated advancement, and with the prestige of holding such jobs. The intrinsic aspects of the work predominated as sources of satisfaction during the second year, and social relationships were reported as having improved. Of course, these are the women who survived all the hassles experienced early in their involvement in male-dominated settings. Women in female-intensive jobs report a lack of hassles, positive relations with others, security, and confidence in their ability to do the job, if detracting factors are not overwhelming (Lopata, Miller, and Barnewolt 1986).

The fact that outside observers may evaluate a job in terms of only its tasks, rather than its social role components, can lead to assumptions of inevitable alienation in many occupations. This leads to questions like Hobson's "Gender Differences in Job Satisfaction: Why Aren't Women More Dissatisfied?" (Hobson 1989). Hobson states that although most women's jobs are inferior in many respects to those of men, the holders express greater satisfaction. One of his tentative explanations is that women use different standards to compare their jobs to those of others. Another is that they focus on different aspects of work for satisfaction than do men (Hobson 1989, 385). However, he ignores the possibility that they see the job in role rather than task terms, while men concentrate on the tasks. Our study of city women in midlife indicates that his first assumption is realistic, since most women did not know enough about jobs from which they were excluded to use them in comparison to their own, judging mainly in terms of jobs similar enough to their own to be visible to their imagination in role-taking terms (Lopata, Barnewolt, and Miller 1985). Thus, our respondents saw their jobs as more complex than the "average job," often contradicting the complexity measures of the *Dictionary of Occupational Titles* (U.S. Department of Labor 1965 and 1977; see more-detailed analyses in Lopata et al., "Job Complexity," 1985). The main reason for this was their perception of the role in terms of the complexities of social relationships. Even the worker in the xeroxing center of a university may see herself as a center of a hub, negotiating priorities. Other studies of women's job satisfaction in different occupations show the importance of perceived complexity and selective job conditions (Miller 1980; Miller et al. 1980).

There are two ways of leaving a job: quitting, or being fired or released. The initiative comes from the worker or the employer. The second aspect of leaving is the direction of movement. One can search for, or be offered, another job, or withdraw from the labor force entirely. Many reasons force or encourage a person toward the latter action, the most typical for women being the desire to focus on other roles or retirement. Historically, women left paid employment to marry, or with the first pregnancy. Employer policies for occupations such as teacher or stewardess used to force women out at these events, and even now class-action suits appear in front of American courts claiming discrimination on such grounds. Women leave their jobs in ever-changing proportions and compositions of the female labor force, with or without pay or guarantee of return, as a result of pregnancy or to care full-time for small children. In the past such women did not return to regular employment except out of financial need, but the probability is now very high that they will.

Of recent interest to economists and sociologists has been the retirement of women with extensive labor force careers (see mainly Szinovacz 1982 and 1989). Previous comments on the effects of retirement on women focused on the husband's leaving his job.

Let us now look at the varieties of work settings by the type of ownership of the territory, ranging from home-based work for pay, to jobs taking the person into the territory of the beneficiary, or to bureaucratically controlled locales such as factories, offices, and multiple settings.

Settings: Home-Based Work

Throughout human history, work has been a bridge between the home and the external world. This holds true also for much of the work now organized into jobs in the formal economic market. By the seventeenth century, Europe had already witnessed the creation of many jobs away from the home, although domestic production has continued into modern times (Boserup 1970). Home production for exchange or for sale involves the whole family, and the role of the paid worker is hard to separate from the roles of homemaker, wife, and mother. The division of labor and assignment of raw material, tools, space, and contributions of others often remained the same for products used at home and those taken out for sale (Clark [1919] 1968). Women organized work groups in the home for the production of crafts or foodstuffs, or the provision of services, such as laundry, and the unit as a whole received the rewards, to be used for its welfare (Boserup 1970). Most job-related work connected with the formal system is different, in that each worker is treated as an individual unit, to be hired, located in the work group, and rewarded for her or his specific contribution.

Early industrialization in England involved the "cottage industry," or "putting out" system. One member of the family would usually go to a central locale to collect the material and bring it back, and then return the finished product (Lopata, Miller, and Barnewolt 1986). Pay was by product, not by worker or hours. Sometimes a middleman (usually a man) delivered to, and picked up from, the home. The introduction of factories did not stop the need for services and goods carried forth in the home. For example, wet-nursing of children of women employed in factories existed in France up until World War I. Customized sewing continues to take place at the home of the seamstress or the customer.

An interesting variation in the history of human production has been the somewhat isolated household operating with relative self-sufficiency, such as farms in the American westward-moving frontier (Pavalko 1988, 174–76). Such a farm required the cooperative work of the whole household, and contact with suppliers was minimal compared to urban households. Special projects required help from neighboring or transitory workers. Flying over the United States, one can still see otherwise isolated farms that are connected to the outside world by roads and to the mass media by television antennas.

Machinery driven by a single farmer has now replaced many farm workers, in contrast to most of the rest of the world where fields are still seasonally populated with laborers of all ages and both genders.

Although the increasing dependence in the world system upon jobs carried forth in places and organizations away from home underemphasizes and undervalues paid work carried forth in the household, that part of economic production contributes in varying proportion to the gross national product. In fact, it is receiving more attention at the present time, with the use of new technologies and entrepreneurial activity for the development of home-based objects and services. Toffler focused on "the electronic cottage" in *The Third Wave* (1981). Due to their own inflexibility, modern corporations have not moved as fast as Toffler predicted they would to develop telecommuting jobs, in which the employee uses electronic means to carry forth her work at a location external to the corporation (Costello 1988, 137). A 1989 *Newsweek* article, "Escape from the Office: High-Tech Tools Spur a Work-at-Home Revolt," also claims that this is the wave of the future, but adds that it is not a major trend at the present because many managers do not trust workers they cannot see (Schwartz and Tsiantar 1989, 59). Some businesses have experimented with supplementary telecommuting work of full-time employees, others with farming out work to self-employed contractors.

Millions of American women, unwilling to conform to the time and energy commitments of the male-based model of jobs at various stages of the life course, have begun to enter home-based paid work that reproduces the "putting out" system of cottage industries, and that of entrepreneurial activity of their own initiative (Christensen 1988c and 1988d). The article in *Newsweek* claimed that the office-at-home market is worth $5.7 billion (Schwartz and Tsiantar 1989, 58), and it has been estimated that 24.9 million people worked at home in 1988 (Holbert 1988). These figures, of course, included both men and women and both entrepreneurial and employee jobs. The latter kind of home-based worker is described by Hope, Kennedy, and de Winter (1976) as

> a person who is employed directly by a firm or by an intermediary or agent of a firm to carry out work in his or her own home, not directly under the control or management of that employer. (P. 88)

Home-based paid workers differ greatly, depending on the type of work and relations to the employer, but they function mainly as a "reserve army" to be used when the employer wishes to call for their work (Milkman 1979). The least advantageous or most exploitive is manual work, as in the garment industry; paid for by product, the employer not even covering such costs as electricity, heat, or damaged goods (Kessler-Harris 1982; Stansell 1986). The employees usually do not receive benefits such as health insurance, paid vacations, maternity leaves, or pensions. They are dependent upon the employer for work, which is often seasonal, always undependable, and invariably underpaid (Allen and Wolkowitz 1987; Brown 1982; Milkman 1979). They are isolated from other circle members of the employer's organization. The power of determining who works when is entirely in the hands of the employer.

Paid home-based work has elicited a great deal of criticism and many attempts to control it throughout American history. Interestingly enough, laws passed to prevent exploitation in the sweatshop types of home-based industries are now actually interfering with the independent entrepreneurial activity (Kleiman 1988). Not only the worker and her household, but also the neighbors, may be disturbed by home-based work. Many communities have passed zoning ordinances relating to people making a living by working at home (Butler 1988). Most of the ordinances are a result of complaints from neighbors about traffic, noise, odors, garbage, fire hazards, advertising signs or other visible demonstrations of the work. In order to satisfy communities, ordinances define home occupations in residential areas, restrict some and regulate conditions under which others may operate, as well as include enforcement procedures (Butler 1988, 192).

Although working conditions can be better for secretaries and others connected by home computer to the organization, the absence of external controls on the employee prevents many organizations from venturing in this direction. There are two types of home-based work in the white-collar domain. One is supplemental, or overflow, work that a regular jobholder occasionally takes home. The other is similar to manual work, in that independent, self-employed workers always work at home, never being located in the employer's office (Kraut 1988; Gerson and Kraut 1988). Such women can do all their work for one employer, in which case they tend to have higher benefits and work assurance, or have arrangements with more than one employer, which can result in a precarious ebb and flow of assignments.

Independent contracting, whether called "freelancing," "consulting," or "telecommuting," has its own variations. Christensen (1988b) found

> that nearly two-thirds of both manufacturing and nonmanufacturing
> firms reported relying on production or administrative support con-
> tracts in 1985. (P. 79)

Involuntary contractors are members of marginal economic groups that cannot obtain regular jobs in employing organizations because of a variety of personal limitations. They would prefer full-time, regular employment (Christensen 1988a, 83). Other independent contractors are in this position voluntarily, most being owners of small, unincorporated businesses, who want the autonomy of being their own bosses.

Whether home workers take such employment by choice or because they have no other alternative, their expanding use has many advantages to the employer. Christensen (1988b) points to structural changes in the U.S. economy as a major set of factors making it worthwhile not to have all workers in the same location. Foreign competition, utilizing cheap labor, provides a strong incentive to cut labor costs here. As the price of space increases in urban centers, having workers work from their own homes can cut all other expenses connected with maintaining a worker in an office or factory. Technological change makes possible the farming out of many white-collar or manual jobs. A third factor Christensen discusses is the shift from an industrial to a service economy, many of whose tasks can be carried out away from an office.

Although many women respond to advertisements and the hype of mass media to take on home-based jobs, feeling they could gain independence and flexibility, and although many are quite satisfied with such an arrangement, others have realized their many disadvantages. In addition to the role conflict similar to that faced by home-working entrepreneurs, employees so situated face isolation from the company's social circle, which means not only loneliness, but also the lack of important organizational information. The same is true for manual workers, whose interaction with the employing firm is formal and relationally minimal. Since so much of a job is contained in social relations, this narrows manual labor down to mainly tasks. Promotions within the system are impossible. And, of course, such workers are at a disadvantage compared to regular employees if they do not have a specified contract guaranteeing a certain amount of work, are paid lower wages or salaries, are not covered by company benefits such as health insurance, and have to use their own space, heat, and other resources.

The Beneficiary's Territory[4]

Another category of jobs requires the social person to enter the territory of the beneficiary—the customer, client, student, or patient—alone or as part of a team, to sell a product or provide a service. Such jobs range from that of a domestic who cleans the homes of her employers, to an interior decorator who transforms a store, a management consultant who develops a plan for the reorganization of a corporation, or a manufacturer's representative selling to a wholesaler or a physician's office. The main locus of power or authority may lie with the beneficiary, who can select the worker and decide what she should do and what her rights are, or she or he may forfeit many of these rights to the incoming "expert" whose knowledge or equipment can solve a major problem.

There are two basic types of beneficiary settings the worker may enter: the home or the organizational setting.

The Beneficiary's Home as the Setting

The jobholder who enters the beneficiary's home can be a performer of services, such as a servant, plumber, doctor, or beautician. Salespersons can provide objects (such as cosmetics) or services (such as insurance). The manager of a household serves as the connecting link between the home and the outside world, utilizing a great variety of services and objects. Those entering the home can do so for very limited amounts of time, once or repeatedly, with differing complexities of duties to the beneficiaries and rights of pay and other benefits.

The characteristics of the social person, the jobholder, are frequently established by agencies other than the customer, who either does not have the knowledge and authority to test ability, or who must accept the proof of tests performed by others. A master plumber who so advertises himself has been apprenticed and trained by the union and licensed by the state; a doctor has been educated by the medical profession and also licensed by the state; a cleaning woman has been trained and bonded by a service agency or accepted on the basis of a word-of-mouth recommendation. The choice of the home entrant by the customer often involves several steps: a local "expert" turned to for advice when several qualified persons are available (Katz and Lazersfeld 1955), a personal interview with a candidate, or a test performance.

The social person entering the home of the main beneficiary must, however, establish trust beyond the formal qualifications that got her there in the first place. The rights of access and movement within the home can be previously established or negotiated at entrance. The patient of a home-visiting doctor can restrict access to certain rooms, while allowing a freedom to manipulate the body that is not offered to people in other jobs, and guaranteeing cooperation of the patient's social circle. At the other extreme is the suspect who must give access to police officers with a search warrant. Other rights and duties of the jobholder must also be negotiated, at least at first contact, if there is to be continued interaction. The circle of the employee includes many more people than the customer.

The subject of private household servants received a great deal of attention from social scientists in the past decades, with the growing shortages of such workers and changes in their relations with employers (see Coser 1973, Katzman 1978, Rollins 1985). This occupation contains some interesting variations, as the power of the social person versus the employer increased with organization. The most powerless have been slaves, legally the property of the owners who could assign them tasks and determine whatever rights they wished (Rodgers-Rose 1980; Malson et al. 1988). In America, descendants of slaves were joined as servants by immigrant women (Katzman 1978).

Several changes on both the employer's and the worker's side have modified this relationship. On the employer's side, the amount of work carried out in the home decreased with urbanization, industrialization, and technology. Soap, bread, clothing, and other goods could be purchased with money, decreasing the need for extra workers in the home. Also, the cost of maintaining servants, in terms of space, clothing, and food, became prohibitive for most households in urban centers. Simultaneously, the dramatically expanding middle class increased the demand for at least partial household help.

On the other hand, fewer and fewer women were willing to work as live-in servants. The spread of democratic ideas and increasing opportunities for alternative occupations decreased the attractiveness of domestic service for all but such women who could not fit into new labor markets, such as older blacks, new immigrants, or imported domestics (Bernard 1981; Coser 1973). The great disadvantages of live-in employment, including the constancy of demands, the lack of privacy on the job, and limits on private life away from it, plus the demeaning nature of the relationship with the employer and related circle members, resulted in a shortage of workers and the modification of demands (Lopata, Miller, and Barnewolt 1986; Rollins 1985).

The changes on both demand and supply sides resulted in a decrease of live-in servants. The combined needs led to an increase in "day workers" who come into the employer's homes to perform more time-limited duties and receive rights more typical of jobs in modern societies (Katzman 1978). This meets the needs of most employers, who can no longer maintain multistaff households, and of the workers, who can live in their own homes. Other changes include the rise of new entrepreneurial businesses that formalize the relationship between the managers of a household and domestic servants, serving as intermediaries, providing workers with very specified duties and definite rights (Lopata, Miller, and Barnewolt 1986). Restaurants, catering businesses, and take-out places have generally replaced the home-based cook, and window-, furniture-, and clothing-cleaning establishments proliferate. Dealing with such organizations reduces the power of the beneficiary, converting an employer into a customer, and diminishes the intensity or primary quality of relations with employees.

The development of a relationship between an employer and a jobholder entering her home is particularly difficult in the direct sales field. The beneficiary knows very little about the seller, so that the first interaction must build trust very rapidly. There are four basic procedures used in direct sales, which mushroomed in the feminine-mystique years when homemakers spent a great deal of time in the home (Cox 1963, 43–45). Some of these have survived into recent times, with variations due to the daytime absence of so many potential customers. The first method follows the traditional door-to-door pattern of the peddler, although the title has been changed to "representative" due to the negative stereotype of high-pressure "foot-in-the-door" salespeople. While such items as vacuum cleaners and household cleaning products have been sold by men to homemakers and couples in the past, manufacturers of goods such as cosmetics, household objects, and jewelry have increasingly used saleswomen. The main reason that it took so long for direct-sales companies to utilize saleswomen, who allegedly would be less threatening at the doorstep than men, is the premodern company's fear of hiring women to travel and enter possibly dangerous places (Lopata, Miller and Barnewolt 1986).

A person in direct sales must rapidly develop a dyadic relationship with the customer and is highly dependent upon her or his cooperation, since she has no supports in the setting or even a team to assist in the presentation (Prus and Frisby 1990). This is undoubtedly one of the most difficult jobs, dependent not so much on the product (although its name does carry weight in building trust) as upon the woman's ability to convert a suspicious stranger into a cooperating teammate.

A second method of direct sales is through referrals and prearranged appointments. Each time a sale is completed, the "demonstrator" asks the customer for names of friends, with a promise of gifts if the recommendation results in a sale. The third procedure is through the "party plan," in which elements of primary relationships are exploited for the secondary goal of making a sale. The whole program is based on home and neighborhood life, in that the dealer enlists hostesses to invite the guests (customers) and provide the homes (salesrooms) and refreshments in exchange for gifts. The dealer presides over the party, leading the games and making a sales presentation. She then takes orders for delivery later to the hostess, who in turn distributes the merchandise to the guests (Cox 1963, 46; see also Peven 1968).

Finally there is a "club plan," which works like a chain letter and is somewhat similar to the referral system, except that the buyer recommends a friend for "club membership." The members actually do not interact with each other, but continue buying items, such as silverware or china, through the seller until they have completed a set.

One of the interesting features of the direct-sales field is the training and selling method, purposely developed for the conversion of former full-time homemakers, with hardly any employment history, into the salesforce. Reinforcement contacts continue for years, in an effort to retain the saleswomen in a field noted for high turnover.[5] Peven (1968) compared the training meetings to religious revival sessions. Employers also provide the salesforce with props, in the form of samples or "gifts," even precanvassing catalogues (Cox 1963). Companies such as Avon have begun to experiment with different ways of merchandising their products, due to the frequent absence of a potential woman customer from the home during daytime hours so that calling "cold" (i.e., without an appointment) is not likely to produce a response (Deveny 1989).

A very difficult form of role strain, between the person and the demands of the job, is often experienced by insurance underwriters due to feelings of intrusion on the privacy of potential customers (Krugman 1969). Successful insurance agents select areas or methods of contacting clients that provide a set of prospects as similar to themselves as possible (Crane 1969).

The easiest aspect of direct selling is that of customer maintenance. For example, milkmen, when this was a frequent occupation, learned complicated methods to establish and retain customers, even to get rid of undesirable ones (Bigus 1972). Like the ballroom dance teacher who must keep the student happy, the milkman uses cultivating tactics of pseudofriendship. At least the teacher has the whole studio and colleagues to support her front- and backstage, a sort of support not available to sales workers (Lopata and Noel 1967).

The Beneficiary's Job Setting

Another type of job involves entering the work setting, rather than the home, of the customer. Some industries and organizations have started hiring women for the male-dominated occupation of sales representative. For example, pharmaceutical manufacturers now send "detail women" to offices of physicians and dentists, and book publishers assign women to universities in an extended territory. Such a person enters an establishment under the control of the potential or repeat customer and has to fit her demeanor to that of the surroundings, while showing genuineness, likeability, toughness, and so forth. She has no close colleagues; all those who do the same thing are competitors or in different locations. She is the only person from her own company, with not even a supervisor to lend support. Knowledge of the product and of the needs of the consumer can be quite complicated, and failure to have been sufficiently prepared is readily apparent.

Such assignments require not only entrance into "foreign territory" of the work space, but also travel, frequently for extended periods of time. Until very recently restaurants, hotels and motels did not know how to handle women business travelers, but now slick travel magazines are running articles showing adjustments being made for them. Prior "protectiveness" toward women, which was partly due to employers' fears that female employees might be sexually assaulted or embarrassed, as well as fears of lawsuits, have decreased (Berheide 1988; Coser 1975b). Women are now traveling independently (although I still get asked if I am going to visit a grandchild when I'm flying to a distant location).

The *City Women* study included two kinds of salesworkers: salesclerks and sales agents (Lopata, Barnewolt, and Miller 1985). The Chicago-area sales agents and representatives are very different from the salesclerks in background, occupational histories, construction of reality, and role clusters. They have more college education, initially and after returns, and more job training in the past and the planned-for future, which is specifically directed toward improving their success in the field. They initially trained to be clerical workers, but somewhere along the line they saw the benefits obtained by male agents in their firms and moved out of clerical work into more independent and profitable jobs. They are very satisfied with the occupation and consider it much more complex than an average job and as very important to the beneficiary. They are career oriented and expect to remain that way in the future. Women sales agents consider themselves to be competent, intelligent, creative, and healthy, and in general they have a higher self-esteem than either full-time homemakers or women in many other occupations, especially salesclerks. In addition, they earn more than two-and-a-half times what other salesworkers make. Thus, they have decrystallized their life patterns in midlife to free themselves from prior constraints and are reaping the benefits. Most do not have small children in the home and are freer than many women to travel and to work unusual and erratic hours. There is one complication in the picture: The husband does not appear to be as pleased by the wife's job as she is. This may be because the changes it has introduced into their married life have disrupted its prior rhythm and, possibly, the rights of the husband to the wife's work and attention. Secretaries may be easier to live with than are sales agents, even if their earnings are inferior. Salesclerks do not report similar problems.

Women now entering the great variety of sales jobs requiring new skills and presentations of self have formed mutual support, local, and national organizations with similarly involved persons. For example, the National Network of Women in Sales has branches in most American cities and suburbs, holding national conventions and publishing literature of interest to members. Much of the activity is very similar to what went on in now-defunct organizations of salesmen: sharing information on sales techniques, building self-esteem, and in general contributing to feelings of morale, esprit de corps, companionship, and similarity of experience. Colleagues in such organizations thus become part of the social circle, the employing organization and customers forming the other two major segments.

Jobholders may also enter as outsiders into organizational territory to perform services. This is true of, for example, accountants or management consultants, fields expanding to include women. A major American consulting firm with hundreds of experts had only one woman until relatively recently, claiming that this was not due to personal taste but to the fact that the clients did not want women telling them how to run their businesses. There were no blacks, male or female, in consulting positions, although such faces were visible in the back rooms of the central settings.

The outsider entering such a "foreign" establishment might have very tightly circumscribed rights of access to space and data, or might be allowed to wander about or to interview people if that is part of the contract. The employees must be told how to cooperate and when to protect the organization from unwelcome disclosure. Even the mass media show the complications of interaction in such situations—the outsider trying to get "guilty knowledge," the locals pretending there is none (Hughes 1971). Here, again, the consultant, accountant, or other specialist is frequently operating alone. However, the firm that tested her for the necessary qualifications, hired her, sent her on the assignment, and pays her is expected to back up her report and defend her actions, if it approves them—but usually not to the point of losing the account.

Outsiders also include office "temps," or temporary workers, sent by mushrooming firms specializing in filling special needs or finding replacements for absent workers, usually in clerical jobs (Gannon 1984). The workers obviously do not have the status of the consultant and face several other difficulties, including learning what needs to be done in the absence of the regular worker and being able to fit into the ongoing system. Social relations can be awkward, especially if the work team suspects that the "temp" may replace their colleague. The experience can be isolating, but women who sign up with the agencies like the flexibility of scheduling and often find the work interesting. Supposedly they are completely free to accept or reject assignments, but frequent rejection will lead to a decrease in calls from the agency.

Organizational Settings

One of the alienating aspects of jobs is the inability to call a setting one's own, with rights to protect it from invasion, particularly by higher-ups. Many jobs are carried forth in relatively large organizations, in space that the worker must personalize to build a setting for herself, such as a factory, prison, store, or office. Manual workers designate boundaries or become frustrated if they cannot do so. Howe (1977) dramatizes the irritation experienced by waitresses in the restaurant she studied over the lack of a safe and private space in which to change into their uniforms and store their street clothes. Attempts to build partial personalized space is evident when pool secretaries insert pictures or permanent flowers on the desk, while the "big shots" have walls to hang art indicating high culture, or at least million-mile awards from airlines (Kanter 1977). Much was made by industrial sociologists, and is now being made by best-seller books, about this allocation and use of space, physical and social, in large (and even small) business firms or factories (Margolis 1979; Pavalko 1988; Whyte 1956).

A very interesting relation between setting and occasional roles exists in "total institutions" (Goffman 1961) such as communities of nuns or armed forces bases. Cloistered nuns lived in their own settings, although owned by the Catholic Church (Ebaugh 1988). There is a great deal of debate concerning the integration of women into the American armed forces, since they are seen as impinging on men's occupations in men's territory (Rustad 1982). It is outside the purview of this volume to deal with such situations, since they encompass more than just the job.

Factories

Probably the most confining setting for a job is the factory floor where manual workers are located. Thanks to scientific management of the transitional times in modernization, assembly work has been divided into the most efficient system judged possible by the experts, with strict schedules. Such a factory setting is not similar to the rest of societal life; it is routinized, specialized, mechanically controlled, and depersonalized (in that each worker is replaceable), with a tight authority structure. Workers are not trusted to do their jobs right, often with cause due to the alienation produced by the setting, and thus supervised tightly without decision-making rights. For example, Cavendish (1982), studying women factory workers, noted that the engineers who came to solve machine problems did not even listen to the women, who knew what was going on. Supervisors have a great deal of control over the allocation of women to jobs and over their acceptance by co-workers (Reskin and Padavic 1988). This is particularly true when they can manipulate the labor force along gender, race, and class lines to prevent work manipulation by workers or organized protest (Hossfeld 1990). Zavella (1987), who studied their jobs and outside lives, reports that Chicano cannery workers in California adjust to going "through hell for three months" of intensive, seasonal employment simply because of the high pay and the unemployment insurance for the months when the canneries do not need them. They must work, and alternative jobs have their own disadvantages.

Work in the canning industries appears to have the same constraints, whether it be in the state of Washington or in Hawaii, or in Delaware in the 1920s and 1930s. The work is tedious, usually carried forth in an unhealthy environment and under constant time pressure. In addition, many of the jobs are dangerous, either in themselves or because of the employer's (and sometimes employees' failure to utilize protective devices (McCurry 1975). This holds true for women miners and those working with hot or heavy machinery (Kingsolver 1989; Walshok 1981; see also Stromberg, Larood, and Gutek's 1987 special volume of *Women and Work* devoted to occupational health issues). Interpersonal relations with co-workers are often limited to off-work hours, and the basic interaction is between the woman and her machine.

Women in factories often face additional problems, modified by their class and racial characteristics, the main one of which is sexual harassment. This is particularly true when they enter territory previously controlled by men. The macho image of so many jobs requires constant reference to subjects with which women are not comfortable, and the harassment can be very personal, even physical. Harassment in female-dominated occupations comes from male supervisors demanding sexual favors and punishing women who do not comply; in male dominated occupations, it takes the form of a constantly demeaning environment.

Attempts to modify the factory work system on the model of, for example, Scandinavian firms have not been very frequent or successful. Such experiments assign greater freedom to work teams to decide rights and duties and to benefit more directly from the economic success of their work. The redefinition, in the 1992 presidential campaign, of the American economic system as being in serious trouble, and the declared future policies of the Clinton administration, may force employers into a more modern organization of factory jobs.

In-depth studies indicate that women do not respond passively to the negative aspects of their jobs. They organize their work scheduling to fool machines and supervisors (see, for example, Cavendish 1982). They form networks and support groups and use the very logic with which the management tries to manipulate them to reconstruct their situation (Hossfeld 1990; Zavella 1987). They even cross racial and class lines to accomplish their purposes vis-à-vis the structure. Kessler-Harris (1982) summarizes women's part in the history of the labor movement in America (see also Kingsolver's 1989 *Holding the Line: Women in the Great Arizona Mine Strike of 1983*). The successful workers studied by Walshok (1981) were very task-oriented, interested in problem solving, skilled, and involved in a "network of competent, savvy peers" who supported them in their risk-taking work.

Men's Prisons

Two studies have recently given us a picture of how women correctional officers handle themselves and others in men's prisons (Jurik 1985; Jurik and Halemba 1984; Zimmer 1987). Women were introduced into the men's prison system in 1978 in an attempt at reform. Dramatic prison revolts and class-action suits led to a mandatory change in the philosophy guiding prisons, a change mainly from coercion to attempts at rehabilitation. Women were supposed to help introduce the reforms. However, extensive cultural and structural barriers—many of which occur in other male-dominated or changing settings—have prevented women from functioning effectively (Jurik 1985). These include the stereotypical image of women as physically and "mentally" weak and unsuited for the job of insuring safety for the staff and conformity by prisoners; polarization of tokenism; the informal "old guard" opportunities for advancement to which they were not admitted; inadequate prior experience (many of the men, but not the women, had been in the armed services or similar prior jobs), training, and on-the-job learning opportunities; ambiguity of the role itself; and inadequate implementation by the external authorities. The prisons were overcrowded, inadequately staffed, and thus dangerous, and the lack of trust from the male guards, who held such strong stereotypes of women, is partially understandable.

The women entering these settings were more educated than their co-workers, but in nonrelevant fields. Many were not married and were attracted to the job by the money and because they wanted to use the training. Thus they used different styles of relationships with the prisoners than were traditional or used by men. For example, they guarded by using communication and persuasion, in order to obtain voluntary cooperation (Zimmer 1987). They decreased the social distance from the prisoners, which the men tried to constantly maintain. Obviously, such differences in styles of interaction produced conflicts with the male guards.

Long Distance Trucks

Women truckers face sexual harassment and must develop their own style of relating with circle members, dock-loading and -unloading workers, truck stop personnel, and other truckers. Although the territory of the truck belongs to the drivers, at least while they are on the road, most women are in a subordinate position, 80 percent of the time driving double, with a boyfriend or husband in the main seat. The women consider themselves to be real truckers, able to solve any problem, but the men, who act as unintentional sponsors, are more interested in female companionship than in driving competency (Lembright and Riemer 1982, 472).

Stores, Restaurants, and Airplanes

Salesclerks are "stationary workers" in a depersonalized setting; their rights over a limited floor space are highly dependent upon characteristics of the establishment for making sales (Mills 1956). The physical arrangements of the store, the location of "stations" to which women are assigned, and the characteristics of the customers who are drawn to the store are not within their control. There is a great variation in settings, ranging from cost-cutting discount outlets that have proleterianized the job into one of merely writing up and packaging the order, to quality stores requiring the clerk to know the merchandise and help customers make selections they are satisfied with. Glazer (1984) points out that in many capitalist establishments, such as stores, the customer now performs some of the work of the employee. Some businesses even set up physical barriers preventing much clerk-customer interaction. On the other hand, many employers intensify the customer interaction of their salesforce, being convinced that service is their main contribution to the beneficiary (Benson 1984, 113). The selection of the social person for this job varies considerably, according to the image the store wants to project, which accounts in a major part for the lag in hiring blacks and other minority women (Benson 1984).

C. Wright Mills (1956, 172–74) classified women salesclerks by the personal styles with which they interact with customers while being careful not to antagonize colleagues. The competition is high when commissions are at stake, but the "saleslady" must constantly relate to the other women in the same job, while customers come and go. Mills also noted the difference between salesclerks in small towns, or shops that draw repeat customers, and those in large city department stores with mainly anonymous sales interaction. We found in the *City Women* study (Lopata, Barnewolt, and Miller 1985) that the job of salesclerk is a catchall, drawing women who consider it a temporary experience. They come from a variety of backgrounds and occupational histories. Most are not career committed and do not see the job as complex or as giving any chance for self-development, control over others, or independence. They are more oriented toward family roles than toward the job, although they do find companionship and their own earnings to be sources of satisfaction (see also Howe 1977). The merchandise is there, the customers come to the store and not to them, and they have few discriminatory decision-making rights. They do think that their performance of the job is more important than the job itself (Lopata, Barnewolt, and Miller 1985). However, there are women among them who have moved up from less prestigeful jobs, and the setting is often pleasant, requiring care of appearance and, if not customer deference, at least polite demeanor. Such salesclerks are much more satisfied with their jobs than are the ones who feel they have moved down in social status.

There is a great deal of gender segregation in the merchandise to be sold. Women are assumed to do better at selling cosmetics or clothes than at selling mechanical gadgets or major appliances

(Donovan [1929] 1974). The perfect example of gender specialization of objects is the car salesroom, which has traditionally been dominated by men, supported by the assumptions of management and clients that women cannot sell cars because they do not understand their mechanical functioning (the accompanying assumption is that all car salesmen do understand this). Lawson's (1990) study of women who are now entering the car salesforce found a high turnover due to the problems and hassles. The job is made especially difficult by the fact that the assisting segment of the circle, in the form of other salespersons, does not cooperate with them. Some women moved into the financial aspects of the business, while those in sales who survived on the floor developed personalized styles of interaction. These styles of relating to the male co-workers resemble stereotypical family roles, labeled as "mothering" and so forth, much as did the women in male-dominated armed-service units studied by Rustad (1982). One reason for the success of some women in this highly competitive field is the increase in female car buyers, who are likely to trust someone of their own gender more than a man. This factor is important, since the public's image of the car salesforce is quite negative.

Waitresses must meet several physical qualifications in order to take orders and bring food and drinks to the diners. The higher the prestige of the restaurant, the more appearances and style are important, although the highest-status establishments (or those trying for such a reputation) usually hire men, who carry, after all, more prestige than the most sophisticated waitress. The waitress deals directly with the beneficiaries, hostesses or maître d's, cooks, bartenders, other waitresses, and "busboys." Whyte's classic 1948 study concluded that the interactional problems of this job are enough to "make waitresses cry." Gender differences among members of the social circle are an important influence on this interaction, and also waitresses have a rather sexist "client classificatory system," according to Howe (1977, 102–3).

A variation on the role of waitress, but with many more complications, is that of flight attendant. Hochschild (1983) devotes a whole book, *The Managed Heart,* to a discussion of the selection, training, duties, and rights of this role. The title refers to the fact that stewardesses, as they used to be called before the title became gender-neutral, are extensively trained to manage their emotions in order to create a relaxed, "homelike" atmosphere in the airplane cabin, controlling difficult passengers without antagonizing them.

The role includes much more than serving food and drinks, although the beneficiaries are often unaware of these duties except in emergencies. The flight attendant can be in contact with the same passengers for extended periods of time, and can see some repeatedly if assigned the same route. Class-action suits have recently been filed against airlines for firing women who married while still on the job. Marital and parental status are no longer asked in hiring procedures, and the women's activities while not on the job are not a subject of concern, unless they embarrass the airline. There has been a shift in selection criteria, with males, older women, and minority women appearing more frequently.

Offices

In discussing the office as a setting of jobs, Pavalko (1988) interestingly limits it to the province of receptionists, secretaries, typists, bookkeepers, file clerks, bank clerks, and so forth. He then adds that this is a feminized work context. This limitation is not surprising, in view of prevalent stereotypes, but it ignores the fact that members of management, university scholars, and persons in many other male- or female-dominated or gender-neutral jobs are also in offices. It is impossible to look at the myriad jobs that are located in offices, so let us first examine those in which such a setting is the main center of activity, and then those for which an office serves only as a "home base" from which the jobholder moves to other locales to fulfill duties and receive rights.

Clerical Workers. Office workers in female-dominated jobs vary in the complexity of their work and social relationships, as well as their control over the setting (Feldberg and Glenn 1979; Lopata, Barnewolt, and Miller 1985; Lopata, Miller, and Barnewolt 1986; Malveaux 1980). There are great differences between the private secretary, who usually has her own office and moves up the organizational ladder with her boss, acquiring territory in fiefdom style as his assistant, and the more stationary pool typist, with limited rights or discretion in her work (Kanter 1977). On the other hand, the pool secretary may need very complex and negotiated interaction just because of her lack of power. File clerks can move around large territories, as illustrated by Howe in *Pink Collar Workers* (1977), having rights of access to other people's space but hardly any space of their own. Some become very possessive about their files, but most must allow others entry even to these (see also Benet 1972). Receptionists and phone operators can extend themselves great distances, as we see in one of the favorite skits by comedienne Lilly Tomlin. Computerization of the secretarial office has had mixed effects, most of which, however, are evaluated by observers as a process of deskilling and degrading, or proletarianization, of the work. One of the ways training schools are trying to upgrade the appearance of this category of jobs is by relabeling: They are now "office support workers." Regardless of the label or location, clerical workers interact with a wide variety of circle members. The organizational structure and size of the establishment obviously influence the relationships and the amount of negotiation necessary to fulfill obligations and receive rights.

Although many disadvantages appear at all levels of clerical jobs, most women are still located in them because it has been white-collar, "socially acceptable employment" (Lillydahl 1986) requiring relatively little education. As younger white women are broadening their horizons and gaining expanded job opportunities, they are decreasing their concentration here, as in other female-intensive occupations. This leaves space for minority women, who are moving into these white-collar positions in great numbers (Braverman 1974; Glenn and Feldberg 1977 and 1979; Sokoloff 1988).

The *City Women* clerical workers varied by the complexity of their jobs from file clerk to receptionist, secretary, and high-level office worker with more complex, executive, or specialized duties. Such employees also came from a variety of backgrounds and were distributed differently within the office setting. The women themselves are highly conscious of internal status differentiation and boundaries, and the ones with higher status are very conscious of the ceiling that prevents them from moving into managerial positions. One of the features that distinguishes their work from that of professional occupations is that few of them interact directly with people outside of the organizational setting except as representatives of management.

Managers and Professionals. The other people who work in offices, but not as part of that female-dominated domain of clericals, are in an even greater heterogeneity of jobs and social-person characteristics. Office-bound jobs tend to be of marginal professional more than managerial character, since management usually requires physical mobility into multiple settings. Office management jobs are actually similar to those of stationary factory employees, in that work must be brought in to the managers and the finished product removed. Many of the "object-focused" professionals in the *City Women* study spend most of their time in offices or their equivalents, such as laboratories—with small office spaces for writing up results—or studios. Here they manipulate data or create objects such as advertisements. The fact that they are focused in one location belonging to a larger organization does not mean that they conduct their roles entirely within its confines; they often go out to meet with colleagues, to conferences with others in the company, or to meetings with people in other organizations. One of the problems of scientists working in bureaucracies is that they have been socialized into cosmopolitan reference and membership groups with whom they continue interaction even when faced with ethical and loyalty conflicts (Gouldner 1957 and 1958; Merton 1968).

Doctors' and dentists' offices are the settings for most of the work of such professionals; the beneficiaries, assistants, and suppliers come to these offices from the outside, although doctors also function in hospital settings. Lawyers are usually required to use multiple locales to accomplish their purposes, but their basic setting is an office. Grade school teachers are often deprived of private offices and tend to convert the classroom into their own space (Lortie 1969 and 1975). The level at which the teacher is hired is dependent upon the match between her knowledge and the children's ages and assumed ability to learn. Teachers of very young children stay mainly in the same room and see the same beneficiaries the academic year 'round. As the age of the children increases, so does specialization by teacher, so that new groups are taught in the same place at different hours of the day. The race of the teacher is often associated with the race of the students, whites being greatly overrepresented in this occupation until recently. Token teachers of a different gender or racial identity than that of the dominant group can become quite isolated and alienated in urban public schools; their colleagues, and even the parents of the children in their classes, cooperate with them only minimally (Dworkin, Chafetz, and Dworkin 1986).

Universities and colleges, with the dual function of developing new knowledge and transmitting it to students and the world, require greater mobility of their professors. The professorial office is visited by students, colleagues, suppliers, building maintenance personnel, and so forth. The professor enters offices of others, classrooms, meeting locales, and food-serving establishments on campus. In fact, ideally, the professor can live a major part of the day and year within the confines of the organization. One way of understanding the real meaning of the resources available to academics in such a setting is to examine the problems facing people who have not acquired full membership (Smith and Hixson 1987).[6] Disadvantages of women adjunct professors not on the tenure track vis-à-vis those on the track, or already past the major career barriers, include inadequate office space and secretarial help, inconvenient course assignments, lack of necessary information for duty performance due to distance from the network, and lack of funds for attendance at professional meetings.

Hochschild (1992) recently studied people at various levels of jobs in a major corporation and noted the significance of placement of photographs upon the allotted spaces. Managers in private offices display formally framed family pictures on the desk or behind it on walls. Secretaries in pool locations stick their unframed pictures into slots of available objects with which they work. Factory workers draw out their photographs from wallets in their pockets.

Multiple Settings

No business, and no organization devoted mainly to other functions, such as a school or church, exists independently of its social milieu—which includes suppliers, external beneficiaries, competitors, and governmental agencies. Therefore, members of the organization who form the connecting link between it and the rest of the world are vital to its welfare. This includes the officers of the firm, the staff whose job is to collect data, and the salesforce, in the case of product or service manufacturers. It may include advertising specialists, lawyers, external accountants, and even managers' wives.

Those connecting-link jobholders may be seen as sufficiently important representatives of the company that the rest of the staff is treated as supportive and responsive to their needs. In other than home settings, the main obligation of the representatives is to make the organization look good or get accounts or new members. Religious personnel are generally expected to seek out and convert potential congregation members.

One of the problems of people in multiple settings that bridge cosmopolitan and local, or other mutually exclusive value systems and norms, is that of person-role strain or role-loyalty conflict (Gouldner 1957 and 1958). If the social circle contains groups that demand different behavior and interaction, the social person can be caught in a psychologically damaging double bind.

Many other jobs require movement from one setting to another, accompanied by changes in social circle and thus in relations and self-presentation. An interesting occupation that combines home, office, and other persons' locales is real estate sales. Traditionally a male-dominated occupation, based on the assumption that males know more about building construction and financial matters, its residential segment has become female-dominated within a relatively short period of time. The explanation for the shift is again in terms of gender qualifications: "Women understand homes better than men," and "women decide on homes and women sales agents are better at finding the right emphasis for persuasion." Realtors establish territories, or "farms," within which they keep track of householders, using word of mouth and other sources of knowledge to spot future vendors or sellers. The office provides the buyers, through advertisements, branches in other locales, or multiple listings. The agent must determine the best match between buyer and seller and negotiate between them, which is often a very delicate process, into which potential agents are carefully trained. Realtors have to be very careful to follow antidiscrimination regulations, while simultaneously not antagonizing colleagues and neighborhoods by selling to "undesirables" (Squires et al. 1987, 9; House 1977).

Kanter and Stein (1979) explain the complexities of multiple settings, made more difficult by male hostility, in a study of women in an industrial salesforce. There were few women in the organization they studied, and so they were highly visible, requiring modifications of behavior and the creation of new relationships by both the women and the various segments of their circles. For example, when out on the road with colleagues, women often felt very uncomfortable in dealing with the "male culture" of jokes, drinking, and general demeanor. Each woman had to develop her own way of dealing with such situations. Most did not find a similar problem with customers, in the latter's location, although awkwardness created by mistaken identity often followed a lack of clarification of the salesperson's gender by appointment arrangers. On the home base of the company, new situations arose with the introduction of women to the salesforce, as in relations with secretaries adjusted to men's style, or the need to develop comfortable relations with the wives of colleagues.

The same need for adjustment exists whenever the social person must change locales or a woman enters a relational context based on a male model of interaction. Relations with colleagues at the home base, with the protection of the organization, must be changed when in public or other settings in which a woman and a man are frequently treated as sexual or at least dating partners. The boundaries of norms of primary or leisure-time interaction and those of secondary relations are often hard to maintain or even understand.

Multiple settings have sometimes been forced upon women by the domination of certain territory by men. The biographies of women scientists, writers, and artists are full of refusals by established research centers or universities to allow them positions or the use of space. This situation was bad enough when the scholar or scientist was doing the same kind of work as her colleagues or husband who had official positions in these centers, but even more difficult when the woman was focused mainly on feminine subjects or viewpoints (Abir-Am and Outram 1987; Harding 1986, 242). As late as 1965, psychiatrist Erik Erikson explained the absence of women from positions in scientific centers and engineering as due to their "inner space," or womb, which makes "scientific training more or less peripheral to the intimate tasks of womanhood and motherhood" (see also Lopata, Miller, and Barnewolt 1984, 213–14). Rossi (1965), attending the same conference on women in the scientific professions, explained their scarcity in more sociological terms: socialization and organizational barriers to preparation and position. Many women who never reached prominence had actually undertaken the preparation for scientific careers, only to withdraw from active involvement later in life. Those who continued faced great problems, especially if their work required a special setting and resources available only at large and endowed centers such as universities.

The white "homosocial" male world of many occupations has made it difficult for persons with other characteristics—not just the female gender—to attain space within their settings at appropriate levels (Lipman-Blumen 1976a, 15). The cooperation of social circles is often absent or minimal, even when jobs are obtained. The difficulties facing people lacking the ideal social-person characteristics, or membership in the desired circle, are still apparent whenever we look at the distribution of workers in the American labor force, or within any large, complex organization such as a corporation, factory, or university.

Summary

Much human work has been organized in the modern world into individually held jobs. Employer and employee much reach an agreement as to the social person characteristics the employee must possess and duties and rights, including the necessary resources the employer must provide the employee. The employer usually has the greater power to define the situation. Beneficiaries of the work can be contacted directly, or so indirectly that the worker considers only the evaluation of a supervisor. Colleagues can be an invaluable asset, making even dreary routines companionate, or they can sabotage all efforts.

Not all women earning an income work outside the home. Some attempt to combine the job with family roles by locating the job in the home. There are two types of home-based paid work: that of entrepreneur and that of employee. The advantages for the woman employee are flexibility and autonomy; disadvantages are low pay, lack of many benefits, social isolation, and conflict with other home-based roles. Few households are organized to protect a woman from interference while she works at her job. The advantages for the employer are low expenses and not having to provide the work space and resources provided to in-company workers; disadvantages are mainly in the lack of control. The entrepreneur faces the same problems of business maintenance as are experienced in any independent economic venture. Independence is curtailed by the rights that must be granted all circle members plus any restrictions coming from governmental policies.

There are other settings within which jobs are carried forth. One is the home or job location of the beneficiaries, such as customers of saleswomen. The home provides more opportunities for the use of primary-relation interaction, while women who travel to the factories and offices of customers often face a heavily male-culture based world.

Organizational settings of jobs also vary, from factory stations to stores and restaurants or offices. Many of these settings are gender-specific, assigned so traditionally and because of stereotypical assumptions of management. Higher status settings tend to be male-intensive and male-dominated. Office-based jobs include those thought of as "feminine," such as clerical support staff, as well as those of most white-collar (dress and suit?) workers, such as professionals and corporate managers. The role, rather than the setting, determines relationships with circle members, but the location either facilitates or hinders these. Workers are highly aware of the importance of the setting as evidenced by the constant demands for "better," often defined in prestige terms, spatial resources on all levels of jobs.

Many jobs are actually carried forth in more than the base location, movement to beneficiaries, colleagues, administrators, or external persons or groups being required or advantageous. Women entering the public domain, in which so many relationships are organized around the male model of interaction, timing, and interest, find some locations easier to work in than others. The tendency to not try, or to withdraw from, jobs and careers that are reputedly hostile or that present too many barriers to success, combined with the very real presence of such barriers, continues the sex-segregated and sex-stratified system. Women who take other than the traditional roles must negotiate variations of style. One of the dramatic trends in recent years has been the willingness of so many of them to try to succeed in an ever-broader range of occupations.

7

Social Roles in the Rest of the World

We have finally reached the social roles of American women outside of the family and economic dimensions: in the rest of societal life and even in the world at large. This includes the roles of student, friend, neighbor, and member of a variety of community groups and social movements. These roles can be carried forth rather informally, or, within a highly structured social circle, they can aim at benefiting the social person, the group, or even larger segments of humanity.

Student

A member of modern societies is often involved with the formal school system at two periods in the life course: as a student in the early years after basic socialization by the family; and later as a parent of a student.

The history of women's involvement in the role of student in America is rather convoluted. Mass education was developed during transitional times with male beneficiaries in mind because the two-sphere ideology placed them in the public sphere of political and economic life for which extensive public knowledge was deemed necessary. It was assumed that women could learn all they needed to know from home, other women, and the church. (See Lopata 1981a, 14, for a summary of that argument). Extension of all but minimal formal schooling to women met with predictions of serious problems. Myerson (1927), for example, blamed higher education (high school and above) of women for the creation of "the nervous housewife": Schooling and employment had already led, and would increasingly lead, girls to refuse to be homemakers or to nervous breakdowns; women's minds were simply less able to absorb the kind of knowledge men's absorb, while educating them would produce individualization and decrease their willingness to contribute to family life. Musterberg (1905), a Harvard psychologist with a strong German background, saw dire consequences for the society at large from the education of women: It would weaken the system and lower the educational, and thus the scientific, achievement of American men, losing this society's ability to compete in the world.[1] Thus, the social-person characteristics in the role of student were deemed masculine, and absent in women or detrimental to their health if they were introduced to them. The social circles in higher education were all male-dominated. However, a new ideological movement of the nineteenth century provided a justification for increasing educational opportunity to women: It would make them better family members. Ehrenreich and English (1979) trace this shift to the idealization of the roles of mother and wife and to the influence of medical experts. Women were now seen as needing more complex knowledge in order to raise intelligent sons and help their husbands (Schwager 1987, 337). Their education was to be limited, however, to home economics and related subjects of use in family and homemaking roles. Thus, higher education was divided into two spheres.

The feminine mystique decades of the twentieth-century that limited women to family roles did little to encourage their involvement in the role of student beyond those legally and culturally prescribed norms, unless it prepared them to teach or nurse others before starting their own families. Women who entered higher education were allegedly looking for a husband who would be successful or, by contrast, they were interested in a career at the sacrifice of family roles. Furthermore, men did not want highly educated wives. For example, the marriage rates of Wellesley graduates between 1889 and 1908 were extremely low, although most of the women did not plan for a career (Frankfort 1977, 58–59). Rossi (1965) found few pioneers in her study of college students as late as in the 1960s. The psychiatrists of various forms influenced by Freud also found scientific and all other demanding careers inappropriate for women (Bettelheim 1965; Erikson 1965; Friedan 1963). In the meantime, Poland and the Soviet Union, needing women in science, engineering, medicine, and dentistry because of the loss of men during World War II, simply redefined women and these fields as appropriate to each other (Sokolowska 1965). These facts show the strength of the social-person stereotypes of areas of life. It is only recently that American universities have begun to reconceptualize science and other knowledge fields in an effort to make them more gender-neutral—mainly due to the direct push from feminists, or new governmental laws and policies. The Civil Rights Act of 1964, the 1972 Education Amendments Act and Title IX of the Equal Rights Amendment helped to force universities and related organizations that obtained federal money to cease discrimination (Mezey 1992; Sochen 1982). Such laws did not mean, however, that the social circle of the established university greeted women students gracefully or facilitated involvement in this role.

In spite of the debate about women and schooling and the hostility of male faculty and students, women were quietly expanding the number of years they spent in schools and the variety of establishments they attended (Solomon 1985). Many observers failed to understand the extent of this change in women's identities and their aspirations to educational achievement. Sewell and Hauser (1975) predicted only a slow change:

> In 1965, 12 percent of the adult male population and 7 percent of the adult women were college graduates. By 1985, these proportions are expected to rise to 18.6 and 12.5 percent, respectively. (P. 10)

Their predictions were pessimistic. By 1979–80 there was a 24 percent increase over 1975–76 in the number of women Ph.D.s (Lopata, Miller and Barnewolt 1986, 210–11). The *Chicago Sun Times* reported (Nelson 1989) that the Department of Education predicted that women would be receiving the majority of doctorates by the year 2000.

However, at all levels of higher education, prejudice and discrimination against women continue, especially in certain fields, due to the myths concerning women's abilities. The characteristics seen as necessary for work in mathematics and natural science are seen as lacking in women. One way of solving this problem is for women to fit the male model of student. Aisenberg and Harrington (1988) caution that a woman must transform herself into an active persona, prepared to be an autonomous expert, in order to succeed in academia. The fight includes changing not only the self, but, even more importantly, relations with all circle members in the role of student in preparation for changes in relations with circle members in succeeding roles. The other solution is the creation of a university, or part of one, that gives equal status to subjects and styles of learning and doing for which women have been already socialized (Howe 1977). This effort started as the very successful women's studies programs and is now pushing for a deconstruction of all traditional areas of knowledge.

An Example of the Effects of Schooling in Transitional Times

The effects of all these constructions of reality concerning education and women can be seen in the Chicago-area studies. The 1950s and 1960s women described in *Occupation: Housewife* (Lopata 1971b) had seldom reached more than a high school education, and few used that schooling to prepare for a multidimensional life space. Even then, however, variations in the consequences of the number of completed years of schooling were dramatic. It became apparent that formal schooling is an extremely important contributor to women's breadth of perspective, self-esteem, and ability to utilize the resources of the society in their involvement in social roles (see also Lopata 1981a, 19). The more education the woman had, the more complex and creative she was in her construction of reality and behavior. Her educational achievement also influenced whom she married and her life during and after marriage.

The same conclusion was reached independently in the widow-hood studies (Lopata 1973a, *Widowhood in an American City,* and 1979, *Women as Widows: Support Systems*). There was, however, one surprise in the findings: The more education a woman achieved, and the more middle-class life-style she and her husband developed while he was living, the more disorganized her life and self-concept became when he died. This is mainly due to such a woman's greater dependence on her husband, being a wife, and on being the wife of that particular husband. On the other hand, the more education she had, and the more middle-class her life-style, the more she was able to reorganize her life patterns and to develop a new social life space.

The reexamination of results from these two sets of studies leads to the conclusion that formal schooling has been of extreme importance to the social involvements of American women, even at a time when knowledge still tended to be organized into gender-specific areas (Lopata 1973a). The less formal schooling a woman achieved even then, the more apt she was to be socially isolated, to be unable to adjust to life changes, and to hold negative attitudes about social relationships. The increasingly voluntaristic nature of social involvement in more-developed and large-scale societies requires of members the kind of knowledge, thought processes, and competence that formal education provides.

The *City Women* study (Lopata, Barnewolt, and Miller 1985) reflected the continuation of a limited use of education for occupational futures by the older, transitional women, but a completely new view of it by the more modern respondents. The latter saw it as an ongoing activity, flexibly used to meet changing needs. Many of the younger women used school to prepare for specific occupations, anticipating life-course changes in other roles. However, a surprising 43 percent of the whole sample returned to school after assuming they had completed education earlier in life (Lopata, Barnewolt, and Miller, 1985).

The Role of Student at Reentry

The traditional educational system of American society was, and basically still is, designed for a young person who has gone through school with only scheduled interruptions since childhood. This applies also to higher education. Such young people are expected to live on campus or nearby and not to have competing marital and parental roles. The ideal of a university locates it in a small town in which it dominates the student's life. The student role is dominant; the circle contains faculty and administrators, service providers, and fellow students organized into classes, majors, and voluntary associations promoting sports, dating, and social life in general.

One of the really dramatic changes in the role of student has been reentry by American women (also men, but not as frequently during the regular schedule) of varied ages.[2] The presence of such students is not reflective of a stage in the "ordinary" life course, nor can it be accounted for in terms of the pleasure of being on campus. It is used as a means of changing role clusters. Reentry is a point of transition, often from full commitment to roles in the family institution and homemaking to expansion in the public sphere (Faver 1984). The midlife student movement is counted in the millions and includes various degrees of involvement and combination with other sets of relations (Schlossberg 1984).

The Chicago-area returnees helped to decrystallize the influence of family background, which had been evident in initial achievements: Women from advantaged households obtained more schooling the first time around than did their less fortunate counterparts. Race had virtually no additional impact on the women's education after parental socioeconomic status, mother's education, and the age of entry into motherhood were taken into account (see also Mott et al. 1977).

The returnees ended up with an average of two years' more schooling than did those with continuous involvement. They most often finished in the school system they started in, and the more education a woman obtained initially, the greater the probability of her return. Interestingly enough, there is a strong association between return to school and divorce. One suspects that either women contemplating divorce decide to prepare themselves occupationally, or return to school so changes the person as to make the marriage stressful or at least no longer satisfactory.

The youngest of our three cohorts of Chicago-area women were much more oriented toward an education that would prepare them for greater involvement in the world outside of the home than had been the older cohorts, but the age thirty-five to forty-five cohort was most apt to return to school and change its life-style, gaining higher incomes and job satisfaction. The same positive results came from specific job training in midlife.

Although both undergraduate and graduate higher educational institutions have become more flexible in the admission of nontraditional students by removing the upper age limits, age remains a pervasive identity affecting the social relationships of the student. An interesting study of the changes introduced in the construction of reality and social circles of older women returning to school is contained in Levy's (1990) analysis of "off-time" students in a prestigious university. Their social circle simply did not know how to handle such older persons in student-faculty or student-student relations. The problems were even more complicated if the older woman entered a male-dominated field, which she was more likely to do than her younger and more occupationally inexperienced counterparts. Friendships were difficult to make with co-students who were in other life-course stages. Problems in relations with younger faculty derived from differences in status, which are accentuated in university settings.

In the meantime, the reentry student goes through several life-course discontinuities in other roles, since formal schooling is usually not considered an appropriate involvement at her age by her other social circles. The problems are illustrated by developments and changes in friendships in settings with which the woman is still affiliated in her nonstudent life (Levy 1990). Involvement in the role of student can disorganize the woman's participation in roles that previously dominated in her life. A subject of interest to sociologists observing this trend toward reentry of adult women into higher levels of the educational institution has been the attitude of the husband. Suitor (1988) reports that, although the more educated husband expresses enthusiasm over his wife's effort, he does not translate this into instrumental support as a member of the student's social circle or in other roles. A less educated husband, who initially expresses worry and mainly negative attitudes, nevertheless extends more support, possibly in anticipation of an increase in family income. The more educated husband may find the changes in his wife's scheduling and commitment to be an inconvenience he does not need. He may also worry about the consequences of his wife's achievements upon their relationship.

Friend

The role of friend is surrounded by many interesting cognitive and emotional nuances in American society. This was apparent when a group of us, sociologists all, got together to talk about the possibility of putting together a book on friendship in the different contexts in which we were studying other roles and relationships (Lopata and Maines 1990). Most of us found a gap between the ideal picture of the perfect friend, totally committed to the relationship, willing to make any sacrifices, aware of all emotional and more practical needs, accepting of all behavior, and providing a very attractive "looking-glass" image of the self and reality in the settings we were studying (Cooley [1902] 1922). At least in American society, emphasis on the value of work for men in proper Protestant-ethic form and the value of "true womanhood" for women, devoted exclusively to the husband, children, and home, defines strong friendship as almost dangerous in that it could interfere with such commitments. In this highly competitive world men allegedly cannot trust each other with disclosures and intimacies, which could expose signs of weakness, while women allegedly are so competitive in their search for, and possessiveness about, men as to make each other unlikely friends. Raymond (1986), in fact, claims that it has been impossible for modern women to enter true friendships with each other in a man-made world, and found it only among lesbians, in convents, or among Chinese marriage resisters of a century ago.

In spite of all these alleged restrictions on friendship in this society, numerous studies point to its presence and variations among women. For example, Bernard documented extensive and multi-level friendships among women in *The Female World* (1981) and Smith-Rosenberg (1979) used letters and diaries of the mid-eighteenth and nineteenth centuries to bring to light networks of friends that provided emotional support, security, and self-esteem and that were central to the members' lives.

A variety of factors influence the social-person characteristics of people selected as friends, the composition of the social circle, and the packages of negotiated rights and duties. Americans vary greatly by stage of life cycle, generation, gender, ethnic and racial background, education, residence, and so forth in whom they identify as a friend. Sociologists have assumed that friendship is most apt to bloom among the elderly, since other roles are less demanding at that time of life. Yet, there is no consensus concerning such a frequency of friendship in old age. Pihlblad and Rosencranz (1968) found some older people in small towns of Missouri claiming all residents as friends, while others claimed to have no friends at all. Other elders spoke of the impossibility of developing relations now that could duplicate those with a lovingly described childhood chum. It appears that old age alone is not a sufficient factor in friendship formation. Physical proximity with people of the same age and marital and life circumstances are facilitating situations, as Hochschild found among women in *The Unexpected Community* (1973). Roberto and Scott (1984–85) tested equity theory on the friendship of elderly women using my support-systems framework and found that those who were "overbenefited," that is, who received more support than they gave, had the lowest morale. Those who were underbenefited, by their terminology, were pleased to be able to help a friend not as well off as themselves. Constraints, such as health or financial problems, can limit the formation of friendship in old age (Rook 1989).

Sources of contact with potential friends depend upon the social involvements of the person; the variety of these is influenced by the complexity of the social life space. During the transitional times of the feminine mystique, restrictions on direct involvement in the public sphere limited the sources to school in childhood, and to the neighborhood and voluntary associations in the roles of wife and mother. Women have expanded their involvements in more modern times, providing greater variations in sources of contact, with mixed results. On the one hand, a job can demand considerable time, especially when combined with the second shift at home, decreasing occasions for developing and maintaining friendships. On the other hand, the job provides opportunities for pleasant interaction, whether limited to such settings or carried into leisure-time activity. The mobility of many women, both social and geographic, almost necessitates a turnover of friends (see also Lopata 1975). It can also bring together people of strongly divergent social classes (Hess 1972; Matthews 1986). The opportunity of finding points of commonalty and divergence, facilitators and barriers, thus differs by setting.

The development of a friendship requires repeated social interaction, preferably, but not necessarily, face-to-face, that can increase perceptions of similarity (Adams and Blieszner 1989; Bell 1981). It is the perceived similarity of interests, reinforced by continued contact, rather than similarity of cultural background, that contributes to friendship formation (Gudykunst 1985, 281). The interaction must be egalitarian, although masters or husbands in asymmetrical relations can claim to be close friends with servants or wives. The person in the subservient position is less likely to so define the relationship.

Once established, friendship acquires a personalistic focus, each partner seeing the other as unique so that intercultural differences recede into the background. Jackson and Crane (1986) studied black-white friendships and concluded that contact is not enough to do away with prejudice and categorical discrimination. Even positive affective dispositions toward a person of another social race is not enough to support equality in the relationship. The best combination appears to include a black of a higher social status than the white, since equality of personal prestige does not offset categorical inferiority. White-black friendships appear more frequent in academia or the entertainment world than in the general population, where equality of interaction and commonalty of interests are less likely.

One of the findings of my various studies in the Chicago area is that some women, usually lower-class and less educated, do not define the role of friend as something that one can develop, assuming either that kin members are the only possible intimates or that such relations can be achieved only in childhood (see also Rubin 1976). The assumption that adults have trouble making friends appears to be prevalent, as evidenced by the existence of numerous for-profit organizations that educate people into the techniques of such development. Dale Carnegie's 1936 book and still popular courses teach people how to "win friends and influence people," etiquette publications abound, and the mass media are full of reports on ways people unaccustomed to developing close nonkin and nonjob relationships with others can learn how to do so. The military and multinational corporations, which force their members into frequent geographic movement, use shortcuts such as enforced socializing to create opportunities for social contact.

The role of friend necessitates not only purposeful development through efforts on both sides, but also maintenance activities (Blieszner 1989; Brown 1990). McCall and Simmons (1978) see friendships as incorporating increasing dimensions of self-identities. Although circumstances can create boundaries, especially when friends are not able to observe each other in other contexts, Little (1990) shows that the sharing of reminiscences, symbolic representations, and even letters can provide insights among buddies who have never seen each other's other selves. Of course, people may wish to segment their friendships, leaving parts of the self uninvolved.

Most observers point to the importance of a positive balance of benefits over costs for a friendship's maintenance. The costs frequently involve strain in relations with significant others who may be jealous of the time and closeness involved in the friend relationship. The benefits include empathetic understanding, even love, acceptance of even less than likable aspects of the self regardless of societal norms, the pleasure of association and sharing activities, protection from unpleasant self-images and sometimes even from unpleasant interaction, the provision of resources for reaching goals, and so forth. Many women stress the importance of friendships in the reconstruction of the self from traditional identities into feminist ones (Acker, Barry, and Esseveld 1990). Factors that underlie the selection of friends may differ from those that sustain or deepen the relationship (Brown 1990, 31–32). In order to exist as a role, of course, a relationship must include more than two people, in a set of friends or a setting of supporting circle members. In fact, a friendship is frequently embedded in a friendship network, with more or less freedom to form closer dyads (Baker and Hertz, 1990). The circle can provide resources, such as space and activity for contact among friends, and can protect them from interference by others. Thus, the relations does not exist in isolation.

Friendships are temporal, changing in characteristics and salience as other aspects of life over which choice is not always possible are modified. This happens, for example, when people move away, for a job or other reasons. Dubin (1956) found factory workers perfectly willing to change jobs even if it meant giving up friendships in the old locale. They knew they could replace them easily enough in the new setting. One of the problems of retirement is the impossibility of maintaining such relationships as the settings vanish.

Commitments to the role of friend, involving "side bets" to anchor this role, are often not sufficiently important to offset commitments to other roles. To paraphrase Janowitz (1968), modern friendships appear to involve limited liability and the willingness to give them up if their benefits fail to satisfy. At the same time, as diffused as friendships appear to be in our society, they also seem to contain rules that, when broken, create strains and often end the relationship (Duck 1986; Rook 1989; Matthews 1986). Violations of such norms include breach of confidence, invasion of privacy, or critical and unresponsive behavior. Sometimes friendships simply face not being revitalized over time. The failure of a dyadic relationship can create problems for the network in which it is embedded.

Whatever meaning the role of friend has for different people, its perceived absence tends to create feelings of social and emotional loneliness (Lopata 1969b; Weiss 1973). People need a variety of relationships (Weiss 1973). People are especially devastated when former friendships are broken off, especially when this does not happen through their own action and they think other people are involved in relations of satisfactory intimacy (see Lopata 1990).

Same-Gender and Cross-Gender Friendships

Two questions are usually raised in discussions of the role of friend: whether, and in what ways, friendships among women differ from those among men, and what are the characteristics of cross-gender relationships.

Although much attention has been given in the mass media and in social science literature to male "bonding" ever since Tiger's *Men in Groups* (1969) appeared, the general consensus appears to be that women form closer, more intimate friendships with each other than do men (Rubin 1985). Men more often lack a best friend or list a woman who does not identify the relationship as symmetrical. A New Zealand study found strong "gender differences in friendship patterns" (Aukett, Ritchie, and Mill 1988). Women's relationships were more intimate and emotional, involving talking, sharing, discussing personal problems, and self-disclosure. Men tended to share activities but to shy away from emotional involvement. Williams (1985) concluded that male colleagues were more instrumental in their support of each other, while women were more expressive.

Even women's same-gender and same-stage-of-life-course friendships can be constrained by involvement in competing roles. Fischer reported in 1982 that marriage restricted the possibilities of non-kin and non-neighbor friendships for women. In addition,

> Children clearly restricted the social involvements of their parents, especially of their mothers. Women with children at home had fewer friends and associates, engaged in fewer social activities, had less reliable social support, and had more localized networks than did otherwise similar women without children. (Fischer 1982, 253)

These conclusions were very similar to those I had reached almost thirty years before, accentuating the importance of looking at a person's role cluster in determining the social psychological aspects of involvement in any one role (Lopata 1971b).

The findings concerning same-gender friendships raise interesting questions concerning cross-gender relationships. Do women gain different benefits from men friends than from women friends? A difference can also be assumed for the men. Several studies address these subjects directly. Women college and graduate university students reportedly prefer same-gender relationships for intimacy and acceptance, but cross-gender friendships for companionship (Rose 1985). The latter is not surprising on a campus where dating is the prevalent companionship activity. Rose (1985) reports that men are more dependent upon significant women in their lives than women are on men. O'Meara (1989) cautions that cross-gender relationships must meet four major challenges:

> These include the private challenges of defining the nature of their emotional bond, regulating the role of sexuality, and dealing with the impact of gender inequality, and the public challenge of presenting the authenticity of the friendship to relevant audiences in the friends' social networks. (P. 539)

The problem of sexuality and the assumption by others in social circles that any relationship between a woman and a man must be based on this element is not surprising in a society that evaluates women mainly as sex objects. Adams (1985) entitled her article on the subject "People Would Talk: Normative Barriers to Cross-Sex Friendships for Elderly Women."

The differences in what women and men offer each other in friendship produce an asymmetrical relationship. Aukett, Ritchie, and Mill (1988) decided that men get more emotional support and therapeutic value from women friends than women get from men friends; women do not benefit equally in their cross-gender relations as they do from same-gender ones. Acker, Barry, and Esseveld (1981) explained that the new feminism in America at first strained cross-gender relationships, as women felt a strong need to develop greater independence from men and anger over their past subservient status, but the authors expect that in the long run it will help the formation of new, egalitarian friendships. Rubin (1985) found that gay men and straight women often were comfortable with each other and able to enter close friendship relations.

Couple-Companionate Friendship

One of the interesting aspects of friendship in this society is the increasing frequency of association between the role of wife and that of friend. Middle-class modern America insists that marital partners should also be "best friends" (Bell 1981; Rubin 1985). In addition, companionate marriage favors what I call "couple-companionate" relations. Women and men who marry are expected to convert their past friendships into relationships involving both mates and to develop new friendships with other couples. For example, change in friendship networks evolves even among college student couples as they deepen their involvement with each other (Milardo 1982). Joint networks help to preserve the couple relationship, while separate friendships "are more invested in one individual or the other than in the couple" (Milardo, 1982; 170).

The friendship conversion process by married couples can be difficult, unless there is sufficient communality among all the people involved in the couples. Block and Greenberg (1985) were wrong when they stated:

> A century ago, few married couples socialized . . . in more recent years, particularly in the last half century, the belief that women and men could be socially compatible emerged. (P. 138)

On the contrary, there is a long history of couple-companionate relations in European and American upper classes (see Veblen [1899] 1953; Znaniecki 1965). Compatible couples have long enjoyed many games and other pastimes together. Couples in modern times tend to do things together on Saturday nights or at other times if retired from paid employment, and share a variety of activities. The role of couple-companionate friend requires that each member treat the others symmetrically in what they do for each other's entertainment and expenses. For example, hospitality in the home should be reciprocated, unless there is an acceptable reason for alternative privileges. It is possible, of course, that the women can have separate personal friendships with each other, but couple-companionate occasions are to be symmetrical, within gender propriety norms.

One of the fascinating aspects of couple-companionate friendships is the source of the contact, the person who brings the other couple into the relationship. Babchuk and Bates (1963) claim that the husbands dominated as the originators of such relationships, at least among urbanites in Nebraska. I found that the wives gave themselves credit in most situations, even when the original contact was through the husband's job (Lopata 1975 and 1990). The wife, who is usually the "social secretary" for the middle-class couple, defines her contribution as the selection of couples from that milieu for close interaction. Claim of contribution gives the originator greater rights and obligations for continued maintenance.

Divorce and widowhood place great strains upon couple-companionate friendships, bringing forth the importance of symmetry and balance (Lopata 1973b, 1975, 1979, etc.). Widows are constantly faced with the fact that their married friends tend to withdraw, or to see them only when their husbands are absent (Adams 1983). Whether accurately or not, widows report that their married women friends are jealous of their possible relations with their husbands (Lopata 1973c). There is an awkwardness over transportation, payment of bills, and other interactional aspects, while past loyalties linger. "His friends" who allegedly became "our friends" revert to their original identity and fail to keep up the contact (Kitson et al. *Divorcees and Widows* 1980). Life circumstances become too different to maintain the feelings of "we-ness." Both widows and divorcees finally turn to other women in the same marital situation, although they feel deprived of male companionship (Adams 1983 and 1985; Adams and Blieszner 1989).

Neighbor

The role of neighbor is another component of a frequent nostalgia for the past. The village or small town is idealized as containing neighbors whom one has known throughout life, who are familiar with the family and all of its history, and who are always there to provide social and emotional support as well as help in emergencies (Fischer 1982). Anyone familiar with such communities, as contained, for example, in Reymont's description (in his Nobel Prize–winning *The Peasants* [1925]) of life in a Polish village, knows better than to accept such portrayals. However, this does not stop much of literature on urbanism from being extremely critical of an alleged lack of such ideally drawn neighboring. At the same time, early observers of suburbia were very negative about that style of life because of "too much" neighboring. Most were horrified by the alleged homogeneity, ease of interaction, and decrease of norms of privacy (Mumford 1961; Riesman, Glaser, and Denney 1950; Whyte 1956). What they neglected to note was that the women were turning to each other to create a new, revolutionary style of life, much as had the women studied by Willmot and Young (1960) who moved from a London borough to a suburb.

222 CIRCLES AND SETTINGS

The concept of neighboring illustrates the difference between availability of a role and actual involvement. Our concern here is with neighbors as people who live within a self- and other-defined geographical "neighborhood," be it composed of apartments, homes within a dense but small territory, or farms scattered on individual acres away from others. It is, of course, possible to talk of people in a work setting or sharing a table at an official event as "neighbors," but I am limiting this discussion to residential proximity. Almost everyone has neighbors, but the role of neighbor involves active exchanges of rights and duties with people considered neighbors. The circle of neighbors may form an integrated network, all members being aware of belonging, communicating, and interacting with each other along established norms.[3] It is this form of neighboring upon which network analysts focus (Fischer et al. 1977; Fischer 1982). It is necessary to note here that our role theory does not negate the presence of such networks but also considers other persons with whom a neighbor may be involved who are not part of the network. For example, being a neighbor may require interaction with the neighbor's children, service and object providers, businesses, school personnel, and so forth.

Neighborhoods vary considerably in the relationships among their residents, as do individuals, communities, even societies. There can be pockets of intense neighboring even in a working-class community with minimal or restricted interaction among those living nearby. The forms and intensity of neighboring vary by the history of interaction, the abilities, desires, and resources of residents, and the competition this role has from other roles in each person's cluster. An important element in neighboring, as in friendship, is the match between the person and the neighbors in social class, race, ethnicity, age, and other common or division-creating characteristics (Lopata 1971b). People living in close proximity almost invariably come into some form of contact, but that can as easily lead to hostility or indifference as to friendly interaction.

The Transitional Form of the Role of Neighbor

Early studies of neighboring in American cities were usually incorporated into research on ethnic communities, prior studies having focused on rural or pioneer relationships. The Chicago school of sociology is famous for such interest in ethnic communities. Wirth's *Ghetto* (1928) is a classic of this type. Scholars studied the influence of increasing size, density, and heterogeneity upon social relations (Wirth 1938). Expansion of large, dense, and heterogeneous cities led scholars such as Stein (1960) to theories of community eclipse.

Social scientists reactivated their interest in neighboring after World War II, with the phenomenal growth of new, and the expansion of old, suburbs surrounding American cities. The G.I. Bill, which helped veterans obtain additional schooling, also assisted them with low-interest loans for the purchase of homes. The housing industry boomed, and mass media as well as sociologists followed people out of the city to see how they lived and related to each other. These various studies contribute to our understanding of factors that activate, or suppress, involvement in the role of neighbor.

For example, builder-designed communities, such as Park Forest, Illinois, were isolated from other settlements, and neighbors were highly dependent upon each other for all kinds of service and emotional supports (Whyte 1956). Upwardly and geographically mobile young residents often came from distances that prevented frequent contact with relatives and friends and made people willing to go through the stages of active neighboring. Most of the women in newly emerging communities developed a quite intensive involvement in the role of neighbor. The fact that urbanists such as Whyte (1956) and his associates and Lewis Mumford (1961) were quite disparaging concerning the women's "fishbowl" existence did not decrease the desire for such relationships, especially in Park Forest. Some of the Park Foresters complained of not having any privacy, but most were thrilled to have such social and support exchanges. Even women not socialized into middle-class forms of social interaction, such as the California residents described in *Working Class Suburb* (Berger 1960) or Levittowners in Pennsylvania, slowly replaced kinfolk with neighbors for support systems (Gans 1967). Active neighboring took place in the Canadian middle-class Crestwood Heights (Seeley, Sim, and Loosely 1956), but the higher status "exurbanites" around New York City engaged in selective interaction with those neighbors they deemed to be of equal status (Spectorsky 1955).

I first became interested in the neighboring relations of American suburban women in the 1950s when my husband and I moved with a small child to a suburb of Chicago (Skokie) while I was finished my dissertation at the University of Chicago. Having been brought up in a much more formal milieu in urban Poland, I was amazed as the informality of interaction in our neighborhood, which

grounds different from one's own, are usually looked upon with suspicion, and few efforts are made to invest in a relationship with them. The behavior of each person and even of other family members may attract or repulse potentially friendly neighbors. People differ not only in their ability to develop closer relationships with neighbors, but also in their interest in doing so.

There is a definite life cycle of the role of neighbor, its forms and intensity varying by the life cycle of the roles of the women and their families and by the cycle of neighboring in a particular area and of that role itself. The birth of a child, a child's entrance into the school system, and the role involvements of the husband/father or the wife/mother can move the role into a more focal place in the cluster or push it out to the outer layers. As children develop more independent sources of contact, the mothers can be deprived of the companionship of other neighborhood mothers. As a neighborhood ages, parks become deserted, and schools can close or consolidate with more distant ones; mothers are freed to enter new roles or reactivate old roles, as in taking a job or becoming a volunteer. A turnover of neighbors can break off a close relationship and result in less willingness to reinvest, or it can introduce people who are much more compatible. Increased income can provide the second car and mobility, decreasing dependence upon those living nearby. Established households require less emergency (and even daily) borrowing, lending, and exchanges of services.

A decrease in opportunities for, and interest in, the role of neighbor can be experienced differentially within a network, often causing strain. Women dependent upon the companionship and other benefits of such involvement can find that neighbors are too busy or wish to change the norms, forms, or intensity of the relationship. A change in leisure-time activities can separate a neighborhood network that played cards within the hearing of young children. Nonlocal friendships can replace the supports of nearby associates. Or someone made uncomfortable with an expansion of neighboring into higher levels may try to cool it, without having adequate techniques for doing so (Goffman 1967). Other problems can arise, as in friendships, making the costs of neighboring disproportionate to the benefits. I found frequent references to conflicts among children or over property rights as main reasons for withdrawal from active neighboring. In fact, such conflicts can split a whole neighborhood into warring camps (Lopata 1971b, 251).

Thus, the person most apt to be involved in the role of neighbor at a somewhat controlled high level in the 1950s and 1960s was a full-time homemaker with small children, a home owner living in a newly developed, middle-class suburb or urban fringe community of similar women. This is particularly true if she had been socialized into developing relationships with virtual strangers, aware of, and following, the norms of reciprocity and privacy. She was not apt to have highly supportive relatives within easy distance upon whom she could depend at all times. She was matched by many characteristics with her neighbors, having common interests and problems, and so developed an egalitarian exchange, not necessarily of the same supports.

The Modern Form of the Role of Neighbor

Suburban life and, to a lesser extent, urban life have been considerably modified since the feminine-mystique days, especially in areas that had previously almost exclusively drawn married full-time homemakers with children (see Stimpson et al. 1981; Lopata 1980a). The boundary between city and suburb has blurred, and living in an outside community is no longer a pioneering venture. Commercial and industrial activity has become more decentralized, providing jobs where only bedroom dwellings existed before.

Many of the women of metropolitan Chicago in 1990 display a different attitude toward the role of neighbor from that of the post–World War II homemakers. Fewer women have small children keeping them in the home and its immediate environment; more women do not marry, do not have children or have fewer than in prior cohorts, and do not stay home even when in the role of mother. The various questions as to forms and levels of neighboring often draw surprised comments—surprised that we expect such strong involvement. Neighboring has often narrowed to an exchange relationship, or close interaction with only one neighbor, and much less network involvement than in the past. Services that are now exchanged include the taking in of packages, mail, or other items in the daily or more lengthy absence of the other, a result of the frequency with which neighbor women are employed. Friendship is less often tied to the role of neighbor, as the women become less constricted to the local area. Education and income, indices of social class, still influence involvement in neighbor networks, especially in a network's size rather than intensity and emotional intimacy. Women of higher levels tend to know more neighbors and to visit more often, but the role is not as significant as among lower-class women, who develop longer lasting friendships with a few neighbors. The mixture of these two roles, friend and neighbor, is hard to separate.

The growing number of retirement communities and retired, leisure-oriented people may be increasing the importance of the neighbor role at that stage of life. More people are living longer and have the economic means to move to climates conducive to outdoor socializing. Retirement hotels or communities make special efforts to provide locales and events for neighboring and encourage the development of such roles as a means of keeping their residents happy (van den Hoonaard 1991). The expansion of such geographical areas in recent years certainly reinforces Rosow's (1967) and Hochschild's (1973) findings that age homogeneity provides an excellent resource for involvement in the role of neighbor.

Suburban and urban social relationships, including those of neighboring, have not been forgotten by social scientists, who still express negative evaluations of life in the outer areas. The strength of the rejection is still tied to an idealized image of the "dream house" in the "dream community." Baumgartner (1988) appears surprised that her affluent suburb of New York City contains people with hostile and indifferent attitudes, who nevertheless avoid open conflict with great restraint. Baldassare (1986) draws our attention to the trouble in paradise, exposing the assumption that paradise should be available in suburbia. Conflicts and anger at the way some communities have developed show involvement, even if negative, and accentuate the fact that the suburbs are not as homogeneous as originally portrayed. There is an increasing interest in the factors that create variations in the role of neighbor, in contrast to the original assumption of high levels of involvement. In spite of all the changes, unemployed women with small children are still most apt to depend on neighbors for social supports, while people involved in a multidimensional life space have broader and less intensive relations (Fischer et al. 1977; Fischer, 1982). Many people in many societies are still seeking the feeling and involvement of community life, judging by the frequency of active neighboring, especially in new towns (Thorns 1976). Women in Middletown were still engaged in neighboring exchanges in the 1980s (Caplow et al. 1982). Urban black communities can be seen as networks involving their residents (Oliver 1988), while neighboring contributes to residential satisfaction in Canadian cities (Michelson 1977). However, many of the recent studies of the role of neighbor in local areas exemplify Janowitz's (1968) thesis of the community of limited liability, in which members have multiple identifications and relationships, so that no single involvement can command strong commitment.

Roles in Communities

There are many social roles within the broader community, defined as a symbolic, territorial, or identity territory in which persons or groups are located (Hunter 1974; Lopata 1976b and 1994; Suttles 1972). This section of the chapter is focused on nonoccupational roles in voluntary associations in local, national and even international communities. Such groups can be identified by manifest (i.e., declared) functions or latent, more hidden functions, or by type of membership. People involved in such groups can be differentiated by level of commitment or position and type of activity. Complex social groups can work toward several purposes, and each member can be involved in one or a combination of them, at any level, at any stage of involvement. For example, a hospital auxiliary can benefit patients by providing objects (such as books) and services (such as companionship), while simultaneously benefiting members by offering social status in the community and activity outside of the home. It can train women in leadership roles or be part of a family's status-production work. Numerous characteristics or pervasive identities of social persons, such as gender, race, religion, ethnicity, and age, can serve as criteria for admission or rejection of potential members. So can interests, such as skiing or stamp collecting. Members may meet frequently or only through representatives. They can move up or down ladders of authority or status positions. In fact, it would be impossible to analyze all the combinations and permutations of characteristics of organizational roles, so I shall concentrate on a limited number of roles organized by breadth of beneficiary. It is important to specify these, because, unlike with the role of mother or wife, the beneficiaries are not always apparent even from the title of the group, and the roles of members are dependent upon these. The first type of group is organized to benefit only the members. The second consists of volunteers whose beneficiaries are external to the group but limited to the local community. The third includes activists or reformers on the national and/or global scale, whose beneficiaries are whole categories of beings, whether people or other species.

The social person characteristics and the activities of each association are more or less formally matched. The criteria of membership of social persons depend on manifest and latent purposes of the group, the duties required, and the rights and privileges offered. These obviously vary so much that generalizations are difficult to make. Some groups have gradations of membership, with scales of duties and rights (Clawson 1986). A woman can take an active part, with other activists, in the campaign to get Nestlé milk products withdrawn from markets in developing countries, without maintaining a lifelong membership in any reform group. Knowledge of the group and willingness to abide by its norms are universal requirements. So is the obligation to treat other members in the expected manner, to allow authoritative actions from those granted leadership privileges, to present the self in a manner not embarrassing to others, and to do the necessary work at the right time in the required setting.

Research on voluntary associations usually focuses on evidence of latent purposes, as in charitable groups that spend so much time selecting the right members and maintaining high-status activities as to indicate that their manifest purpose is really secondary in importance to social status. Only a careful examination of the actual criteria used to select members and the relative importance of activities can bring to light the conscious, or sometimes even unconscious, functions. Evaluative research can also focus on dysfunctional activities that interfere with main goals. Some researchers try to determine the reasons people join or avoid joining a particular group, or a category of such groups. This is especially true of associations designed to benefit people who often fail to take advantage of the benefits, as is true of those devoted to the elderly or the handicapped (Fisher et al. 1989).

The significance for women of participation in all kinds of voluntary associations has not been carefully researched. In studies devoted to the whole social life space, the role usually does not appear as the most important in women's role clusters, but this varies considerably by social class or special group affiliation. Some women and some groups have intensive interconnections, the networks functioning as a constant background to other roles, or even in a central location of the role cluster (see also the special issue of

Signs, Women in the American City [Stimpson et al. 1980]). What a person gains from membership and activity varies, of course, by the same sociopsychological aspects of involvement that apply to other roles.

Several researchers have recently studied the differences in the role of member in voluntary organizations as carried forth by women and by men. McPherson and Smith-Lovin (1982) drew on a large sample of noninstitutionalized adults in Nebraska and found differences having extensive consequences upon life and social influence. Women were members of smaller and different kinds of groups than were men. Small size in itself had negative consequences, in that it limited the number of potential contacts. Although they had the same mean number of memberships as did the men, the women limited themselves to "domestic, including youth, church-related, social charitable, neighborhood and community organizations," while men belonged to job-related organizations (union, professional, or business) or nondomestic organizations (fraternal, sports, veterans, political, hobby, and service and civic; McPherson and Smith-Lovin 1982, 901). The researchers accounted for the differences in terms of selective recruitment by high-powered, prestige organizations, which prefer high-status, high-income, high-mobility men, or selective joining by women in traditionally defined roles. They conclude that women join organizations that value their skills and interests, which tend to be local and small in size. These cannot "provide access to information about jobs, business opportunities or chances for professional advancement" and thus place women at a disadvantage vis-à-vis that world. This analysis fits beautifully into our role theory, in that it documents the importance of social person and social circle selection processes and the criteria.

We could say that such gender variation may be typical of Nebraskans but certainly not of such a cosmopolitan environment as New York City! It appears, however, that there are also status differences in the type and level of involvement by women in organizations in that city. Lawson and Barton (1980) studied the tenant movement in New York, which included organizations in buildings, neighborhoods, and larger federations. The movement was started by women on the local level and then spread geographically and horizontally. The authors found that the higher the level of the positions in the larger units that required negotiation with bureaucracies, and the higher the income of the tenants, the more the leaders were apt to be men (235).

The explanation for the divergence follows traditional gender roles. The fact that women started the tenant movement on the building level is due to their responsibility for the domestic sphere with its related problems. Such involvement brings them into contact with other women residents who share similar activities and content. Local participation is also more socially acceptable for them than is citywide activism. There is an additional gender difference in involvement in the movement. The men who enter, usually at a less local and higher level of leadership, are in the movement mainly for career reasons. Their expertise and knowledge of "bureaucratic manipulations" is transferable to other organizations, and they tend to move on. This rapid turnover at higher positions enables the women, who learn from them, to finally move into leadership positions. In making policy recommendations, the authors suggested that men should learn to utilize the local skills of women and combine these with formal, large-organization skills in developing and maintaining social movements. The opposite direction of organizational advantages was not recommended for the women.

A study of two organizations in the women's movement, however, provides guidelines stressing the advantages of a "formalized or bureaucratic structure." Staggenborg (1989) followed the history and format of the Chicago Women's Liberation Union, which did not survive, and the Chicago chapter of the National Organization for Women, which is still in existence. The former allowed more innovation, but was undermined by a lack of formalized structure and centralized division of labor. Although Chicago NOW is seen as disadvantaged by too much centralization and lack of contribution by subunits, its paid staff and organizational techniques are judged to assist continuity. These kinds of studies are sociologically interesting because of the underlying assumption that women are not able to organize effectively. Such a hypothesis is erroneous, in view of the history of women's groups the world over.

Member of Voluntary Associations

Women have been involved in community roles for centuries, although the definition of these varies by society and time. Religious communities abounded in Europe and have a complicated history in America. Women also participated in a variety of ways in courts of rulers. It is safe to say, however, that only a tiny proportion of past populations were involved in any but local groups. The vast majority participated in, without choosing, village life and informal group-ings, the church being the main formal organization. Thomas and Znaniecki (1918–20) described the Polish peasant of the early twen-tieth century as limited in the perspective to the *okolica,* the local area within which his or her reputation was contained. In spite of nationalistic movements by political rulers and the intelligentsia, most Europeans did not see, and were not interested in, the wider national cultural society, let alone the world.

The same can be said of the majority of less educated Americans. In addition, the emergence of the "Cult of True Womanhood" in the nineteenth century discouraged women from participation in public sphere activities that fell into the province of men. Foreign travelers like de Toqueville ([1835] 1936) and Harriet Martineau ([1837] 1966) were astounded by the lack of opportunity for women to be in-volved in the world outside of the home. In actuality, however, there were many local groups, formal and informal, of women who shared work or leisure time and church activities in colonial America. These groups blurred the boundaries between the role of neighbor and that of member of an association, with its formal characteristics of title, tests of membership, declared function, division of labor, and hierarchy of status. The increasing numbers of middle- and upper-class women in larger communities became involved in associations providing the role of volunteer in a wider arena:

> Volunteering broke it [the Cult of True Womanhood], for generations of leisured women who created new, unpaid jobs for themselves outside the home. It gave them public lives, ended their domestic isolation, and gave rise to organizations of women dedicated to insti-tutional reform in education, health care, and criminal justice, as well as the cultural and "moral" enrichment of society. (Kaminer 1984, 24)

Charity circles, anti-vice societies, and educational and politically oriented groups that were organized on a national scale helped the poor, insured the welfare of children, and worked to change the position and life of women. Antislavery and women's rights groups preceded and followed the Civil War. The Young Women's Chris-tian Association, the Women's Christian Temperance Union, and the National Consumers League are examples of early associations with a wide range of beneficiaries. It is interesting to note a basic difference between even these groups with broad goals: Some were oriented toward maintenance of the status quo, partly by solving some of its problems, while others were determined to reform the system itself. A few, but not many, were revolutionary, in that they aimed to overthrow the system and substitute a different one.

The role of status-maintaining volunteer remains even in modern times. Susan Ostrander (1985) comments on it in the world of upper-class women:

> The evidence presented in this chapter demonstrates that volunteer work provides certain personal advantages to upper-class women (such as the opportunity to advance to leadership positions without formal credentials, and to balance home and family responsibilities). But these personal advantages do not explain their overall commitment to this work . . . the women focus on class-specific reasons for doing volunteer work, such as noblesse oblige (which justifies privilege) and family tradition (which carries on the traditions of the class). These are the fundamental reasons for their commitment. (P. 138)

The level of commitment to this work is high, although the women downplay its importance to the community at large. Ostrander interestingly notes that

> upper-class women are not, for the most part, involved in direct service kinds of volunteer work. . . . Instead . . . [they] move quickly into leadership positions on the boards of their organizations. (P. 112)

However, volunteers managed by these upper-class women, who are themselves at least upper-middle-class in community status, contribute time and effort directly to the beneficiaries or at least raise funds used to do so. And the work civic leaders do definitely benefits the community, which could not exist in its modern form without it (Daniels 1988). Although their effort and careers within this world are mainly invisible, they can produce large sums of money, enabling the maintenance and growth of major community agencies. The patriarchal nature of the society is evident in the male dominance over the "important" positions in the same groups. The women's work and contributions are "backstage," while that of the males are front or center stage (Daniels 1988, 270). The backstage is in itself important, as it provides opportunities for others to accomplish the visible work, and it maintains the values of community, encouraging active participation of many other people. In general:

> These women fund, organize and manage school, church, and neighborhood services. . . . All these efforts focus on two major lines of interest: voluntary activities in social reform and community welfare and cultural interests, community beautification, or "uplift." (Daniels 1988, xx)

Actually, their social reform efforts are limited to cleaning up any dysfunctional or inefficient aspects of the social system, rather than reforming the system itself.

Many of the traditional volunteer organizations also provide the female equivalent to the proverbial "old boy network" for the concentration of informal and even formal sources of power in the community. Domhoff concluded in *Who Rules America?* (1967) and *Who Rules America Now?* (1983) that persons listed in *Who's Who of American Women* were almost inevitably involved in a wide range of social groups with welfare, cultural, and civic activities. Membership roles carry appropriate obligations and rights of information and influence, as well as careful observance of norms of deference and demeanor (Ostrander 1985). Duties to fellow members include recognition and respect and strict adherence to the activities for which the group is known in the community. Unless the group is secret, which the vast majority are not, the need to maintain its reputation carries the obligation to meet its purposes, regardless of competition from other roles.

The presence of such status quo-maintaining organizations should not blind us to the recognition of many broader, reform-oriented women's associations. There is a whole history of more or less organized women's social movements pushing for dramatic change in American institutions, including those aimed at suffrage, protective legislation, mothers' rights over their children, the environment, and a variety of other economic and political rights for all Americans, as well as movements aimed against war and militarism. Those have not been the goals of groups maintaining the status quo.

Communities that depend upon volunteer workers and leaders are now facing major problems, as the same women who had the knowledge and ability to organize and carry out so many local activities are the very ones who can do similar work in a job. Wendy Kaminer concludes in *Women Volunteering: The Pleasure, Pain, and Politics of Unpaid Work from 1830 to the Present* (1984) that a community who "lived on its volunteers" is finding it hard to find substitutes (212). Certainly associations can hold meetings on eve-

nings and weekends, and some fathers are increasing their participation in "traditional women's things," but that still leaves much
daytime work undone. Who is to be a Brownie leader? The whole
ideology of volunteerism is questioned when people have to be
hired to do the work. It is the same problem that O'Donnell and
Stueve (1983) noted about the failure of employed middle-class
mothers to serve as the social agents connecting children to the
community. From the vantage point of the community itself, the
absence of these women has created a major void inadequately
filled by paid workers. Of course, not all women are employed;
many women of the upper and middle classes continue their activities with limited help. Attempts are made to socialize women of the
lower classes into less passive stances vis-à-vis their communities,
housing, and schools. An example of such efforts is the Organization
of the NorthEast in two of Chicago's most heterogeneous and prob-
lem-ridden neighborhoods. Women who traditionally did not venture out of home, church, and maybe a job have become active in
a variety of activities under the motto "Our Hope for the Future,"
meaning the children (Nyden et al. 1922). Men will undoubtedly be
forced to do more of the backstage work in the absence of women
who did it in the past.

One source of volunteers for traditional community work is
expanding in recent years. The developing concern over the graying
of America has resulted in a closer look at the voluntary association
membership of the elderly. The extensive survey *Older Minnesotans: What Do They Need? How Do They Contribute?* found many of
the elderly making volunteer contributions to others (Fisher et al.
1989). Their work was segregated to a certain degree by gender.
Women did welfare work of a personal nature, visiting people,
bringing food, helping the church function—all of which are extensions of family and homemaking activity. Men helped with male-
intensive work, such as house repairs, and were more active in
organizational management. Thus, gender assignment or selection
of activity, including leadership, does not end in old age.

Whatever the beneficiaries of the role of volunteer gain from this
activity, the social person also receives rewards. Involvement in the
role prevents, or at least delays, the "cycle of social breakdown,"
which Bengtson and Kuypers developed as a model of problems
associated with aging due to role loss and ambiguity of norms. Being
a volunteer with obvious duties and rights reconstructs feelings of

status and competence (Payne 1977). Activity in voluntary associations assists integration into the community, even at the lower-class levels, as Clemente, Rexroad, and Hirsch (1975) found among elderly black women. Ethnic and religious communities also provide resources for continued social involvement throughout the life course (Kitano 1988; Sklare 1971). The Polish Women's Alliance, founded in the 1880s and still active, has maintained a completely female staff of leaders, doctors, and lawyers (Lopata 1976b and 1993b). Problems occur if the community moves away to a secondary settlement, leaving behind the elderly, usually widowed women, who may be completely alienated from the new residents and their networks and thus become socially isolated (Lopata 1988a). In general, however, researchers find that voluntary associations are very important in the lives of the elderly, providing positive feedback to people who no longer have demanding roles upon which to focus (Cutler 1976).

In the meantime, women have been forming new types of associations based on new interests of their members. A major category of such groups has emerged from involvement in the more prestigeful and knowledge-demanding occupations. Occupational groups provide "networking" or contacts, information about jobs, and success stories as well as pointers. The newspapers and magazines of local communities, and occupational and professional journals, abound with announcements of meetings, training seminars, and opportunities for informal exchanges of problems and solutions (Kleiman 1980). I have recently been attending numerous meetings of Women in Sales, Women in Marketing, Women in Publishing, Women Business Owners, and so forth. Branches in different cities arrange for national meetings that much resemble those of the previously all-male National Sales Executives, except that the participants are much more open about barriers, lack of personal tools, and "helpful hints." These are examples of new forms of associations aimed at helping the members themselves. The main obligation of the member role is to transmit knowledge and skills useful in the occupation, as similar men's groups have done for years.

An example of an organization furthering the careers of members is the relatively new Sociologists for Women in Society. Consisting mainly of women (but with male members), it provides a journal aimed at making women and feminist theories more visible, conducts annual conferences with refereed scientific papers, has a mentoring program, and maintains a hotel suite at the American

Sociological Association's and related meetings for members to come together, talk, and arrange for social events. An important benefit to members is ease of involvement in a profession that traditionally was male-based and ignored women except as objects of sexual interest.

One of the new types of organizations in America (although similar, informal groups have usually existed in every community) is in the form of self-and-other help. These groups bring together people who have gone through a disorganizing experience, be it winning the lottery or the death of a significant other, or who are trying to solve personal problems. The most famous, and one of the oldest, is Alcoholics Anonymous (Denzin 1987a and 1987b). Silverman (1987) organized the initial Widow-to-Widow program at Harvard Medical School and studied similar groups as they sprang up all over the United States. Such organizations consist of widows who serve as mentors providing information about resources and confidante interaction at times of intense grief, as well as other widows to get together with to share experiences (Lopata 1973c and 1979). Self- or mutual-help groups are now being organized by women homemakers, according to Andre (1982). Their activities include food or baby-sitting cooperatives, cottage industries, and so forth.

Another part of the women's movement is aimed at opening up gender-restricted associations, much as the civil rights movement worked toward democratizing other restrictive groups. The pioneers have been tokens in groups composed mostly of the dominant gender or racial members. Clawson (1986) presents a historical picture of the Freemasons' and other quasi-Masonic groups' responses to women's demands for membership. The fraternals were purposely organized to exclude, and separate themselves, from, female influence. The formation of auxiliaries such as Eastern Star, as a compromise, allowed the membership in the main body to remain male-only. Wives of Rotarians can be "Rotary Anns"; American women could not join the Rotary itself until the U.S. Supreme Court declared such a membership policy unconstitutional. That decision created an uproar in some of the chapters. The June 1990 issue of *The Rotarian* contained a special section on women in Rotary. Although the cover story was titled "Women—Are They Changing Rotary?" the question was never really answered. Opposition is still strong among many male members, although one respondent said he had "mellowed a bit" (Nugent 1990, 27).

Member of Reform or Revolutionary Movements

Women's reform groups are often vaguely identified as part of the feminist movement, working for humanitarian and equal-rights causes (Mueller 1988). Although there have been some revolutionary groups at different times in American history since independence, they have not been as influential as groups that have limited themselves to reform.

Most historians trace the feminist movement to the Seneca Falls Declaration of 1848 (Sochen 1982). Women also organized farmers' alliances and employee groups, such as the International Ladies Garment Workers Union, and pushed for the vote for civil rights legislation (Hansen 1990). The activities of the Women's Christian Temperance Union certainly influenced political and private life (Gusfield 1963). Black women have been active in abolition, suffrage, and crusades against lynching, and for women's rights movements. Aptheker's *Tapestries of Life* (1989; see also Aptheker 1982) shows how resistance to patriarchal, racist, and class restrictions operates in the daily lives of women. Angela Davis (1988) reminds audiences all over the country of the importance of fighting racism and violence against women on the global scale.

Hartman, in *From Margin to Mainstream: American Women and Politics since 1960* (1989, vii), identifies three eras of the women's movement in America. The first lasted from "the birth of the nation to 1920," a period when women were not citizens and thus were unable to vote, hold office, or participate in party activities, so they had to exert influence indirectly, as did Abigail Adams. The second era lasted from 1920 till the 1960s—women had the vote but were not really integrated into the political system. Hartman dates the third era from the 1960s, when women began mobilizing actively to change major political policies toward their gender. Many scholars have analyzed these activities, successes, and failures (see, for example, Garland 1988, *Women Activists: Challenging the Abuse of Power*).

Examples of women's leadership in environmental protection abounded in the Public Broadcasting System's ten-hour program "Race to Save the Planet" in October 1990 (see *TV Guide*, 6–12 October 1990, 100). Women have organized to protest the militarization of this society, based on the mythology of maleness, which actually hurts the very people who play "war games" against real or hypothetical enemies (Allatt 1983; Enloe 1987). The Boston Women's Health Collective has three times published *Our Bodies, Ourselves* (1971, 1984, 1992), teaching women about the care of their bodies, and numerous protest groups have formed around the subject of human health.

An ongoing example of one form of women's pressure on the economic system is consumer activism (Bloom and Smith 1986). Some of the actions have been individual, such as complaints or personal boycotts against products, brands, or sellers, and legal action. Much, however, is organized through a variety of groups (see Warland, Herrmann, and Moore 1986 for a survey of such actions). The most dramatic has been the pressure to stop the distribution of Nestlé infant formula to less-developed countries because it resulted in a high mortality rate (Post 1986). Nestlé filed a defamation lawsuit in Switzerland to stop the boycott, but had to bow to pressure and settle out of court.

As Steinberg (1990) points out:

> Women have become an institutionalized force in American politics, with dramatic results: in the 1970s Congress passed 71 laws that were part of the feminist political agenda. Gains have been greatest in the extension of legal entitlement in employment and education, among them equal pay for work of comparable worth. (508)

Bernard (1979) summarized the extensive reform activity of various groups of women and their goals of the 1970s:

> They wanted protection for themselves against rape; they wanted an end to discrimination against them in education, vocational training, job opportunities. They wanted protection against "displacement" as housewives in middle life. They wanted recompense for their work in the home. They wanted credit on the same terms as men. They wanted into the social security system in their own names. They wanted a better public image in the media. An end to putdowns; changes in language, in forms of address. . . . They found issues that stunned the world, so long had they been swept under the carpet. (P. 285)

Participation in social movements can be undertaken at various levels and in various social roles. There is usually a core group of highly committed women who are involved in a variety of activities. It often includes both charismatic leaders, who draw new members or at least passive support for the cause, and bureaucratic leaders, who develop constitutions and organize activities. Around the cadre can be found specialists with unique talents who carry forth such work as publicity or special events and wider rings of participants, many of whom are involved only temporarily. The role of activist requires political savvy of a different type than is needed in the role of volunteer in local communities. Yet many of the social person skills are similar, in that a major function of such roles is to "educate" the powers that be, locally or in Washington, who are not interested in women's issues or who are bombarded by opposing groups. Newsletters, such as those produced by the National Organization of Women, have often been read by, and informed, male legislators (Hartman 1989).

Yet women have a long way to go (in spite of the Virginia Slims ads) to achieve equity, as is obvious from the gender distributions in all aspects of American life. Gelb and Palley (1982) claim that women still need to professionalize and even bureaucratize the members of their pressure groups if they are to be more effective in influencing national or state political leaders. The failure to pass the Equal Rights Amendment is an indication that women have not sufficiently coordinated their efforts. Of course, one problem is that women do not form a single block, having many, often contradictory, definitions of social problems and of their solutions, as is clearly evidenced in the abortion issue.

The absence of women in the seats of economic and political power in the United States reflects the strength of the dual-sphere world of the past and, obviously, in the present. Where are the women in high political offices? Other societies, such as Israel, Pakistan, India, and Britain, have elected women to their highest political positions—sometimes, but definitely not always, in consequence of class and political manipulation by stronger powers and the women's connections to powerful males. Even in those countries there is a large gap between the women in the top positions and those further down. Communist societies, which had an ideology of meritocracy, lacked a proportional representation of women in the ruling elite, or even in the next layers of officials. Although Papandreau (1988) states that "feminism is the most powerful revolutionary force in the world today," she adds: "Yet, significant numbers of women have not yet been able to break into that bastion of male power, the traditional political arena—electoral politics" (p. xiii). Those who comment on the failure of women the world over to acquire power point to the importance of both grass-roots and national organization and of funding for political office campaigns (Papandreau 1988). Flammang (1984), Mueller (1988), and various American mass-media publications keep counting the number of women holding various political offices in their own right (and not because of their connection as daughters, wives, or widows to strong males). Although contributors to Flammang 1984 and Mueller 1988 find a rather dramatic increase of women on the local and state levels, the few women reaching national attention have not been very successful in their bids for office. Women in their struggle to get access to power still face enormous barriers (Epstein and Coser 1981; see also Lipman-Blumen 1984). The painful experiences of watching Ferraro and Schroeder be defeated in their campaigns for the highest offices in the United States remind observers of the distance women have yet to come. So does even a glance at the corporate structure of the business world.

On the other hand, the mass media are full of the very recent movement of women into the political arena, which can be explained in part as a reaction to several national events that have dramatized inequality and the obvious degradation of women by American men. A front-page article in the 21 October 1992 issue of the *New York Times*, entitled "Women Advance in Politics by Evolution, Not Revolution," pointed out that even if all 108 women who were running for the 103d Congress had won, that would still have left Congress 80 percent male (Manegold 1992, 1A). The rather dramatic increase in the number of women who had at least won the primaries was accounted for by the financial help and training given to candidates by the National Women's Political Caucus, the National Organization for Women, the Women's Campaign Fund, Emily's List, and the Wish List, all of which have been formed in the last twenty-some years. These groups have also learned to distribute the millions of dollars they have raised to candidates who have a good possibility of winning, rather than to all women who are running for office.

Summary

The social roles discussed in this chapter are, or can be, interrelated. Social relationships do not exist alone, but are interwoven into larger fabrics. What is common to all these roles is the element of volunteerism, freedom from the kinds of pressures facing women in traditional society and even now in family roles. Friends are persons converted from strangers or acquaintances through a series of negotiations. Living next to someone does not necessitate entrance into the role of neighbor, nor does residence in a community or the world at large demand active membership in the activities of their groups. At the same time, all these roles require a social circle of same-minded persons who interweave their rights and duties through a division of labor in order to meet their mutual goals. Few friendships can exist without the support of others. The same is true of the circle of a neighbor or of an association member. No matter how one wants to revolutionize one's world, one needs the cooperation of many other persons, who can enter the social circles of each role with a whole range of their own sociopsychological forms of involvement.

When it comes to push and shove, American culture usually justifies neglect of any of these roles if they interfere with what are considered to be more important sets of relations, such as, for women, those of wife or mother. And yet, as the world widens and education and the mass media help broaden the *okolica*, or the arena within which women and men locate their social life spaces, involvement in all kinds of roles is unavoidable. Presumably the connection between the domestic arena and the larger community outside is constantly reinforced by children and friends' sharing activities, by neighborhood interaction, movement in and out of the role of student, and involvement in all sorts of groups at all stages of the life course. Thus, the boundaries between primary and secondary roles are also indeterminate and subject to negotiation with all involved.

The conclusions one can draw from women's involvements in roles outside of the family and occupations are similar to those developed in previous chapters. The overall pattern reflects the movement from traditional, ascribed involvements in the local scene, entered into with little choice and without awareness of the broader world by the majority of women. Transitional times, supported by increased education and individuation, freed women from being automatically embedded in these local relationships. This had a dual effect, expanding the number of women concerned with the larger community while simultaneously expanding the number and variety of social groups helping women achieve personal goals. However, structural and two-sphere restrictions still abounded. It appears that "modern" women are becoming more established in their broader and flexible identities and are turning their attention to concern with the world community through a variety of nonfamilial roles.

8

Life Spaces and Self-Concepts

American society has gone through tremendous changes, purposely introduced or felt repercussively since its traditional times. The processes of modernization and increased scale of organization or social development—whatever concept we use to summarize all the modifications—have been introducing a different way of life, experienced and contributed to by dissimilar people from the past (Coser 1991; Inkeles 1981; Inkeles and Smith 1974). We have been examining the roles of women, who have experienced and contributed to these changes differently than men have. Each gender has been affected in multiple ways, depending on social class with its racial and ethnic subgroups, the degree of urbanization, and, especially, education. Since men and women live together in that they share daily life in many settings, each is influenced by what happens to the other. In addition, since each social role contains circle members who, in turn, can now come from a variety of backgrounds and are involved in other social roles, what they do constantly affects their relationships. All these developments make it dysfunctional, even impossible, to adhere to social roles as fixed patterns of behavior.

The more rigid and inflexible the social person or circle members, the greater the probability of extreme role strain for both the changer and those living in the past. As we have noted throughout, role strain is anyway inevitably built into sets of relations, due to the complexity of demands and the needs for synchronization. It is impossible to be a traditional mother in transitional or modern times if the child is exposed to other types of interaction with other members of the mother's circle who do not cooperate with traditional rights and duties.

Not only role strain, but also role conflict, is inevitable in anyone's role complex, let alone when roles are changing in different ways or all the people involved are experiencing life at varied stages of modernization. Add to this people's need to be socialized and constantly resocialized to the world around them, and it is easy to see multiple sources of role conflict.

Interestingly enough, Americans individually and as a society either do not seem to realize all the consequences of changes they are experiencing, or are unwilling to introduce collective solutions to some of the problems, even when they publicly wring their hands about them. A perfect example of the inadequacy of the definition of current life is contained in the stereotypical view of role conflicts of modern [actually transitional] women.

Role Conflict

Much discussion of present-day American women focuses on the subject of role conflict (that is, conflict among the roles in which they are involved at any stage of life) as if it were a new situation and as if men did not face it. There are two basic sources for such a concern. One is nostalgia for the past that encompasses the strange idea that role conflict did not occur in the "good old days," because of institutional integration with clearly-set priorities (Coontz 1992). The second is a rather simplistic view of human beings. According to the first imagery, men and women had definitely defined, mutually congruent roles that connected activities in all institutions. Women, for example, were wives, mothers, homemakers, kin keepers, grandmothers, producers, members of religious congregations, neighbors, and so forth in a whole fabric moving along the life course, all circle members in each role supporting the rest. One need only read the ever-growing number of biographies and recently resurrected autobiographies of women in the U.S. past and in other societies to know how unrealistic that image was.[1] Role conflict abides in all known situations.

The fact that complex, "developed" societies contain relatively separated and segmented institutions and structures with highly divergent value and behavioral systems leads some observers to the assumption that uncontrolled role conflict is inevitable. Human beings, and especially women, are seen as incapable of dealing with complex social life spaces. Most of the current literature assumes, or even clearly states, that "modern" [actually transitional] societies force onto women much role conflict and that this is detrimental to their welfare.

On the other hand, some scholars, such as Simmel (1955), Sieber (1974), Long and Porter (1984), Marks (1977), and Rose Coser (1975a and 1991), find complex social systems to have positive consequences, allowing the development of complex human personality, and find traditional and more homogeneous cultures to be limiting. I agree with them in many ways and will return to this point.

One cannot deny the complexities of multiple role involvement in large societies. Most of their institutions have grown dissimilar in many values and role hierarchies, and most people's roles are not encompassed within a single institution. People are involved in more than one area of life and are thus faced with competing values and behavioral demands. For example, many scientists must give up some of their commitment to scientific openness and to control over their findings, which are required for membership in the scientific community, in return for a salary from a business company. Women lawyers trying to bring feminist norms into their practice face resistance even from women clients and secretaries who have been socialized into the male model of the lawyer role (Epstein 1983). In addition, circle members of one role often do not allow demands of another role to take precedence, insisting that duties to them take precedence over duties toward the other circle. Duties to clients on the job may be judged by employers as being more important than duties to children.

Awareness of at least partial segmentation of institutions in modern societies could lead to an understanding of the difficulties of involvement in roles that are located in different value systems that do not allow strong alternative commitments. Being a mother of small children and being a lawyer in a Wall Street firm are still almost mutually exclusive involvements (Epstein 1971 and 1983). It is hard to meet the standards of two greedy institutions at the same time (L. Coser 1974; Coser and Coser 1974; see also Pearson 1990).

There are two major settings of possible conflict inherent in the role clusters of American women, as seen from the perspective of "ideal typical" models only, that is, through the framing of selected characteristics. These are among roles within the family institution and between roles in it and in other institutions (Weber 1949).

Role Conflict within the Family Institution

Americans still require that women give highest priority to family roles, alternating between those of wife and mother. It is apparent from previous discussion that these two roles can easily conflict, as when the husband wants to make love but the wife/mother worries about waking the children (Rubin 1979). Much of the literature on the problems created by the birth and presence of children within a marriage focuses on the emotional, attentional, time, and energy demands on the husband and wife team versus the father and mother team. As Bettelheim (1962) noted when describing the advantages of the kibbutzim method of childrearing, the marital couple in the kibbutz system have time to themselves without interruptions from children, and the time devoted to the offspring is not interfered with by duties of housekeeping or husband-tending. He also pointed out that each child gets the attention needed for its stage of development without having to compete with other children of the same mother who have different needs. The role of mother is entered into by a woman each time separately for each child, unless she treats them as a single unit. Each child tends to place her at the center of her or his needs, treating her as a mother separate from the mother the other children have. Add to this the fact that the same man can be a multiple of fathers, as well as a husband to her, and the complexities increase.

In addition, a partial resolution of role conflicts at one stage of life may not work for long. The concept of "empty nest" somehow implied that role conflicts for mothers with several children and between that role and other roles subsided when offspring grew into adulthood. The life-course literature shows us how oversimplified that assumption was. The children may continue to need help in competition with each other, and the husband may resent the woman's continued focus upon motherhood. Although a husband does require "tending," and although his schedule and demands complicate life (see chapter 2), his removal from the household through divorce or death creates new sources of conflict for the woman. Vestiges of the role of wife that interfere with other relationships and her ambivalent emotions are apt to complicate adjustment to new life-styles and, for example, the role of mother. Of course, divorced and widowed women can experience feelings of freedom and competence and new ways of enjoying life.

Family roles can involve other forms of conflict. Add to the nuclear family the mother of the husband, and the complications can be unbearable, especially if she becomes one of the beneficiaries of the homemaker by moving in with them. Her idea of how her son should be treated or the children raised can conflict with all or some of the family members' ideas. The role of daughter may conflict with that of wife and mother. Differences in values, norms, and ideologies among people of different generations, cultural backgrounds, genders, and relationships, when brought into a close interactional setting, can result in emotional explosions, no matter how much people try to manage their feelings (Hochschild 1983).

There is likely to be another role conflict involved: that between the homemaker and the beneficiaries of her role who are also her husband, children, and so forth. Whatever she does to make the house socially presentable to evidence her expertise in that role is likely to interfere with their needs for play space or informality of clothes placement (otherwise known as "messing up" the bathroom and bedroom). Of course, the role of homemaker does not fit in the family institution in the first place, although it is usually so placed by all involved. That role really falls into the economic institution, being an occupational role, allegedly judged in this society by some of the same standards as other jobs. The homemaker is supposed to keep the home within certain appearance and comfort levels, clean and germ-free as much as possible, operating efficiently, rationally and according to all the norms of scientific management. At least, that is what the home economics movement and the mass media portray, pointing out that modern conveniences make this cognitively run system operative. Current observations by sociologists document the confusion between the contributions of technological change and the interpersonal dynamics of the role (see Cowan 1983, Hardyment 1988, and chapter 5 for examples). To state the main problem bluntly, the activities of homemaking have been organized into a role, taken out of the family and placed into the occupational system in its set of behavioral norms, while it remains in the family institution in the minds of the beneficiaries—if they are not paid lodgers and boarders in secondary relationship to the social person. The household beneficiaries often want the woman to run the home along economical and efficient norms, but giving priority to her obligations as wife and mother.

Although a number of observers have addressed themselves to role conflicts experienced by women within the family institution, it is the problem of carrying forth roles in different institutional settings that draws most attention. There are some comments about such role conflicts for American men with greedy jobs and family responsibilities (see J. Pleck 1983; also Pleck and Pleck 1980; Kimmel and Messner 1992), but it is the women who are pinpointed as suffering it to an almost debilitating extent.

Conflict between Family Roles and
Those in Other Institutional Dimensions

The early literature on role conflicts of American women focused upon the roles of wife and jobholder, especially if the job made strong commitment demands or was of higher social status than that of her husband (see, e.g., Bird 1979; Ferber and Huber 1979).

Bird (1979) described "the personal, sometimes painful side" of the wife-jobholder conflicts in *The Two-Paycheck Marriage*. The titles of some of her chapters illustrate conflicts: "Coping with the Dream of a Perfect Home," "The Truth about the Money She Earns," "The Age Thirty Bind," and "The Two-Career Collision Course." The book was written from the woman's point of view and the problems are seen as hers, with relatively little attention to the man's reality. Whether the woman is a defiant working wife preferring to be employed although the husband wants her at home full-time, a reluctant jobholder although neither she nor her spouse wants her in that role, or a submissive employee pushed out of the home by the demands of the husband, she faces several role conflicts. Bird (1979) found that many couples are not comfortable with the money earned by the wife because they do not openly acknowledge the need, especially if it is large enough to threaten the man.[2] Regardless of size, it is often treated as not sufficiently significant to warrant the husband's cooperation in the wife's "second shift" of homemaking and parental roles. Bird's chapter on the two-career collision course focuses on the conflicting demands of the marital partners' greedy occupations in terms of time, energy, and attention commitment, solution of emergencies, transfers, and so forth. Whose crisis is the most important? When does love conquer all, including ambition? Bird notes:

> Most of the married women in *Who's Who in America* have husbands who are not listed in their own right, including anti-feminists Phyllis Schlafly and Marabel Morgan, author of *Total Woman*. . . . A man who gives up his own career for his wife's can expect raised eyebrows— and so can his wife. (P. 208)

One of the concerns of this gender-stratified society is that the wife's higher education and occupational activity can decrease the husband's productivity, an additional commentary on how much the men are dependent upon backup wives and may suffer when such demands are made upon them. Ferber and Huber (1979) actually found support for this anxiety among academic men. Those with wives of higher role status outside of the marriage produced less than those with wives without demanding occupations. Ostrander (1985) and Daniels (1988) also explain that upper-class women cannot even allow their volunteer roles to interfere with their more direct obligations to the husband, although he is a beneficiary of even that work. A wife's friendships can be seen as competing with the husband's demands for attention, especially if he feels left out and considers the wife as his "best friend," which many men seem to do in the absence of male confidants.

The lack of equality between husband and wife in carrying forth life-sustaining and life-style work, which produces role conflict for women, is documented by many other social scientists, such as Hertz (1986; see also the contributions to Gerstel and Gross 1987a and 1987b). Hochchild's analysis in *The Second Shift* (1989) focuses on the problems of work and personal interaction facing a couple when both the husband and the wife are employed. Interviewing both partners, and even observing them at great length in the home, Hochschild analyzed not only the sources of conflict but also the methods by which different couples managed to survive without breaking up. The problems include the fact that few marriages actually involve the sharing of the home shift, although the woman is definitely overextended in her duties and obligations. Hochschild found some very interesting ways in which both husbands and wives justify the husband's not sharing in responsibilities, which she labels "gender ideologies." Each human being exists within a constructed reality, that is, within a process of constructing meaning in all of life's situations. Each couple then must create a mutual constructed reality at least to an extent that makes coexistence possible. According to Hochschild, such a construction is often forged at great cost to the wife. It is basically the wife who needs greater help from the husband, while both of them either do not see or else explain away the asymmetry.

Thus, personal conflict often occurs between the employed husband and the employed wife concerning his resistance to her strong outside commitments and efforts to change home maintenance into a shared activity, that is, to make the role of homemaker one of joint responsibility and work. Men resist simply because they do not want to give up all the benefits of a superior position, especially if these have been previously established (Goode 1982). Although many men (though not all) admit that they need, or else that they use, the "extra" income brought in by an employed wife, the fact that this income is usually smaller than the husband's provides the justification for not sharing the work. The realization by middle-class men that the wife's lower pay is not her fault, and that the couple has frequently favored his search for occupational advantages at the cost of her job, does not diminish his use of greater earnings as a reason for dispensation from work and responsibility (Gerson 1985). It does make a difference, however, whether the job held by the wife preceded marriage or was undertaken after the family patterns became established with a full-time homemaker as the backup to a greedy family (Coser and Coser 1974). It is difficult for the woman to unhinge the prior dependence upon her, just as it is hard for the middle-aged wife and mother to separate her identity from dependence upon the husband and children (Rubin 1979).

Most literature on the role conflicts of American women focuses not on those between an occupation and the role of wife, but on the conflicts between an occupation and the role of mother, or even potential mother. The mass media, at least, worry that some women may not want to be mothers at all. The panic created by the "biological clock," which eventually cuts off the possibility of becoming a mother (whether in fact or psychologically) was already a major subject of the 1970s. It has become increasingly so in recent years as women postpone role conflict with careers by postponing pregnancy. The panic over role conflict is mainly due to the definition of the role of mother. The demands of motherhood in American society are such that they are expected to interfere with any activity away from the home base, be it of a volunteer, an organizational, or an occupational nature. Children get sick, and it is the mother who must transport them from wherever this occurs and stay home with them. School, doctor, service, and activity appointments for the offspring are usually available only during working hours, on the assumption that a mother is always available. School closings for whatever reason neglect the problems of empty houses, and indignation over "latchkey kids" neglects the fact that some mothers cannot leave work when children return from school. Middle-class mothers are also expected to have time to serve as the social agents linking children to the community (O'Donnell and Stueve 1983).

Going as far back as Komarovsky's *Women in the Modern World* (1953) we find that about a third of highly educated post–World War II women avoided possible role conflict by becoming unmarried career women and another third became full-time homemakers. The women who combined career and motherhood felt guilt but had good help with the care of children by live-in, trained servants. Any other method of dealing with problems of child care in the absence of a full-time mother or full-time cooperation from other family members was reportedly extremely difficult. The occasional "career woman" of the past familistic era had not only servants but also support from many sources because she was so unusual (Hunt and Hunt 1982). It was also helpful to have an unusually cooperative husband (Holmstrom 1973). Having a complex support network is also typical of successful women in the public sphere in other societies, most of whom come from upper-class families.

Of course, problems can occur when people are involved in more than one role in institutions other than the family. Some of these appear endemic to American women; others are faced by both genders. Friendship can be seen as interfering with occupational roles, especially in bureaucracies. As mentioned in connection with institutional separation, people working for a bridging organization may experience conflicting demands from groups in the two neighboring institutions. In addition, they may face role conflict within their life course, as when the job requires behavior contrary to what they learned in the role of student or what they expect to follow in future roles.

Societal Solutions to Role Conflicts of Women

American society of the transitional times has not admitted, or even understood, how it has created and contributed to the role conflicts of its women, nor has it taken on as much responsibility as other countries for creating solutions. It fails to recognize that women's "personal troubles" arise out of societal changes and that these have serious social problems as consequences (Mills 1956). Although it acknowledges that modernization, especially industrialization and urbanization, has made inevitable many of these social problems, its value system and power structure do not allow adequate assistance to people who are going through them. In fact, the main solution to the dramatic changes of the last two centuries, the division of the world into the private and the public, is itself a major cause of role conflict for its members. Society has allowed its men to solve role conflicts by neglecting the private aspects of self and life—roles of husband, father, friend, and neighbor. It has pushed and socialized women to solve them by neglecting involvement in roles defined as public. It also ignores the fact that this is an artificial division and that women are constantly in the public sphere in what are called "private" roles or in almost invisible public roles. This the society does by defining women's public involvements as secondary both for them and for the whole, while preventing their access to powerful roles.

The artificial boundaries between public and private lead to the pretense that private and public are separate and ought to be occupied by separate types of persons. In fact, the ideology contains major contradictions. On the one hand, the private is defined as sacredly immune from interference, especially in the form of public responsibility for its welfare. On the other hand, American society impinges upon the alleged private sphere with its laws and policies any time it wishes to do so. In the case of policies concerning women, it tries to keep women out of important roles in the public sphere, ignores their actual presence in that sphere, and interferes with their roles of wife, mother, and homemaker.

Kamerman and Kahn (1978; see also Kamerman 1977; Kahn and Kamerman 1975) studied family policies of the major industrializing societies and found the United States to be the least cooperative. It is most unwilling to introduce policies that could alleviate or at least decrease social problems, blaming these instead on the relatively powerless mother/wife/homemaker/employee. Solutions are left to individual action, although the problems are often, if not usually, beyond personal control.

In fact, the late 1980s and the 1990s have been witnessing an allegedly strong backlash against women's efforts at breaking down the barriers between private and public domains (Faludi 1991). Deep in its heart, this society wants women back in the home, in nineteenth-century fashion, even when they cannot maintain themselves economically from that setting and although modern life and education have considerably changed pervasive and role identities. The theme Rose Coser pointed to in "Stay Home Little Sheba" (1975b) has not been revised much since then. Americans worry about the effects on the children of having an employed mother, in spite of the conclusion by many researchers that there are no serious negative effects (see the summary of this research in Hoffman 1987). They do not worry about the effects of a father so engaged, nor does the worry result in the provision of alternative community or governmental solutions. The mass media favorably publicize stories of women who decide to give up their careers to stay home (Trost 1990a, B1). These traditional attitudes were brought into the open by the conservative, religious right during the 1992 presidential campaign. It is now trying to organize a grass-roots movement to offset any governmental policies aimed at decreasing conflicts for family members that might be introduced by the Democratic administration.

It is interesting, if worrisome to symbolic interactionists, to note that all the concern over stressful role conflict of women focuses on a limited range of time and thus neglects sixty or so years in their lives (see also Long and Porter 1984). This backlash ignores women who do not have any children and most of the life course of those who do. It generalizes to all women and is strongest in rejecting those who are entering occupations or the political, religious, or other spheres of life in influential roles. The underlying assumption is that all of a woman's life must be organized around these few years when the demands for exclusive commitment to each major role are highest. This happens when she is building a career, entering a love relationship that is still expected to last many decades (with all the negotiations with the social circle that that entails), and being a mother to one or more young children. The failure of American society to recognize and adjust to this life squeeze makes the years between entering the major roles and reaching a stabilized stage difficult. It is possible that, at some time in the future, the scheduling of the life cycles of major roles will be sufficiently sequenced to interfere less with each other. It is also possible that role commitment will not be so "greedy" as to exclude strong (but not twenty-four-hours-a-day) involvement in more than one role.

Of course, one way women's temporary role conflicts during greedy stages of role involvements could be eased is through actions of the employing organizations, rather than governmental agencies, but the economic institution has been organized around a model of male workers who can commit themselves to the job without regard for other commitments (see also Coser 1991). The male worker is seen as either not responsible for any dependents, be they disabled relatives or children, or as having a backup person to solve all the troubles arising from such involvements. Women who are also committed to other roles besides the job and thus refuse to meet the male model of behavior, or who are expected by employers to do so, are kept in inferior positions at inferior pay or in unstable jobs. It is going to take some time, and the revolt of many employees, for employers to reorganize work to meet employee needs because they realize such action will also benefit the company (Schwartz 1992). Arrangements that would make life easier for employees include: flextime, flexplace, part-time employment with benefits, job sharing, temporary assignments, and leaves for medical, parental, and other reasons. Most of these variations on the traditional work schedule actually benefit the organization, according to a survey by the American Marketing Association; they produce higher morale, reduced tardiness, reduced turnover, and easier recruitment of new employees (Rothman and Marks 1987, 196). An extensive article in the *Wall Street Journal* indicates that some bosses are adjusting (Hymowitz 1990). Some employing organizations even set up child-care centers nearby (Trost 1990a). And yet Rothman and Marks (1987) reported several years ago that only 12 percent of employing organizations have developed some form of flexible work schedule to accommodate the needs of employees arising from role conflicts. This figure had risen to just about 15 percent by the middle of 1990 (Trost 1990b).

The reexamination of work and career scheduling has not been helped by existing powerful pressure groups and other organizations whose leaders could introduce changes but do not, or by male members of other circles of women. Economic and political institutions have a long way to go to make life more humane for the society's members, including men.

Role-Conflict Solutions by Women

There are two major ways in which women can ease some of the life squeeze of role conflicts: through collective action and through individual action. Transitional women organized the fight for freedom from traditional restrictions, for abolition of slavery, and for suffrage and equality of opportunity, but they sought individual solutions to their personal role conflicts and felt inadequate or guilty if the problems remained. Part of their problem has been an ambivalence concerning basic values, and possibly a belief in the reality of a two-sphere world. In view of their inner conflicts , how did, and how do, these women, who are still far from being able to negotiate a modern life, deal with experienced role conflicts? The vast number of studies that document problems faced by women in "modern" times who are wives, mothers, homemakers, and jobholders come to the same conclusion: Women are the only ones who are assigned, and take on, the responsibility of solving role conflict. Many women are aware of this and make hard choices (Gerson 1985) along the way, trying to decide which roles to enter, and balancing costs and rewards, including not just the quality and benefits of the job, but also the types of sharing they can expect from "understanding bosses" or cooperative husbands/fathers/home-co-maintainers. Many career-oriented women simply postpone or decide not to enter competing roles, especially that of mother, but even that of wife. However, the pressure toward motherhood is high in this society, and usually comes also from the husband, although the pressure toward fatherhood does not appear to translate into shared parenting. Women have usually succumbed to this pressure and taken the path of least resistance by becoming mothers and giving up careers, even jobs, in spite of the low status of full-time homemakers (Bird 1979; Gerson 1985). Some, as we saw earlier, consciously sequence their role involvements, but often at a cost to success, given the rigid career lines of many occupations.

Many mothers settle for inferior jobs, as numerous studies have documented (see Lopata, Miller, and Barnewolt 1984; Lopata,

Barnewolt, and Miller 1985). The same is true in Britain, where the price of convenient hours or location is a woman's inability to get a job that is either as rewarding as the job she gave up to become a mother or equal to her prior training (Sharpe 1984). Certain occupations in both countries, mainly in service industries, have benefited considerably from this cheap and expendable labor, and an ideology about women's unreliability has grown to justify discrimination in hiring, firing, and job assignment.

Women who insist on following demanding careers in combination with family roles also find individual solutions.[3] Extended families, especially their female members who have traditionally been the main supports of mothers with competing roles, are decreasingly available with increasing geographical mobility and labor force participation. Given sufficient income, many women hire "nannies" or other servants, although the problems associated with this action are legion, according to all mass-media and social science reports. The pool of women willing to take on those roles in preference to other jobs is shrinking; often the remaining candidates have only passing interest in the job or have inferior social person characteristics.

Women decrease conflict between homemaking and other roles by simply decreasing the amount of work they do in the home, adding more assistants to provide such services as cleaning, food preparation, and purchasing and delivering goods. Entertaining company at home is one of the first activities to be given up by multirole women, decreasing or simplifying the numbers of beneficiaries of the role (Bird 1979). The delegation of work to others, avoidance of duties and rights deemed unnecessary, and compartmentalization of time and mind are effective strategies for many women. In the meantime, the woman whose roles are all in the expanding stage who does feel stressed can only do the best she can and hope for the plateau stage, when skills have been learned, negotiations bring satisfactory sequences of relationships, and changes flow into each other.

Some couples have worked out alternate scheduling to insure that the children have a parent present whenever they need one. However, most husbands and wives work matching schedules (Pleck and Staines 1982). Some couples have returned to the world of Mom-and-Pop businesses, working together out of the home or in a manner enabling family care (see chapter 6). Hunt and Hunt (1982) call these "integrators," couples who are able to bring together businesses and family roles.

Whatever the individual solutions, the net result is overall inefficiency for the society as a whole and for each woman who must reinvent the wheel of solutions common to so many others at the same stage of the life course. (Spalter-Roth and Hartmann 1990; documented *in Unnecessary Losses: Costs to Americans by the Lack of Family and Medical Leave* ; see also Hyde and Essex 1990 for multiple analyses). And this in a society that prides itself on rationality and efficiency in solving problems!

The Complexity of Social Life Spaces

There are two aspects of this situation that need closer examination. One is the questionable assumption that complex life spaces inevitably produce problems; the second is the general image of American women that permeates American culture.

Although the mass media and much of social science literature portray Americans as living in too complex a world, facing serious role conflicts, constantly stressed, harried, nervous, and in a difficult relationship with each other, there are some voices of dissent. These speak of the advantages of complex roles and multidimensional life spaces. Rose Coser takes this idea even further in "The Complexity of Roles as a Seedbed of Individual Autonomy" (1975a) and her book *In Defense of Modernity: Role Complexity and Individual Autonomy* (1991). Segmented social roles provide a variety of role partners differently positioned and not equally involved, which necessitates constant negotiation. People in such life spaces need to constantly articulate their stances, to think out the consequences of their actions in view of their empathetic understanding of others' constructions of reality. Coser refers to Kohn and Schooler's (1983) work showing that complexity of the work environment is associated with complexity of personality and with intellectual flexibility. Referring back to George Herbert Mead (1934), Coser illustrates the effects of social complexity with his game stage of social development. The more complex the game, the more positions a person must understand in order to plan her present and future behavior. Even conflict creates the need for distancing and thinking out one's rights and duties, which can result in greater flexibility and individual enrichment.

The same can be said of complexity of the role cluster—its spread into multiple institutional dimensions, visualized as a social life space. One role may actually support another, as when member-ship in a professional organization and friendship among scientists assist scientific production. Crane (1968), Merton (1968), and Lewis Coser (1984) found the most productive scientists to be ones with complex sociometric connectedness networks, who are involved in many interactions and roles that communicate and disseminate knowledge. People with complex kinship roles may obtain emer-gency and regular help with any role, including work brought home from a job.

The growing number of social scientists who have undertaken a life-course perspective also point to the importance of complex role involvements (Moen, McClain and Williams 1989). Contributors to Baruch and Brooks-Gunn's *Women in Midlife* (1984), especially Baruch (1984) herself, stress the psychological well-being that accom-panies multiple roles in those years, as Payne (1977) had observed regarding the elderly. Baruch, Barnett, and Rivers (1983) found women pleased to have multiple roles, mastery over their lives, and independence. Such women had a strong sense of selfhood and self-worth that came from successful role performance and the ability to coordinate involvements. They were freed from depen-dence upon the husband's approval for their feelings of mastery, a dependence which was more typical of married full-time home-maker (Baruch, Barnett, and Rivers 1983, 40). In fact, the authors state:

> But one of the most positive findings of our study is that involvement in multiple roles has a strengthening effect on well-being—for both Mastery and Pleasure— for women. This contradicts the conventional wisdom so directly that it made us ask why. Where did those old notions come from? (P. 140)

They answer this question with references to the mental health field, which assumed there would be serious problems when women left the home to enter the labor force (see also Friedan 1963 and Harris 1979). According to Baruch and her associates, the expectation of great stress came from what they called a "limited model" of resources available to human beings. This model refers to energy as being drained by each effort leaving less energy for other activities. Neglected are the stimulating and energizing aspects of many activities. Inter-estingly enough, they also found that the limited-resources model is applied more frequently to women than to men, possibly flowing from nineteenth-century medical imagery of the "frail lady" (140–41). Mental health experts gave greater weight to stress emanating from role conflicts of women with external commitments than to stress based on domestic involvements.

Marks (1977) calls this a "scarcity" approach to energy, time, and commitment, tracing it back to Freud and numerous other theoreticians who use the metaphors of spending, draining, leaking out, or dribbling away of energy. The result of both the theoretical and the empirical work is the conviction that people in modern society are overwhelmed by demands from multiple roles (Marks 1977, 973).

Marks (1977, 926) favors the expansion approach to human energy, following Durkheim, who saw complex social involvement as enriching and revitalizing. Marks applies the same argument to time and commitment, pointing out that many activities are stimulating and can be carried out simultaneously. He argues that concerns about role strain and role conflict limit the view of human potential for complex behavior. The conclusion that people can wither when faced with a simplistic life after more complex social involvement is recognized by everyone who finds inadequate the Cumming and Henry (1961) thesis that people "disengage" voluntarily from social roles as they grow older.

Returning now to Simmel (1955) , Sieber (1974), Coser (1975a and 1991), and Long and Porter (1984), and developing their ideas further, we find a very optimistic view of modern life. Simmel (1955) pointed out that conflict is not inevitably debilitating. In fact, the segmentation of institutions and social structures has enabled modern individualism. It gives people much more freedom to choose and negotiate, to have a unique life-style, than is possible in more homogeneous societies with a greater interdependence of institutions. One can carry the feeling of being a unique individual wherever one goes, in contact with a variety of others who are also unique and thus able to create or modify social roles to fit themselves and circle members, rather than conforming to culturally established norms of behavior (see also Turner 1962, 1968, 1978, and 1981).

Gains of role accumulation can include the acquisition of new rights, status security and enhancement, ego gratification, and feeling of competence. The rights may include greater authority and resources (Sieber 1974). However, there is a serious question as to whether women are as yet gaining all these benefits from increased role accumulation, since so may find that adding a job and contributing to the family economic welfare do not guarantee rights and privileges, certainly not within the family (Long and Porter 1984). One can but optimistically predict that the cumulative effects will come as all the roles of women's social life spaces increase in importance and as America enters the modern world at least in this aspect of its life and social structure.

Sociopsychological Aspects of Social Life Spaces

The questions remain, how do social roles influence the self-concepts women carry around with them through the life course, and how have these changed with shifts from traditional to transitional and modern societal times? These questions cannot be adequately answered at the present time, because there is not enough data from carefully worked research, but some insights can be gained from my ongoing studies of Chicago-area women, begun in 1956. As mentioned before, the reexamination of results from all this work points strongly to the significant effects of formal schooling on the social involvement of American women. Schooling definitely affects the complexity with which women perceive and act in the roles of wife, mother, kin member, friend, and participant in voluntary associations. In addition, the less formal schooling a woman achieves, the more apt she is to be socially isolated, to hold negative attitudes about social relationships, and to be unable to adjust to life changes. The increasingly voluntaristic nature of social involvement in more socially developed and large-scale societies requires of members the kind of knowledge, thought processes, and competence that formal education provides. This conclusion is reinforced by comparative studies of support systems of widows in different societies (Lopata 1987c and 1987d).

Modernization or social development of complexity brought expanded education, in terms of the percentage of the population being educated and the amount of knowledge transmitted to it. We can posit that women (and men, too, of course) in a modern society, having received a formal education that involves the manipulation of abstract ideas, have learned to think out and plan their lives and to participate in the larger world. Abstract thinking enables the person to anticipate the consequences of alternative decisions, without having to experience them in concrete form. Women can make their decisions autonomously (Coser 1975a; Inkeles 1981; Inkeles and Smith 1974; Simmel 1971), but in cooperation with circle members of the roles they choose to enter. They are not isolated human beings and are not dependent upon a single, or limited, source of social involvement and thus identities (Troits 1986). Social roles contain social relationships, and modernization does not necessarily lead to isolated independence, as some thinkers have claimed; it can lead to negotiated and voluntary interdependence based on self-development (Cancian 1978). Of course, this idealized image of development of human potential assumes a society that has removed tradition-based barriers to individual achievement and has stopped forcing dysfunctional stereotypes upon the young.

The ideal typical woman in such a modern, developed society is able to build a congruent construction of reality that brings into the framework her generalized and specialized conceptions of herself, her commitments, her actual role involvements, the positively evaluated benefits of such, the pleasure of such role complexity, and the support she perceives herself to receive from circle members in each of the roles within her role cluster (Lopata 1980b; 1993a).

However, not all members of an allegedly modern society, even in its urban centers, have been sufficiently socialized and educated to take advantage of available resources to build individualistically congruent constructions of their own reality. This is particularly true of women in patriarchal, rapidly changing settings. We can hypothesize that two types of women will have the most internally congruent constructions of reality at the present time. One type would be located in less changing and more homogeneous pockets of such a society, the second near the forefront of social change. What factors influence such settings, and what happens to women in the transitional middle, caught by both traditional and modern views of women and opportunities for role involvements?

The traditional women whom I interviewed in the 1950s and 1960s were married home owners in new, or new areas of older, suburbs with at least one pre–high school child and no outside employment. They represented the vast majority of women in such settings, being there with the help of the GI Bill and often socially mobile husbands. Of roles such as careerwoman, artist (or other self-expressive role), concerned citizen, or neighbor, or even member of a religious group, none was considered anywhere near as important as roles in the home. Their constructions of reality, including commitments, perceptions, and self-concepts, within the family and homemaking roles, varied considerably by social class and especially by education, but were highly traditional when it came to outside involvements (Lopata 1971b). The more educated respondents perceived their world and themselves and their homemaking and family roles in much more complex and creative ways than did their less educated counterparts. Those married to more educated husbands in more-prestigious jobs tended to place the role of wife above that of mother, while the working-class women definitely stressed the role of mother, often forgetting to mention that of wife. However, Spock (1957) was very much evident among the middle-class women who worried about their ability to meet all the requirements of good motherhood. The husbands of the less-educated respondents were seen mainly as breadwinners, while they themselves ranked high the role of homemaker (Lopata 1966). The questioning of this whole value system and the restriction of women to the home—a questioning brought forth by Friedan in *The Feminine Mystique* (1963)—had not yet surfaced, and the women's main concerns were financial or maternal.

The transitional women whom I have studied since the 1970s have been much more heterogeneous along several dimensions in addition to social class. They vary considerably in how they sequenced the entrances and exits of their roles and in how well they had anticipated the consequences of their choices upon the goals they visualized with more or less clarity. Many were socialized into a circumscribed world by parents with little education or other resources, many of whom were themselves socialized in foreign countries or American rural areas, and simply followed the traditional patterns of life, completing limited schooling, working for pay and having some "cheap amusements" along the way, marrying and/or having children, and deviating little from the standard (Peiss 1986). They resemble the 1950s women in their home orientation more than any other group, except that they feel much more restricted, being aware of the alternative life-styles publicized by the mass media. Others of a similar background have been able to decrystallize the effects of such a background, mainly by entering occupations that offered a new look at what women can do, achieving new educational levels or job training, and becoming resocialized into new life-styles and self-concepts (see Epstein 1992 for changes in the self-concept). A third category had all the advantages of higher social class, which built positive self-images, and either went the traditional route or committed themselves early to educational and occupational involvement that enabled them to enter multidimensional life spaces. Some of the advantaged women also went back to school. In fact, the higher her original educational achievement, the more likely is the woman to return to school or obtain new or further job training in later years. Divorce has often been associated with occupational or educational change, in chicken-or-egg sequence. Many women now combine roles in their cluster in a variety of ways and with degrees of flexibility, changing their life spaces in response to life-course shifts.

Since so much of the concern over American women is focused on the alleged conflict between full-time homemakers and full-time employees, I will limit my discussion here to the construction of reality centered around these two mutually exclusive forms of commitment (see also Lopata and Barnewolt 1984).

There appears to be an increasing number of "modern" women who have created relatively internally congruent realities, in that they are involved in the roles they rank as very important and that they prefer. They can be either full-time homemakers or full-time employees. They see many advantages to their involvements, they have a comparatively high self-esteem, and they perceive their environments (particularly the husband, if there is one) as supportive. They fit other roles around their basic commitment.

The most highly congruent homemakers are relatively young and educated, with a background of comparatively high-status jobs. They are married and mothers of small children, which is why they choose to be at home. They are able to do so, but not necessarily because of a high family income. In fact, need, as established by family income without the wife's earnings in comparison to other respondents, is not a significant factor. This finding surprised us, in view of the frequent assertion that all employed mothers must work for financial reasons. Such mothers scaled down their expenses from preparenthood times and learned how to live on more limited incomes. Of course, each had an employed husband. What is important is the conscious decision these mothers of younger children have made to leave the labor force, at least temporarily, because they consider such action necessary for the welfare of their families. They find their husbands supportive of this decision. The generalized characteristics and areas of competence in their self-concept reflect a much higher self-esteem than that of older and less educated full-time homemakers, who usually scored lower than did the employees (see Lopata 1980b; Lopata, Barnewolt, and Miller 1985). A surprising conclusion, in view of the 1956 study, is that these voluntary homemakers do not find their role highly complex, in spite of their having higher levels of education than the less congruent homemakers. It is possible that they do not define homemaking as equivalent in complexity to that of prior or future jobs.

I had expected to find other types of homemaker with congruent constructions of reality, and I found one: mothers of large families, with a husband and three or more children, in the full-house plateau stage of that role. They have been socialized to be homemakers and have mastered the role sufficiently to look upon themselves as successful and to experience relatively little role conflict. They are pleased with their situations, although they often live on relatively restricted incomes and in rather flat social life space. They tend not to be geographically or socially mobile, but they are not sufficiently bothered by the mass media's image of the "modern woman" as having an outside career to question themselves. They are quite different from the first category of congruent homemakers and are critical of what they consider the others' "uptight" life-style, especially what they see as the others' pushing their children in developmentally detrimental ways. They express traditional values and are also critical of the actions of the congruent employed women.

The least congruent transitional full-time homemakers are not involved in that role at its expanding circle or full-house plateau stages, in that the home does not contain small children but may have a husband. They appear to lack justification for being out of the labor force, and often express the wish to get a job. However, the older ones do not have the skills and knowledge to get employment, having been disadvantaged early in life in terms of family and educational background. They never did hold a good job and do not visualize themselves as able to function successfully in the world of work outside of the home. On the other hand, they do not find homemaking complex. They do not hold images of themselves as leaders or as successful or competent women, and so they have a very different content to their self-concepts than do the congruent employees or the more congruent homemakers.

The most congruent employees can be either unmarried or married, but most do not have small children in the household (although there are some with that combination in the role cluster who have worked it all out). Most are apt to have been employed a longer proportion of time since finishing school in more prestigious and better paying jobs than the less congruent jobholders or homemakers at any but the highest level of congruence. In fact, they appear either to have avoided roles that compete with their career commitment or to have reached a stage in life course, external supports, or self-confidence where they do not feel major conflicts. They like their jobs, find them complex, and find many advantages to employment. If married, they are very apt to report that the husband is supportive, although he seldom shares equally in home-making or child rearing, a not surprising find in view of all the reports of other researchers. Those with the cluster of wife-mother-career explain with great satisfaction how they maintain this.

The least congruent employees are working for pay because they feel they have to, although they would rather stay home; or they try to stick to a career although they are unable to resolve guilt or role conflict with motherhood. Some report supportive attitudes on the part of the husband for such employment; others do not. Some simply do not like their jobs and see many advantages to full-time homemaking. Others worry about the children and about not having enough time and energy to carry forth the home-based roles the way they would like to. These represent the typification of the "modern, conflict ridden" women of the mass media and public outcry. However, they are only one of many different categories of women along this congruence dimension. It must be remembered that they are being studied at one point in their life course and in their role's life cycle. Some may change considerably due to person-ally or externally induced events.

In spite of all the negative evaluations of this society and of women's role modifications in all spheres of life, positive changes are evident throughout the life spaces of Americans. Both women and men are entering new roles or developing negotiated flexibility in old ones. There is excitement surrounding those people and groups that experience voluntarily introduced and even repercus-sive reconstructions of reality in their own world and those of circle members in a variety of roles.

In the long run, a major influence of "the female world" (Ber-nard 1981) upon transitional American society may be the conse-quence of the different activities of many different women and their associations. This influence can remove the artificial division be-tween the public and the domestic spheres simply by the way women's pervasive identities express themselves in all interaction— as the ranges of relationships expand, so do the various forms of these identities. Douglas in *The Feminization of American Culture* (1977) and Lenz and Myerhoff in *The Feminization of America: How*

Women's Values Are Changing Our Public and Private Lives (1985)
document changes in this society and its way of life. Lenz and
Myerhoff trace women's influence on language, friendship, politics,
the workplace, religion, the arts, the family, health care, and the
protection of life through pressure for peace and against war. The
emerging men's movement may work toward the same goals from
the other direction, making roles and relationships more flexible
and negotiable, less norm-restricted (see Turner 1978 and 1981).

Conclusions

We have examined the major roles of American women, in historical
perspective and with the help of a symbolic interactionist social role
framework. The ways the roles of wife, mother, kin member, daughter, sister, and grandmother in the family dimension and the roles of
women in other institutional dimensions have evolved are ingrained
in the evolution of American society and are now influencing where
it goes. This interdependence of social changes has been deeply
affected in recent decades (a very short period of time in human
history) by the feminist movement and the actual behavior of women
vis-à-vis social roles outside of the family institution. Women previously marginal to the occupational world have entered the labor
force, almost before the development of an ideology questioning
past barriers to the public domain. They have also pushed for
greater involvement in the local, national, and international political,
religious, scientific, military, health, and nonoccupational economic
spheres of life. In fact, most of the changes have been forced on
society by women, with little help from their male companions,
public agencies, or economic establishments.

The interdependence of women's involvement in all roles of
their social life spaces have decrystallized the effects of their backgrounds, early socialization, and prior choices, making more flexible the life cycle of each role and the women's whole life course.
The processes and rapidity of personal changes and of changes in
the public sphere have produced many role strains and conflicts,
which have been loudly commented upon by the mass media and
objected to by those who benefited from the status quo. Educational
institutions have been more responsive to demands for modification
than have other areas of life, with pockets of slow adjustment in
academic roles. Occupational structure appears to have been very

slow to change, taking advantage of power to perpetuate convenient stereotypes and practices. Religious groups are accepting token women and token reformulations, but have a long way to go.

And so it is—a great deal of change and a great deal of resistance. Women have taken advantage of openings, modified prior involvements, and fought vestiges of the transitional past by individual actions and in cooperation with others. Some have been pushed in directions they did not choose or with which they are still uncomfortable. Some have taken advantage of former and new resources to build complex, flexible social life spaces with involvements in many roles in several institutions. Some experience a great deal of stress, especially in view of the minimal encouragement and assistance they receive from their circles and the society at large. Many men in their social circles have resisted new demands that threaten their advantages. They are often fearful of responding to the demands of their female partners in many roles, braced by the inflexibility of images of masculinity and of the structures of greedy institutions to which they feel committed by necessity.

The idea that these are times of transition assumes that we know what the next model of role involvement will be. Futurists attempt to paint the picture of various types of utopias. In the meantime, the growing pressure of social groups and of individual choices appears to be gradually moving mainstream American social structure and culture into a more open system of role involvement for both women and men. All the intelligentsia's talk of a postmodern society neglects the fact that most Americans have yet to create and take advantage of a fully modern one.

A major conclusion of this book is that the potential for role conflict exists whenever human beings are involved in more than one role. The degree and frequency of conflict depend on many factors, including the coexistence of high-intensity stages in multiple role involvements. The frequently heard statement among Americans that role complexity is necessarily debilitating, producing major problems for people in multidimensional social life spaces, is based on a limited or scarcity model of human resources: of time, energy, love, commitment, and so forth. The view of American women as overwhelmed by multiple role involvements is based upon this model and upon the nineteenth-century picture of women as frail and unable to meet the challenges of public life. It is thus tied to the image of a two-sphere world. Downplaying role conflicts within the family institution, the current concern over the activities of modern women focuses upon their entrance into the public sphere. It generalizes to women of all ages, although it is explained in terms of the coexistence of high-intensity stages in the roles women undertake in only a small time period of their life course. In other words, women are still discouraged from strong commitments in the occupational and related worlds, from investing in side bets of education and training, and from sequencing roles, on the assumption that, sooner or later, they will face tremendous role conflicts. All of the life course is thus ideally constricted by the fact that certain years of certain women's lives might require strong commitments in more than one role. Simultaneously, little effort is made by the occupational world, or the society at large, to modify the timing of career stages to enable sequencing of high-intensity stages in more than one role.

An almost inevitable conclusion of the mass media and many social scientific studies of the disastrous consequences of role conflicts for American women is that women should avoid such conflicts by not entering, or by withdrawing from, situations that might bring them about. Since total responsibility motherhood is so highly valued, the withdrawal they appear to be demanding is from the public world of occupations, politics, and other community involvement. Other solutions, ones that might actually benefit men and establishments in the public sphere, are not seriously considered. The Protestant ethic is doing well in the corporate, managerial, and professional worlds—employing high-status and high-pay people. These greedy organizations demand that the lives of their workers be organized around one model of work scheduling. Yet it is possible that flexibility will be introduced in the future, and make the worst forms of role conflict obsolete. Until then, women in increasing numbers are showing that they are able to manage in complex social life spaces, and that their response to challenge is to become invigorated rather than pathetically wilted or withdrawn.

Notes

Chapter 1. Social Roles of American Women

1. This book is not the place to argue the pros and cons of modernization or social development theory, or whether American society at large is now in the postmodern stage. I am simply using the concepts of traditional, transitional, and modern to cover sweeping changes in the roles of women.

2. Turner (1962, 24) refers to roles as "meaningful groupings of behavior," but my emphasis on sets of relations is more appropriate to interactionist perspectives.

3. Znaniecki (1965), whose definition of social role is, with modifications, the basis of this study, used the concept of social circle rather than social group, since people associated in a social role may not form an organized whole, as exemplified by the patients of a doctor. Social circle is a more useful concept than that of role set, which is used by Merton (1957 and 1968) and his followers because it shows the interrelationships among its members, as well as the person's relationships with its segments.

4. The symbolic interactionist perspective on social roles, as here developed, is very different from the analysis that deals "only with institutionalized roles, linked to recognized social status" (and is thus limited to a social structural

framework), as presented by Mirra Komarovsky (1973, 649). Although our definition pulls together the micro and macro levels of sociological analysis, it approaches the subject as a set of negotiated relations within established patterns. The culture of a particular group provides the model for the relationships. The traditional view of social role, based on Linton's (1936) anthropological analysis of status as position and role as the more or less conformist *behavior* of one person in that position, is used by Komarovsky (1973), Parsons (1937, 1951), and others, as brought together by Biddle and Thomas (1966).

Also frequent, but impossible to use in studies of human interaction, is the view of social role as a set of expectations of behavior by the position holder. That use requires additional concepts to explain what actually occurs in life— the interaction rather than the expectation. The symbolic interactionist perspective makes irrelevant the artificial polarization of sociology and psychology into which Komarovsky (1973) pushes herself. The differences between the analysis used here and other perspectives on social roles will be increasingly apparent as we examine the shift from the traditionally conformist to the negotiated roles of American women.

5. Of course, the mother must wait for many of the rights from the children to be activated until the children are socialized into their roles. In the meantime, others ideally contribute to the rights later carried forth by the children, such as dressing and feeding them.

6. My original formulation of the concepts of role cluster, institutional richness, and social life space first appeared in the original manuscript of *Occupation: Housewife*, which was written in the late 1960s but was not used in the final product by Oxford University Press. I used abbreviated versions in Lopata 1969b and 1987e.

7. Many languages introduce great variations in noun, pronoun, verb, and adverb by gender, making gender-neutral communication impossible. For example, my mother, an American with English as her first language, frequently evoked smiles among Poles when she spoke their language, since she imitated my father's vocabulary. The need for specifying gender is important when variations in imagery must be acknowledged. Even English, which is quite simple as far as gender allocations are concerned, requires caution in the use of singular pronouns. I will use the female pronoun throughout, unless there is a reason to bring forth a male image, since this book is devoted to the social roles of women.

8. I am drawing on a number of my own studies as material for this theoretical reformulation of existing knowledge of the history and contemporary roles of women. All the studies took place in the metropolitan Chicago area. The first of these was conducted in the 1950s and 1960s and involved in-depth interviews with suburban and urban homemakers and urban employees. *Occupation: Housewife*, published by Oxford University Press in 1971, contains the insights derived from these studies. I then entered two major research projects focused on widows as women who had reached a stage of life that required modifications of their social roles. *Widowhood in an American City* (Lopata

1973c) involved women aged fifty to sixty-four and sixty-five plus. *Women as Widows: Support Systems* (Lopata 1979) developed a support-systems framework that was replicated in studies in many countries of the world (see Lopata 1987c, 1987d). The next project that makes theoretical and data contributions to this volume focused on the changing commitments of American women to paid work and family roles. Emphasis on background, occupational reality, and role clusters was developed in a two-volume work entitled *City Women: Work, Jobs, Occupations and Careers*. The first volume, subtitled *America* (Lopata, Miller, and Barnewolt 1985), analyzed various sources of knowledge about the occupational history and present involvements of women in America; the second, subtitled *Chicago* (Lopata, Barnewolt, and Miller 1985), drew upon an extensive sample of 1,877 Chicago-area women aged twenty-five to fifty-four. Cheryl Allyn Miller looked at the background, school, and work histories of the women, organized into twenty-six occupational categories. I analyzed their occupational construction of reality, and Debra Barnewolt examined their role cluster. A study now in process concerns itself with the social integration of modern suburban women in the suburb, their homes, and the role of homemaker. I shall be referring to these studies from time to time in this book.

Chapter 2. The Role of Wife

1. Bernard Farber (1966) claims that the complexities of modern times require serial marriages through the life course, each stage experienced with a partner of different characteristics. Of course, the same individual may change to meet the needs of each stage.

2. Komarovsly documented in *Blue-Collar Marriage* (1964) that "blue-collar or manual workers (skilled, semi-skilled and unskilled) constituted, in 1963, 48.9 percent of employed white persons and 79.7 percent of employed Negroes" (4). The families were involved mainly in traditional lifestyles, or the slow process of transitional change.

Chapter 3. The Role of Mother

1. Feldmen (1981) found that intentionally childless couples have more highly interactive marriages than intentional parents, but that these groups were "similar in their levels of marital happiness and in the extent to which they have egalitarian marriages" (593, 598).

2. Berrueta-Clement (1984) followed three- to four-year-old children receiving early childhood education into age nineteen to determine the consequences of a special Perry Preschool program. One conclusion is the importance of the quality of the program, which includes parent (mainly mother) involvement. The second conclusion is the undeniable benefit of early educational

preparation, especially of children living in poverty. They note that it is unfortunate that the vast majority of children in poor families, who are most at risk for later educational failure, are not served by similar programs.

3. Barbara Ehrenreich and Deirdre English document the extensive growth of "experts," especially since "the century of the child" in *For Her Own Good: 150 Years of Experts' Advice to Women* (1979). The end result has been the treatment of "motherhood as pathology." I found the women reported on in *Occupation: Housewife* (Lopata 1971b) to be very concerned over the role of mother, seeking experts whenever they could find them, although they often received contradictory advice. It is not that the newly expanding knowledge on child development was scientifically wrong, but that it was presented in such piecemeal fashion, and in such a style, as to create anxiety on the part of conscientious mothers unable to develop their own style of relationship with their children. Ehrenreich and English predict greater self-assertiveness on the part of women who insist on their right to define their duties.

Chapter 4. Social Roles in Kinship Networks

1. I have decided not to enter here into discussion of the complex topic of network analysis. Interest in the establishment of network methodologies and characteristics, started by anthropologists, appears to have peaked in the 1970s. Schneider (1980) uses the concepts of kin groups and networks interchangeably, although the degree of organization varies considerably in these social units.

2. Students in several family classes whom I asked to trace family histories often reported that their informants simply lacked information about whole branches of the mother's or father's kinfolk. This is particularly true in cases of divorce, which often cut off the relatives of the noncustodial parent.

3. As I will document in chapter 8, there is an increasing tendency for young women to decrystallize the effects of family background, mainly through the use of education, which supplies knowledge, skills, and self-confidence to operate in a larger world with more choices than predicted on the basis of the background limitations.

4. Of course, the easy movement of children to grandmothers for varying amounts of time among Native American families in the Southwest (Nelson 1988; Schlegel 1988) was facilitated by the matrilineal nature of some of these societies. The women trusted each other with their children since they belonged to the same lifelong kinship unit.

Chapter 5. Occupation: Homemaker

1. Matthews (1987). "If one could accurately pinpoint the exact time when the phrase 'Just a housewife,' made its first appearance, it seems likely that the

period under discussion [1920s] might have been that time. Certainly the likelihood that domesticity could be a fully adequate prop for female self-esteem had greatly diminished by 1930. The consumer culture along with the hedonism it spawned sounded the death knell both for housewifery as a skilled craft and for mother as the moral arbitrator. And yet the overwhelming majority of American women were still housewives for the better part of their lives" (pp. 193–94).

My original title for the *Occupation: Housewife* book was *I'm Just a Housewife*, because that was the phrase most often used by women asked to identify themselves during the 1950s and 1960s (Lopata 1971b; see also Friedan 1963). The publisher, Oxford University Press, considered that title insufficiently dignified at that time, although it recently came out with a book titled *Just a Housewife* (Matthews 1987). It appears that the negative identification and its connotations have not died out even in the 1990s.

2. It is surprising that the feminist efforts to redefine the role of homemaker have been so dependent upon this economic framework. Trying to determine how much a family would have to pay for the various activities performed by the homemaker reduces her role to that of hired helper, ignoring commitment and interactive components.

3. *Glamour* magazine (1989, 110) recently listed information on timesaving services under the title "Ease Holiday Pressures: Let Someone Else Do It":

> In a season filled with pressures and obligations, fitting yet another last-minute errand into your overloaded schedule can be the last straw. More and more businesses provide time-saving services—particularly pickup and delivery—to ease your load. And the price you pay is often as low as a $2 tip. As you write out your "do it" list, think again: What could someone else do for me? Many dry cleaners and laundries now offer pickup and delivery. There are video stores that pick up, pet food stores that deliver and diaper services that provide disposable as well as cloth diapers. Grocery stores and many restaurants (not just pizza and Chinese) deliver, of course, as do some drugstores. You can order stamps and tickets and check your bank balance by phone. Some hairdressers and manicurists will come to you to save waiting at a salon. If your SOS requires more than convenience, a personal service firm may be the way to go. These jacks-of-all-trades will do almost anything—from Christmas shopping to party planning to waiting in line to renew a driver's license. Just having someone come in to clean—especially before or after a party—could salvage your holiday spirit. Some companies charge by the task; others by the hour ($10–25 is average) — not cheap, but sometimes, your time—and sanity—are worth it.

Chapter 6. The Job: Settings and Circles

1. The occupations in *City Women: Work, Jobs, Occupations, Careers,* volume 1, *America,* and volume 2 *Chicago,* were organized by level of complex-

ity. For example, the professionals were aggregated into those in "object-focused (statisticians, sculptors)" teaching, health/welfare, and in "people-focused (counselors, ministers)" jobs.

2. Susan Berkun, a young lawyer with two small children, explained some of the problems of running her practice from the home, problems that have driven her back into a law firm. She had originally developed a successful career line in a prestigeful, large, Chicago-area firm. After the birth of the children she tried to negotiate a more flexible schedule with this definitely greedy institution. This proved impossible, so she quit to start her own legal practice, specializing in tax law, which is her forte. The presence of children in the home made it impossible to do professional counseling on the telephone—she couldn't persuade clients or other lawyers to her argument with screaming children in the background. Her work was constantly interrupted, and the problems of maintaining professional behavior with the constant impingement of the mother role was impossible. She recommends that any professional or business entrepreneur arrange for members of the family to be absent during hours of occupational work. A further difficulty was the tendency of clients and others in the social circle of the lawyer to call at all hours, which they could not do in an office with established hours.

3. I will never forget how fast my husband, a management consultant, was pulled off of a job when I unwillingly told his age to an older representative of a major manufacturing company whom he was advising. The man was furious that such a "youngster" was telling him how to run his department.

4. It is difficult to find a term other than *beneficiary* that covers the segment of the social circle toward which the activity is directed and that is assumed to be most benefited. I also use the terms *customer* and *client* in this chapter, when appropriate. Sometimes the people assumed by the social person and/or the organization to be the beneficiary do not construct reality the same way, as in the case of men prisoners in the circle of prison officers. The social person can be the beneficiary of her own work, as is true of students and patients.

5. Any organization experiencing rapid employee turnover is concerned with this problem, trying to solve it at various points in employee search or career. Direct-sales companies such as Tupperware invest heavily in training and constant reinforcement. See Peven's (1968) comparison of its training procedures to religious revival events.

6. My mother, who obtained her law degree from the University of Chicago in 1915, had to sit outside the classroom in several courses because the professors were worried that her presence might distract the male students.

Chapter 7. Social Roles in the Rest of the World

1. De Tocqueville stated in his *Democracy in America* ([1835] 1936) that if egalitarian education were spread "over whole earth, the human mind would

gradually find its beacon lights grow dim and men would fall back into darkness" (p. 421).

> [De Tocqueville] favored the aristocratic system by which upper-class families provided extensive education to their youth, at home with tutors and governesses or in special schools. Peasants and other class members were assumed by him to obtain all the learning they needed from role models at home or in the apprenticeship system. (Lopata 1981a, 12)

2. My husband was initially rejected by Northwestern University when he applied for the Ph.D. program in economics at an over-thirty-five age, although he had completed an M.S. in that field at the age of twenty-two. His was not a unique situation, as most universities until rather recently were operating on a short-life-span model and did not want to "waste" resources on people who could not devote their entire adulthood to a career. There were also questions as to the desirability of students who changed their minds in midlife, rather than an appreciation of personal flexibility of career involvement. Although increasing numbers of midlife women started returning to school during the 1970s, it was not until such prestigious colleges as Radcliffe or Mundelein, specifically addressed themselves to such a potential student body that this became a publicly acknowledge group of persons in higher education. Loyola University of Chicago has a whole program of counseling and socialization for returning students, regardless of age. Davis and Bumpass (1976) questioned the traditional sequencing of school, marriage, and employment.

3. Although network analysis has been extensively used in research on neighborhoods, the concept of social circle enables us to see how non-neighbors, such as service providers, are brought in to facilitate or hinder neighboring. For example, we can see how neighbors can decrease interdependence with the expansion of shopping facilities or the introduction of voluntary associations which draw upon a selected number of co-residents.

Chapter 8. Life Spaces and Self-Concepts

1. *The Peasants: Fall, Winter, Spring, Summer* by Ladislaw Reymont (1925), a Nobel Prize–winning novel of life in a small Polish village, provides a perfect description of families involved in highly emotional role conflicts.

2. The fact that husbands may not be supportive of high earnings of wives comes from the *City Women: Chicago* (Lopata, Barnewolt, and Miller 1985) study. Our sample contained two sets of salesworkers: clerks and agents. The agents entered that occupation later in life, having left mainly secretarial jobs and obtained specialized training. They are now earning much more than before, and two-and-a-half times what the salesclerks make. However, few report that their husbands think work is "good for the wife" or that it is an "advantage to

have a working wife." Salesclerks regard their husbands as appreciative of the money they bring home. The lack of support by the husbands of sales agents may be due to the inconvenience placed on the family by the irregular hours and work patterns of sales agents, but we wonder how much the increase in earnings by the women contributes to it.

3. Carolyn Heilbrun (Amanda Cross), a professor of literature at Columbia University and also an author of murder mysteries, responded, when asked during a speech at Wellesley College how she finds time to do everything: "There are only two of us at home, and we meet our children in restaurants."

References

Abbott, Grace. 1938. *The Dependent and the Delinquent Child.* Vol. 2 of *The Child and the State.* Chicago: University of Chicago Press.

Abir-Am, Pnina G. and Dorinda Outram, eds. 1987. *Uneasy Careers and Intimate Lives: Women in Science, 1989–1979.* New Brunswick, N.J.: Rutgers University Press.

Acker, Joan, Kate Barry, and Joke Esseveld. 1990. "Feminism, Female Friends, and the Reconstruction of Intimacy." In *Friendship in Context,* 75–108. *See* Lopata and Maines 1990.

Adams, Bert. 1968. *Kinship in an Urban Setting.* Chicago: Markham.

————. 1988. "Fifty Years of Family Research. What Does It Mean?" *Journal of Marriage and the Family* 50:5–17.

Adams, Frances McLeavey. 1972. "The Role of Old People in Santo Thomas, Mazaltepec." In *Aging and Modernization. See* Cowgill 1972.

Adams, Rebecca. 1983. "Friendship and Its Role in the Lives of Elderly Women." Ph.D. diss., University of Chicago.

————. 1985. "People Would Talk: Normative Barriers to Cross-Sex Friendships for Elderly Women." *The Gerontologist* 25:605–11.

Adams, Rebecca, and Rosemary Blieszner, eds. 1989. *Older Adult Friendship: Structure and Process*. Beverly Hills, Calif.: Sage.

Aisenberg, Nadya, and Mona Harrington. 1988. *Women of Academe: Outsiders in the Sacred Grove*. Amherst: University of Massachusetts Press.

Aldous, Joan, ed. 1982. *Two Paychecks: Life in Dual-Earner Families*. Beverly Hills, Calif.: Sage.

Allatt, Patricia. 1983. "Men and War: Status, Class, and the Social Reproduction of Masculinity." In *The Public and the Private*, edited by Eva Gamarnikow, David H. J. Morgan, June Purvis, and Daphne Taylorson, 47–61. London: Heinemann.

Allen, Sheila, and Carol Wolkowitz. 1987. *Homeworking: Myths and Realities*. New York: Macmillan Education.

Anda, Diane de, and Rosina M. Becerra. 1984. "Support Networks for Adolescent Mothers." *Social Casework* 65:172–81.

Andersen, Margaret L. 1983. *Thinking about Women: Sociological and Feminist Perspectives*. New York: Macmillan.

Andre, Rae. 1982. *Homemakers: The Forgotten Workers*. Chicago: University of Chicago Press.

Anspach, Donald F. 1976. "Kinship and Divorce." *Journal of Marriage and the Family* 38:323–30.

Aptheker, Bettina. 1982. *Woman's Legacy: Essays on Race, Sex, and Class in American History*. Amherst: University of Massachusetts Press.

———. 1989. *Tapestries of Life: Women's Work, Women's Consciousness, and the Meaning of Daily Experience*. Amherst: University of Massachusetts Press.

Ardener, Shirley, ed. 1981. *Women and Space: Ground Rules and Social Maps*. New York: St. Martin's.

Aries, Philippe. 1965. *Centuries of Childhood*. New York: Random House.

Armstrong, Peter. 1982. "If It's Only Women It Doesn't Matter So Much." In *Women, Work, and the Labor Market*, edited by Jackie West, 27–43. London: Routledge & Kegan Paul.

Aukett, Richard, Jane Ritchie, and Kathryn Mill. 1988. "Gender Differences in Friendship Patterns." *Sex Roles* 19:57–66.

Avioli, Paula Smith. 1989. "The Social Support Functions of Siblings in Later Life." *American Behavioral Scientist* 33:45–57.

Babchuk, Nicholas, and Alan P. Bates. 1963. "Primary Relations of Middle-Class Couples: A Study of Male Dominance." *American Sociological Review* 28:374–84.

Babcock, Barbara Allen, Ann Freedman, Eleanor Holmes Norton, and Susan C. Ross. 1975. *Sex Discrimination and the Law: Causes and Remedies*. Boston: Little, Brown.

Backett, Katheryn C. 1982. *Mothers and Fathers*. New York: St. Martin's.

Bahr, Harvey M. 1976. "The Kinship Role." In *Role Structure and Analysis of the Family,* edited by F. I. Nye, 61–79. Beverly Hills, Calif.: Sage.

Baker, Wayne, and Rosanna Hertz. 1990. "Communal Diffusion of Friend-ship: The Structure of Intimate Relations in an Israeli Kibbutz." In *Friendship in Context. See* Lopata and Maines 1990.

Baldassare, Mark. 1986. *Trouble in Paradise: The Suburban Transformation in America.* New York: Columbia University Press.

Bank, Stephen, and Michael D. Kohn. 1982. "Intense Sibling Loyalties." In *Sibling Relationships. See* Lamb and Sutton-Smith 1982.

Barnes, Denise R. 1987. "Wives and Widows in China." In *Widows: The Middle East, Asia, and the Pacific. See* Lopata 1987c.

Barnett, Rosalind C. 1988. "On the Relationship of Adult Daughters to Their Mothers." *Journal of Geriatric Psychiatry* 21:37–50.

Barnewolt, Debra. 1986. "Social Role Importance: An Interplay of Experi-ence and Expectation in the Lives of Chicago Area Women." Ph.D. diss., Department of Sociology, Loyola University of Chicago.

Bart, Pauline. 1971. "Depression in Middle-aged Women." In *Woman in Sexist Society,* edited by Vivian Gornick and Barbara K. Moran, 163–86. New York: Basic Books.

Baruch, Grace. 1984. "The Psychological Well-Being of Women in the Middle Years." In *Women in Midlife. See* Baruch and Brooks-Gunn 1984.

Baruch, Grace, and Jeanne Brooks-Gunn, eds. 1984. *Women in Midlife.* New York: Plenum.

Baruch, Grace, Rosalind Barnett, and Caryl Rivers. 1983. *Lifeprints: New Patterns of Love and Work for Today's Women.* New York: McGraw-Hill.

Baumgartner, M. P. 1988. *The Moral Order of a Suburb.* New York: Oxford University Press.

Beach, Betty. 1989. *Integrating Work and Family Life: The Home-Working Family.* Albany: State University of New York Press.

Becerra, Rosina M. 1988. "The Mexican American Family." In *Ethnic Families in America. See* Mindel, Habenstein, and Wright 1988.

Becker, Howard S. 1951. "The Professional Dance Musician and His Audi-ence." *American Journal of Sociology* 57:136–44.

———. 1953. "Becoming a Marijuana User." *American Journal of Sociology* 59:235–42.

———. 1960. "Notes on the Concept of Commitment." *American Journal of Sociology* 66:32–42.

Bedford, Victoria. 1989a. "Understanding the Value of Siblings in Old Age." *American Behavioral Scientist* 33, 33–44.

————. 1989a. "Sibling Research in Historical Perspective: The Discovery of a Forgotten Relationship." *American Behavioral Scientist* 33:6–18.

Bedford, Victoria H. and Debra T. Gold, eds. 1989. *Siblings in Later Life: A Neglected Family Relationship.* [Special issue]. *American Behavioral Scientist* 33 (September/October).

Beecher, Catherine E., and Harriet Beecher Stowe. 1870. *The American Woman's Home.* New York: J. B. Ford.

Bell, Robert R. 1981. *Worlds of Friendship.* Beverly Hills, Calif.: Sage.

Benet, Mary Kathleen. 1972. *The Secretarial Ghetto.* New York: McGraw-Hill.

Bengtson, Vern L., and E. deTerre. 1980. "Aging and Family Relations: A Decade Review." *Marriage and Family Review* 3:51–76.

Bengtson, Vern L., and Joan Robertson, eds. 1985. *Grandparenthood.* Beverly Hills, Calif.: Sage.

Bennett, Amanda. 1983. "Population Lid: China Cajoles Families and Offers Incentives to Reduce Birth Rate." *Wall Street Journal,* 6 July, 1 and 16.

Benson, Susan Porter. 1984. "Women in Retail Sales Work: The Continuing Dilemma of Service." In *My Troubles Are Going to Have Trouble with Me,* edited by Karen Brodkin Sacks and Dorothy Remy, 113–24. New Brunswick, N.J.: Rutgers University Press.

Berger, Bennett. 1960. *Working Class Suburb.* Berkeley: University of California Press.

Berger, Peter, and Hansfried Kellner. 1970. "Marriage and Construction of Reality." In *Patterns of Communicative Behavior,* edited by Hans Dreitzel, 50–73. London: Collier-Macmillan.

Bergmann, Barbara R. 1986. *The Economic Emergence of Women.* New York: Basic Books.

Berheide, Catherine-White. 1988. "Women in Sales and Service Occupations." In *Women Working: Theories and Facts in Perspective,* edited by Ann Helton Stromberg and Shirley Harkess, 2d ed., 241–57. Mountain View, Calif.: Mayfield.

Berk, Richard A., and Sarah Fenstermaker Berk. 1979. *Labor and Leisure at Home: Content and Organization of the Household Day.* Beverly Hills, Calif.: Sage.

————. 1985. *The Gender Factory: The Apportionment of Work in American Households.* New York: Plenum.

Bernard, Jessie. 1973. *The Future of Marriage.* New York: Bantam.

————. 1974. "The Housewife: Between Two Worlds." In *Varieties of Work Experience,* edited by Phyllis L. Steward and Muriel G. Cantor, 49–66. New York: Wiley.

————. 1979. "Women as Voters: From Redemptive to Futurist Role." In *Social Roles and Social Policy: A Complex Social Science Equation,* edited by Jean Lipman-Blumen and Jessie Bernard, 279–86. Beverly Hills: Sage.

———. 1981. *The Female World*. New York: Free Press.

———. 1983. "The Good Provider Role: Its Rise and Fall." In *Family in Transition*, edited by Arlene S. Skolnick and Jerome H. Skolnick, 155–75. Boston: Little, Brown.

Berrueta-Clement, John R. 1984. *Changed Lives*. Ypsilanti, Mich.: High/Scope Press.

Bettelheim, Bruno. 1962. "Does Communal Education Work? The Case of the Kibbutz." *Commentary* 33:117–25.

———. 1965. "The Commitment Required of a Woman Entering a Scientific Profession in Present-Day American Society." In *Women and the Scientific Professions*, 4–17. *See* Rossi 1965.

Biddle, Bruce J., and Edwin J. Thomas. 1966. *Role Theory*. New York: Wiley.

Bieder, Robert E. 1973. "Kinship as a Factor in Migration." *Journal of Marriage and the Family* 35:429–39.

Bigus, Odis. 1972. "The Milkman and His Customers." *Urban Life and Culture* 1:131–65.

Bird, Caroline. 1976. *Enterprising Women*. New York: New American Library/Mentor.

———. 1979. *The Two-Paycheck Marriage*. New York: Rawson Wade.

Blake, Judith. 1974. "Coercive Pronatalism and American Population Policy." In *The Family: Its Structure and Functions*, 2d ed., edited by Rose Coser, 276–317. New York: St. Martin's.

Blieszner, Rosemary. 1989. "Developmental Processes of Friendship." In *Older Adult Friendship*, 108–26. *See* Adams and Blieszner 1989.

Block, Joel, and Diane Greenberg. 1985. *Women and Friendship*. New York: Franklin Watts.

Bloom, Paul N., and Ruth Belk Smith, eds. 1986. *The Future of Consumerism*. Lexington, Mass.: Lexington Books.

Bluestone, Barry, and Bennett Harrison. 1982. *The Deindustrialization of America*. New York: Basic Books.

Blumer, Herbert. 1969. *Symbolic Interactionism: Perspective and Method*. Englewood Cliffs, N.J.: Prentice-Hall.

Blumstein, Philip, and Pepper Schwartz. 1983. *American Couples: Work, Money, Sex*. New York: Morrow.

Bohannan, Paul J. 1963. *Social Anthropology*. New York: Holt, Rinehart & Winston.

Borg, Susan, and Judith Lasker. 1988. *When Pregnancy Fails: Families Coping with Miscarriage, Stillbirth, and Infant Death*. Rev. ed. Boston: Beacon.

Bose, Christine. 1980. "Social Status of the Homemaker." In *Women and Household Labor,* 69–87. *See* Berk 1980.

Boserup, Ester. 1970. *Woman's Role in Economic Development.* New York: St. Martin's.

Boston Women's Health Collective. [1971] [1984] 1992. *The New Our Bodies, Ourselves.* New York: Simon & Schuster.

Bott, Elizabeth. 1957. *Family and Social Network.* London: Tavistock.

Boverman, C. E., and R. M. Dobash. 1974. "Structural Variations in Inter-Sibling Affect." *Journal of Marriage and the Family* 36:48–54.

Braverman, Harry. 1974. *Labor and Monopoly Capital.* New York: Monthly Review Press.

Brody, Elaine M. 1989. *Women in the Middle: Their Parent Care Years.* New York: Springer.

Brody, Elaine M., Christine Hoffman, Morton Kleban, and Claire Schoonover. 1989. "Caregiving Daughters and Their Local Siblings: Perceptions, Strains, and Interactions." *The Gerontologist* 29:529–38.

Brown, Bradford B. 1990. "A Life-Span Approach to Friendship." In *Friendship in Context,* 23–50. *See* Lopata and Maines 1990.

Brown, Clair (Vickery). 1982. "Home Production for Use in a Market Economy." In *Rethinking the Family: Some Feminist Questions,* 151–67. *See* Thorne 1982.

Bucher, Rue, and Joan G. Stelling. 1977. *Becoming Professional.* Beverly Hills, Calif.: Sage.

Burton, Linda M., and Vern L. Bengtson. 1985. "Black Grandmothers: Issues of Timing and Continuity of Roles." In *Grandparenthood,* 61–77. *See* Bengtson and Robertson 1985.

Butler, JoAnn C. 1988. "Local Zoning Ordinances Governing Home Occupations." In *The New Era of Home-Based Work,* 189–200. *See* Christensen 1988c.

Cain, Virginia, and Sandra L. Hofferth. 1989. "Parental Choice of Self-Care for School-Age Children." *Journal of Marriage and the Family* 51:65–77.

Callan, Hilary, and Shirley Ardener. 1984. *The Incorporated Wife.* London: Croom Helm.

Cancian, Francesca. 1987. *Love in America: Gender and Self-Development.* New York: Cambridge University Press.

Caplow, Theodore, Howard M. Bahr, Bruce A. Chadwick, Reuben Hill, and Margaret Holmes Williamson. 1982. *Middletown Families: Fifty Years of Change and Continuity.* New York: Bantam.

Carlson, Margaret. 1992. "All Eyes on Hillary." *Time,* 14 September, 28–33.

Carlson, Patricia, Marian Simacek, William F. Henry, and Ida M. Martinson. 1984. "Helping Parents Cope: A Model Home Care Program for the

Dying Child." In *Childhood and Death,* edited by Hannelore Wass and Charles A. Corr, 113–27. New York: Hemisphere.

Carnegie, Dale. 1936. *How to Win Friends and Influence People.* New York: Simon & Schuster.

Cavendish, Ruth. 1982. *Women on the Line.* London: Routledge & Kegan Paul.

Chafe, William Henry. 1972. *The American Woman: Her Changing Social, Economic and Political Roles, 1920–1970.* New York: Oxford University Press.

Chapman, Jane Roberts, and Margaret Gates. 1977. *Women into Wives: The Legal and Economic Impact of Marriage.* Beverly Hills, Calif.: Sage.

Chatters, Linda M., Robert Joseph Taylor, and Harold W. Neighbors. 1989. "Size of Informal Helper Network Mobilized During a Serious Personal Problem among Black Americans." *Journal of Marriage and the Family* 51:667–76.

Cherlin, Andrew J. 1981. *Marriage, Divorce, Remarriage.* Cambridge: Harvard University Press.

Cherlin, Andrew J. and Frank F. Furstenberg. 1986. *The New American Grandparent: A Place in the Family, A Life Apart.* New York: Basic Books.

Chodorow, Nancy. 1978. *The Reproduction of Mothering: Psychoanalysis and the Sociology of Gender.* Berkeley: University of California Press.

Chodorow, Nancy, and Susan Contratto. 1982. "The Fantasy of the Perfect Mother." In *Rethinking the Family,* 54–75. *See* Thorne 1982.

Christensen, Kathleen. 1988a. "Independent Contracting." In *The New Era of Home-Based Work. See* Christensen 1988c.

———. 1988b. "Introduction: White-Collar Home-Based Work—The Changing U.S. Economy and Family." In *The New Era of Home-Based Work. See* Christensen 1988c.

———, ed. 1988c. *The New Era of Home-Based Work: Directions and Policies.* Boulder, Colo.: Westview.

———. 1988d. *Women and Home-Based Work.* New York: Henry Holt.

Cicirelli, V. G. 1982. "Sibling Influence throughout the Life Span." In *Sibling Relationships,* 455–62. *See* Lamb and Sutton-Smith 1982.

Clark, Alice. [1919] 1968. *Working Life of Women in the Seventeenth Century.* New York: Kelley Reprints.

Clavan, Sylvia. 1978. "The Impact of Social Class and Social Trends on the Role of Grandparent." *The Family Coordinator* 27:351–57.

Clawson, Mary Ann. 1986. "Nineteenth-Century Women's Auxiliaries and Fraternal Orders." *Signs* 12, 40–61.

Clemente, Frank, Patricia A. Rexroad, and Carl Hirsch. 1975. "The Participation of Black Aged in Voluntary Associations." *Journal of Gerontology* 30:469–72.

Cohler, Bertram J. 1988. "The Adult Daughter-Mother Relationship: Perspectives from Life-Course Family Study and Psychoanalysis." *Journal of Geriatric Psychiatry* 21:51–72.

Cooley, Charles Horton. [1902] 1922. *Human Nature and the Social Order.* New York: Scribner's.

Coontz, Stephanie. 1992. *The Way We Never Were: American Families and the Nostalgia Trip.* New York: Basic Books.

Corcoran, Mary, Greg J. Duncan, and Martha S. Hill. 1988. "The Economic Fortunes of Women and Children: Lessons from the Panel Study of Income Dynamics." In *Black Women in America,* 97–113. *See* Malson et al. 1988.

Coser, Lewis. 1973. "Servants: The Obsolescence of an Occupational Role." *Social Forces* 52:31–40.

———. 1984. *Refugee Scholars in America: Their Impact and Their Experiences.* New Haven: Yale University.

———. 1974. *Greedy Institutions.* New York: Free Press.

Coser, Lewis, and Rose Laub Coser. 1974. "The Housewife and Her 'Greedy Family.'" In *Greedy Institutions. See* Coser 1974.

Coser, Rose Laub. 1975a. "The Complexity of Roles as a Seedbed of Individual Autonomy." In *The Idea of Social Structure: Papers in Honor of Robert K. Merton,* edited by Lewis A. Coser, 237–630. New York: Harcourt Brace Jovanovich.

———. 1975b. "Stay Home Little Sheba: On Placement, Displacement, and Social Change." *Social Problems* 22, 470–80.

———. 1991. *In Defense of Modernity: Role Complexity and Individual Autonomy.* Stanford, Calif.: Stanford University Press.

———. 1992. Personal Correspondence.

Costello, Cynthia B. 1988. "Clerical Home-Based Work: A Case Study of Work and Family." In *The New Era of Home-Based Work,* 135–45. *See* Christensen 1988c.

Cott, Nancy F. 1977. *The Bonds of Womanhood: Women's Sphere in New England, 1780–1885.* New Haven: Yale University Press.

Cowan, Ruth Schwartz. 1983. *More Work for Mother: The Ironies of Household Technology from Open Hearth to the Microwave.* New York: Basic Books.

Cowgill, Donald O. 1972. "The Role and Status of the Aged in Thailand." In *Aging and Modernization,* edited by Donald O. Cowgill and Lowell D. Holmes, 91–101. New York: Appleton-Century-Crofts.

Cox, Claire. 1963. *How Women Can Make Up to $1000 a Week in Direct Selling*. New York: Van Nostrand.

Crane, Diana. 1968. "Social Structure in a Group of Scientists: A Test of the 'Invisible College' Hypothesis." *American Sociological Review* 34:335–352.

Crane, Lauren Edgar. 1969. "The Salesman's Role in Household Decision-Making." In *Salesmanship: Selected Readings,* edited by John M. Rathwell, 98–110. Homewood, Ill.: Irwin.

Csikszentimihalyi, Mihaly, and Eugene Rochberg-Halton. 1981. *The Meaning of Things: Domestic Symbols and the Self.* New York: Cambridge University Press.

Cumming, Elaine, and William E. Henry. 1961. *Growing Old: The Process of Disengagement.* New York: Basic Books.

Cutler, Stephen. 1976. "Membership in Different Types of Voluntary Associations and Psychological Well-Being." *The Gerontologist* 16:335–39.

Danco, Leon A. 1982. *Inside the Family Business.* Englewood Cliffs, N.J.: Prentice-Hall.

Daniels, Arlene Kaplan. 1988. *Invisible Careers: Women Community Leaders in the Volunteer World.* Chicago: University of Chicago Press.

Davis, Angela Y. 1988. *Women, Culture, and Politics.* New York: Random House.

Davis, Kinsley. 1940. "The Sociology of Parent-Youth Conflict." *American Sociological Review* 5:523–35.

———. [1949] 1966. "Status and Related Concepts." In *Role Theory. See* Biddle and Thomas, 1966.

Davis, Nancy J., and Larry Bumpass. 1976. "The Continuation of Education after Marriage among Women in the United States." *Demography* 3:161–74.

Demos, John. 1973. *A Little Commonwealth: Family Life in Plymouth Colony.* New York: Oxford University Press.

Denzin, Norman K. 1987a. *The Alcoholic Self.* Newbury Park, Calif.: Sage.

———. 1987b. *The Recovering Alcoholic.* Newbury Park, Calif.: Sage.

Deutsch, Helene. 1977. *The Psychology of Women.* New York: Grune & Stratton.

Deutsch, Morton. 1954. "Field Theory in Social Psychology." In *Handbook of Social Psychology,* edited by Gardner Lindsey, 412–487. Cambridge, Mass.: Addison-Wesley.

Deutscher, Irwin. 1964. "The Quality of Postparental Life." *Journal of Marriage and the Family* 26:52–59.

Deveny, Kathleen. 1989. "Can Avon Get Wall Street to Answer the Door? *Business Week,* 20 March, 123–24.

Dobrofsky, Lynne R., and Constance T. Patterson. 1977. "The Military Wife and Feminism." *Signs* 2:675–84.

Domhoff, G. William. 1967. *Who Rules America?* Englewood Cliffs, N.J.: Prentice-Hall.

———. 1983. *Who Rules America Now: A View for the '80s*. Englewood Cliffs, N.J.: Prentice-Hall.

Donovan, Frances R. [1929] 1974. *The Saleslady*. New York: Arno.

Douglas, Ann. 1977. *The Feminization of American Culture*. New York: Avon Books.

Dubin, Robert. 1956. "Industrial Workers' World: A Study of the Central Life Interests of Industrial Workers." *Social Problems* 3:131–42.

Dulles, Foster Rhea. 1965. *A History of Recreation: America Learns to Play*. New York: Appleton-Century-Crofts.

Duncan, James. 1982. *Housing and Identity: Cross-Cultural Perspectives*. New York: Holmes & Meier.

Duvall, Evelyn. 1954. *In-Laws: Pro and Con*. New York: Association Press.

Dworkin, Anthony Gary, Janet Saltzman Chafetz, and Rosalind J. Dworkin. 1986. "The Effects of Tokenism on Work Alienation among Urban Public School Teachers." *Work and Occupations* 13:399–420.

Ebaugh, Helen Rose Fuchs. 1988. *Becoming an Ex: The Process of Role Exit*. Chicago: University of Chicago Press.

Edwards, Richard. 1979. *Contested Terrain: The Transformation of the Workplace in the Twentieth Century*. New York: Basic Books.

Ehrenreich, Barbara. 1983. *The Hearts of Men: American Dreams and Flight from Commitment*. Garden City, N.Y.: Anchor.

Ehrenreich, Barbara, and Deirdre English. 1979. *For Her Own Good*. Garden City, N.Y.: Anchor.

Eichler, Margrit. 1973. "Women as Personal Dependents." In *Women in Canada,* edited by Marylee Stephenson, 36–55. Toronto: New Press.

Eisenstein, Zillah. 1979. *Capitalist Patriarchy and the Case for Socialist Feminism*. New York: Monthly Review Press.

Elder, Glen H., Jr., and Charles E. Bowerman. 1963. "Family Structure and Child-Rearing Patterns: The Effect of Family Size and Sex Composition." *American Sociological Review* 28:891–906.

Emmerman, Lynn. 1990. "Mixed Blessings: Five Couples Talk about Their Interracial Marriages." *Chicago Tribune Magazine,* 9 September, 13–18.

England, Paula, and George Farkas. 1986. *Household, Employment, and Gender: A Social, Economic, and Demographic View*. New York: Aldine.

Enloe, Cynthia. 1987. "Feminists Thinking about War, Militarism, and Peace." In *Analyzing Gender: A Handbook of Social Science Research,* edited by Beth B. Hess and Myra Marx Ferree, 526–47. Beverly Hills, Calif.: Sage.

Entwisle, Doris, and Susan G. Doering. 1981. *The First Birth: A Family Turning Point.* Baltimore: Johns Hopkins University Press.

Epstein, Cynthia. 1970. *Women's Place: Options and Limits in Professional Careers.* Berkeley: University of California Press.

————. 1971. "Encountering the Male Establishment: Sex-Status Limits on Women's Careers in the Professions." In *The Professional Woman,* edited by Athena Theodore, 42–73. Cambridge, Mass.: Schenkman.

————. 1983. *Women in Law.* Garden City, N.Y.: Anchor.

————. 1988. *Deceptive Distinctions: Sex, Gender, and the Social Order.* New Haven: Yale University Press.

————. 1992. "Changes in Structure: Changes in the Self." Paper presented at the annual meeting of the American Sociological Association, Pittsburgh, 22 August.

Epstein, Cynthia, and Rose Coser, eds. 1981. *Access to Power: Cross-National Studies of Women and Elites.* London: Allen & Unwin.

Erikson, Erik H. 1965. "Concluding Remarks." In *Women and the Scientific Professions,* 232–45. *See* Rossi 1965.

Eskilson, Arlene, and Mary Glenn Wiley. 1987. "Parents, Peers, Perceived Pressure, and Adolescent Self-Concept: Is a Daughter a Daughter All of Her Life?" *Sociological Quarterly* 28:135–45.

Faludi, Susan. 1991. *Backlash: The Undeclared War against Women.* New York: Crown.

Farber, Bernard. 1966. "Kinship Laterality and the Emotionally Disturbed Child." In *Kinship and Family Organization,* edited by Bernard Farber, 69–78. New York: Wiley.

Farber, Bernard, Charles H. Mindel, and Bernard Lazerwitz. 1988. "The Jewish American Family." In *Ethnic Families in America,* 400–437. *See* Mindel, Habenstein, and Wright 1988.

Faver, Catherine A. 1984. *Women in Transition: Career, Family, and Life Satisfaction in Three Cohorts.* New York: Praeger.

Feldberg, Roslyn, and Evelyn Nakano Glenn. 1979. "Male and Female: Job versus Gender Models in the Sociology of Work." *Social Problems* 26:524–38.

Feldman, Harold. 1981. "A Comparison of Intentional Parents and Intentionally Childless Couples." *Journal of Marriage and the Family* 43:593–600.

Ferber, Marianne, and Joan Huber. 1979. "Husbands, Wives, and Careers." *Journal of Marriage and the Family* 41:315–25.

Ferree, Myra Marx. 1976. "Working-Class Jobs: Housework and Paid Work as Sources of Satisfaction." *Social Problems* 23:431–41.

————. 1980. "Satisfaction with Housework: The Social Contract." In *Women and Household Labor,* 89–112. *See* Berk 1980.

―――. 1987. "Family and Job for Working-Class Women: Gender and Class Systems Seen from Below." In *Families and Work,* 289–301. *See* Gerstel and Gross 1987a.

Finch, Janet. 1983. *Married to the Job: Wives' Incorporation in Men's Work.* Boston: Allen & Unwin.

Finch, Janet, and D. Groves. 1983. *A Labour of Love.* Boston: Routledge & Kegan Paul.

Finley, Nancy J. 1989. "Theories of Family Labor as Applied to Gender Differences in Caregiving for Elderly Parents." *Journal of Marriage and the Family* 51:79–86.

Fischer, Claude. 1982. *To Dwell among Friends: Personal Networks in Town and City.* Chicago: University of Chicago Press.

Fischer, Claude, Robert Max Jackson, C. Ann Steve, Kathleen Gerson, Lynne McCallister Jones, and Mark Baldassare. 1977. *Networks and Places: Social Relations in the Urban Setting.* New York: Free Press.

Fisher, Lucy Rose. 1983. "Mothers and Mothers-in-Law." *Journal of Marriage and the Family* 45:187–92.

―――. 1986. *Linked Lives: Adult Daughters and Their Mothers.* New York: Harper & Row.

Fisher, Lucy Rose, Daniel P. Mueller, Philip W. Cooper, and Richard A. Chase. 1989. *Older Minnesotans: What Do They Need? How Do They Contribute?* St. Paul, Minn.: Amherst H. Wilder Foundation.

Flammang, Jane A., ed. 1984. *Political Women: Current Roles in State and Local Government.* Beverly Hills, Calif.: Sage.

Foerstner, Abigail. 1987. "Home Again: Increasingly Businesswomen Are Finding There's No Place Like It." *Chicago Tribune,* 12 April, 6–15.

Forcey, Linda Rennie. 1987. *Mothers of Sons: Toward an Understanding of Responsibility.* New York: Praeger.

Fowlkes, Martha R. 1980. *Behind Every Successful Man.* New York: Columbia University Press.

Frankfort, Roberta. 1977. *Collegiate Women.* New York: New York University Press.

Friedan, Betty. 1963. *The Feminine Mystique.* New York: Norton.

Frohock, Fred M. 1986. *Special Care: Medical Decisions at the Beginning of Life.* Chicago: University of Chicago Press.

Fromm, Eric. 1947. *Man for Himself.* New York: Rinehart.

Furstenberg, Frank, Jr. 1990. "As the Pendulum Shifts: The National History of Teenage Childbearing as a Social Problem." The Duvall Distinguished Lecture, National Council on Family Relations, 11 November, Seattle.

Furstenberg, Frank Jr., Leon Gordis, and Milton Markowitz. 1969. "Birth Control Knowledge and Attitudes among Unmarried Pregnant Adolescents: A Preliminary Report." *Journal of Marriage and the Family* 31:34–42.

Furstenberg, Frank, Jr. and Graham Spanier. 1984. *Recycling the Family: Remarriage after Divorce.* Beverly Hills, Calif.: Sage.

Galbraith, John Kenneth. 1973. "The Economics of the American Housewife." *Atlantic Monthly,* August, 78–83.

Gallup, George H., Jr. and Frank Newport. 1990. "Who Wants Kids? Nearly Everybody." *Chicago Sun Times,* 3 June, 3.

Gannon, Martin J. 1984. "Preferences for Temporary Workers: Time, Variety, and Flexibility." *Monthly Labor Review,* August, 26–28.

Gans, Herbert. 1962. *The Urban Villagers: Group and Class in the Life of Italian-Americans.* New York: Free Press.

———. 1967. *Leavittowners.* New York: Pantheon.

Garland, Anne Witte. 1988. *Women Activists: Challenging the Abuse of Power.* New York: Feminist Press, City University of New York.

Gates, Margaret. 1977. "Homemakers into Widows and Divorcees: Can the Law Provide Economic Protection? In *Women into Wives,* 215–32. *See* Chapman and Gates 1977.

Gelb, Joyce, and Marian Lief Palley. 1982. *Women and Public Policies.* Princeton: Princeton University Press.

Genevie, Louis, and Eva Margolies. 1987. *The Motherhood Report: How Women Feel about Being Mothers.* New York: Macmillan.

Gerhardt, Uta. 1980. "Toward a Critical Analysis of Role." *Social Problems* 27:556–69.

Gerson, Judith M., and Robert E. Kraut. 1988. "Clerical Work at Home or in the Office: The Difference It Makes." In *The New Era of Home-Based Work,* 49–64. *See* Christensen 1988c.

Gerson, Kathleen. 1985. *Hard Choices: How Women Decide about Work, Career, and Motherhood.* Berkeley: University of California Press.

Gerson, Menachem. 1978. *Family, Women, and Socialization in the Kibbutz.* Boston: Lexington Books.

Gerstel, Naomi, and Harriet Engel Gross, eds. 1987a. *Families and Work.* Philadelphia: Temple University Press.

———. 1987b. "Introduction to Work in and from the Contemporary Home." In *Families and Work,* 153–61. *See* Gerstel and Gross 1987a.

Gibson, Geoffrey. 1972. "Kin Family Networks: Overheralded Structure in Past Conceptualizations of Family Functioning." *Journal of Marriage and the Family* 34:13–24.

Giles-Sims, Jean, and Margaret Crosbie-Burnett. 1989. "Stepfamilies." *Family Relations* 38:19–23.

Gilligan, Carol. 1982. *In a Different Voice: Psychological Theory and Women's Development.* Cambridge: Harvard University Press.

Gilman, Charlotte Perkins. [1898] 1966. *Women and Economics.* New York: Harper Torchbook.

Glamour. 1989. "Private Time: Ease Holiday Pressures: Let Someone Else Do It." December, 110.

Glazer, Nona. 1978. "Housework: A Review Essay." In *Family Factbook,* edited by Helena Z. Lopata, 87–93. New York: Marquis Academic Media.

———. 1980. "Everyone Needs Three Hands: Doing Unpaid and Paid Work." In *Women and Household Labor,* 249–73. *See* Berk 1980.

———. 1984. "Servants to Capital: Unpaid Domestic Labor and Paid Work." *Review of Radical Political Economics* 16:61–87.

———. 1988. "Overlooked, Overworked: Women's Unpaid and Paid Work in the Health Services "Cost Crisis."" *International Journal of Health Services* 18:119–37.

Glazer, Nona, Linda Majka, Joan Acker, and Christine Bose. 1979. "The Homemaker, the Family, and Employment: Some Inter-relationships." In *Women in the Labor Force,* edited by Ann Foote Cahn, 155–169. New York: Praeger.

Glenn, Evelyn Nakano. 1986. *Issei, Nisei, War Bride: Three Generations of Japanese American Women in Domestic Service.* Philadelphia: Temple University Press.

Glenn, Evelyn Nakano, and Roslyn L. Feldberg. 1977. "Degraded and Deskilled: The Proletarianization of Clerical Work." *Social Problems* 25:52–64.

———. 1979. "Clerical Work: The Female Occupation." In *Women: A Feminist Perspective,* edited by Jo Freeman, 2d ed., 313–38. Palo Alto, Calif.: Mayfield.

Glenn, Norval D., and Charles N. Wever. 1988. "The Changing Relationship of Marital Status to Reported Happiness." *Journal of Marriage and the Family* 50:317–24.

Glick, Paul C. 1989. "Remarried Families, Stepfamilies, and Stepchildren: A Brief Demographic Profile." *Family Relations* 38:24–47.

Goetting, Ann. 1989. "Patterns of Support among In-Laws in the United States." Paper presented at the Eighty-Fifth Annual Meeting of the American Sociological Association, San Francisco, August.

Goffman, Erving. 1961. *Asylums: Essays on the Social Situation of Mental Patients and Other Inmates.* New York: Anchor.

———. 1967. *Interaction Ritual: Essays on Face-to-Face Behavior.* Garden City, N.Y.: Doubleday.

Gold, Deborah. 1987. *Siblings in Old Age: Their Roles and Relationships.* Chicago: Center for Applied Gerontology.

Goode, William. 1960. "A Theory of Role Strain." *American Sociological Review* 25:483–96.

———. 1963. *World Revolution and Family Patterns.* New York: Free Press.

————. 1982. "Why Men Resist." In *Rethinking the Family*, 131–50. *See* Thorne 1982.

Goody, Jack. 1983. *The Development of the Family and Marriage in Europe.* Cambridge: Cambridge University Press.

Gouldner, Alvin W. 1957. "Cosmopolitans and Locals." *Administrative Science Quarterly* 2 (December): 281–306; 2 (March 1958): 444–80.

Grubb, Norton W. and Marvin Lazerson. 1982. *Broken Promises: How Americans Fail Their Children.* New York: Basic Books.

Gudykunst, William B. 1985. "An Exploratory Comparison of Close Intracultural and Intercultural Friendships." *Communications Quarterly* 33:270–83.

Guillemin, Jeanne Harley, and Lyda Lytle Holmstrom. 1986. *Mixed Blessings: Intensive Care for Newborns.* New York: Oxford University Press.

Gujral, Jaya Sarma. 1987. "Widowhood in India." In *Widows: The Middle East, Asia, and the Pacific*, 43–55. *See* Lopata 1987c.

Gusfield, Joseph. 1963. *Symbolic Crusade: Status Politics and the American Temperance Movement.* Urbana: University of Illinois Press.

Gutmann, David L. 1985. "Deculturation and the American Grandparent." In *Grandparenthood*, 173–81. *See* Bengtson and Robertson 1985.

Halem, Lynne Carol. 1982. *Separated and Divorced Women.* Westport, Conn.: Greenwood.

Halpern, Sydney A. 1989. *American Pediatrics: The Social Dynamics of Professionalism, 1880–1980.* Berkeley: University of California Press.

Hansen, Karen V. 1990. "Women's Unions and the Search for Political Identity." In *Women, Class, and the Feminist Imagination*, 213–38. *See* Hansen and Philipson 1990.

Harding, Sandra. 1986. *The Science Question in Feminism.* Ithaca, N.Y.: Cornell University Press.

Hareven, Tamara K. 1987a. "The Dynamics of Kin in an Industrial Community." In *Turning Points*, edited by J. Demos and S. Boocock, 151–81. Chicago: University of Chicago Press.

————. 1978b. *Transitions: The Family and the Life Course in Historical Perspective.* New York: Academic Press.

Hareven, Tamara K., and Randolph Langenbach. 1978. *Amoskeag: Life and Work in an American Factory-City.* New York: Pantheon.

Harragan, Betty Lehan. 1977. *Games Mother Never Taught You: Corporate Gamesmanship for Women.* New York: Warner.

Harris, Barbara. 1979. "Careers, Conflict, and Children: The Legacy of the Cult of Domesticity." In *Career and Motherhood: Struggles for a New Identity*, edited by Alan Roland and Barbara Harris, 55–86. New York: Human Sciences Press.

Hartman, Susan M. 1989. *From Margin to Mainstream: American Women and Politics since 1960*. New York: Knopf.

Hartmann, Betsy. 1987. *Reproductive Rights and Wrongs: The Global Politics of Population Control and Contraceptive Choice*. New York: Harper & Row.

Hartmann, Heidi. 1981. "The Family as the Locus of Gender, Class, and Political Struggle: The Example of Housework." *Signs* 6:366–94.

———. 1990. "Capitalism, Patriarchy, and Job Segregation by Sex." In *Women, Class, and the Feminist Imagination*, 146–81. *See* Hansen and Philipson 1990.

Haug, Marie R., and Marvin B. Sussman. 1968. "Professional Autonomy and the Revolt of the Client." *Social Problems* 17:153–61.

Hayden, Delores. 1981. *The Grand Domestic Revolution: A History of Feminist Designs for American Homes, Neighborhoods, and Cities*. Cambridge: MIT Press.

Heisel, Marsel A. 1987. "Women and Widows in Turkey: Support Systems." In *Widows: The Middle East, Asia, and the Pacific*, 79–105. *See* Lopata 1987c.

Henze, Lura, and John Hudson. 1974. "Personal and Family Characteristics of Cohabiting and Noncohabiting College Students." *Journal of Marriage and the Family*. 36:722–26.

Hertz, Rosanna. 1986. *More Equal than Others: Women and Men in Dual-Career Marriages*. Berkeley: University of California Press.

Hess, Beth. 1972. "Friendship." In *Aging and Society*, vol. 3: *A Sociology of Age Stratification*, edited by Matilada Riley, M. Johnson, and Anne Foner, 357–93. New York: Sage.

Hess, Beth, and Joan M. Waring. 1978a. "Changing Patterns of Aging and Family Bonds in Later Life." *Family Coordinator* 27: 303–14.

———. 1978b. "Parent and Child in Later Life." In *Child Influences on Marital and Family Interaction*, 241–74. *See* R. Lerner and Spanier 1978.

Hobson, Randy. 1989. "Gender Differences in Job Satisfaction: Why Aren't Women More Dissatisfied?" *Sociological Quarterly* 30:385–99.

Hochschild, Arlie. 1969. "The Role of the Ambassador's Wife: An Exploratory Study." *Journal of Marriage and the Family* 31:73–87.

———. 1973. *The Unexpected Community*. Englewood Cliffs, N.J.: Prentice-Hall.

———. 1983. *The Managed Heart*. Berkeley: University of California Press.

———. 1989. *The Second Shift: Working Parents and the Revolution at Home*. New York: Viking Penguin.

———. 1992. "Beyond the Second Shift: Denying Needs at Home or Contesting Rules at Work." Paper presented at the annual meetings of the National Council on Family Relations. 8 November, Orlando.

Hoffman, Lois. 1987. "The Effects on Children of Maternal and Paternal Employment." In *Families and Work,* 362–95. *See* Gerstel and Gross 1987a.

Holbert, Ginny. 1988. "If You Must Work, There's No Place Like a Home Office." *Chicago Sun Times,* 16 October, B.M. 3.

Holmstrom, Linda L. 1973. *The Two-Career Family.* Cambridge, Mass.: Schenkman.

Hoonaard, Deborah van den. 1991. "The Aging of a Retirement Community." Ph.D. diss., Department of Sociology, Loyola University of Chicago.

Hope, Emily, Mary Kennedy, and Anne De Winter. 1976. "Homeworkers in North London." In *Dependence and Exploitation in Work and Marriage,* edited by Diana Leonard Barker and Sheila Allen, 88–108. London: Longman.

Horgan, Ellen Somers. 1988. "The American Catholic Irish Family." In *Ethnic Families in America,* 45–75. *See* Mindel, Habenstein, and Wright 1988.

Horner, Matina S. 1972. "Towards an Understanding of Achievement-related Conflicts in Women." *Journal of Social Issues* 28 (February):157–76.

Horowitz, Amy. 1985. "Sons and Daughters as Caregivers to Older Parents: Differences in Role Performance and Consequences." *The Gerontologist* 25:612–17.

Hossfeld, Karen J. 1990. "Their Logic against Them: Contradictions in Sex, Race, and Class in Silicon Valley." In *Women Workers and Global Restructuring,* edited by Kathryn Ward, 149–78. Ithaca, N.Y.: Cornell University Press.

House, J. D. 1977. *Contemporary Entrepreneurs: The Sociology of Residential Real Estate Agents.* Westport, Conn.: Greenwood.

Houseknecht, Sharon K. 1987. "Voluntary Childlessness." In *Handbook of Marriage and the Family,* 369–95. *See* Steinmetz 1987.

Howe, Louise Kapp. 1977. *Pink Collar Workers: Inside the World of Women's Work.* New York: G. P. Putnam's Sons.

Huber, Joan. 1980. "Will U.S. Fertility Decline toward Zero?" *Sociological Quarterly* 21:481–92.

Hughes, Everett C. 1971. *The Sociological Eye.* Chicago: Aldine Atherton.

Hughes, Helen MacGill. 1977. "Wasp/Woman/Sociologist." *Society/Transaction.* August, 69–80.

Hunt, Janet G., and Larry L. Hunt. 1982. "Dual-Career Families: Vanguard of the Future or Residue of the Past?" In *Dual Paychecks* 41–62. *See* Aldous 1982.

Hunter, Albert. 1974. *Symbolic Communities: The Persistence and Change of Chicago's Local Communities.* Chicago: University of Chicago Press.

Hurtado, Aida. 1989. "Relating to Privilege: Seduction and Rejection in the Subordination of White Women and Women of Color." *Signs* 14:833–55.

Hyde, Janet Shibley, and Marilyn J. Essex. 1990. *Parental Leave and Child Care: Setting a Research and Policy Agenda.* Philadelphia: Temple University Press.

Inkeles, Alex. 1981. *Exploring Individual Modernity.* New York: Columbia University Press.

Inkeles, Alex, and David H. Smith. 1974. *Becoming Modern: Individual Change in Six Developing Countries.* Cambridge: Harvard University Press.

Irish, Donald P. 1964. "Sibling Interaction: A Neglected Aspect in Family Life Research." *Social Forces* 42:279–88.

Jackson, Mary R., and Marie Crane. 1986. "'Some of My Best Friends Are Black . . .': Interracial Friendships and Whites' Racial Attitudes." *Public Opinion Quarterly* 50:459–86.

Janowitz, Morris. 1968. "The Community of Limited Liability." In *The American City,* edited by Anselm Strauss, 368–72. Chicago: Aldine.

Jarrett, Robin. 1990a. "A Comparative Examination of Socialization Patterns among Low-Income African-Americans, Chicanos, Puerto Ricans, and Whites: A Review of the Ethnographic Literature." New York: Social Science Research Council.

———. 1990b. "Gender Roles among Low-Income Black Women." Manuscript, Chicago: Loyola University of Chicago.

———. 1992. "A Family Case Study: An Examination of the Underclass Debate." In *Qualitative Methods in Family Research,* edited by Jane Gilgun, Kerry Daly and Gerald Handel. 172–97. Newbury Park, Calif.: Sage.

Joffe, Carole E. 1977. *Friendly Intruders: Childcare Professionals and Family Life.* Berkeley: University of California.

John, Robert. 1988. "The Native American Family." In *Ethnic Families in America,* 325–63. *See* Mindel, Habenstein, and Wright 1988.

Johnson, Colleen Leahy. 1985. *Growing Up and Growing Old in Italian-American Families.* New Brunswick, N.J.: Rutgers University Press.

———. 1988. *Ex Families: Grandparents, Parents, and Children Adjust to Divorce.* New Brunswick, N.J.: Rutgers University Press.

Johnson, Elizabeth S. 1981. "Older Mothers' Perceptions of Their Child's Divorce." *The Gerontologist* 21:395–401.

Johnson, Miriam M. 1988. *Strong Mothers, Weak Wives: The Search for Gender Equality.* Berkeley: University of California Press.

Jurik, Nancy C. 1985. "An Officer and a Lady: Organizational Barriers to Women Working as Correctional Officers in Men's Prisons." *Social Problems* 32:375–88.

Jurik, Nancy C., and Gregory J. Halemba. 1984. "Gender, Working Conditions, and Job Satisfaction of Women in a Non-traditional Occupation:

Female Correction Officers in Men's Prisons." *Sociological Quarterly* 25:551–66.

Kahn, Alfred J., and Sheila B. Kamerman. 1975. *Not for the Poor Alone: European Social Services*. New York: Harper Colophon.

Kamerman, Sheila B. 1977. "Public Policy and the Family: A New Strategy for Women as Wives and Mothers." In *Women into Wives*, 195–214. See Chapman and Gates 1977.

——. 1980. *Parenting in an Unresponsive Society*. New York: Free Press.

Kamerman, Sheila B., and Alfred J. Kahn. 1978. *Family Policy: Government and Families in Fourteen Countries*. New York: Columbia University Press.

——. 1989. *Privatization and the Welfare State*. Princeton: Princeton University Press.

Kaminer, Wendy. 1984. *Women Volunteering: The Pleasure, Pain, and Politics of Unpaid Work from 1830 to the Present*. Garden City, N.Y.: Doubleday.

Kammeyer, Kenneth. 1967. "Sibling Position and the Feminine Role." *Journal of Marriage and the Family* 29:494–99.

Kanter, Rosabeth Moss. 1977. *Men and Women of the Corporation*. New York: Basic Books.

Kanter, Rosabeth Moss, and Barry A. Stein. 1979. "The Gender Pioneers: Women in an Industrial Sales Force." In *Life in Organizations*, edited by Rosabeth Moss Kanter and Barry A. Stein, 134–60. New York: Basic Books.

Kantrowitz, Barbara, and Pat Wingert. 1980. "Step by Step." Special Issue on *The 21st Century Family: Who We Will Be, How We Will Live. Newsweek*, Winter/Spring, 14–17.

Katz, Elihu, and Paul E. Lazarsfeld. 1955. *Personal Influence*. New York: Free Press.

Katzman, David M. 1978. *Seven Days a Week: Women and Domestic Service in Industrializing America*. New York: Oxford University Press.

Kessler-Harris, Alice. 1981. *Women Have Always Worked: A Historical Overview*. New York: Feminist Press.

——. 1982. *Out to Work: A History of Wage-Earning Women in the United States*. New York: Oxford University Press.

Kidwell, Jeannie S. 1981. "Number of Siblings, Sibling Spacing, Sex, and Birth Order: Their Effects on Perceived Parent-Adolescent Relationships." *Journal of Marriage and the Family* 43:315–32.

Kimmel, Michael S., and Michael A. Messner. 1992. *Men's Lives*, 2d ed. New York: Macmillan.

Kingsolver, Barbara. 1989. *Holding the Line: Women in the Great Arizona Mine Strike of 1983*. New York: ILR (International Labour Review).

Kitano, Harry H. L., 1988. "The Japanese American Family." In *Ethnic Families in America, 258–75. See* Mindel, Habenstein, and Wright, 1988.

Kitano, Harry H. L., Wai-Tsang Yeung, Lynn Chai, and Herbert Tatanaka. 1984. "Asian-American Interracial Marriage." *Journal of Marriage and the Family* 46:179–90.

Kitson, Gay, Helena Z. Lopata, William Holmes, and Suzanne Meyering. 1980. "Divorcees and Widows: Similarities and Differences." *American Journal of Orthopsychiatry* 50:291–301.

Kleban, M. H., Elaine Brody, Claire Schoonover, and Christine Hoffman. 1989. "Family Help to the Elderly: Sons-in-Law Perceptions of Parent Care." *Journal of Marriage and the Family* 51:303–12.

Kleiman, Carol. 1980. *Women's Networks.* New York: Lippincott & Crowell.

———. 1986. "Women Climb Off the Corporate Ladder to Build Their Own." *Chicago Tribune,* 30 June, 5–10.

———. 1988. "Cottage Industries Battle to Stay In-Home." *Chicago Tribune,* 29 August, section 4, 6.

Knapp, R. J. 1986. *Beyond Endurance: When a Child Dies.* New York: Schocken.

Kohn, Melvin L. 1977. *Class and Conformity: A Study of Values.* 2d ed. Chicago: University of Chicago Press.

Kohn, Melvin L., and Carmi Schooler. 1983. *Work and Personality: An Inquiry into the Impact of Social Stratification.* Norwood, N.J.: Ablex.

Komarovsky, Mirra. 1953. *Women in the Modern World: Their Education and their Dilemmas.* Boston: Little, Brown.

———. 1962. *Blue Collar Marriage.* New York: Vintage Books.

———. 1973. "Presidential Address: Some Problems in Role Analysis." *American Sociological Review* 38:649–62.

Koo, Jasoon. 1987. "Widows in Seoul, Korea." In *Widows: The Middle East, Asia, and the Pacific,* 56–78. *See* Lopata 1987c.

Kourvetaris, George. 1988. "The Greek American Family." In *Ethnic Families in America.,* 76–108. *See* Habenstein, and Wright 1988.

Krauskopf, Joan M. 1977. "Partnership Marriage: Legal Reform Needed." In *Women into Wives,* 93–121. *See* Gates, 1977.

Kraut, Robert E. 1988. "Homework: What Is It and Who Does It?" In *The New Era of Home-Based Work,* 30–48. *See* Christensen 1988c.

Kriesberg, Louis. 1970. *Mothers in Poverty: A Study of Fatherless Families.* Chicago: Aldine.

Krugman, Herbert E. 1969. "Salesman in Conflict: A Challenge to Marketing." In *Salesmanship,* 25–28. *See* Crane 1969.

Lamb, Michael E. 1978. "Influence of the Child on Marital Quality and Family Interaction during the Prenatal, Perinatal, and Infancy Periods." In *Child*

Influences on Marital and Family Interaction, 137–63. *See* R. Lerner and Spanier 1978.

Lamb, Michael E., and Brian Sutton-Smith. 1982. *Sibling Relationships: Their Nature and Significance across the Lifespan.*Hillsdale, N.J.: Erlbaum.

Landers, Ann. 1976. "If You Had It to Do Over Again—Would You Have Children?" *Good Housekeeping,* June, 100–101, 215–16, 223–24.

Langman, Lauren. 1987. "Social Stratification." In *Handbook of Marriage and the Family,* 211–49. *See* Steinmetz 1987.

Larwood, Laurie, Ann H. Stromberg, and Barbara A. Gutek, eds. 1985. *Women and Work.* Vol. 1. Beverly Hills, Calif.: Sage.

Laslett, Barbara. 1973. "The Family as a Public and Private Institution: An Historical Perspective." *Journal of Marriage and the Family* 35:480–92.

———. 1978. "Family Membership, Past and Present." *Social Problems* 25:476–91.

Laslett, Peter. 1971. *The World We Have Lost: England before the Industrial Age.* New York: Scribner's.

Lauritzen, Paul. 1990. "What Price Parenthood?" *Hastings Center Report,* March/April, 39–46.

Lawson, Helene. 1990. "Service Values-Profit Goals: The Divided Selves of Car Sales Women." Ph.D. diss., Loyola University of Chicago.

Lawson, Ronald, and Stephen E. Barton. 1980. "Sex Roles in Social Movements: A Case Study of the Tenant Movement in New York City." *Signs* 6:230–47.

Lee, Gary R. 1980. "Kinship in the Seventies: A Decade Review of Research and Theory." *Journal of Marriage and the Family* 42:923–34.

Lembright, Muriel Faltz, and Jeffrey W. Riemer. 1982. "Women Truckers' Problems and the Impact of Sponsorship." *Work and Occupations* 9:457–74.

Lenz, Elinor, and Barbara Myerhoff. 1985. *The Feminization of America: How Women's Values Are Changing Our Public and Private Lives.* New York: St. Martins.

diLeonardo, Micaela. 1987. "The Female World of Cards and Holidays: Women, Families, and the Work of Kinship." *Signs* 12:440–53.

Lerner, Daniel. 1958. *The Passing of Traditional Society.* New York: Free Press of Glencoe.

Lerner, Richard M., and Graham B. Spanier. 1978. *Child Influences on Marital and Family Interaction: A Life-Span Perspective.* New York: Academic Press.

Levinson, Daniel J. 1978. *The Seasons of a Man's Life.* New York: Ballantine.

Levy, Judith. 1990. "Friendship Dilemmas and the Interaction of Social Worlds: Re-Entry Women on the College Campus." In *Friendship in Context,* 143–70. *See* Lopata and Maines 1990.

Liebow, Elliot. 1967. *Tally's Corner.* Boston: Little, Brown.

Lillydahl, Jane H. 1986. "Women and Traditionally Male Blue-collar Jobs." *Work and Occupations* 13:307–23.

Lindgren, Ralph J., and Nadine Taub. 1988. *The Law of Sex Discrimination.* New York: West.

Linton, Ralph. 1936. *The Science of Man.* New York: Appleton-Century.

Lipman-Blumen, Jean. 1976. "Toward a Homosocial Theory of Sex Roles: An Explanation of the Sex-Segregation of Social Institutions." In *Women and the Workplace: The Implications of Occupational Segregation,* edited by Martha Blaxall and Barbara Reagan, 15–31. Chicago: University of Chicago Press.

Little, Roger. 1984. *Gender Roles and Power.* Englewood Cliffs, N.J.: Prentice-Hall.

———. 1990. "Friendship in the Military Community." In *Friendship in Context,* 221–35. *See* Lopata and Maines 1990.

Litwak, Eugene. 1965. "Extended Kin Relations in an Industrial Democratic Society." In *Social Structure and the Family: Generational Relations,* edited by Ethel Shanas and Gordon Streib, 290–23. Englewood Cliffs, N.J.: Prentice Hall.

Long, Judy, and Karen L. Porter. 1984. "Multiple Roles of Midlife Women: A Case for New Directions in Theory, Research, and Policy." In *Women in Midlife,* 15–31. *See* Baruch and Brooks-Gunn 1984.

Lopata, Helena Znaniecka. 1966. "The Life Cycle of the Social Role of Housewife." *Sociology and Social Research* 51:5–22.

———. 1969a. "Loneliness: Forms and Components." *Social Problems* 17:248–62.

———. 1969b. "Social Psychological Aspects of Role Involvement." *Sociology and Social Research* 53:285–98.

———. 1971a. "Living Arrangements of Urban Widows and their Married Children." *Sociological Focus* 5:41–61.

———. 1971b. *Occupation: Housewife.* New York: Oxford University Press.

———. 1972. "Role Changes in Widowhood: A World Perspective." In *Aging and Modernization.* edited by Donald Cowgill and Lowell Holmes, 275–303. New York: Appleton-Century-Crofts.

———. 1973a. "The Effect of Schooling on Social Contacts of Urban Women." *American Journal of Sociology* 79:604–19.

———. 1973b. "Self-Identity in Marriage and Widowhood." *Sociological Quarterly* 14:407–18.

———. 1973c. *Widowhood in an American City.* Cambridge, Mass.: Schenkman.

————. 1975. "Couple Companionate Relationships in Marriage and Widowhood." In *Old Families/New Families,* edited by Nona Glazer-Malbin, 119–49. New York: Van Nostrand.

————. 1976a. "The Expertization of Everyone and the Revolt of the Client." *Sociological Quarterly* 17:435–47.

————. 1976b. *Polish Americans: Status Competition in an Ethnic Community.* Englewood Cliffs, N.J.: Prentice-Hall.

————. 1978. "Contributions of Extended Families to the Support Systems of Metropolitan Area Widows: Limitations of the Modified Kin Network." *Journal of Marriage and the Family* 40:355–64.

————. 1979. *Women as Widows: Support Systems.* New York: Elsevier/North-Holland.

————. 1980a. "The Chicago Woman: A Study of Patterns of Mobility and Transportation." *Signs* 5 (Spring): S161–S169. Special issue entitled "Women and the American City."

————. 1980b. "The Self-Concept: Characteristics and Areas of Competence." Paper presented at the annual meeting of the American Sociological Association, New York.

————. 1981a. "American Women: Education and the Construction of Reality." *Quarterly Journal of Ideology* 3:11–24. Special issue entitled "Gender and Ideology".

————. 1981b. "Widowhood and Husband Sanctification." *Journal of Marriage and the Family* 43:439–50.

————. 1984. "Social Construction of Social Problems over Time." *Social Problems* 31:249–72.

————. 1987a. "Widowhood and Social Change." In *Widows: The Middle East, Asia, and the Pacific,* 217–29. *See* Lopata 1987c.

————. 1987b. "Widowhood: World Perspectives on Support Systems." In *Widows: The Middle East, Asia, and the Pacific,* 1–23. *See* Lopata 1987c.

————, ed. 1987c. *Widows: The Middle East, Asia, and the Pacific.* Durham: Duke University Press.

————. 1987d. *Widows: North America.* Durham: Duke University Press.

————. 1987e. "Women's Family Roles in Life Course Perspective." In *Analyzing Gender: A Handbook of Social Science Research,* edited by Beth B. Hess and Myra Marx Teree, 381–407. Newbury Park, Calif.: Sage.

————. 1988a. "Polish American Families." In *Ethnic Families in America,* 17–42. *See* Mindel, Habenstein, and Wright, 1988.

————. 1988b. "Support Systems of Widowhood." *Journal of Social Issues* 44:220–28.

————. 1990a. "Friendship: Historical and Theoretical Perspectives." In *Friendship in Context*, 1–19. *See* Lopata and Maines 1990.

————. 1990b. *Current Research on Occupations and Professions: Societal Influences*. Greenwich, Conn.: JAI Press.

————. 1991a. "Role Theory." In *Social Roles and Social Institutions: Essays in Honor of Rose Laub Coser*, edited by Judith R. Blau and Norman Goodman, 1–11. Boulder, Colo.: Westview.

————. 1991b. "Which Child? The Consequences of Social Development on the Support Systems of Widows." In *Growing Old In America*, 4th ed., edited by Beth B. Hess and Elizabeth W. Markson, 39–49. New Brunswick, N.J.: Transaction.

————. 1993a. "The Interweave of Public and Private: Women's Challenge to American Society." *Journal of Marriage and the Family* 55:176–90.

————. 1993b. "Career Commitments of American Women: The Issue of Side Bets." *Sociological Quarterly* 34:257–77.

————. 1994. *Polish Americans,* 2d rev. ed., New Brunswick, N.J.: Transaction.

Lopata, Helena Znaniecka, and Debra Barnewolt. 1984. "The Middle Years: Changes and Variations in Social-Role Commitments." In *Women in Midlife*, 83–108. *See* Baruch and Brooks-Gunn 1984.

Lopata, Helena Znaniecka, Debra Barnewolt, and Kathryn Harrison. 1987. "Homemakers and Household Composition." In *Current Research on Occupations and Professions,* edited by Helena Z. Lopata, 219–45. Greenwich, Conn.: JAI Press.

Lopata, Helena Znaniecka, Debra Barnewolt, and Cheryl Allyn Miller. 1985. *City Women: Work, Jobs, Occupations, Careers.* Vol. 2: *Chicago.* New York: Praeger.

Lopata, Helena Znaniecka, and Henry Brehm. 1986. *Widows and Dependent Wives: From Social Problem to Federal Policy.* New York: Praeger.

Lopata, Helena Znaniecka, and David Maines, eds. 1990. *Friendship in Context.* Greenwich, Conn.: JAI Press.

Lopata, Helena Znaniecka, Cheryl Miller, and Debra Barnewolt. 1984. *City Women: Work, Jobs, Occupations, Careers.* Vol. 1: *America.* New York: Praeger. Published in paperback in 1986 as *City Women in America.*

Lopata, Helena Znaniecka, and Joseph R. Noel. 1967. "The Dance Studio: Style without Sex." *Transaction/Society,* 4 (January/February): 10–17.

Lopata, Helena Znaniecka, Kathleen F. Norr, Debra Barnewolt, and Cheryl Allyn Miller. 1985. "Job Complexity as Perceived by Workers and Experts." *Sociology of Work and Occupations* 12:295–415.

Lopata, Helena Znaniecka, and Barrie Thorne. 1978. "On the Term 'Sex Roles'." *Signs* 3:718–21.

Lorber, Judith. 1984. *Women Physicians: Careers, Status, and Power.* New York: Methuen.

Lortie, Dan C. 1969. "The Balance of Control and Autonomy in Elementary School Teaching." In *The Semi-Professions and their Organization,* edited by Amitai Etzioni, 1–53. New York: Free Press.

Lortie, Dan C. 1975. *Schoolteacher.* Chicago: University of Chicago Press.

Losh-Hesselbart, Susan. 1987. "Development of Gender Roles." In *Handbook of Marriage and the Family,* 535–63. *See* Steinmetz 1987.

Ludwig, Constance. 1977. "The Social Role of the Grandmother among Puerto Ricans on the Mainland." M.A. thesis, Department of Sociology, Loyola University of Chicago.

Luxton, Meg. 1980. *More than a Labour of Love: Three Generations of Women's Work in the Home.* Toronto: Women's Educational Press.

Lynes, Russell. 1963. *The Domesticated Americans.* New York: Harper & Row.

Malson, Micheline R., Elisabeth Mudimbe-Boyi, Nean F. O'Barr, and Mary Wyer, eds. 1988. *Black Women in America: Social Science Perspectives.* Chicago: University of Chicago Press.

Malveaux, Julianne M. 1980. "Moving Forward, Standing Still: Women in White Collar Jobs." In *Women in the Workplace,* edited by Phillis Wallace, 101–29, Boston: Auburn.

Manegold, Catherine S. 1992. "Women Advance in Politics by Evolution, not Revolution." *New York Times,* 21 October, 1A, 15.

Margolis, Diane Rothbard. 1979. *The Managers: Corporate Life in America.* New York: Morrow.

Marks, Stephen R. 1977. "Multiple Roles and Role Strain: Some Notes on Human Energy, Time, and Commitment." *American Sociological Review* 42:921–36.

Marotz-Baden, Ramona, and Deane Cowan. 1987. "Mothers-in-Law and Daughters-in-Law: The Effects of Proximity on Conflict and Stress." *Family Relations* 36:385–90.

Martin, Elmer P., and Joanne Mitchell Martin. 1978. *The Black Extended Family.* Chicago: University of Chicago Press.

Martineau, Harriet. [1837] 1966. *Society in America,* edited by Seymour Martin Lipset. Garden City, N.Y.: Doubleday.

Masnick, George, and Mary Jo Bane. 1980. *The Nation's Families 1970–1990.* Boston: Auburn.

Matthews, Glenna. 1987. *Just a Housewife: The Rise and Fall of Domesticity in America.* New York: Oxford University Press.

Matthews, Sarah. 1986. *Friendship through the Life Course.* Beverly Hills, Calif.: Sage.

deMause, Lloyd. 1974. "The Evolution of Childhood." In *The History of Childhood,* edited by Lloyd deMause, 1–73. New York: Psychohistory Press.

McAdoo, Harriet Pipes. 1980. "Black Mothers and the Extended Family Support Network." In *The Black Woman,* 125–44. *See* Rodgers-Rose 1980.

McCall, George J., and J. L. Simmons. 1978. *Identities and Interactions.* New York: Free Press.

McCurry, Dan. 1975. *Cannery Captives: Women Workers in the Produce Processing Industry.* New York: Arno.

McGhee, Jerrie L. 1985. "The Effects of Siblings on Life Satisfaction of the Rural Elderly." *Journal of Marriage and the Family* 47:85–91.

McIlwee, Judith S. 1982. "Work Satisfaction among Women in Nontraditional Occupations." *Work and Occupations* 9:299–355.

McKain, Walter. 1969. *Retirement Marriage.* Storrs, Conn.: University of Connecticut.

McPherson, J. Miller, and Lynn Smith-Lovin. 1982. "Women and Weak Ties: Differences by Sex in the Size of Voluntary Organizations." *American Journal of Sociology* 87:883–904.

Mead, George Herbert. 1934. *Mind, Self, and Society, from the Standpoint of a Social Behaviorist,* edited by Charles Morris. Chicago: University of Chicago Press.

Merton, Robert. 1957. "The Role Set." *British Journal of Sociology* 8:106–20.

———. 1968. *Social Theory and Social Structure,* enlarged ed. New York: Free Press.

Mezey, Susan. 1992. *In Pursuit of Equality: Women, Public Policy and the Federal Courts.* New York: St. Martin's.

Michaels, Gerald and Wendy Goldberg, eds. 1988. *The Transition to Parenthood.* New York: Cambridge University Press.

Michelson, Williams. 1977. *Environmental Choice, Human Behavior, and Residential Satisfaction.* New York: Oxford University Press.

Milardo, Robert M. 1982. "Friendship Networks in Developing Relationships: Converging and Diverging Social Environments." *Social Psychology Quarterly* 45:162–72.

Milkman, Ruth. 1979. "Women's Work and the Economic Crisis: Some Lessons from the Great Depression." In *A Heritage of Her Own,* edited by Nancy F. Cott and Elizabeth H. Pleck, 507–41. New York: Simon & Schuster.

Miller, Barbara. 1981. *The Endangered Sex: Neglect of Female Children in Rural North India.* Ithaca, N.Y.: Cornell University Press.

Miller, Brent C. 1987. "Marriage, Family, and Fertility." In *Handbook of Marriage and the Family,* 565–95. *See* Steinmetz, 1987.

Miller, Cheryl Allen. 1981. "The Life Course Patterns of Chicago Area Women." Ph.D. diss., Department of Sociology, Loyola University of Chicago.

Miller, Joanne. 1980. "Individual and Occupational Determinants of Job Satisfaction." *Sociology of Work and Occupations* 7:337–66.

Miller, Joanne, Carmin Schooler, Melvin Kohn, and Karen Miller. 1980. "Women and Work: The Psychological Effects of Occupational Conditions." *American Journal of Sociology* 85:66–94.

Mills, C. Wright. 1956. *White Collar*. New York: Oxford University.

Min, Pyong Gap. 1988. "The Korean American Family." In *Ethnic Families in America,* 199–229. *See* Mindel, Habenstein, and Wright 1988.

Mindel, Charles H., Robert W. Habenstein, and Roosevelt Wright, Jr., eds. 1988. *Ethnic Families in America*. 3d ed. New York: Elsevier.

Model, Suzanne. 1982. "Housework by Husbands: Determinants and Implications." In *Two Paychecks*, 193–205. *See* Aldous 1982.

Moen, Phyllis, Donna Dempster McClain, and Robin Williams, Jr. 1989. "Social Integration and Longevity: An Event History Analysis of Women's Roles and Resilience." *American Sociological Review* 54:635–47.

Monagle, Katie. 1989. "Court Backs Two-Mom Family." *MS*, October, 69.

Mosher, Steven W. 1983. "Why Are Baby Girls Being Killed in China?" *The Wall Street Journal,* 25 July, 9.

Mott, Frank, Steven Sansell, David Shapiro, Patricia Brito, Timothy Carr, Rex Johnson, Carol Jusenius, Peter Koenig and Sylvia Moore. 1977. *Years for Decision: A Longitudinal Study of the Educational, Labor Market, and Family Experiences of Young Women, 1968 to 1973*. Columbus: Ohio Center for Human Resource Research, College of Administrative Science, Ohio State University.

Mueller, Carol M. 1988. "Continuity and Change in Women's Political Agenda." In *The Politics of the Gender Gap: The Social Construction of Political Influence,* edited by Carol M. Mueller, 284–99. Newbury Park, Calif.: Sage.

Mumford, Lewis. 1961. *The City in History*. New York: Harcourt Brace & World.

Musterberg, Hugo. 1905. "The American Woman." In *The Making of America,* vol. 1, edited by John D. Morris and Robert M. Lafollette, 402–96. Chicago: John D. Morris.

Myerson, Abraham. 1927. *The Nervous Housewife*. Boston: Little, Brown.

Nelson, Dale. 1989. "Women to Get Most Doctorates, Study Shows." *Chicago Sun Times,* 28 December, 8.

Nelson, Sarah M. 1988. "Widowhood and Autonomy in the Native American Southwest." In *On Their Own: Widows and Widowhood in the American*

Southwest 1848–1939, edited by Arlene Scadron, 22–41. Urbana: University of Illinois Press.

Neugarten, Bernice. 1973. *Middle Age and Aging.* Chicago: University of Chicago Press.

Neugarten, Bernice, and Karen K. Weinstein. 1964. "The Changing American Grandparent." *Journal of Marriage and the Family* 26:199–204.

Newman, Katherine S. 1988. *Falling from Grace: Experiences of Downward Mobility in the American Middle Class.* New York: Free Press.

Nilson, Linda Burzotta. 1978. "The Social Standing of a Housewife." *Journal of Marriage and the Family* 40, no. 3:541–48.

Nugent, Jo. 1990. "We're All Rotarians." *Rotarian,* June, 26–27.

Nyden, Philip, Joanne Adams, and Maryann Mason. 1992. *Our Hope for the Future: Youth, Family, and Diversity in the Edgewater and Uptown Communities.* Chicago: Loyola University of Chicago.

Oakley, Ann. 1974a. *The Sociology of Housework.* Bath, England: Pitman.

———. 1974b. *Women's Work: A History of the Housewife.* New York: Pantheon.

———. 1981. *Subject Women.* New York: Pantheon.

O'Bryant, Shirley L. 1987. "Attachment to Home and Support Systems of Older Widows in Columbus, Ohio." In *Widows: North America,* 48–70. *See* Lopata 1987d.

O'Donnell, Lydia, and Ann Stuave. 1983. "Mothers as Social Agents: Structuring the Community Activities of School-Aged Children." In *Research on the Interweave of Social Roles: Families and Jobs,* 112–29. *See* E. Pleck 1983.

O'Farrell, Brigid. 1988. "Women in Blue-Collar Occupations: Traditional and Nontraditional." In *Women Working,* 258–72. *See* Berheide 1988.

Oliver, Melvin L. 1988. "The Urban Black Community as Network: Toward a Social Network Perspective." *Sociological Quarterly* 29:623–745.

O'Meara, J. Donald. 1989. "Cross-Sex Friendship: Four Basic Challenges of an Ignored Relationship." *Sex Roles* 21:525–43.

Omolade, Barbara. 1986. *It's a Family Affair: The Real Lives of Black Single Mothers.* Latham, N.Y.: Kitchen Table: Women of Color Press.

O'Neill, William. 1969. *Everyone Was Brave.* Chicago: Quadrangle.

Osborn, D. Keith, and Janie D. Osborn. 1978. "Childhood at the Turn of the Century." *Family Coordinator* 27:27–32.

Ostrander, Susan A. 1984. *Women of the Upper Class.* Philadelphia: Temple University Press.

Overvold, Amy Zucherman. 1988. *Surrogate Parenting.* New York: Pharos Books.

Papandreau, Margarita. 1988. "Foreword. Feminism and Political Power:

Some Thoughts on a Strategy for the Future." In *Women, Power, and Policy: Toward the Year 2000,* edited by Ellen Boneparth and Emily Stoper, xi–xix. New York: Pergamon.

Papanek, Hanna. 1973. "Men, Women, and Work: Reflections on the Two-Person Career." *American Journal of Sociology* 78:852–72.

———. 1979. "Family Status Production: The 'Work' and 'Nonwork' of Women." *Signs* 4:775–81.

Papanek, Hanna, and Gail Minault. 1982. *Separate Worlds: Studies of Purdah in South Asia.* Delhi: Chanakya.

Parsons, Talcott. 1951. *The Social System.* Glencoe, Ill.: Free Press.

———. 1943. "The Kinship System in the Contemporary United States." *American Anthropologist* 31:22–38.

Parsons, Talcott, and Robert Bales. 1955. *Family: Socialization and Interaction Process.* Glencoe, Ill.: Free Press.

Paskowicz, Patricia. 1982. *Absentee Mothers.* New York: Universe Books.

Pavalko, Ronald M. 1988. *Sociology of Occupations and Professions.* Itasca, Ill.: Peacock.

Payne, Barbara P. 1977. "The Older Volunteer: Social Role Continuity and Development." *The Gerontologist* 17:355–61.

Pearlin, Leonard. 1975. "Sex Roles and Depression." In *Proceedings of the Fourth Life-Span Developmental Psychology Conference: Normative Life Crisis,* edited by Nancy Datan and Leon Ginsberg, 191–208. New York: Academic.

Pearson, Kandace. 1990. "Illusion and Reality: An Examination of the Position of Women in Small Law Firms." M.A. thesis, Department of Sociology, University of Wisconsin, Milwaukee.

Peiss, Kathy Lee. 1986. *Cheap Amusements: Working Women and Leisure in Turn-of-Century New York.* Philadelphia: Temple University Press.

Peterson, Gary W., and Boyd C. Rollins. 1987. "Parent-Child Socialization." In *Handbook of Marriage and the Family,* 471–507. *See* Steinmetz 1987.

Peven, Dorothy. 1968. "The Use of Religious Revival Techniques to Indoctrinate Personnel: The Home-Party Sales Organization." *Sociological Quarterly* 9:97–106.

Pfohl, Stephen J. 1978. "The 'Discovery' of Child Abuse." *Social Problems* 3:310–23.

Pfouts, Jane H. 1976. "The Sibling Relationships: A Forgotten Dimension." *Social Work* 21:200–204

Pihlblad, T., and Howard Rosencranz. 1968. *Old People in the Small Town.* Columbia: University of Missouri.

Pinchbeck, Ivy. [1930] 1969. *Women Workers and the Industrial Revolution, 1750–1850.* London: Bass.

Pineo, Peter. 1966. "Disenchantment in Later Years of Marriage." In *Kinship and Family Organization*, 229–39. *See* Farber 1966.

Piven, Frances Fox, and Richard A. Cloward. 1977. *Poor People's Movements: Why They Succeed, How The Fail*. New York: Pantheon.

Pleck, Elizabeth H. 1983. "The Old World, New Rights, and the Limited Rebellion: Challenges to Traditional Authority of Immigrant Families." In *Research on the Interweave of Social Roles: Families and Jobs*, 91–112. See Lopata and Pleck 1983.

Pleck, Elizabeth H., and Joseph H. Pleck. 1980. *The American Man*. Englewood Cliffs, N.J.: Prentice-Hall.

Pleck, Joseph. 1983. "Husband's Paid Work and Family Roles: Current Issues." In *Research on the Interweave of Social Roles: Families and Jobs*, 251–333. *See* Lopata and Pleck, 1983.

Pleck, Joseph, and Graham L. Staines. 1982. "Work Schedules and Work-Family Conflict in Two-Earner Families." In *Two Paychecks*, 63–88. *See* Aldous 1982.

Polit, Denise F., and Toni Falbo. 1987. "Only Children and Personality Development: A Quantitative Review." *Journal of Marriage and the Family* 49:309–25.

Post, James E. 1986. "International Consumerism in the Aftermath of the Infant Formula Controversy." In *The Future of Consumerism*, 165–78. *See* Bloom and Smith 1986.

Prus, Robert, and Wendy Frisby. 1990. "Persuasion as Practical Accomplishment: Tactical Maneuverings at Home (Party Plan) Shows." In *Current Research on Occupations and Professions*, vol. 4, edited by Helena Z. Lopata, 133–652. Greenwich, Conn.: JAI Press.

Pyun, Chong Soo. 1972. "The Monetary Value of a Housewife." In *Women in a Man-Made World*, edited by Nona Glazer-Malbin and Helen Youngelson Waehrer, 187–93. Chicago: Rand McNally.

Rainwater, Lee, Richard P. Coleman, and Gerald Handel. 1959. *Workingman's Wife: Her Personality, World, and Life Style*. New York: Oceana.

Rapp, Rayna. 1982. "Family and Class in Contemporary America: Notes toward an Understanding of Ideology." In *Rethinking the Family*, 168–87. *See* Thorne 1982.

Rapping, Elayne. 1990. "The Future of Motherhood: Some Unfashionably Visionary thoughts." In *Women, Class, and the Feminist Imagination*, 537–48. *See* Hansen and Philipson 1990.

Raymond, Janice G. 1986. *A Passion for Friends: Toward a Philosophy of Female Affection*. Boston: Beacon Press.

Reiss, Ira, and Gary R. Lee. 1988. *Family Systems in America*. New York: Holt, Rinehart & Winston.

Reskin, Barbara F., and Heidi I. Hartmann, eds. 1986. *Women's Work, Men's Work: Sex Segregation on the Job*. Washington, D.C.: National Academy Press.

Reskin, Barbara F., and Irene Padavic. 1988. "Supervisors as Gatekeepers: Male Supervisors' Response to Women's Integration in Plant Jobs." *Social Problems* 35:536–50.

Reymont, Ladislas. 1925. *The Peasants: Fall, Winter, Spring, Summer*. 4 vols. New York: Knopf.

Riesman, David, Nathan Glaser, and Reuel Denney. 1950. *The Lonely Crowd*. New Haven: Yale University Press.

Roberto, Karen A., and Jean Pearson Scott. 1984–85. "Friendship Patterns among Older Women." *International Journal of Aging and Human Development* 19:1–10.

Robertson, Joan. 1977. "Grandparenthood: A Study of Role Conceptions." *Journal of Marriage and the Family* 39:165–74.

Rodgers-Rose, La Frances, ed. 1980. *The Black Woman*. Beverly Hills, Calif.: Sage.

Rodman, Hyman. 1990. "The Social Construction of the Latchkey Children Problem." *Sociological Studies of Child Development* 3:163–74.

Rodman, Hyman, and David J. Pratto. 1987. "Child's Age and Mother's Employment in Relation to Greater Use of Self-Care Arrangements for Children." *Journal of Marriage and the Family* 49:573–78.

Rogers, Barbara. 1980. *The Domestication of Women: Discrimination in Developing Countries*. London: Tavistock.

Rollins, Judith. 1985. *Between Women: Domestics and Their Employers*. Philadelphia: Temple University Press.

Rook, Karen S. 1989. "Strains in Older Adults' Friendship." In *Older Adult Friendship*, 166–94. *See* Adams and Blieszner 1989.

Rosaldo, Michelle Zimbalist. 1974. "Women, Culture, and Society: A Theoretical Overview." In *Women, Culture, and Society*, edited by Michelle Zimbalist Rosaldo and Louise Lamphere, 17–42. Stanford, Calif.: Stanford University Press.

Rose, Suzanna M. 1985. "Same- and Cross-Sex Friendships and the Psychology of Homosociality." *Sex Roles* 12:63–74.

Rosen, Ellen Israel. 1987. *Bitter Choices: Blue-Collar Women In and Out of Work*. Chicago: University of Chicago Press.

Rosen, Lawrence, and Robert R. Bell. 1966. "Mate Selection in the Upper Class." *Sociological Quarterly* (Spring): 157–66.

Rosenberg, George S., and Donald F. Anspach. 1973. *Working-Class Kinship*. Lexington, Mass.: Lexington Books.

Rosenberg, Morris. 1979. *Conceiving the Self*. New York: Basic Books.

Rosenthal, Carolyn J. 1985. "Kinkeeping in the Family Division of Labor." *Journal of Marriage and the Family* 47:965–74.

Rosow, Irving. 1967. *The Social Integration of the Aged.* New York: Free Press.

Ross, Arlene. 1961. *The Hindu Family in Its Urban Setting.* Toronto: University of Toronto Press.

Rossi, Alice. 1965. "Barriers to the Career Choice of Engineering, Medicine, or Science among American Women." In *Women and the Scientific Professions,* edited by Jacquelyn A. Mattfelt and Carol G. Van Aken, 51–127. Cambridge: MIT Press.

———. 1968. "Transition to Parenthood." *Journal of Marriage and the Family* 30:26–39.

———. 1985. "Gender and Parenthood." In *Gender and the Life Course,* edited by Alice Rossi, 161–91. New York: Aldine.

Rossi, Peter. 1955. *Why Families Move.* Glencoe, Ill.: Free Press.

Rothman, Barbara Katz. 1986. *The Tentative Pregnancy: Prenatal Diagnosis and the Future of Motherhood.* New York: Penguin.

Rothman, Sheila M. 1978. *Woman's Proper Place: A History of Changing Ideals and Practices, 1879 to the Present.* New York: Basic Books.

Rothman, Sheila M., and Emily Menlo Marks. 1987. "Adjusting Work and Family Life: Flexible Work Schedules and Family Policy." In *Families and Work,* 469–77. *See* Gerstel and Gross 1987a.

Rubin, Lillian. 1976. *Worlds of Pain: Life in the Working-Class Family.* New York: Basic Books.

———. 1979. *Women of a Certain Age.* New York: Harper & Row.

———. 1983. *Intimate Strangers: Men and Women Together.* New York: Harper & Row.

———. 1985. *Just Friends: The Role of Friendship in Our Lives.* New York: Harper & Row.

Russell, Diana E. H. 1984. *Sexual Exploitation: Rape, Child Sexual Abuse, and Workplace Harassment.* Sage Library of Social Research, no. 155. Beverly Hills, Calif.: Sage.

———. 1986. *The Secret Trauma: Incest in the Lives of Girls and Women.* New York: Basic Books.

Rustad, Michael L. 1982. *Women in Khaki: The American Enlisted Woman.* New York: Praeger.

Ryan, Mary P. 1979. *Womanhood in America: From Colonial Times to the Present.* 2d ed. New York: New Viewpoints.

Sanchez-Ayendez, Melba. 1988. "The Puerto Rican American Family." In *Ethnic Families in America,* 173–95. *See* Habenstein and Wright 1988.

Scanzoni, John H., and Leta Scanzoni. 1981. *Men, Women, and Change.* 2d ed. New York: McGraw-Hill.

Schlegel, Alice. 1988. "Hopi Family Structure and the Experience of Widowhood." In *On Their Own: Widows and Widowhood in the American Southwest 1848–1939,* edited by Arlene Scadron, 42–64. Urbana: University of Illinois Press.

Schlossberg, Nancy. 1984. "The Midlife Woman as Student." In *Women in Midlife,* 315–39. *See* Baruch and Brooks-Gunn 1984.

Schnaiberg, Allan, and Sheldon Goldenberg. 1989. "From Empty Nest to Crowded Nest: The Dynamics of Incompletely-Launched Young Adults." *Social Problems* 36:251–69.

Schneider, David. 1980. *American Kinship: A Cultural Account.* 2d ed. Chicago: University of Chicago Press.

Schooler, Carmi. 1984. "Serfdom's Legacy: An Ethnic Continuum." In *Work and Personality,* 261–77. *See* Kohn and Schooler 1984.

Schooler, Carmi, Melvin L. Kohn, Karen A. Miller, and Joanne Miller. 1984. "Housework as Work." In *Work and Personality,* 242–60. *See* Kohn and Schooler 1984.

Schooler, Carmi, Joanne Miller, Karen A. Miller, and Carol N. Richtand. 1984. "Work for the Household: Its Nature and Consequences for Husbands and Wives." *American Journal of Sociology* 90:97–124.

Schroedel, Jean Reich. 1985. *Alone in a Crowd: Women in the Trades Tell Their Stories.* Philadelphia: Temple University Press.

Schwager, Sally. 1987. "Educating Women in America." *Signs* 12:333–72.

Schwartz, Felice. 1992. *Breaking with Tradition.* New York: Warner Books.

Schwartz, John, and Dody Tsiantar. 1989. "Escape from the Office: High-Tech Tools Spur a Work-at-Home Revolt." *Newsweek,* 24 April, 58–60.

Scott, Marvin, and Stanford Lyman. 1968. "Accounts." *American Sociological Review* 33:46–62.

Secombe, Wally. 1974. "The Housewife and Her Labour under Capitalism." *New Left Review* 83 (January–February): 3–24.

Seeley, John R., Alexander Sim, and Elizabeth W. Loosely. 1956. *Crestwood Heights.* New York: Basic Books.

Segura, Denise A. 1989. "Chicano and Mexican Immigrant Women at Work: The Impact of Class, Race, and Gender on Occupational Mobility." *Gender and Society* 3:37–52.

Selingmann, Jean. 1990. "Variations on a Theme." *Newsweek,* Winter/Spring. Special Issue entitled *The 21st Century Family: Who We Will Be, How We Will Live.*

Settles, Barbara H. 1987. "A Perspective on Tomorrow's Families." In *Handbook of Marriage and the Family,* 157–80. *See* Steinmetz 1987.

Sewell, William H., and Robert M. Hauser. 1975. *Education, Occupation, and Earnings.* New York: Academic Press.

Shae, Nancy. 1941. *The Army Wife*. Rev. ed. New York: Harper's Brothers.

Shanas, Ethel. 1977. "Family-Kin Networks and Aging in Cross-Cultural Perspective." In *The Family*, edited by Peter Stein, Judith Richman, and Natalie Hannon, 300–307. Reading, Mass.: Addison-Wesley.

————. 1979a. "The Family as a Social Support System in Old Age." *The Gerontologist* 19:169–74.

————. 1979b. "Social Myth as Hypothesis: The Case of the Family Relations of Old People." *The Gerontologist* 19:3–9.

————. 1980. "Older People and Their Families: The New Pioneers." *Journal of Marriage and the Family*. 42:9–15.

Sharpe, Sue. 1984. *Double Identity: The Lives of Working Mothers*. New York: Penguin.

Shehan, Constance. 1984. "Wives' Work and Psychological Well-Being: An Extension of Gove's Social Role Theory of Depression." *Sex Roles* 11:881–99.

Shehan, Constance, Mary Ann Burg, and Cynthia A. Rexroat. 1986. "Depression and the Social Dimensions of Full-Time Housewife Role." *Sociological Quarterly* 27:403–21.

Sicherman, Barbara. 1975. "Review Essay: American History." *Signs* 1:461–85.

Sieber, Sam D. 1974. "Toward a Theory of Role Accumulation." *American Sociological Review* 39:567–78.

Silverman, Phyllis. 1987. "Widowhood as the Next Stage in the Life Course." In *Widows: North America*, 171–90. *See* Lopata 1987d.

Simmel, George. 1955. *Conflict and the Web of Group Affiliations*, edited by D. Levine. Chicago: University of Chicago Press.

Simon, Barbara Levy. 1987. *Never Married Women*. Philadelphia: Temple University Press.

Sklare, Marshall. 1971. *American Jews*. New York: Random House.

Skolnick, Arlene S. 1983. *The Intimate Environment: Exploring Marriage and the Family*. Boston: Little, Brown.

Smith, Catherine Begnoche, and Vivian Scott Hixson. 1987. "The Work of University Professor: Evidence of Segmented Labor Markets inside the Academy." In *Current Research on Occupations and Professions,* vol. 4, edited by Helena Z. Lopata, 159–80. Greenwich, Conn.: JAI Press.

Smith, Dorothy. 1987. *The Everyday World as Problematic: A Feminist Sociology*. Boston: Northeastern University Press.

Smith, Shelley A., and Marta Tienda. 1988. "The Doubly Disadvantaged: Women of Color in the U.S. Labor Force." In *Women Working,* 61–80. *See* Berheide 1988.

Smith-Rosenberg, Carroll. 1979. "The Female World of Love and Ritual." In *A Heritage of Her Own,* edited by Nancy F. Cott and Elizabeth H. Pleck, 311–42. New York: Simon & Schuster.

Sochen, June. 1982. *HerStory: A Record of the American Woman's Past.* 2d ed. Palo Alto, Calif.: Mayfield.

Sokoloff, Natalie J. 1988. "Evaluating Gains and Losses by Black and White Women and Men in the Professions, 1960–1980." *Social Problems* 35:36–53.

Sokolowska, Magdalena. 1965. "Some Reflections on the Different Attitudes of Men and Women toward Work." *International Labor Review* 92:35–50.

Solnit, Albert J. 1984. "Parenthood and Child Advocacy." In *Parenthood: A Psychodynamic Perspective,* edited by Rebecca S. Cohen, Bertram J. Cohler, and Sidney H. Weismann, 227–38. New York: Guilford.

Solomon, Barbara Miller. 1985. *In the Company of Educated Women.* New Haven: Yale University Press.

Sommerville, John. 1982. *The Rise and Fall of Childhood.* Beverly Hills, Calif.: Sage.

Spalter-Roth, Roberta, and Heidi J. Hartmann. 1990. *Unnecessary Losses: Costs to Americans of the Lack of Family and Medical Leave.* Washington D.C.: Institute for Women's Policy Research.

Spectorsky, A. C. 1955. *The Exurbanites.* Philadelphia: Lippincott.

Spender, Dale. 1980. *Man Made Language.* London: Routledge & Kegan Paul.

Spicer, Jerry W., and Gary D. Hampe. 1975. "Kinship Interaction after Divorce." *Journal of Marriage and the Family* 17:113-119.

Spock, Benjamin. 1957. *Baby and Child Care.* New York: Cardinal/Pocket.

Spradley, James, and Brenda Mann. 1975. *The Cocktail Waitress: Women's Work in a Man's World.* New York: Wiley.

Sprey, Jetse, and Sarah H. Matthews. 1982. "Contemporary Grandparenthood: A Systematic Transition." *Annals, AAPSS* 464 (November): 91–103.

Squier, Ann D., and Jill S. Quadagno. 1988. "The Italian American Family." In *Ethnic Families in America,* 109–37. *See* Mindel, Habenstein, and Wright 1988.

Squires, Gregory D., Larry Bennett, Kathleen McCourt, and Philip Nyden. 1987. *Chicago: Race, Class, and the Response to Urban Decline.* Philadelphia: Temple University Press.

Stack, Carol B. 1975. *All Our Kin.* New York: Harper & Row.

Staggenberg, Suzanne. 1989. "Stability and Innovation in the Women's Movement: A Comparison of Two Movement Organizations." *Social Problems* 36:75–92.

Stansell, Christine. 1986. *City of Women: Sex and Class in New York 1780–1860.* New York: Knopf.

Staples, Robert. 1988. "The Black American Family." In *Ethnic Families in America,* 303–324. *See* Mindel, Habenstein, and Wright 1988.

Staples, Robert, and Alfredo Mirande. 1980. "Racial and Cultural Variations among American Families: A Decennial Review of the Literature on Minority Families." *Journal of Marriage and the Family* 42:887–903.

Stein, Maurice. 1960. *The Eclipse of Community.* Princeton: Princeton University Press.

Steinberg, Ronnie. 1982. *Wages and Hours: Labor and Reform in Twentieth-Century America.* New Brunswick, N.J.: Rutgers University Press.

———. 1990. "Radical Challenges in a Liberal World: The Mixed Success of Comparable Worth." In *Women, Class, and the Feminist Imagination,* 508–34. *See* Hansen and Philipson, 1990.

Steinmetz, Suzanne. 1987. "Family Violence: Past, Present, and Future." In *Handbook of Marriage and the Family,* edited by Marvin Sussman and Suzanne Steinmetz, 725–65. New York: Plenum.

Stephan, Cookie White, and Walter G. Stephan. 1989. "After Intermarriage: Ethnic Identity among Mixed-Heritage Japanese-Americans and Hispanics." *Journal of Marriage and the Family* 51:507–19.

Stimpson, Catharine R., Elsa Dixler, Martha J. Nelson, and Kathryn B. Yatrakis, eds. 1981. *Women and the American City.* Chicago: University of Chicago Press.

Stoller, Eleanor Palo. 1983. "Parental Caregiving by Adult Children." *Journal of Marriage and the Family* 45:851–58.

Stone, Gregory. 1962. "Appearance and the Self." In *Human Behavior and Social Process,* edited by Arnold Rose, 86–117. Boston: Houghton Mifflin.

———. 1981. "Appearance and the Self: A Slightly Revised Version." In *Social Psychology through Symbolic Interaction,* edited by Gregory P. Stone and Harvey A. Farberman, 187–202. New York: Wiley.

Strasser, Susan. 1978. "The Business of Housekeeping: The Ideology of the Household at the Turn of the Twentieth Century." *Insurgent Sociologist* 7:147–63.

———. 1982. *Never Done: A History of American Housework.* New York: Pantheon.

Stromberg, Ann H., Laurie Larood, and Barbara A. Gutek. 1987. *Women and Work.* Newbury Park, Calif.: Sage.

Stryker, Sheldon. 1980. *Symbolic Interactionism: A Social Structural Version.* Palo Alto, Calif.: Benjamin/Cummings.

Sue, Stanley, and James K. Morishima. 1982. *The Mental Health of Asian Americans.* San Francisco: Jossey-Bass.

Suitor, J. Jill. 1988. "Husbands' Educational Attainment and Support for Wives' Return to School." *Gender and Society* 2:482–95.

Sussman, Marvin B. 1962. "The Isolated Nuclear Family: Fact or Fiction." In

Selected Studies in Marriage and the Family, edited by Robert Winch, 49–57. New York: Holt, Rinehart & Winston.

———. 1965. "Relationships of Adult Children with Their Parents in the United States." In *Social Structure and the Family: Generational Relations,* edited by Ethel Shanas and Gordon Streib, 62–72. Englewood Cliffs, N.J.: Prentice-Hall.

Suttles, Gerald. 1972. *The Social Construction of Communities.* Chicago: University of Chicago Press.

Sutton, John R. 1983. "Social Structure, Institutions, and the Legal Status of Children in the United States." *American Journal of Sociology* 88:915–47.

Sweet, James A., and Larry L. Bumpass. 1987. *American Families and Households.* New York: Russell Sage Foundation. Boston: Auburn House.

Szinovacz, Masimiliane, ed. 1982. *Women's Retirement: Policy Implications of Recent Research.* Beverly Hills, Calif.: Sage.

———. 1989. "Retirement, Couples, and Household Work." In *Aging and the Family,* edited by S. J. Bahr and E. T. Peterson, 33–58. Lexington, Mass.: Lexington Books.

Taylor, F. W. 1911. *Scientific Management.* New York: Harper and Row.

Teachman, Jay D., Karen A. Polonko, and John Scanzoni. 1987. "Demography of the Family." In *Handbook of Marriage and the Family,* 3–36. *See* Steinmetz 1987.

Thomas, W. I., and Florian Znaniecki. 1918–20. *The Polish Peasant in Europe and America.* Boston: Richard G. Badger.

Thorne, Barrie. 1982. "Feminist Rethinking of the Family: An Overview." In *Rethinking the Family: Some Feminist Questions,* edited by Barrie Thorne with Marilyn Yalom, 1–25. New York: Longman.

Thorne, Barrie, Cheris Kramarae, and Nancy Henley, eds. 1983. *Language, Gender, and Society.* Rowley, Mass.: Newbury House.

Thorns, David C. 1976. *The Quest for Community: Social Aspects of Residential Growth.* London: Allen & Unwin.

Tiger, Lionel. 1969. *Men in Groups.* New York: Random House.

Tilly, Louise A., and Joan W. Scott. 1978a. *Women, Work, and Family.* New York: Holt, Rinehart & Winston.

———. 1978b. *Working Life of Women in the Seventeenth Century.* New York: Holt, Rinehart & Winston.

Toffler, Alvin. 1981. *The Third Wave.* New York: Bantam.

Tocqueville, Alexis de. [1835] 1936. *Democracy in America,* edited by J. P. Mayer. Garden City, N.Y.: Doubleday.

Touba, Jacqueline Rudolph. 1987. "The Widowed in Iran." In *Widows: The Middle East, Asia, and the Pacific,* 106–32. *See* Lopata 1987c.

Treas, Judith, and Vern L. Bengtson. 1987. "The Family in Later Years." In *Handbook of Marriage and the Family,* 625–48. *See* Steinmetz 1987.

Troits, Peggy A. 1986. "Multiple Identities and Psychological Well-Being: A Formulation and Test of the Social Isolation Hypothesis." *American Sociological Review* 48:174–87.

Troll, Lillian E. 1983. "Grandparents: The Family Watchdogs." In *Family Relationships in Later Life,* edited by Timothy Brubaker, 63–74. Beverly Hills, Calif.: Sage.

———. 1985. "The Contingencies of Grandparenting." In *Grandparenting,* 135–49. *See* Bengtson and Robertson 1985.

Trost, Cathy. 1990a. "Careers Start Giving in to Family Needs." *Wall Street Journal Marketplace,* 18 June, B1.

———. 1990b. "Marketing-minded Child-Care Centers Become More than 9–5 Baby Sitters." *Wall Street Journal Marketplace,* 18 June, B1.

Trost, Jan. E. 1979. *Unmarried Cohabitation.* Vasteras, Sweden: International Library.

Turner, Ralph. 1962. "Role Taking: Process versus Conformity." In *Human Behavior and Social Processes,* edited by Arnold Rose, 20–40. Boston: Houghton Mifflin.

———. 1968."The Self Conception in Social Interaction." In *The Self in Social Interaction,* edited by Chad Gordon and Kenneth Gergen, 93–106. New York: Wiley.

———. 1978. "The Role and the Person." *American Journal of Sociology* 84:1–23.

———. 1981. "The Real Self: From Institution to Impulse." In *Social Psychology through Symbolic Interaction,* 203–20. *See* Stone 1981.

U. S. Department of Labor. 1965. *Dictionary of Occupation Titles.* Vol. 1, *Definitions of Titles.* 3d ed. Washington, D.C.: U.S. Government Printing Office.

Vandepol, Ann. 1982. "Dependent Children, Child Custody, and the Mother's Pensions: The Transformation of State-Family Relations in the Early 20th Century." *Social Problems* 29:220–35.

Vandervelde, Maryanne. 1979. *The Changing Life of the Corporate Wife.* New York: Mecox.

Vanek, Joann. 1978. "Housewives as Workers." In *Women Working,* 392–414. *See* Berheide 1988.

Veblen, Thorstein. [1899] 1953. *The Theory of the Leisure Class.* New York: Mentor.

Veevers, Jeanne E. 1980. *Childless by Choice.* Toronto: Butterworth.

Visher, Emily B., and John S. Visher. 1979. *Stepfamilies: A Guide to Working with Stepparents and Stepchildren.* New York: Brunner/Mazel.

Walker, Kathryn, and William H. Gauger. 1973. *The Dollar Value of Household Work*. Ithaca, N.Y.: Cornell University.

Wallis, Claudia. 1985. "Children Having Children." *Time,* 9 December, 78–90.

———. 1992. "The Nuclear Family Goes Boom." *Time,* Fall, 42–44. Special issue.

Walsh, Mary Roth. 1977. *Doctors Wanted—No Women Need Apply: Sexual Barriers in the Medical Profession*. New Haven: Yale University Press.

Walshok, Mary Lindenstein. 1981. *Blue-Collar Women: Pioneers on the Male Frontier*. Garden City, N.Y.: Doubleday Anchor.

Ward, Barbara. 1963. *Women in New Asia*. Paris: UNESCO.

Ward, John. 1987. *Keeping the Family Business Healthy*. San Francisco: Jossey-Bass.

Warland, Rex H., Robert O. Herrmann, and Dan E. Moore. 1986. "Consumer Activism, Community Activism, and the Consumer Movement." In *The Future of Consumerism,* 85–95. *See* Bloom and Smith 1986.

Warren, Carol. 1987. *Madwives: Schizophrenic Women of the 1950s*. New Brunswick, N.J.: Rutgers University Press.

Wearing, Betsy. 1990. "Leisure and Crisis of Motherhood: A Study of Leisure and Health amongst Mothers of First Babies in Sydney, Australia." In *The Family as an Asset,* edited by Stella Quah, 122–55. Singapore: Times Academic Press.

Weber, Max. 1949. *The Methodology of the Social Sciences,* edited by E. Shils and H. Finch. Glencoe, Ill.: Free Press.

———. [1904] 1958. *The Protestant Ethic and the Spirit of Capitalism*. New York: Scribner's.

Weinbaum, Batya, and Amy Bridges. 1979. "The Other Side of the Paycheck: Monopoly Capital and the Structure of Consumption." In *Capitalist Patriarchy and the Case for Socialist Feminism,* 190–205. *See* Eisenstein 1979.

Weisner, Thomas S. 1982. "Sibling Interdependence and Child Caretaking: A Cross-Cultural View." In *Sibling Relationships,* 305–27. *See* Lamb and Sutton-Smith 1982.

Weiss, Robert S. 1973. *Loneliness: The Experience of Emotional and Social Isolation*. Cambridge: MIT Press.

Weitzman, Lenore. 1981. *The Marriage Contract: Spouses, Lovers, and the Law*. New York: Free Press.

———. 1985. *The Divorce Revolution: The Unexpected Social and Economic Consequences for Women and Children in America*. New York: Free Press.

Whyte, William F. 1948. *Human Relations in the Restaurant Industry*. New York: McGraw-Hill.

————. 1955. *Street Corner Society: The Social Structure of an Italian Slum.* Chicago: University of Chicago Press.

Whyte, William H., Jr. 1956. *The Organization Man.* New York: Simon & Schuster.

Wilkinson, Doris Y. 1988. "Mother-Daughter Bonds in Later Years: Transformation of the 'Help Pattern'." In *Family and Support Systems Across the Life Span,* edited by Suzanne K. Steinmetz, 183–95. New York: Plenum.

Williams, Dorie Giles. 1985. "Gender, Masculinity-Femininity, and Emotional Intimacy in Same-Sex Friendship." *Sex Roles* 12:586–600.

Williams, Norma. 1990. *The Mexican American Family: Tradition and Change.* Dix Hills, N.Y.: General Hall.

Willie, Charles, and Susan L. Greenblatt. 1978. "Four 'Classic' Studies of Power Relationships in Black Families: A Review and Look to the Future." *Journal of Marriage and the Family* 40:691–94.

Wilmott, Peter, and Michael Young. 1964. *Family and Class in a London Suburb.* London: Routledge & Kegan Paul.

Wilson, William Julius. 1987. *The Truly Disadvantaged.* Chicago: University of Chicago Press.

Winch, Robert, Scott Greer, and Rae Lesser Blumberg. 1967. "Ethnicity and Extended Familism in an Upper Middle Class Suburb." *American Sociological Review* 32:265–76.

Winch, Robert, and Rae Lesser Blumberg. 1968. "Societal Complexity and Familial Organization." In *Selected Studies in Marriage and the Family,* edited by Robert F. Winch and Louis Wolf Goodman, 70–92. New York: Holt, Rinehart & Winston.

Wirth, Louis. 1928. *The Ghetto.* Chicago: University of Chicago Press.

————. 1938. "Urbanism as a Way of Life." *American Journal of Sociology* 44:1–24.

Wittner, Judith. 1977. "Households of Strangers: Career Patterns of Foster Children and Other Wards of the State." Ph.D. diss., Department of Sociology. Northwestern University.

————. 1980. "Domestic Labor as Work Discipline: The Struggle over Housework in Foster Homes." In *Women and Household Labor,* 229–47. *See* Berk 1980.

————. 1990. "A Resource for Women? Domestic Violence Court and Feminist Research." Manuscript, Loyola University of Chicago.

Wong, Morrison G. 1988. "The Chinese American Family." In *Ethnic Families in America,* 230–57. *See* Mindel, Habenstein, and Wright 1988.

Wood, Vivian, and Joan Robertson. 1973. "The Significance of Grandparenthood." In *Time, Roles, and Self in Old Age,* edited by Jay Gubrium, 278–304. New York: Behavioral Publications.

Wrobel, Paul. 1979. *Our Way: Family, Parish, and Neighborhood in a Polish-American Community*. Notre Dame. University of Notre Dame Press.

Wylie, Philip. 1955. *Generation of Vipers*. New York: Holt, Rinehart & Winston.

Yogev, Sara. 1981. "Do Professional Women Have Egalitarian Marital Relationships?" *Journal of Marriage and the Family* 43: 865–71.

Young, Malcolm. 1984. "Police Wives: A Reflection of Police Concepts of Order and Control." In *The Incorporated Wife*, edited by Hilary Callan and Shirley Ardener, 67–88. London: Croom Helm.

Zavella, Patricia. 1987. *Women's Work and Chicano Families: Cannery Workers of the Santa Clara Valley*. Ithaca, N.Y.: Cornell University Press.

Zelizer, Viviana. 1981. "The Price and Value of Children: The Case of Children's Insurance." *American Journal of Sociology* 86:1036–56.

———. 1985. *Pricing the Priceless Child: The Changing Social Value of Children*. New York: Basic books.

Zicklin, Gilbert. 1983. *Counterculture Communes: A Sociological Perspective*. New York: Greenwood.

Zimmer, Lynn. 1987. "How Women Reshape the Prison Guard Role." *Gender and Society* 1:415–31.

Znaniecka, Zofia Pin de Saint Pau. 1872. Unpublished diary.

Znaniecki, Florian W. 1965. *Social Relations and Social Roles*. San Francisco: Chandler.

Index